1. Make a log sheet for clients
2. Copy relaxation tapes
   & give to clients.
3. Observe administration of DES
4. Informed consent form
5 make eval form for practice clients
   remind of the issue + ask them to assess it now

D0386769

McCann + Peartman, 1990

EYE MOVEMENT DESENSITIZATION AND REPROCESSING

Basic Principles, Protocols, and Procedures

• • •

FRANCINE SHAPIRO, Ph.D.

THE GUILFORD PRESS
New York   London

Published by The Guilford Press
A Division of Guilford Publications, Inc.
72 Spring Street, New York, NY 10012

Printed in the United States of America

This book is printed on acid-free paper.

Last digit is print number: 9   8   7   6   5

Library of Congress Cataloging-in-Publication Data

Shapiro, Francine.
      Eye movement desensitization and reprocessing: Basic principles,
protocols, and procedures / Francine Shapiro.
         p.   cm.
      Includes bibliographical references and index.
      ISBN 0-89862-960-8
      1. Eye movement densitization and reprocessing. 2. Post-
traumatic stress disorder—Treatment.   3. Psychic trauma—
Treatment.   I. Title.
      RC552.P67S44   1995
      616.85'210651—dc20   94-41750
                                                                  CIP

*With gratitude for the
guiding lights of each generation*

*In memory of my grandparents,
Charles and Lena Sumner,
and my sister, Debra P. Shapiro*

*and for the loving support of my parents,
Daniel and Shirley Shapiro,
and one of my life's greatest blessings,
Bob Welch*

◆ ◆ ◆

Freedom is what you do with what's been done to you.
Jean-Paul Sartre

$$\cdot \quad \cdot \quad \cdot$$

Acknowledgments

This book could not have been written without the unswerving support of Robbie Dunton, who freed my time and mind for the task. I am thankful for her organizational skills but even more for her loving-kindness and generosity of spirit which have never failed me. Special thanks go also to Robert Welch and Margot Silk Forrest, who put their great intelligence and skill into editing these chapters. My gratitude goes also to Pat Ryley, who skillfully created a number of the illustrations, and to A. J. Popky, who has consistently provided valuable technical support.

The content of this book is based on the clinical experiences of hundreds of clinicians, and I hope I have done them justice. The task of communicating the information was aided by many people, but special thanks go to Howard Lipke and Steven Silver, who served as the primary readers of many of the versions of most of the chapters.

I am grateful to the many people who took the time to read different chapters or who offered suggestions at various stages of the book's development. These people, in alphabetical order, are Lonnie Barbach, Pat Boudewyns, Jac Carlson, Robbie Dunton, Catherine Fine, Gary Fulcher, Eirin Gould, Tom Horvath, Lee Hyer, Steven Lazrove, Marilyn Luber, Jeri Marlowe, Sandra Paulsen, Gerald Puk, Curt Rouanzoin, Mark Russell, Roger Solomon, Landry Wildwind, and Walter Young.

Many thanks to the Guilford staff and especially to my editors, Kitty Moore, for her astute suggestions, and Anna Brackett, for her careful shepherding of the book through the production process.

Introducing an innovation to the psychology community is notoriously difficult, but I have been blessed with an expanding circle of openhearted, masterful clinicians whose ability and integrity reassure me that we are on the right path. To those EMDR trainers, facilitators, and clinicians who had the vision to try something new and the courage to spread the word about their experiences—although it may seem like hubris to thank you for things you did out of a sense of personal responsibility and purpose—I will be endlessly grateful.

$$\bullet \quad \bullet \quad \bullet$$

Preface

Blessed is he who has found his work. Let him seek no
other blessedness.

Thomas Carlyle

THE PATH OF DISCOVERY

We went from Kitty Hawk to a man on the moon in little more than 50
years, yet we have not had a major paradigm shift in psychology since
Freud, nearly a century ago. Clearly, attitudes shift more slowly than
technology. Sometimes we have to be forced out of what is comfortable
in order to change. Sometimes changes that seem like the worst
tragedies hold gifts we cannot imagine. It certainly seems so in my life.

I made the initial discovery that led to the development of Eye
Movement Desensitization and Reprocessing (EMDR) in 1987. The path
to that discovery had begun nearly ten years before. In 1979 I was
completing a doctorate in English literature at New York University and
had already published extensively in the field. It felt like important work
to be one of those who shed light on our culture, and literature—with
its delicate nuances, rich textures, and the intricate lives of characters—
held me in constant fascination.

At the same time, I had long been interested in behavior therapy
owing to my early readings of Andrew Salter and Joseph Wolpe. The
idea of a focused, predictable, cause-and-effect approach to human
psychology seemed fully compatible with the concepts of literary character and plot development. After all, many well-known authors had
intimated that if characters are drawn true to life and set loose, they
then create their own plots. I had fascinating discussions with my
English professors on the interaction between the rich, multifaceted
texts I was reading and the physiological cause-and-effect implications
of behavioral formulations. But psychology was only a side interest of
mine. I held staunchly with those authors who believed in the perfecti-

bility of man. I reveled in the glory of human suffering transformed into art via the masterworks of English literature, and I looked forward to a long and fruitful career as a literary critic and scholar. Then, right before launching into my dissertation on the poetry of Thomas Hardy, I was diagnosed with cancer.

When a potentially fatal disease strikes, it can be a watershed that marks a change in the course of one's life. For me, time took on a new dimension. Life no longer stretched out endlessly before me. Suddenly, the behaviorists' "physiological cause and effect" took on new meaning. I became focused on the interplay of mind and external stressors. I also wondered why we had come so far technologically but seemed unable to advance in ways to master our own minds and bodies.

Fortunately, I discovered the works of Norman Cousins and others in the field of psychoneuroimmunology, which was just emerging. The idea that there is a connection between disease and stress now seemed obvious to me, but what to do about it was another matter. By now, according to my physicians, my cancer was cured, but there was no guarantee it wouldn't happen again. I remember their communication to me as something like this: "Your cancer is gone, but X percent get it back. We don't know who and we don't know how, so good luck."

Now the question of which psychological and physiological methods actually worked to enhance physical health became primary. I believed there had to be some useful psychological and physiological approaches already developed, but why weren't they well known? Suddenly, finding these methods and disseminating the information about them to others with life-threatening illnesses became more important to me than studying and communicating about 19th-century literature. I left New York in search of workshops and seminars on mind, body, and psychological methods to enhance physical and mental well-being.

After a while, I sponsored workshops myself for the general public on everything I found that offered tangible ways to help people lead less stressful lives. During that time I also enrolled in a doctoral program in clinical psychology to complete my formal education. The eventful walk in the park that led to the discovery of the effects of the eye movements occurred just as I was beginning to look for a dissertation topic. In that single moment my cross-country search for mechanisms of mental change and my need for a doctoral research project neatly converged.

The rest of the story of the development of EMDR will be covered in Chapter 1. For now, suffice it to say that my discovery of the effects of the eye movements was followed by the development of a methodology that grew rapidly in complexity and application. Today positive clinical results with EMDR are being reported consistently by the vast majority of the 10,000 clinicians who have been trained in its use. Our clinical work with EMDR shows us that suffering *can* be transformed—not only into art but into life.

This book is a product of my eight years of personal experience refining and teaching EMDR; it includes case histories as well as cautions derived from the experience of EMDR-trained practitioners.

THE NEED FOR TRAINING

Because the emphasis of my life since 1979 has been on disseminating to the general public procedures that really work to enhance mental health, it's no surprise that my primary concern now is with the client. Clients are best served by clinicians who are willing to learn, expand their skills, and experiment with innovative methods. They are also clearly best served when clinicians are licensed in the field of mental health and trained in the methods they are using and when adequate research is done to validate and improve upon those methods. These beliefs are at the heart of EMDR and are the foundation upon which EMDR's success—as well as its training policies—has been built. I have been blessed to have met many clinicians who share these beliefs.

An explanation of EMDR training policies is the subject of a position paper of the EMDR Professional Issues Committee (an independent watchdog group that oversees training), which is included in Appendix B. The rest of the rationale for these policies springs from logic and compassion. A survey of the first 1,200 clinicians trained in EMDR showed that only 3% considered the supervised training unnecessary. What's more, results of this survey (which are reproduced in Appendix D) indicated that 85% of the clinicians found that clients had more "repressed" memories emerge with EMDR than with any other method. It seems reasonable to conclude that if dysfunctional memories consistently emerge from EMDR sessions, complete with a high level of abreactive disturbance, clinicians should be educated in the method that precipitates these memories and has the potential to resolve them. To reiterate more succinctly, clients are best served if their clinicians are trained. The bottom line is helping people.

Of course, training does not ensure success with every client. EMDR is not a cure-all; treatment failures occur, as they do with any method. However, the American Psychological Association ethics code states that training and supervision are necessary to achieve competency before treating clients or doing research. Adequate training means greater likelihood of success—and less likelihood of harm. Therefore, although this book provides the necessary written instructions to begin using EMDR, I strongly believe that it should be used in conjunction with appropriate supervision and training. I will repeat this refrain throughout the text.

PRINCIPLES AND PROCEDURES

As the saying goes, it is better to teach a hungry man how to fish than to give him a fish. Likewise, it is better to provide practitioners with a conceptual framework or model to serve as a guide to their clinical practice than merely to give them an inflexible step-by-step procedure for implementing EMDR.

Early articles (Shapiro, 1989a, 1989b) that attempted to offer a series of circumscribed steps for doing EMDR have proved inadequate, according to reports both by clinicians and by clients treated by therapists whose only EMDR "training" was to read those articles. So, along with step-by-step directives, this text offers clinicians a new way of thinking about pathology and therapeutic treatment and a comprehensive set of therapeutic alternatives that have evolved from clinical applications consistent with the theory.

One of the basic premises of EMDR is that most psychopathologies are based on early life experiences. The goal of EMDR treatment is to rapidly metabolize the dysfunctional residue from the past and transform it into something useful. Essentially, with EMDR the dysfunctional information undergoes a spontaneous change in form and meaning—incorporating insights and affect that are enhancing rather than self-denigrating to the client. Clinicians should find that the information covered in this book provides the components and strategies necessary for this process, wherein the client's innate information-processing system is called into play to bring about this resolution.

THE NAME OF THE METHOD

While EMDR was initially named for the eye movements, which in 1987 appeared to be the most salient part of the method, over the past few years the name has appeared to unduly limit the appreciation and application of the methodology. As this book indicates, EMDR is a complex methodology that includes many components; in addition, many other stimuli besides the eye movements have proven useful. If I had it to do over again, I might name it simply Reprocessing Therapy. Nonetheless, because of the extensive worldwide name recognition I have decided to maintain the abbreviation and the original designation, with the understanding that it may serve ultimately to be of historical, rather than descriptive, significance. (As examples, Coca-Cola retained its designation even after the cocaine derivative it was named for was removed from the contents, and the diagnostic category of schizophrenia was maintained even after it was no longer viewed as "split mind." The name Eye Movement Desensitization and Reprocessing may meet the same fate.) The abbreviation EMDR should therefore be used with the understanding that the eye movements are merely one of many dual-attention stimuli used to activate the client's information-processing system and achieve treatment effects.

USE OF THIS BOOK

Only licensed mental health professionals, or those under direct supervision of licensed clinicians, should use the procedures and protocols in this book. This caution is important because, as a psychological treatment, EMDR should only be used within the context of a complete and detailed treatment plan and with the appropriate safeguards that trained and licensed clinicians are schooled to be aware of. Instructors of clinical graduate students will probably want to engage their students in a supervised internship program before teaching the method to them. While suggestions for the form and timing of supervised practice in EMDR are included in this book, in all instances a formal training course with licensed, trained, experienced EMDR instructors is considered the most appropriate forum for learning the method.

This book has been written with four kinds of readers in mind: academicians, researchers, clinicians, and clinical graduate students. I have attempted to make the language and organization appropriate for all (with varying degrees of success). Those readers especially interested in the history, supportive data, research, theory, and the placement of EMDR in the field of trauma therapies will find Chapters 1, 2, and 12 of particular relevance. Although therapists primarily interested in learning the method will find important clinical material in various sections of those three chapters (particularly Chapter 2), such material is most heavily concentrated in the remainder of the text.

GENDER

In order to avoid sexism without the stylistic awkwardness of phrases such as *he or she*, the personal pronouns have been alternated throughout the text.

RESEARCH AND EVOLUTION

The continued evolution of EMDR from a simple technique to a complex methodology has been based largely on clinical observation. The need for research to provide further validation of the EMDR method is indisputable, since clinical evaluation is susceptible to many of the distortions and fallacies of personal observation. Nevertheless, there are at present more positive controlled studies on EMDR than on any other method used in the treatment of psychological trauma. These studies, along with research implications and suggestions for further investigation, are discussed in depth in Chapter 12.

Clearly, there is no substitute for well-designed and well-implemented controlled clinical outcome research, and more of it is needed. However, such research is notoriously scarce and traditionally lags far behind clinical practice. For instance, no controlled clinical outcome research has yet been published on victims of molestation, natural disasters, or accidents. The implications of this paucity of "hard data" in the field of trauma in general will be explored in Chapter 12.

It is important for clinicians to remember that until extensive comparative research validates EMDR, it should be treated as a newly developed method, with appropriate information provided to the client for the purpose of informed consent. While there is already much promising evidence, the efficacy of EMDR is not yet a universally proven fact. This is another reason for limiting EMDR training to licensed mental health professionals. If EMDR does not work in a given situation, such clinicians have at their disposal a repertoire of more traditional procedures they can use.

The unfortunate split between the clinical community, which finds EMDR highly successful, and the academic and research community, which demands further study of EMDR before it is used on clients, is essentially a false dichotomy. Naturally, all clinicians would prefer to have their tools verified by research. However, the pressing daily need to treat their clients' suffering comes first, and clinical practice simply cannot wait for the research to catch up.

In the meantime, while EMDR continues to evolve through research and clinical observation, the primary principles and substance of current practice are presented in this book. The reader is urged to keep an appropriately skeptical, yet open, mind. Changing ingrained ways of doing psychotherapy may not be easy. This book is only the beginning of a learning process and, I hope, of a rewarding journey of exploration. And while clinical evaluations and personal observations are far from infallible, they are also indispensable to sound scientific findings—and to the joy of healing.

. . .

Contents

CHAPTER 1

• • •

Background

There is a principle which is a bar against all
information, which is proof against all arguments
and which cannot fail to keep a man in everlasting
ignorance—that principle is contempt prior to
investigation.

Herbert Spencer

Since its discovery in 1987, Eye Movement Desensitization and Reprocessing (EMDR) has found widespread acceptance by much of the clinical community. Understandably, the use of directed eye movements as part of a therapeutic intervention has not found immediate acceptance within much of academia. Nothing in the traditional psychological modalities has pointed to their use. The initial use of eye movements in therapy was based on neither theory nor experimental data but, rather, on a chance observation. The subsequent development of the method and its theoretical framework grew from an exploration of consistently achieved treatment effects, an exploration that refined the use of the eye movements and additional elements of the procedure. However, as we shall see, the current method and theory incorporate many aspects that should prove familiar to most clinicians, academicians, and researchers.

Although EMDR is best known and named for its eye movements, it is vital that we approach it as a whole system. The eye movements are only one component of the method. For instance, before attempting any EMDR work with a client, clinicians must establish the appropriate therapeutic relationship and take a full history. They must use different protocols depending on the type of pathologies and follow different therapeutic procedures depending on the type and number of traumas the client has experienced. Although EMDR can rapidly relieve distress caused by a single trauma, clinicians must carefully consider a number of factors before using it.

For example, when treating a victim of a single rape, the clinician identifies the different aspects of the trauma that are disturbing the client. These might include intrusive images; negative thoughts or beliefs the client has about herself or her role in the rape; negative emotions such as fear, guilt, or shame and their associated body sensations; and, conversely, the precise way the client would prefer to think about herself instead. The rape victim may begin by feeling intense fear and shame. She may have constant images of the rape intruding on her present life and may experience negative thoughts such as "I am dirty" or "It was my fault." After her clinician has worked with her using eye movements focused on specific internal responses, the rape victim may be able to recall the rape without feelings of fear and shame. She may, in fact, feel empowered and may be able to say, "I did very well. He was holding a knife at my throat, and I managed to stay alive." In addition to this positive change in her thoughts and beliefs, she may no longer have intrusive images of the rape. If she later recalls the event, her associated emotions, thoughts, and body sensations may be neutral or positive rather than disturbing. As one rape victim who received EMDR treatment said of her attack, "It's still an ugly picture but not because I did anything wrong."

A DAY OF DISCOVERY

EMDR is based on a chance observation I made in May 1987. While walking through the park one day, I noticed that some disturbing thoughts I was having suddenly disappeared. I also noticed that when I brought these thoughts back to mind, they were not as upsetting or as valid as before. Previous experience had taught me that disturbing thoughts generally have a certain "loop" to them; that is, they tend to play themselves over and over until you consciously do something to stop or change them. What caught my attention that day was that my disturbing thoughts were disappearing and changing without any conscious effort.

Fascinated, I started paying very close attention to what was going on. I noticed that when disturbing thoughts came into my mind, my eyes spontaneously started moving very rapidly back and forth in an upward diagonal. Again the thoughts disappeared, and when I brought them back to mind, their negative charge was greatly reduced. At that point I started making the eye movements deliberately while concentrating on a variety of disturbing thoughts and memories, and I found that these thoughts also disappeared and lost their charge. My excitement grew as I began to see the potential benefits of this effect.

A few days later I started to try it out with other people: friends, colleagues, and participants in psychology workshops I was attending. They had a wide range of nonpathological complaints and, like the rest of the population, had had varying amounts of psychotherapy. When I asked, "What do you want to work on?" people brought up disturbing memories, beliefs, and present situations, with complaints ranging from early childhood humiliations to present-day work frustrations. Then I showed them how I had moved my eyes rapidly back and forth, and I asked them to duplicate those eye movements while simultaneously holding their problem in mind. The first thing I discovered was that most people do not have the muscle control to continue the eye movement for any length of time. Still determined to investigate, however, I asked them to follow my fingers with their eyes while I moved my hand back and forth until their eye movements duplicated the speed and direction I had used that day in the park. This worked much better. However, the next thing I discovered was that people would start feeling better but would then get stuck in the disturbing material. To overcome this, I tried different kinds of eye movements (faster, slower, in different directions) and I asked people to concentrate on a variety of different things (such as different aspects of the memory or the way it made them feel). As we proceeded I began to learn which strategies were most likely to get positive and complete results. In addition, I started to find standard ways of opening and closing the eye movement sessions that seemed to contribute to positive effects.

In short, by working with some 70 people over the course of about 6 months, I developed a standard procedure that consistently succeeded in alleviating their complaints. Because my primary focus was on reducing anxiety (as that had been my own experience with the eye movements) and my primary modality at that time was behavioral, I called the procedure Eye Movement Desensitization (EMD).

THE FIRST CONTROLLED STUDY

In the winter of 1987 I decided to see if EMD would prove successful under controlled conditions. In my initial work I had used EMD most easily and most effectively with old memories. Therefore, I decided that for my first official study I wanted to find a homogeneous grouping of people who had difficulty with old memories. The people who first came to mind were rape victims, molestation victims, and Vietnam veterans who fit the diagnosis for Posttraumatic Stress Disorder (PTSD) as defined by the then current *Diagnostic and Statistical Manual of Mental Disorders*, third edition (DSM-III, 1980). At first this seemed an ideal population because of their old memories, but there was a catch: I did not know if the eye movements would prove effective in resolving traumatic memories, since I had not yet tried them with any pathological conditions. What if the brain stored traumatic memories in a different way? What if they could not be accessed by the eye movements in the way that disturbing but nontraumatic memories could?

To test whether EMD would work with people who had traumatic memories, I decided to find a volunteer who had suffered combat trauma. "Doug" was a counselor at a local Veterans Outreach program. Although he was generally very well adjusted and successful, he had one recurring memory that continued to upset him tremendously. On a tour of duty in Vietnam back in the 1960s, Doug had served as an infantryman. One day while he was unloading dead soldiers from a rescue helicopter, a buddy came up and gave him very upsetting news about one of the bodies he had just handled. I asked Doug to hold the memory of that moment in his mind while he followed my hand with his eyes. He did this and after two or three sets of eye movements he reported that the scene had changed: The auditory part of the memory had vanished. Instead, all he saw was his buddy's mouth moving; no sound came out. After several more sets of eye movements, Doug told me that the scene had been transformed in his mind's eye until it looked like "a paint chip under water" and that he now felt calm. "I can finally say the war is over and I can tell everyone to go home," he said. When I later asked him to think of Vietnam, the image that emerged was—instead of one of dead bodies—a memory of the first time he had flown over the country, when it had looked to him like "a garden paradise." This was the first time in 20 years that Doug had remembered that positive image of Vietnam. Six months later, when I checked back with him, Doug told me that the positive effects had lasted. The disturbing image had not intruded since his treatment. Moreover, when he deliberately retrieved the memory, it looked like the "paint chip," and he felt no distress when he saw it.

My success with Doug seemed to confirm that decades-old traumatic memories could be accessed and resolved by the method. With that encouragement, I began a controlled study with 22 victims of rape, molestation, or Vietnam combat who were suffering from traumatic memories. The subjects ranged in age from 11 to 53 years old, with an average age of 37. The amount of time since the traumatic experience ranged from 1 to 47 years, with an average of 23 years, and the amount of previous therapy ranged from 2 months to 25 years (in the case of a psychiatrist suffering from early trauma), with an average of 6 years of treatment.

The criteria for inclusion in the study were a self-reported traumatic memory and one or more pronounced symptoms (such as intrusive thoughts; flashbacks, which are vivid recollections that include the feeling that the event is actually occurring; sleep disturbance; or relationship problems) occurring over at least a 1-year period. In addition, I assessed the severity of the complaint by determining the number of pronounced symptoms of PTSD occurring per week (such as nightmares, flashbacks, and intrusive thoughts). Most of the subjects were diagnosed with PTSD and had been referred by therapists or community agencies dealing with traumatic problems. A few subjects were not undergoing therapy but were themselves counselors at the referring agencies who volunteered for the study in hopes of resolving past traumatic incidents. The subjects were randomly assigned to the treatment or control groups.

I used EMD with the treatment group, and I gave the subjects in the control group (group A) a "placebo" by asking them to describe their traumatic memory in detail. I interrupted subjects in both groups approximately the same number of times for scoring the anxiety level and for feedback, using the same questions (e.g., "What do you get now?"). The purpose of having a control group was to allow for the possibility of positive effects resulting merely from the subjects' having the direct attention of a researcher and spending a similar amount of time exposed to the memory. This exposure, in which the subject holds the memory in focused consciousness for a prolonged time, might be regarded as a modified flooding condition, but I considered it a placebo condition because positive treatment effects are not expected with direct therapeutic exposure (DTE) of a single session's duration (Keane & Kaloupek, 1982).

I asked subjects in both treatment groups individually to tell me about the disturbing image of their traumatic memory, along with whatever negative thoughts and beliefs they had about the situation or their participation in it (such as "I'm dirty," "I'm worthless," "I'm not in control"). I call this the negative cognition. Then I asked subjects to recall the memory and the negative cognition and to rate their anxiety level using an 11-point Subjective Units of Disturbance (SUD) Scale, where 0 represents neutral intensity and 10 equals the highest possible anxiety (Wolpe, 1991). I also asked subjects to verbalize a positive thought or belief they would like to have about themselves (such as "I'm worthwhile," "I'm in control," or "I did the best I could"). Finally, I asked them to rate how true they felt this positive belief was by means of a 7-point semantic differential scale—designated the Validity of Cognition (VOC) Scale—where 1 represents "completely false" and 7 means "completely true." I cautioned subjects to use their gut feeling as the basis for their judgment rather than some intellectual analysis. EMD was applied for 15 to 90 minutes to the treatment group. Results are shown in Figures 1 and 2.

The treatment group showed two marked changes: Anxiety levels decreased, showing a pronounced desensitization effect, and there was a marked increase in subjects' perceptions of how true their positive beliefs were, showing a strong cognitive restructuring. The control

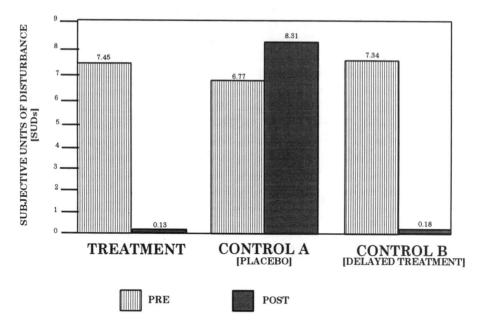

FIGURE 1. Mean SUDs for treatment group, control group A, and control group B at first session.

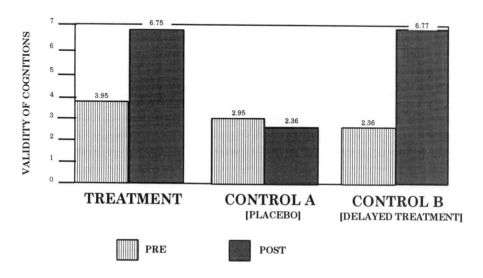

FIGURE 2. Mean validity of cognitions for treatment group, control group A, and control group B at first session.

group initially showed increased anxiety, which is consistent with the responses to initial phases of flooding procedures found by other researchers (Boudewyns & Shipley, 1983). Additionally, as the control subjects' anxiety increased, it was not unusual for their sense of self-efficacy to decrease. For ethical reasons, EMD was administered to the control group after they had participated in the placebo condition, and positive treatment effects were obtained with the delayed treatment (control B) condition. Although providing treatment for the control group prevented a between-groups analysis of follow-up results, it did allow for a limited comparison of immediate versus delayed treatment conditions.

Despite the fact that subjects in the treatment group were treated in only a single session, reports of both the SUD and VOC levels immediately after treatment and at 1-month and 3-month follow-ups, as shown in Figures 3 and 4, indicated that substantial desensitization and pronounced cognitive restructuring of perceptions regarding the traumatic event had been achieved. In addition to these quantitative self-re-

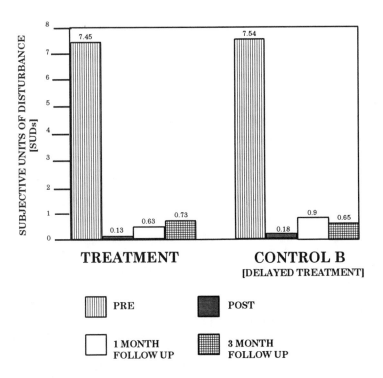

FIGURE 3. Mean SUDs for treatment group and control group B at first session, 1-month follow-up, and 3-month follow-up.

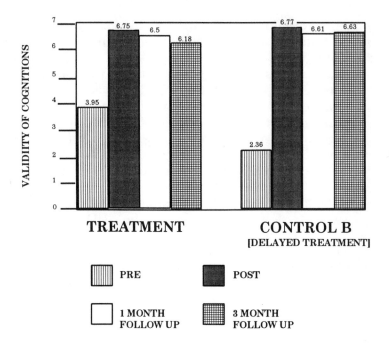

FIGURE 4. Mean validity of cognitions for treatment group and control group B at first session, 1-month follow-up, and 3-month follow-up.

port measures, I sought verification of changes in the subjects' pronounced symptoms. In all but 4 of the 22 subjects, the behavioral shifts and changes in symptomatology reported by the subjects were verified by a spouse, parent, or primary therapist. An informal 6-month follow-up session with approximately half of the subjects indicated that the treatment effects had been maintained.

Primary complaints such as flashbacks and intrusive thoughts were also assessed. Subjects reported that flashbacks were totally eliminated; that intrusive thoughts were either fully eliminated or far fewer in number; and that when intrusive thoughts of the traumatic memory did occur, they were without anxiety and the pretreatment negative cognition no longer applied.

Complaints of sleep disturbances were also greatly reduced. A subject who had a lifelong history of one or two violent, fearful dreams per week reported that he had a violent dream on the night following EMD treatment but that on this occasion he had felt no fear and in the dream had "ritually bowed to [his] Samurai enemies." They had then "joined forces," and he had had no subsequent violent or fearful dreams. He stated that this was, as far as he could remember, the first period of his life in which he had no nightmares and felt consistently "good and confident, without breaks." His wife corroborated that he no longer thrashed around in bed.

A Vietnam veteran who had had flashbacks, intrusive thoughts, and nightmares for 21 years about a particular incident also reported only one subsequent nightmare, one that had "no power to it." Moreover, he confided, "I realized that the person in the dream cutting my throat was me." He had had no other frightening dreams. He acknowledged that he had occasional intrusive thoughts but claimed, "None have power anymore." He also described himself as calmer on all related issues and memories. This report was verified by an independent investigator 2 years later.

The study, including the 1-month and 3-month follow-ups, was completed in 1988. The results, along with a description of the fundamental procedure, were published in the *Journal of Traumatic Stress* (Shapiro, 1989a). (Critiques of this study, which appeared 3 years later; additional research; and suggestions for future investigations will be covered in detail in Chapter 12.) A more detailed description of the procedure (albeit only two and a half pages), along with a report of the study and a case example, was published in the *Journal of Behavior Therapy and Experimental Psychiatry* (Shapiro, 1989b).

EMD BECOMES EMDR

In response to the positive results of the 1989 study and the numerous requests from clinicians who had heard me present my findings at various conferences, I decided to teach the procedure to licensed mental health professionals. In the interests of client safety, I determined to limit training to those who had the credentials to diagnose mental illness, maintain safe boundaries, work with the kind of material potentially stimulated by this treatment, and who had a full clinical repertoire from which to choose if the procedure failed. In March 1990, with the help of three colleagues I had already instructed in the method, I taught a 2-day workshop for 36 clinicians who had requested training. Subsequent workshops were scheduled as word of mouth spread and clinicians using the procedure referred their colleagues for training.

During the procedure's first "official" year as a treatment intervention, I learned several things, thanks to feedback from participants in the training programs and reports from the clients of untrained clinicians who had used the journal articles as their guides. First, it became clear that the application of the procedure was much more complex than I had originally thought and that in teaching the procedure I needed to address factors involving client vulnerability and timing that I had taken for granted. Second, I found that clinicians needed additional variations of the method and corresponding protocols as the types of clinical populations expanded and more resistant and difficult patients were encountered. Third, in order for the method to achieve full therapeutic effectiveness and to prevent relapse, I needed to refine some of its existing components and add new ones that paid greater attention to residual body tension. Fourth, I saw that training needed to include supervised practice, since many of the aspects of using the method successfully with clients—including timing, decision points, and nonverbal feedback indicators—had to be demonstrated. Finally, it was clear that clients were at risk of being retraumatized by the disturbing material if untrained clinicians attempted to use the method (see Appendix B).

One outcome of the training experience and the subsequent evaluation of hundreds of case reports from trained clinicians was the full realization that the optimal procedure included the simultaneous desensitization and cognitive restructuring of memories and personal attributions, all of which appeared to be byproducts of the adaptive processing of the disturbing memories. This realization led to my renaming the method Eye Movement Desensitization and Reprocessing (EMDR). More than just a change in name, this was a shift in paradigm and perspective that would take EMDR far beyond its original clinical conceptualization as a treatment for PTSD. The continued refinement of the principles, protocols, and procedures that make up EMDR came to clearly define it as a methodology for a new approach to psychotherapy. This will become clearly delineated in the remainder of this text.

FURTHER CLINICAL
AND EXPERIMENTAL OBSERVATIONS

The successful clinical results achieved with EMDR by the approximately 10,000 clinicians trained to date indicate the wide range of applicability of the method. For example, a survey approved and partially funded by a Department of Veterans Affairs (DVA) medical center targeted EMDR-trained clinicians who had treated over 10,000 clients. It found that approximately 74% of the clinicians cited more beneficial treatment effects with EMDR than with other methods used, while only 4% indicated less success (Lipke, 1992b; see Appendix D). Published case studies and conference presentations have described successful EMDR treatment effects with a wide range of clinical populations, including the following:

1. Combat veterans from Desert Storm, the Vietnam War, the Korean War, and World War II who were formerly treatment resistant and who no longer experience flashbacks, nightmares,

and other PTSD sequelae (Carlson, Chemtob, Rusnak, & Hedlund, in press; Daniels, Lipke, Richardson, & Silver, 1992; Lipke & Botkin, 1992; Perry, in press; Taber, in press; Thomas & Gafner, 1993; Viola & McCarthy, 1994; Young, in press).

2. Persons with phobias who revealed a rapid reduction of fear and/or symptomatology (Doctor, 1994; Kleinknecht, 1993; Lohr, Tokin, & Kleinknecht, in press-a, in press-b).

3. Sufferers of panic disorder who are recovering at a rate more rapid than that achieved by other treatments (Goldstein & Feske, 1993, 1994; O'Brien, 1993).

4. Crime victims and police officers who are no longer disturbed by the aftereffects of violent assaults (Baker & McBride, 1991; Kleinknecht, 1992; Page & Crino, 1993; Shapiro & Solomon, in press; Solomon, 1995).

5. People relieved of excessive grief due to the loss of a loved one or to line-of-duty deaths, such as engineers no longer devastated with guilt because their train unavoidably killed pedestrians (Puk, 1991a; Solomon, 1994, 1995; Solomon & Shapiro, in press).

6. Children healed of the symptoms caused by the trauma of assault or natural disaster (Abruzzesse, 1994; Cocco & Sharpe, 1993; Greenwald, 1994; Pellicer, 1993; Shapiro, 1991a).

7. Sexual assault victims who are now able to lead normal lives and have intimate relationships (Gould, 1994; Parnell, 1994; Puk, 1991a; Shapiro, 1989b, 1991a, 1994a; Spector & Huthwaite, 1993; Wolpe & Abrams, 1991).

8. Accident and burn victims who were once emotionally or physically debilitated and who are now able to resume productive lives (McCann, 1992; Puk, 1992; Solomon & Kaufman, 1994).

9. Victims of sexual dysfunction who are now able to maintain healthy sexual relationships (Levin, 1993; Wernik, 1993).

10. Clients at all stages of chemical dependency who now show stable recovery and a decreased tendency to relapse (Kitchen, 1991; Shapiro, Vogelmann-Sine, & Sine, 1994).

11. People with dissociative disorders who progress at a rate more rapid than that achieved by traditional treatment (Fine, 1994; Lazrove, 1994; Marquis & Puk, 1994; Paulsen, in press; Paulsen, Vogelmann-Sine, Lazrove, & Young, 1993; Puk, 1994; Rouanzoin, 1994; Young, 1994).

12. Clients with a wide variety of PTSD and other diagnoses who experience substantial benefit from EMDR (Cohn, 1993; Fensterheim, 1994a; Figley & Carbonell, 1995; Forbes, Creamer, & Rycroft, 1994; Marquis, 1991; Puk, 1991b, 1994; Spates & Burnette, in press; Vaughan, Wiese, Gold, & Tarrier, 1994; Wolpe, 1991).

While there are many positive controlled studies of EMDR that have been presented at professional conferences, most of them have not yet been published. Unfortunately, the results of the controlled experiments on EMDR that have appeared in print so far have proven more equivocal than those studies or the clinical reports. Because appropriate research is mandatory, I will offer a detailed explication of research problems and suggestions in Chapter 12, after the reader has a better understanding of the methodology. In the meantime, it is important for EMDR practitioners to remember that although there are insufficient comparative experimental data to validate the method fully, there is enough evidence to warrant judicious clinical application and exploration, particularly in the area of PTSD. It is not unusual for research to lag far behind clinical application. For example, at the time EMDR was introduced in January 1989 at the International Stress Conference in Tel-Aviv, there were no published controlled studies validating flooding in the treatment of PTSD, as defined in DSM-III in 1980, despite the fact that this procedure was being used throughout the Department of Veterans Affairs system. And as of June 1994 there were more reported randomized controlled studies on EMDR than on any other method (including flooding) used in the treatment of PTSD. While we await the results of yet more controlled experiments on EMDR, appropriately trained clinicians are providing useful data in the form of pre- and posttreatment measures, together with follow-up assessment and behavioral measures. This is discussed more fully in Appendix C.

PARADIGM SHIFT

The change of name from EMD to EMDR in 1990 included a change in orientation from the initial behavioral formulation of simple desensitization of anxiety to a more integrative information-processing paradigm. This paradigm includes the application to clinical practice of the terminology and some of the concepts of information processing and associative networks originally presented by Lang (1977) and Bower (1981). While there are a number of other information-processing theories that hold great merit (Chemtob, Roitblat, Hamada, Carlson, & Twentyman, 1988; Foa & Kozak, 1986; Horowitz, 1979; Litz & Keane, 1989), the EMDR model is both compatible with them and distinct in its elements and applications. Observation of many EMDR treatment sessions has identified certain patterns of information processing and memory association that have led to the formulation of certain principles, which in turn guided the continued development and refinement of the specific practice, protocols, and procedures of EMDR.

One principle that is crucial to EMDR practice (but not specified in other theories) and which is suggested by the consistent application of the procedure is that there is a system inherent in all of us that is physiologically geared to process information to a state of mental health. This adaptive resolution means that negative emotions are relieved and that learning takes place, is appropriately integrated, and is available for future use. The system may become unbalanced due to a trauma or through stress engendered during a developmental period, but once it is appropriately activated and maintained in a dynamic state by means of EMDR, it transmutes information to a state of therapeutically appropriate resolution. Desensitization and cognitive restructuring are viewed as byproducts of the adaptive reprocessing taking place on a neurophysiological level.

This principle in no way contradicts my originally held behavioral orientation, which included a recognition of the interaction of learned material, conditioned responses, physiological concomitants, and the therapist's ability to intervene in a structured manner for behaviorally observable results. Indeed, many behaviorists may interpret EMDR solely in terms of conditioning and/or exposure. However, while research over the next decade will undoubtedly shed much light on the underlying mechanisms of EMDR, clinicians currently need the most useful clinical heuristic we can provide. The information-processing paradigm, which I have termed the Accelerated Information Processing model, provides a way to explain EMDR's treatment effects as well as to successfully predict the appropriate application of the method to a variety of presenting problems. The next section briefly describes the parameters of the model. A more extensive discussion is offered in Chapter 2.

ACCELERATED INFORMATION PROCESSING

The Accelerated Information Processing model was developed to explain the rapidity with which clinical results are achieved with EMDR and the consistency of the many patterns of response to it. On the basis of the observation of thousands of EMDR treatment sessions, the earlier desensitization paradigm was replaced by this model, which appears not only to explain treatment outcomes more effectively but to accurately predict more beneficial clinical effects when certain variations are used. Hence, the therapeutic application of principles, protocols, and procedures consistent with the new information-processing model results in treatment effects that are much better than those produced by the initially described EMD (Shapiro, 1989a, 1989b; see Beere, 1992; Lipke & Botkin, 1992; Shapiro, 1991a, 1993).

Briefly stated, the model regards most pathologies as derived from earlier life experiences that set in motion a continued pattern of affect, behavior, cognitions, and consequent identity structures. (We will explore this in detail in Chapter 2.) The pathological structure is inherent within the static, insufficiently processed information stored at the time of the disturbing event. From cases of simple PTSD and phobias to more complex conditions such as panic disorders, some forms of depression, dissociation, and personality disorders, pathology is viewed as configured by the impact of earlier experiences that are held in the nervous system in state-specific form.

The continued influence of these early experiences is due in large part to the fact that present-day stimuli elicit the negative affect and beliefs embodied in these memories and cause the client to continue acting in a way consistent with the earlier events. Although a client's memory may be of an event that actually took place and of behavior that may have included responses that were, at the time, appropriate for the disturbing situation, the lack of adequate assimilation means that the client is still reacting emotionally and behaviorally in ways consistent with the earlier disturbing event. For example, a child may understandably feel fear and lack of control when threatened by an adult, but an identical reaction by an adult to a similar situation is generally inappropriate. Likewise, an adult may feel fear and lack of control during a hurricane, but an identical reaction to a stiff breeze months later is pathological. The dysfunctional nature of traumatic memories, including the way in which they are stored, allows the negative affect and beliefs from the past to pervade the client in the present. EMDR processing of such memories allows the more positive and empowering present affect and cognitions to generalize to the associated memories throughout the neurophysiological network and leads spontaneously to more appropriate behaviors by the client. Clinical pathologies are therefore viewed as amenable to change if the clinician appropriately targets the information that has been stored dysfunctionally in the nervous system. Part of the clinical history-taking process is to identify the memories that have helped form the client's negative self-concepts and behaviors. Even pronounced personality disorders are viewed as susceptible to change by virtue of reprocessing the memories that set in motion the dysfunctional characteristics, the memories, for instance, that cause a paranoid personality to be suspicious of people and an avoidant personality to feel unsafe.

Adopting the Accelerated Information Processing model can facilitate the ability of many EMDR-trained clinicians to achieve the highest possible level of treatment effects. For some clinicians this may appear to be a natural integration of already held beliefs; for others it may demand a paradigm shift. There are a number of critical elements of the proposed paradigm. I mention them here, but they will be much more thoroughly developed in Chapter 2.

1. *The possibility of direct, nonintrusive, physiological engagement with the stored pathological elements:* Observation of EMDR treatment effects suggests that pathologies are represented by dysfunctional information that is physiologically stored and that can be accessed and transformed directly, without the use of medication. For instance, rather than targeting the client's *reaction* to the disturbing event—as biofeedback, flooding, or relaxation training does—EMDR focuses on the memory itself. The resulting transmutation of the information in the targeted memory appears to occur spontaneously, leading to a change in client reaction.

The observations of EMDR-produced shifts in the memory itself and the way it is stored are consistent with recent independent conjectures regarding the different manifestations of declarative (narrative) and nondeclarative memory (Lipke, 1992a; van der Kolk, 1994). For instance, before EMDR treatment a traumatic target memory is manifested by a picture, cognition, affect, and physical sensations that are in the state-specific and disturbing form in which they were acquired. These factors indicate that the traumatic memory is held in nondeclarative memory. After EMDR treatment, however, the memories are stored with a less disturbing picture, a positive cognition and the appropriate affect. In addition, there are no attendant disturbing physical sensations. Perhaps the processing of the information allows its appropriate storage in declarative memory, a development that also means freedom from pathological reactions.

2. *An information-processing system that is intrinsic and adaptive:* It appears that an innate information-processing system exists and that pathologies occur because this mechanism is blocked. Therefore, if the traumatic memory is accessed and the system is activated, the information is taken to an adaptive resolution. The observations of thousands of EMDR treatment sessions appear to bear out this conjecture. Apparently, the system is configured to process the information and restore mental health in much the same way the rest of the body is geared physiologically to heal when injured. This belief is the basis for EMDR's primarily client-centered model, which assumes that the client's shifting cognitions and levels of affect during an EMDR treatment will move to an optimal level with minimal clinician intrusion.

The suggestion that trauma itself in some way causes an imbalance that prevents adequate processing was presented by Janet (1889/1973) and Pavlov (1927) and has been made in contemporary studies on the effects of neurotransmitters (van der Kolk, 1994; Watson, Hoffman, & Wilson, 1988; Zager & Black, 1985). In addition, the hypothesis that the traumatic information itself will move to a positive plateau once the system is activated has grown from the consistent observations of EMDR treatment sessions. For instance, there are no reports of a rape victim who is at peace with the event who subsequently moves through EMDR to a level of self-loathing. However, rape victims entering treatment in a state of shame and guilt have evolved to positive states, such as self-acceptance and peace. While EMDR clients may break through feelings of dissociation and denial and temporarily feel more disturbed, this is merely a transitional stage toward healthy resolution.

This movement toward a positive state when the information-processing system is maintained in dynamic form through the use of EMDR is certainly consistent with conjectures by Maslow (1970). On the other hand, it is also consistent with the assumptions of the medical model, wherein medications and interventions are used to unblock or accelerate the body's natural healing properties. In the EMDR treatment of trauma, an analogous healing is assumed if the information-processing mechanism is unblocked.

3. *Identity constructs change as the embedded information shifts:* As the disturbing information is transformed, there is a concomitant shift in cognitive structure, behavior, affect, sensation, and so forth. Clinical experience has shown that once specific memories are reprocessed, the client's sense of self-worth and self-efficacy automatically shift. This leads spontaneously to new, more self-enhancing, behaviors. The Accelerated Information Processing model holds that underlying dysfunctional memories are primarily responsible for pathological personality characteristics and that they can be structurally altered. The theory accurately predicted and is consistent with findings of EMDR clinicians that even severe personality disorders may be amenable to comparatively rapid change through the targeting and reprocessing of key memories (with the obvious exception of chemically or organically based conditions).

4. *A release from previously accepted temporal limitations:* EMDR has the ability to facilitate profound therapeutic change in much less time than has been traditionally assumed to be necessary, regardless of the number of years since the traumatic event occurred. In EMDR the clinical emphasis is on facilitating therapeutic effects through the adaptive connection of associative neurophysiological networks in the information-processing system. The close physical proximity of these networks logically dictates that treatment outcomes need not be rigidly time-bound. For example, cases of single-session reprocessing effects, noted as complete desensitization and cognitive restructuring of traumatic memories, in hitherto treatment-resistant Vietnam veterans have been reported by a number of DVA Medical Center program directors (Daniels et al., 1992).

Let me underscore that it was the observation of the *spontaneously* generated eye movements that led to my belief that I had stumbled upon an inherent physiological mechanism that influences cognitive processes. This initial evaluation was particularly important because it became the underpinning of the subsequent theoretical framework and my willingness to accept the rapid and profound therapeutic changes that occurred more and more consistently as the method evolved. It seemed logical that using the eye movement to deliberately engage an inherent physiological mechanism that had evolved to process disturbing information could offer treatment effects comparable to, if not surpassing, psychopharmacological interventions. The chemical alteration of synaptic receptors or biochemical/electrical concomitants to treat PTSD was clearly an accepted area of investigation. EMDR differs primarily from the more conventional neurobiological treatment approaches, which advocate benzodiazepines, carbamazepine, or lithium, in its use of a body mechanism rather than a chemical intervention to initiate treatment effects. Even if other mechanisms besides eye movements (as described in Chapter 3) prove to have an equal effect, the whole discipline of physical therapy shows that inherent physiological processes can be mobilized by more than just biochemical means. Clinical observations with EMDR during the past 8 years certainly support this conjecture.

Since all clinical modalities can be defined as ultimately working with information stored physiologically in the brain, the information-processing paradigm provides an integrative approach that can include and interpret key aspects of such different modalities as psychodynamic, behavioral, cognitive, Gestalt, and body-oriented therapies (including psychopharmacology).

THEORETICAL CONVERGENCES

The use of EMDR can be fully compatible with most of the known psychological modalities. The importance of early childhood memories clearly fits into the psychodynamic model (Freud, 1900/1953; Jung, 1916), while the importance of the focused attention to current dysfunctional reactions and behaviors is completely consistent with the conditioning and generalization paradigms of classical behaviorism (Salter, 1961; Wolpe, 1991). In addition to being a client-centered approach (Rogers, 1951), EMDR addresses the concept of positive and negative self-assessments, which has firm roots in the field of cognitive therapy (Beck, 1967; Ellis, 1962; Meichenbaum, 1977; Young, 1990), and its emphasis on the physical responses related to a client's presenting dysfunction (Lang, 1979) is proving to be an important element in its full therapeutic utilization.

Posttraumatic Stress Disorder

EMDR began as a therapy specifically for the treatment of people with PTSD. As such, the fundamental approach and a number of the treatment components were based on research reports regarding this population. For instance, studies done with Vietnam combat veterans called attention to the traumatic event itself, indicating that the psychological reactions to stress are expected to persist as a direct function of the magnitude of the stressor (Figley, 1978b; Kadushin, Boulanger, & Martin, 1981; Laufer et al., 1981; McDermott, 1981; Strayer & Ellenhorn, 1975; Wilson, 1978).

There is a consensus in the therapeutic community working with trauma survivors that the amelioration of PTSD is accomplished by coming to grips with the traumatic incident, and a wide range of treatment techniques are employed. Unfortunately, there are few controlled studies in the literature to corroborate the efficacy of any of them. Most of the published work in this area entails etiological, epidemiological, or theoretical conjectures, usually based on uncontrolled case studies and enumerations of promising treatment techniques (Blake, Abueg, Woodward, & Keane, 1993; Hyer, 1994b; Malloy, Fairbank, & Keane, 1983; Solomon, Gerrity, & Muff, 1992). Nevertheless, various aspects of a number of the theories and treatments were incorporated into EMDR practice and have proved to be quite efficacious.

Biochemical Approaches

One promising area of research concerns the hypothesis that PTSD results from stress-induced changes in the biochemistry of the central nervous system, or CNS (Anisman, 1978; Christi & Chesher, 1982). It is conjectured that the "learned helplessness" paradigm in laboratory animals subjected to inescapable shock is the same as the behavioral effects of PTSD (van der Kolk, Greenberg, Boyd, & Krystal, 1985). It is also proposed that trauma induces changes in the CNS norepinephrine level, a development that leads to a decrease in functioning and such symptoms as diminished motivation and constricted affect. This paradigm also accounts for symptoms of hyperactivity and increased emotional lability caused by a consequent noradrenergic hypersensitivity. Given this understanding, van der Kolk proposed that treatment for PTSD entail a forced exposure similar to that used to extinguish the effects of inescapable shock in laboratory animals.

Other theories also suggest that physiological changes lead to the hyperarousal and oversensitivity of PTSD victims. Kolb (1987) hypothesized cortical changes in the mechanisms that regulate sleep and aggressive-control functions. Van der Kolk (1987) and Friedman

(1988) suggested "kindling" (progressive sensitivity) as a cause of PTSD's arousal states. These biochemical models are consistent with the Accelerated Information Processing model, which posits that physiologically blocked processing is responsible for the pathology and that EMDR's rapid, positive treatment effects result from electro-biochemical changes that rebalance an inherent physiological system responsible for healthy assimilation of the traumatic event.

Psychodynamic Approaches

Also compatible is the psychodynamic information-processing model (Horowitz, 1979), which proposes that one's natural "completion tendency" continues to rework the traumatic information in active memory until it can be reconciled with one's internal models of the world. Unless the trauma can be incorporated into existing schemata, the information will remain in active memory and will break through in intrusive thoughts. This process alternates with numbing and avoidance until some integration results.

The psychodynamic approach attempts to reintegrate the traumatic experience using a variety of techniques geared to specific stages of the disorder (or the therapeutic process), as well as to the personality development of the client (Blackburn, O'Connell, & Richman, 1984; Brende, 1981; Brende & McCann, 1984; Crump, 1984; Horowitz, 1973, 1974; Horowitz & Kaltreider, 1980). Therapeutic interventions include "covering" techniques (such as stress management) for stages involving intrusive memories and "uncovering" techniques (such as psychodrama) during denial stages (Horowitz, 1973, 1974). Unfortunately, studies that have investigated the effectiveness of the psychodynamic approach (Horowitz, Marmar, Weiss, Dewitt, & Rosenbaum, 1984; Lindy, Green, Grace, & Titchener, 1983) remain hampered by the lack of control groups and the mixed-subject pool in which only a portion of the clients are diagnosable as having PTSD. However, the "completion tendency" theory is clearly compatible with EMDR's blocked-processing paradigm, and the utilization of various strategies for effective relief is consistent with the multimodality approach of EMDR, which includes self-control techniques, the incorporation of stages of imagined reenactment, and the adoption of alternative behaviors.

Behavioral Approaches

The behavioral approach to PTSD has been elucidated by Keane, Zimering, and Caddell (1985) and follows Mowrer's (1960) two-factor learning theory, which incorporates both classical and operant conditioning. Proponents of this theory argue that there is an analogous relationship between the development of the fear and avoidance behavior found in PTSD and that found in laboratory-conditioned animals (Keane, Zimering, & Caddell, 1985; Kilpatrick, Veronen, & Resick, 1982; Kolb, 1984).

The first factor in Mowrer's theory involves learning by association, or classical conditioning, as in Pavlov's early experiments where a bell, termed a conditioned stimulus (CS), was paired with a shock, or unconditioned stimulus (UCS). This pairing leads to an aversive emotional state (such as fear) at the sound of the bell (Pavlov, 1927). The second factor is instrumental learning, or avoidance behavior, which entails consistent avoidance by the organism of both the conditioned stimulus (bell) and unconditioned stimulus (shock). In this paradigm the fear generated by gunfire in wartime or by rape is associated with other presenting cues. All such cues, such as loud noises or dark streets, are then avoided by the victim whenever possible. Two controlled studies of veterans' responses to combat cues have supported this conditioning model (Blanchard, Kolb, Pallmayer, & Gerardi, 1982; Malloy et al., 1983). Further, success has been reported in a number of therapeutic interventions that are based on this learning theory (Fairbank & Nicholson, 1987).

Diagnostic criteria for PTSD include intrusive thoughts regarding traumatic events, flashbacks, and nightmares that include specific details of the trauma. Therefore, behavioral techniques have been adapted to increase exposure to the conditioned stimulus in order to cause experimental extinction of the concomitant anxiety/fear behavior and physiological arousal. Since the existence of the traumatic incident is the basis of the psychological and behavioral maladaptation, behavioral approaches have employed direct therapeutic exposure (DTE; Boudewyns & Shipley, 1983) techniques, also known as flooding (Malleson, 1959) and implosion (Stampfl, cited in London, 1964), for the alleviation of PTSD. These procedures have been used in a number of case studies (Black & Keane, 1982; Fairbank, Gross, & Keane, 1983; Fairbank & Keane, 1982; Johnson, Gilmore, & Shenoy, 1982; Keane, Fairbank, Caddell, Zimering, & Bender, 1985; Keane & Kaloupek, 1982; Miller & Buchbinder, 1979; Schindler, 1980; Scrignar, 1983) and in four outcome studies (Boudewyns & Hyer, 1990; Boudewyns, Hyer, Woods, Harrison, & McCranie, 1990; Cooper & Clum, 1989; Keane, Fairbank, Caddell, & Zimering, 1989).

In the DTE treatment of PTSD, traumatic memories are often relived over several sessions until the anxiety is reduced. The intention is to produce the maximum amount of anxiety in the client for the most sustained period. The treatment is based on the assumption that forced exposure that prohibits the usual avoidance response to an anxiety-producing stimulus (which is not reinforced by an unconditioned aversive stimulus) will cause the anxiety to be extinguished (Levis, 1980; Stampfl & Levis, 1967). Representative is the case of a Vietnam combat veteran disturbed by the memory of a traumatic event in which he was the only survivor of a five-man team; nine sessions of 60 to 70 minutes each were required for successful treatment (Fairbank et al., 1983).

While the intensity of the evoked anxiety and the number of sessions necessary to reach desensitization with DTE might indicate a likelihood of dropouts from treatment, there are as yet no data available on the rate of attrition. However, the therapeutic community continues to voice concern about the forced elicitation of high-anxiety responses in clients for such prolonged periods (Fairbank & Brown, 1987b; Pitman et al., 1991). Fortunately, EMDR offers an alternative method for the treatment of traumatic memories that does not demand prolonged exposure to high-anxiety-producing stimuli and yet desensitizes the traumatic event rapidly.

In many regards, EMDR can be considered an exposure method because the client is asked to maintain the traumatic event in consciousness for direct treatment effect. However, the amount of exposure needed in EMDR appears to be much less than the prolonged exposure required by DTE techniques for the inhibition process to develop and for the client to show signs of decreased anxiety (Daniels et al., 1992; Wilson, Covi, Foster, & Silver, 1995; Wilson, Becker, & Tinker, in press). In addition, in EMDR there is no attempt to exacerbate or increase the level of anxiety, as there is in DTE, a difference that appears to make EMDR more satisfactory to many clinicians (Lipke, 1992b).

However, consistent with the cited research, the need for some exposure to the traumatic event is undeniable, as is the need to decondition the associated stimuli. For these reasons, EMDR protocols incorporate a three-pronged approach that entails the reprocessing of the primary events, the present stimuli and the negative reactions to projected future behaviors.

Cognitive–Behavioral Approaches

The incorporation into EMDR of aspects of cognitive therapy, along with the desensitization phase, was based on research reports involving the treatment of rape victims. Rape victims constitute the largest population of PTSD sufferers and the only homogeneous group besides combat veterans that has been the focus of controlled clinical outcome research. Treatment often involves multimethod approaches, including the teaching of coping skills, cognitive interventions, and stress management techniques and the dispensing of information that dispels social myths that exacerbate the victim's negative self-statements (Forman, 1980; Kilpatrick & Veronen, 1983; Pearson, Poquette, & Wasden,

1983; Veronen & Kilpatrick, 1983). A three-stage stress-inoculation program has been used, which includes an educational stage; a rehearsal stage, where relaxation and cognitive coping skills are explored; and an application stage (Meichenbaum, 1977). It is during the application stage—or by themselves—that exposure techniques have been successfully used (Pearson et al., 1983; Rychtarik, Silverman, Van Landingham, & Prue, 1984; Wolff, 1977).

Although there is a heavy emphasis on the cognitive aspect of the therapeutic process, an examination of the literature indicates that exposure techniques are often used either as part of a total treatment package or as the major treatment component (Fairbank & Brown, 1987a). Systematic desensitization, which entails a combination of graduated exposure to low-level anxiety and relaxation (Wolpe, 1958), has been used successfully with rape victims, where treatment focuses on rape-related cues and the client's feelings of fear and anxiety. The technique has been successfully used with a variety of cases to alleviate fear, anxiety, and depression and to increase social adjustment (Frank et al., 1988; Frank & Stewart, 1983a, 1983b; Pearson et al., 1983; Turner, 1979; Wolff, 1977). However, lack of control groups and small sample size mar much of the research. In addition, the successful use of DTE has been documented in a study of four sexual assault victims (Haynes & Mooney, 1975) and in a case of incest in which treatment required five 80-to-90-minute treatments on consecutive days (Rychtarik et al., 1984).

While desensitization to the traumatic cues appears effective, the therapeutic community seems particularly concerned about the use of DTE on rape victims because of its failure to specifically address irrational cognitions or to provide alternative coping strategies and because of the likelihood of a high dropout rate owing to the prolonged anxiety it produces (Kilpatrick et al., 1982; Kilpatrick & Best, 1984) in a population already known to have a high treatment attrition rate (Veronen & Kilpatrick, 1983). While these points have been systematically rebutted (Rychtarik et al., 1984), there remains a scarcity of reports in the literature regarding the use of DTE with rape victims (Steketee & Foa, 1987), possibly because of the strong level of anxiety that must be evoked and maintained for a successful treatment. The one controlled comparative study with this PTSD population (Foa, Rothbaum, Riggs, & Murdock, 1991) compared supportive counseling (SC), stress inoculation therapy (SIT), and prolonged exposure (PE), a variant of flooding. Immediately following treatment, SIT was found to be superior to PE, but this was reversed at the 4-month follow-up. Both PE and SIT were superior to SC; however, 45% of the subjects (who received seven sessions of either PE or SIT) still retained the diagnosis of PTSD 3.5 months after treatment. Therefore, this study (plus the findings of Frank et al., 1988) seems to indicate that a combination of exposure and cognitive restructuring would be the most effective method of treatment (a view that has recently received experimental support; see Resick & Schnicke, 1992).

As with the literature on combat-related PTSD, there are few controlled group studies published on rape-related PTSD (Foa et al., 1991; Resick & Schnicke, 1992) but a variety of individual case reports. Another difficulty in searching the published literature to assess the effectiveness of treatment procedures with this population is that many of the treatments are inaugurated during the first 3 months after the assault, during which time spontaneous recovery from PTSD symptoms is likely to occur (Fairbank & Brown, 1987b; Kilpatrick & Calhoun, 1988). Despite the difficulties, however, there seems to be a significant indication of the need for cognitive restructuring of the rape/incest victim owing to the societally reinforced self-denigrating thoughts and self-assessments of rape victims, cognitions that are reflected by feelings of self-blame, guilt, and shame (Bart & Scheppele, 1980; Burgess & Holmstrom, 1974; Forman, 1980; Hepper & Hepper, 1977; Scheppele & Bart, 1983; Veronen & Kilpatrick, 1980).

Recurrent themes in cases of rape, such as sadness over loss, discomfort over vulnerability, fear of attack, and guilt about responsibility, need to be dealt with (Krupnick & Horowitz, 1981). Attention should be directed to the three basic beliefs or assumptions that may be shattered by victimization: personal invulnerability, the perception of the world as meaningful, and positive self-image (Janoff-Bulman, 1985). Cognitive therapy has been successful in reducing fear, depression, and anxiety in research with rape victims (Frank, Turner, & Duffy, 1979; Frank & Stewart, 1983b; Resick, Jordan, Girelli, Hutter, & Marhoerfer-Dvorak, 1988; Turner & Frank, 1981), and one study (Frank et al., 1988) comparing cognitive therapy and desensitization indicates equivalent treatment effects. However, the lack of adequate control groups limits the conclusions that can be drawn about its efficacy.

Integrative Approach

The consensus in the research literature is that some form of exposure to the traumatic cues to prevent avoidance and allow desensitization is necessary for the successful treatment of PTSD (see Fairbank & Brown, 1987a; Fairbank & Nicholson, 1987). However, as indicated above, research shows that a combined cognitive and exposure approach might be more effective than exposure alone, as is also the case in the treatment of phobia (Rachman, 1978). There is considerable similarity in the reported treatments of phobias and PTSD (Fairbank & Brown, 1987a; Kuch, 1987). In light of these observations, EMDR was developed as a method that would specifically help integrate new desirable self-statements while allowing for rapidly desensitizing traumatic cues. Within this paradigm, a cognitive reassessment that includes redefining the event, finding meaning in it, and alleviating the inappropriate self-blame (Janoff-Bulman, 1985) is an important aspect of the EMDR treatment of trauma survivors. A recent study in which clients were exposed to memories of the traumatic event while changes in their physiology were monitored (Wilson et al., 1995) indicates that the desensitization (and cognitive restructuring) observed in EMDR may be caused by an intrinsic relaxation response. This response pairs a profound relaxation with anxiety (causing deconditioning) in a manner that is similar to but more rapid than systematic desensitization and that certainly causes less prolonged distress than does DTE. Also incorporated within EMDR is a rapid way of helping the client integrate the new information, coping skills, and behaviors offered by the clinician.

EYE MOVEMENTS

It has been observed clinically that similar processing effects may be derived from the use of stimuli other than the directed eye movements of EMDR; examples are hand taps, lights, and auditory cues (Shapiro, 1993). In fact, since 1990 we have instructed clinicians taking EMDR training in the use of hand taps and auditory cues as alternatives to the directed eye movements. However, further investigation may find that eye movements have a unique status as a stimulus that is also an observable inherent physiological manifestation of some types of cognitive processing. For instance, in addition to spontaneously generated rapid eye movements, whose effect on disturbing thoughts I observed initially (Shapiro, 1989a), there are also involuntary rhythmical eye movements, known as nystagmus, which have been noted during concentration in psychotherapy patients (Teitelbaum, 1954) and an observed relationship among eye movements, attention, and anxiety (Day, 1964). An association between eye movement and problem solving has also been reported (Amadeo & Shagass,1963; Antrobus & Singer, 1964), and there is extensive research on the relationship of eye movement to cognitive process and cortical function (Gale & Johnson, 1982; Leigh & Zee, 1983; Monty, Fisher, & Senders, 1978; Monty & Senders, 1976; Ringo, Sobotka, Diltz, & Bruce, 1994).

Although EMDR was not originally derived from a theoretical basis, there appears to be a possible link between its effects and those of the rapid eye movement (REM) stage of sleep (Neilsen, 1991; Shapiro, 1989a, 1989b). This stage was named for the rapid eye movements that occur during periods in which subjects when awakened are likely to report that they were dreaming (Aserinsky & Kleitman, 1953). A number of researchers have postulated that the REM state serves to process information, including emotional, stress-related, and survival material (Gabel, 1987; Greenberg, Katz, Schwartz, & Pearlman, 1992;

Winson, 1990, 1993), and there is evidence that PTSD patients attempt to make more use of REM sleep than do normal subjects (Ross et al., 1994).

The observation that other stimuli, such as rhythmic tapping or forced fixation, may have the effect of activating the proposed information-processing mechanism does not detract from the EMDR/REM hypothesis. Clearly, the body in sleep is not capable of producing auditory stimuli or other forms of focused attention, and clinicians can certainly provide more choices for activating this kind of information processing in the waking state. Moreover, independent research in the field of sleep behavior has produced results that appear to support the EMDR/REM hypothesis. While earlier research suggested that REM patterns might be associated with scanning the dream environment, a recent study (Hong, Gillin, Callaghan, & Potkin, 1992) indicates that the amount of REM is correlated with the intensity of the emotional state. In addition, supporting the connection between REM (and, consequently, eye movements) and cognitive processing are studies (Karni, Tanne, Rubenstein, Askenasi, & Sagi, 1992; Mandai, Guerrien, Sockeel, Dujardin, & Leconte,1989; Tilly & Empson, 1978) that reveal a relationship between the learning of new material and uninterrupted REM. That is, if subjects are taught a new skill, they do not assimilate it well if their REM sleep is disturbed. In addition, my earlier suggestions (Shapiro, 1989a, 1989b) that the eye movements may have an inhibiting effect on stress (and, reciprocally, that excessive stress may inhibit the eye movements) appear supported by the conclusion of other investigators that disrupted REM sleep is a cardinal feature of PTSD (Ross et al., 1990). For example, instead of fully processing a traumatic combat experience while they sleep, combat veterans with PTSD awaken in the middle of a nightmare.

It is possible that the eye movements that occur during REM sleep are an indication of concomitant cognitive processes rather than their cause. Alternatively, the deliberate instigation of eye movements may stimulate the corresponding cortical functions, leading in turn to the cognitive processes. It is important to understand, however, that the EMDR/REM hypothesis is merely a conjecture and not a necessary correlate of the observed treatment effects. Indeed, the similarity of states in EMDR and REM sleep may prove to be more usefully viewed as an analogue than as evidence of a direct, unique causal connection between the eye movements and processing.

METHOD COMPLEXITY

Some of the controversy and resistance to the reports of clinical effects of EMDR may be due to the mistaken view that this form of psychotherapy is a simplistic behavioral technique. However, as this book makes quite clear, EMDR contains many components besides the eye movements. Indeed, it is a complex clinical intervention directed toward all aspects of memory and dysfunction, as well as toward ways of generalizing the positive effects. Every EMDR treatment session includes attention to negative and positive self-attributions, somatic manifestations, issues of self-control and self-esteem, and much more. EMDR components are embedded in the clinical approach, the framing of client participation, the protocols, and the procedures themselves. As we will explore more fully in Chapter 12, the fact that research has focused on the directed eye movement alone is a simplification and reductive of the method; such a research focus is misleading because clinical effectiveness is built into every component of EMDR, not just the eye movements.

In fact, even without the eye movements, EMDR has shown itself to be an efficient and structured approach to pathology that offers positive therapeutic benefit. It is important to understand EMDR as a complex methodology and to give significant weight to each of its components (the use of negative and positive cognitions, the use of SUD and VOC scales, and so on) and to its eight treatment phases. While the apparent effect of the eye movements became the impetus for the development of EMDR, each of its components has evolved and been refined over time to maximize treatment effects. Clinicians who attempt to use truncated versions of the method or who apply it without the appropriate supervised instruction do a disservice to the method and to the clients who depend upon us for educated assistance. These same cautions apply to researchers and will be more fully explored in the final chapter of this book.

SUMMARY AND CONCLUSIONS

The origin of EMDR, initially called EMD, was my observation of the apparent desensitizing effect of spontaneous repeated eye movements on unpleasant thoughts. The use of directed eye movements with 70 volunteers with nonpathological complaints proved variably effective in reducing disturbance. During these trials the procedure was elaborated to maximize its effects for use on a clinical population. A controlled study, published in the *Journal of Traumatic Stress* in 1989, of 22 subjects suffering from PTSD symptomatology indicated that the procedure was highly beneficial for desensitization, cognitive restructuring, and elimination of pronounced intrusions stemming from the traumatic event.

The change of name from EMD to EMDR occurred when it became apparent that the procedure entailed an information-processing mechanism rather than a simple desensitization treatment effect. The integrative Accelerated Information Processing model underscores a physiologically based methodology that stimulates the presumed self-healing mode of an inherent information-processing system. Early memories are considered to be the primary basis for many present pathologies, and EMDR effects are viewed as rapidly changing the impact of these memories in order to alter the current clinical picture.

Many of the components of EMDR were derived from PTSD studies and case reports in the field of biochemistry and in psychotherapies with psychodynamic, cognitive, and behavioral orientations. While this book is based primarily on clinical observations, there is theoretical and research support in many related scientific areas, including the study of sleep and dreaming. However, while the effects of REM sleep are suggested analogues to the effects of directed eye movements, both hand taps and auditory cues are useful alternative stimuli. It should be noted for both clinical and research purposes that EMDR is a complex method with a variety of components that are necessary for full effectiveness. The next chapter continues with a more detailed explication of the model for clinical use.

CHAPTER 2

Accelerated
Information Processing

THE MODEL AS A WORKING HYPOTHESIS

> As far as the laws of mathematics refer to reality, they are
> not certain; as far as they are certain, they do not refer to
> reality.
>
> *Albert Einstein*

As described in Chapter 1, EMDR is based on my empirical observation
of the effect of eye movements on emotional–cognitive processing. I
developed the basic procedural steps through trial and error by observing clinical results. The rapid, observable effects allowed me to delineate
various patterns of clinical response and naturally led me to formulate
various theories in an attempt to explain them. Refining these theoretical principles allowed me to predict and test new applications of the
procedures, which in turn molded the method's ongoing development.
While we cannot be sure that the resultant theories represent what is
going on physiologically, they are consistent with observations and help
to guide clinical decisions by the logical application of the primary
principles. In addition, for many, the model can be viewed as a paradig-
matic shift in understanding the nature of therapeutic change.

In this chapter I will describe Accelerated Information Processing,
which helps to provide an explanation of how EMDR therapy works.
First, I will explain how EMDR fits into the Accelerated Information
Processing model, and then I will show how it can be used to gain access
to and have an impact on material that is dysfunctionally stored in the
brain. A transcript of an actual client session will highlight some
important aspects of this exposition. I will also review the nature of
psychopathology, a variety of clinical applications, and the integrated
nature of the EMDR treatment approach.

While this chapter presents in detail the current model that guides
the use of EMDR, it is important to understand that *this model is offered as*

a working hypothesis only and is subject to modification based on further laboratory and clinical observation. Note that although the model applies to clinical practice, it utilizes the terminology of neurophysiological information processing introduced by Bower (1981) and Lang (1979). In addition, I use psychophysiological concepts by employing the term *neurophysiological* or *neuro networks*. This construct will subsume the way the term *neural networks* is currently being used by neuropsychologists and extend it to an additional strata of cognitive/emotional processing. Using a term that does not have a precise neurophysiological referent is particularly important to underscore the point that the efficacy of EMDR is not based on the validity of the physiological model being offered. This is relevant because we must remember that the physiology of the brain is not yet sufficiently understood to confirm the validity of the model at that level. However, the model does not appear to contradict anything known to be true, is congruent with the observed treatment effects of EMDR, and serves as a clinical road map for treating a wide range of pathologies. So far, the model has proved explanatory and highly predictive of therapeutic response in new areas of application.

INFORMATION PROCESSING

While EMDR is a specific therapeutic method, Accelerated Information Processing (Shapiro, 1993, 1994c) represents the general model that provides the theoretical framework and principles for this method. Thus, a set of Accelerated Information Processing treatments includes EMDR as one method. As a method, EMDR includes principles, procedures, and various protocols for a wide range of pathologies. Within the set of Accelerated Information Processing treatments, other methods may certainly arise that entail their own protocols and procedures. Indeed, there have already been reports of other methods, including forms of electrical stimulation (Schmitt, Capo, & Boyd, 1986) and photo arousal (Ochs, 1993), that are being used to good purpose.

The Accelerated Information Processing model is consistent with Freud's (1919/1955) and Pavlov's (1927) early understanding of what is now referred to as information processing. Specifically, there appears to be a neurological balance in a distinct physiological system that allows information to be processed to an "adaptive resolution." By adaptive resolution I mean that the connections to appropriate associations are made and that the experience is used constructively by the individual and is integrated into a positive emotional and cognitive schema. Essentially, what is useful is learned and stored with the appropriate affect and is available for future use. For example, let us say that something negative happens to us, such as a humiliation at work, and we are bothered by it. We think about it, dream about it, and talk about it. After a while, we are no longer bothered by it, and the experience may be used appropriately as information to guide our future actions. Thus, we learn something about ourselves and other people, we better understand past situations, and we are better able to handle similar situations in the future.

When someone experiences a severe psychological trauma, it appears that an imbalance may occur in the nervous system, caused perhaps by changes in neurotransmitters, adrenaline, and so forth. Due to this imbalance, the system is unable to function and the information acquired at the time of the event, including images, sounds, affect, and physical sensations, is maintained neurologically in its disturbing state. Therefore, the original material, which is held in this distressing, excitatory state-specific form, continues to be triggered by a variety of internal and external stimuli and is expressed in the form of nightmares, flashbacks, and intrusive thoughts—the so-called positive symptoms of PTSD.

The hypothesis is that the eye movements (or alternative stimuli) used in EMDR trigger a physiological mechanism that activates the information-processing system. Various mechanisms by which this activation and facilitation of processing occurs have been proposed, including the following:

1. Activation and facilitation of information processing due to the client's dual focus of attention as he simultaneously attends to the present stimuli and the past trauma
2. A differential effect of neuronal bursts caused by the various stimuli, which may serve as the equivalent of a low-voltage current and directly affect synaptic potential (Barrionuevo, Schottler, & Lynch, 1980; Larson & Lynch, 1989)
3. Deconditioning caused by a relaxation response (Shapiro, 1989a, 1989b; Wilson et al., 1995)

Therefore, in EMDR when we ask the client to bring up a memory of the trauma, we may be establishing a link between consciousness and the site where the information is stored in the brain. The eye movements (or alternate stimuli) activate the information-processing system and rebalance it. With each set of eye movements, we move the disturbing information—at an accelerated rate—further along the appropriate neurophysiological pathways until it is adaptively resolved. For instance, resolution may come when the previously isolated disturbing information is brought into contact with currently held adaptive information (such as "It wasn't my fault my father raped me"). One of EMDR's main assumptions is that activating the processing of the trauma memory will naturally move it toward the adaptive information it needs for resolution.

Inherent in the Accelerated Information Processing model is the concept of psychological self-healing, a construct based on the body's healing response to physical injury. For instance, when you cut your hand, your body works to close and heal the wound. If something blocks the healing, such as a foreign object or repeated trauma, the wound will fester and cause pain. If the block is removed, healing will resume. A similar sequence of events seems to occur with mental processes. That is, the natural tendency of the brain's information-processing system is to move toward a state of mental health. However, if the system is blocked or becomes imbalanced by the impact of a trauma, maladaptive responses are observed. These responses may be triggered by present stimuli or perhaps by the attempt of the information-processing mechanism to resolve the material. For instance, the rape victim may automatically continue to recall images of the rape in a blocked attempt to reach resolution and complete processing (Horowitz, 1979). If the block is removed, processing resumes and takes the information toward a state of adaptive resolution and functional integration. This resolution is manifested by a change in the images, affect, and cognitions the client associates with the event. Metaphorically, we can think of the processing mechanism as "digesting" or "metabolizing" the information so that it can be used in a healthy, life-enhancing manner.

I theorize that the information-processing system is adaptive when it is activated because abuse victims begin an EMDR treatment with a negative self-concept in regard to the event and consistently end with a positive sense of self-worth. Moreover, the opposite does not occur. That is, EMDR treatments reveal an accelerated progression toward health (positive emotions and higher self-regard), but not toward dysfunction (inappropriate blame and self-loathing). The notion of activating the adaptive information-processing mechanism is central to EMDR treatment and has been critical in its application to a variety of pathologies.

Alternate Stimuli

As noted earlier, there are other stimuli besides directed eye movements that can activate the information-processing system. For instance, hand taps and the repetition of auditory cues have also proven effective (Shapiro, 1994b). While it is not yet clear if such stimuli are as effective as the directed eye movements, the possibility should not be precluded inasmuch as the dual-focus hypothesis mentioned earlier may prove to be the most useful explanation of EMDR effects. Specifically, the information-processing mechanism may be activated by the act of concentrating on maintaining the eye movement (or attending to hand taps or auditory cues) or by the act of merely fixating a stimulus. Simultaneously focusing on the traumatic memory may cause the activated system to process the dysfunctionally stored material. Alternatively, if it is the neuro-electrical stimulation generated by the eye movements themselves that activates the information-processing system, we might expect other rhythmical movements or forms of sustained or repeated stimulation to have a similar effect.

In fact, clinicians have reported positive therapeutic results when certain alternatives to eye movements are used in selected cases. These alternatives will be described in Chapter 3, and their research implications will be discussed in Chapter 12.

As previously mentioned, I am offering a theoretical model to interpret the clinical effect, not to prove its existence. For example, the REM hypothesis only attempts to explain the apparent role of the eye movements in the treatment effects; it does not preclude the possible usefulness of other stimuli, such as hand taps or auditory cues. Even if directed saccadic or tracking eye movements do prove to stimulate a mechanism that also operates during REM sleep, this finding does not discount the potential effectiveness of other stimuli used in the waking state. Obviously, there may be other choices of stimuli, even though the body in a sleep state is incapable of generating auditory stimuli, hand taps, blinking lights, or other external fixating devices. Regardless of the exact mechanism that brings about EMDR's effects, it is the activation of the information-processing system that provides the clinical focus for treatment. Therefore, although the terms *sets* and *eye movements* are used throughout this text, they are meant to refer to sets of other effective stimuli as well.

MEMORY NETWORKS

Our hypothesis about the brain's innate information-processing system leads us to the concept of memory networks. In very simple terms, a memory network represents an associated system of information. No one knows what memory networks actually look like, but we can picture them metaphorically as a series of channels where related memories, thoughts, images, emotions, and sensations are stored and linked to one another.

EMDR treatment is conceptualized as progressing through memory networks, a configuration that is illustrated in Figure 5. When using EMDR, we ask the client to focus on a target, that is, a specific memory or dream image; a person; an actual, fantasized, or projected event; or some aspect of experience such as a body sensation or thought. In the Accelerated Information Processing model, this target is called a node because it has a pivotal place among the physiologically associated material. For instance, if the client's response to her boss is the presenting complaint, the clinician might target an image of the boss's face, which would be considered a node because of the constellation of associated

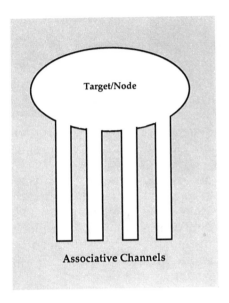

FIGURE 5. A graphic representation of the progression of EMDR treatment through the memory network.

experiences around it. If the client reacts to the target with undue anger or anxiety, it is because of the associations linked to it. These associations may include certain experiences with the boss or with other authority figures, such as the client's father. Therefore, if the goal of therapy is for the client to react calmly to the target, it is necessary to "clean out" each channel by reprocessing all of the dysfunctionally stored material connected to that node. The reprocessing is done during each set of eye movements (or other stimuli), and we view each progressive stage of reprocessing as a plateau where images, thoughts, and emotions complete a shift in their progress toward greater therapeutic resolution.

A SAMPLE EMDR SESSION

To illustrate the concepts underlying EMDR, let us look at the transcript of part of an actual treatment session. The client is a Vietnam veteran who had already been treated for a number of combat-related traumatic experiences. The client had suffered moderate PTSD symptoms since the war, despite many years of therapy, including occasional inpatient treatment. In four previous EMDR sessions he reprocessed his disturbing memories, and his intrusive thoughts subsided. The client's presenting complaint in this session is his negative reaction to an incompetent coworker. Although incompetence in a coworker is bound to be unpleasant for anyone, this client was reacting with such great anger and anxiety that he was incapable of working with the person. The client had been fighting his anger and frustration for weeks and finally asked for assistance because he could not escape working with his colleague on an ongoing project. The very thought of this coworker had become such a source of discomfort to the client that we used the coworker, rather than any specific interaction, as the target. As you will see, the clinician works with the client by using sets of eye movements to process the information causing his distress.

First, the therapist asks the client to visualize the incompetent coworker's face and to get in touch with the anxiety this generates. Then she asks him for a rating of any negative feelings he has, expressed in terms of the SUD (Subjective Units of Disturbance) Scale, where *0* represents a neutral or calm feeling and *10* equals the most disturbance he can imagine. Next, the therapist asks the client to begin the set by visually following a rhythmical motion made by her fingers. (Specific instructions on how to do this are given in Chapter 3.) The clinician checks in with the client between sets to determine the client's condition and to ask if any new information has emerged. The clinician assesses the information revealed after each set to determine if the client is processing the information and evolving to a more adaptive plateau.

At the end of each set, the therapist reinforces the client by saying, "Good." Then she instructs him to blank out what was last in mind and asks, "What do you get now?" The client then reports his most dominant thought, emotion (or intensity level), sensation, or image so that the therapist can get a reading on the new information plateau. On the basis of what she learns, the clinician will direct the client's attention either to the new information or to the original target. Figure 6 shows the node (the incompetent coworker) with the associated channels of information that are revealed by the client's successive responses. The first designation in each column (e.g., major anxiety, comical) reflects the initial response of the client when the target was brought to mind; below each such designation are the associations that emerged after each subsequent set was initiated. Only one phase (desensitization) of the treatment session will be illustrated.

Partial Transcript of the Sample Session

The client is "Eric," age 39. He is a computer programmer.

THERAPIST: So let's start with seeing the man you consider to be incompetent at work. Just look at him and see his face and feel how incompetent he is. From 0 to 10, how does it feel?

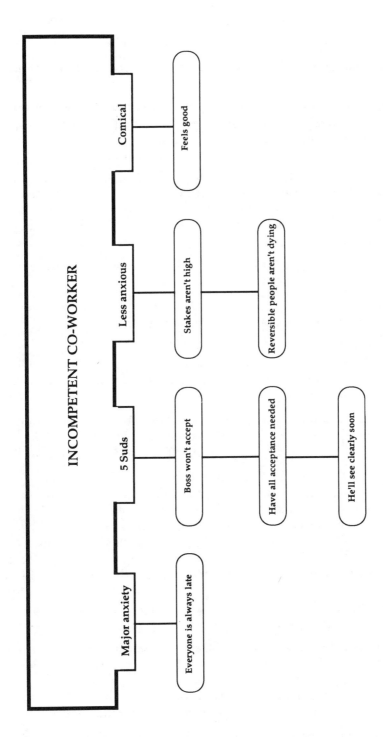

FIGURE 6. Diagram of a target (the incompetent co-worker) and the channels of information that emerge with EMDR treatment, in the form of the client's responses and the sequential associations related to those responses.

ERIC: 7.

[The client imagines the face of the coworker and gives an initial rating of 7 on the SUD Scale.]

THERAPIST: Concentrate on the feeling and follow my fingers with your eyes. (*leads client in a set of eye movements*) Good. Blank it out and take a deep breath. What do you get now?

ERIC: I don't know. I guess it feels a little bit better. Before coming in today I worked through some of the things and at least on an intellectual level I realized . . . well, it's work and you know I'm going to be late on the schedule and people are going to be upset at it, but that's always going to be true. I mean in the computer business someone is always late. So I started making some connections with that.

[This is the first channel that opens up. The therapist decides to return to the original target.]

THERAPIST: Right. When you bring up his face now and get into the sense of his incompetence, from 0 to 10, where is it?

ERIC: Probably a 5.

THERAPIST: Hold that. (*Again the clinician leads the client in a set of eye movements.*) Good. Blank it out and take a deep breath. What do you get now?

[As we will see, a new channel opens up because the client was brought back to the original target. This second channel indicates a chain of associated material linked by the concept of "personal acceptance."]

ERIC: One thing that comes up is, part of the reason that it's frustrating is that because of my boss's situation, he can't evaluate the other guy's ability. I guess it feels a little better in that other people can. I mean there are other people that see it and are frustrated by it. But I guess it's like I need everybody to realize what's going on. And since my boss can't recognize it, and agree to it, I guess it gets back to me needing to be competent and having other people feel I'm competent.

THERAPIST: Think of all of that. (*leads client in another set of eye movements*) Good. Blank it out and take a deep breath. What do you get now?

ERIC: Probably a 4 or a 3. Slowly but surely I'm starting to have periods where I realize I don't need other people's acceptance. I have a lot of people's acceptance and those are probably the ones that are important. It's difficult right now because my boss is one of them that I probably don't have, but that's his problem, not mine. (*laughs*)

[At this point a clinician using traditional therapy might be tempted to start a discussion focused on helping the client with his attitude. However, in EMDR, this response is contraindicated. Rather, the clinician asks the client to hold in mind what he just said and then leads him in another set of eye movements to stimulate further processing. The client then provides another reading on what is happening for him. As we will see, this client has reached a new plateau and the information has evolved to a more adaptive form.]

THERAPIST: Okay. Think of that. (*leads client in another set of eye movements*) Good. Blank it out and take a deep breath. What do you get now?

ERIC: I guess that I've got enough of his acceptance. I've got as much as I need. I mean, he needs me really badly right now, so certainly my job isn't in danger. So I've probably got as much as I need.

THERAPIST: Okay. Think of that. (*leads client in another set of eye movements*) Good. Blank it out and take a deep breath. What do you get now?

ERIC: Ah . . . the thing that occurs to me is that probably in the next couple of months the pressure's going to let up on the project and by that time he'll be able to see.

THERAPIST: Okay. Hold that one. (*leads client in another set of eye movements*) Good. Blank it out and take a deep breath. What do you get now?

ERIC: About the same.

[When the client indicates no change and is relatively comfortable, the clinician assumes he has "cleaned out" that second channel and brings him back to the original target.]

THERAPIST: Okay. Now what happens when you go back to the man's face that you feel is incompetent? What do you get now?

ERIC: It bothers me. I know I'm going to be frustrated by him in the future, but I think I'm going to be less likely to lose sight of what's going on.

[Note that although the client's level of anxiety has dropped, it is still bothersome. During the next set of eye movements the processing stimulates information stored associatively in a third channel. Here we discover the impact of Vietnam combat material: If someone was incompetent in Vietnam, it meant people could die.]

THERAPIST: Just see him again and feel the incompetence. (*leads client in another set of eye movements*) Good. Blank it out and take a deep breath. What do you get now?

ERIC: The thing that came to mind is, in this case the stakes aren't high. I mean, assuming I'm right and he is incompetent in this area and he gets in and screws everything up. So what? (*laughs*) I mean, we can turn it around.

THERAPIST: Really. Hold that one. (*leads client in another set of eye movements*) Good. Blank it out and take a deep breath. What do you get now?

ERIC: Um, it's just nice to know . . . it's nice to think about the stakes and realize that it's just a bunch of computers and obviously the issue is people aren't dying because that you can't reverse.

THERAPIST: So if you bring up his picture again, what do you get?

ERIC: Um, it's sort of comical!

[Once again, since the previous two responses were the same and the client is relatively comfortable, the third channel is considered cleared and the original target is elicited. We see that the client's reaction to the incompetent coworker is now quite different. Only after the psychological pressures of the Vietnam experience were released could the client react in a more relaxed manner.]

THERAPIST: Yes.

ERIC: I mean he's a very bright guy. He's a very capable guy. It's just that when I look at the kinds of errors he makes, they're comical, and they're the same ones we all made when we first tried this stuff out. You know you found a problem, you solved a little bitty piece of the problem. There's this giant problem out there, but you went, "Yeah! Great, I solved it" because it was the only thing you could find. (*laughs*) And so you're so excited you found it, you pretended that was the whole thing. And other people are seeing it as well, and they've been handling it better than I have. I think they've always been at the chuckling level. You know, "Well what do you want him to do at the level he's at?" They just handle it better, but they all see it as well, and I think it's sort of cute that he thinks he can solve the world.

THERAPIST: Okay. Think of that. (*leads client in another set of eye movements*) Good. Blank it out and take a deep breath. What do you get now?

ERIC: About the same.

THERAPIST: Great.

ERIC: Yeah, it feels good. It's nice to not be lost in the frustration and anger, and that's where I was last week. I was losing it and I felt like there was nothing I could do about it. I tried to sort of detach myself but I couldn't.

Evaluation of the Sample Session

The final sense of understanding and self-efficacy shown by the client in the sample session is the hallmark of a successful EMDR session.

However, this kind of unimpeded and uneventful information process-ing (i.e., processing without the need for additional clinical guidance) occurs with EMDR only about half the time. For the remainder, the eye movements are insufficient and the progression ceases, requiring the clinician to intervene at a number of points or risk having the client retraumatized by the highly charged, disturbing information. Alterna-tive EMDR strategies to unblock information processing are especially important when using the method with highly disturbed clients (see Chapters 7 and 10).

Which associations the client might have cannot be completely predicted. For instance, if Eric had seen a friend die in combat because of someone's incompetence, he might have launched into an intense abreaction, or a reliving, of the experience. Clinicians, therefore, should observe an EMDR session involving highly charged material before attempting EMDR with a client, and they should proceed with caution if they are not experienced at handling abreactive responses. Further-more, clinicians must always use EMDR in a clinically safe environment and with sufficient time for the client either to process an event fully or to return to a state of equilibrium. Again, there is no way of knowing if a channel contains dissociated material that will emerge full-blown once the processing is started. In other words, the client's level of disturbance can get much worse before it gets better, and the clinician must be fully prepared for this (see the discussion on history taking and cautions, covered in Chapter 4, and on the preparation phase, covered in Chapter 5, both of which are mandatory to lay the appropriate therapeutic groundwork).

DYSFUNCTIONAL TO FUNCTIONAL

Trained therapists consistently report that during EMDR treatment their clients' negative images, affect, and cognitions become more diffuse and less valid while positive images, affect, and cognitions become more vivid and more valid. A good metaphor for clinicians to apply here is that of a train traveling along its route. Initially, the information starts off in a dysfunctional form. When information processing is stimulated, it moves like a train down the tracks. During the accelerated processing that takes place with each set, the train travels one more stop along the line. At each plateau, or stop, some dysfunctional information drops off and some adaptive (or less problematic) information is added, just as some passen-gers disembark and others get on a train at each stop. At the end of EMDR treatment, the target information is fully processed and the client reaches an adaptive resolution. Metaphorically speaking, the train has arrived at the end of the line.

Clinicians should remember that until processing is complete, the client's statements regarding the targeted material will not be fully functional. These verbalizations only manifest, or describe, the immediate plateau; they indicate the current state of the processed information. These interim nonadaptive statements may tempt the clinician to challenge the client verbally or to use cognitive restructuring. This would be a mistake, however, because it is equivalent to inviting the client to get off the train at an intermediate (and upsetting) stop. Because of EMDR's emphasis on self-healing, any premature attempt by the therapist to intervene may slow or stop the client's information processing. In fact, when moving from one plateau of information to the next set, the clinician should direct the client (as much as possible) simply to think of the previous statement and should not attempt to repeat it. The client knows what he has just reported. Again, metaphorically, when we open the information-processing system, we allow the train to proceed down the line. The clinician's job is, whenever possible, to stay off the tracks.

DISPARATE NEURO NETWORKS

To reiterate, our working hypothesis is that the symptoms of PTSD are caused by disturbing information stored in the nervous system. This information is stored in the same form in which it was initially experienced, because the information-processing system has, for some reason, been blocked. Even years later, the rape victim may still experience the fear, see the rapist's face, and feel his hands on her body, just as if the assault were happening all over again. In effect, the information is frozen in time, isolated in its own neuro network, and stored in its originally disturbing state-specific form. Because its biological/chemical/electrical receptors are unable to appropriately facilitate transmission between neural structures, the neuro network in which the old information is stored is effectively isolated. No new learning can take place because subsequent therapeutic information cannot link associatively with it. Therefore, when thoughts of the incident arise, they are still connected to all the negative attributions of the original event. The results of years of talk therapy, of reading self-help books, and of experiencing counterexamples are also stored, but they reside in their own neuro network. It is in part the disparity between this therapeutic information and the dysfunctionally stored information that impels the client into the therapist's office for treatment and has him say, "I shouldn't be this way."

Although combat veterans, sexual molestation victims, and rape victims may know intellectually that they are not to blame for what happened to them, they often continue to struggle with the negative cognitions and disturbing affect. Again, this conflict appears to be due to the fact that the disparate information is stored in separate neuro networks. The Accelerated Information Processing model suggests that the moment of insight and integration comes when the two neuro networks link up with each other. When the information-processing system is activated and maintained in dynamic form, the appropriate connections between the two networks can be made. Clinicians can observe a transmutation of information after each set as the target material links up with and is reshaped by the more positively oriented information. At the end of an EMDR treatment, the clinician asks the client to access the original target; after a successful session that memory will emerge spontaneously in a more positive form and will be integrated with appropriate affect and self-attribution.

APPLICATIONS OF EMDR TO OTHER DISORDERS

EMDR's successful results with trauma victims have led to its application to a wide range of disorders. Essentially, the already stated principles of reprocessing apply. The Accelerated Information Processing model predicts that most kinds of disturbing life experiences can be success-fully treated, regardless of their origin.

A trauma, such as rape, sexual molestation, or combat experience, clearly has an impact on its victims in terms of how they behave, think, and feel about themselves and in their susceptibility to pronounced symptomatology, such as nightmares, flashbacks, and intrusive thoughts. These victims will have self-attributions such as "I'm power-less," "I'm worthless," or "I'm not in control." Of course, clients who have not experienced such traumas may also have dominant negative self-attributions, such as "I'm worthless," "I'm powerless," or "I'm going to be abandoned." These clients seem to have derived their negative self-statements from early childhood experiences. Therefore, when they are asked to rate on a 0-to-10 scale how they feel about a representative event from their family of origin that helped give them these beliefs, they may report an 8, 9, or 10. Like trauma victims, they see the event, feel it, and are profoundly affected by it.

Such clients were not, of course, blown up in a mine field or molested by a parent. Nevertheless, a memory of something that was said or that happened to them is locked in their nervous system and seems to have an effect similar to that of a traumatic experience. An indication of the dysfunction is the fact that the memory of the event still elicits the same negative self-attributions, affect, and physical sensations as existed on the day the memory was originally created. The therapeutic target is the disturbing memory as it is currently stored, because the dysfunctional information has set the groundwork for the present pathology. While a wide variety of conditions are amenable to change, the specific diagnosis is less important than the appropriate targeting of the earlier experiences that are generating the client's dysfunctional symptoms, characteristics, and behaviors.

STATIC EXPERIENCE:
AFFECT AND BELIEF STATEMENTS

The disturbing aspects of dysfunctionally stored memories are statically associated together because the memories cannot make new, appropriate connections. The information stored in the neuro network may be manifested by all elements of the event: images, physical sensations, tastes and smells, sounds, affect, and such cognitions as assessment and belief statements. When the unresolved trauma is stimulated, the client not only sees what occurred but may also reexperience the affect and physical sensations that were felt at the time. Some researchers believe that maintenance of the disturbing elements, including strong physical sensations, is due to inappropriate storage in short-term memory rather than in the appropriate long-term memory (Horowitz & Becker, 1972) or to storage in nondeclarative (motoric) systems rather than in declarative (narrative) systems (Lipke, 1992a; van der Kolk, 1994). If so, successful EMDR treatment includes a dynamic shifting of the information to functional storage in memory as it is metabolized and assimilated, which means that what is useful is learned and is made available, with appropriate affect, for future use.

Although the person's negative beliefs and self-attributions are transformed simultaneously with the other manifestations of the trauma, they are not given greater weight than sensory experiences. They are termed meta-perceptions because they are not sensory experience but, rather, are interpretive of the experience and entail language.

Language is not a necessary component of the original trauma, as seen, for example, by the negative effects of sexual and physical abuse on preverbal infants. For instance, many children are locked in closets and abused before they can speak, yet they clearly have symptoms of PTSD. Some cognitive therapists might say that a child placed in a room with a tiger would not fear the beast unless the child was old enough to know that a tiger is dangerous. However, it seems clear that if the tiger turned and roared at the child, no matter what its age, fear and possibly traumatization would result. This illustrates one of the genetically encoded responses in human beings, responses that have developed through evolution and do not require the stimulus of language. Thus, while a person's beliefs, stated via language, are clinically useful distillations of experience, it is the affect feeding them that is the pivotal element in the pathology.

The concept that past experiences lay the groundwork for present dysfunction is far from new, but let us examine it in the context of EMDR, specifically, in terms of memory storage and information processing. Imagine that a little girl is walking beside her father and reaches up for his hand. At that moment the father deliberately or inadvertently swings his arm back and hits the child in the face. The child experiences intense negative affect, which might be verbalized as "I can't get what I want; there is something wrong with me." (This self-blame is almost predictable: Children typically seem to take the blame for their parents' mistakes or flaws, a fact that is most painfully obvious in the case of sexual molestation victims who blame themselves for their abuse. This tendency may also be caused by evolutionary processes that encode the submission to authority as a necessary adjunct to survival.) The affect, perhaps intense feelings of worthlessness and powerlessness, and the images, sounds, and the pain of the blow are stored in the child's nervous system. This experience becomes a touchstone, a primary self-defining event in her life; in the Accelerated Information Processing model we call it a node. Since memories are clearly stored associatively, the next event that represents a similar rejection is likely to link up with the node in the ongoing creation of a neuro network that will be pivotal to the girl's definition of her self-worth. Subsequent experiences of rejection by mother, siblings, friends, and others may all link up with the node in channels of associated information. Even before language is adequately developed, all the different childhood experiences containing similar feelings of powerlessness, despair, and inadequacy are stored as information linking into a neuro network organized around the node of the earlier touchstone experience. Positive experiences are not assimilated into the network because the node is defined by the negative affect.

When there is sufficient language to formulate a self-concept, such as "I can't get what I want; there is something wrong with me," verbalization is linked associatively with the network by the affect that the meaning of those words engenders. In essence, once the affect-laden verbal conceptualization is established in the neuro network, it can be viewed as generalizing to each of the subsequent experiences stored as information in the network. The process continues in adolescence, such as when, for instance, the girl in our example experiences a rejection by a teacher or a boyfriend. Thus, all subsequent related events may link to the same node point and take on the attributions of the initial experience. Therefore, the assessment associated with such an event is not limited to a function-specific statement (e.g., "I can't get what I want in this instance"), but is linked to the dysfunctional generalized statement "I can't get what I want; there is something wrong with me."

What happens when the girl reaches adulthood and something happens that seems like—or even threatens to become—a rejection? This new information is assimilated into the neuro network, and the concept "I can't get what I want; there is something wrong with me" and its affect generalize and become associated with it. Over time, the accumulated related events produce a self-fulfilling prophecy; thus, any hint or chance of rejection can trigger the neuro network with its dominant cognition of "There is something wrong with me." This person's consequent behavior and attributions in the present are dysfunctional because what motivates and fuels them is the intense affect, fear, pain, and powerlessness of that first experience, now compounded by all of the subsequent experiences. Thus, the pain of childhood continues to be triggered in the present, and because of the associational nature of memory and behavior the woman's current responses and assessments of herself and the world will be dysfunctional. When the woman enters a social or business situation and desires something, the neuro network with the affect that is verbalized by "I can't get what I want; there is something wrong with me" will be stimulated, and the associated affect, level of disturbance, and self-denigrating belief will severely hamper her functional behavior in the present.

RESOLUTION

Resolution of disturbance is achieved through the stimulation of the client's inherent self-healing processes. As previously discussed, one of the primary principles of the Accelerated Information Processing model is the notion of a dynamic drive toward mental health. The information-processing mechanism is physiologically designed to resolve psychological disturbances just as the rest of the body is geared to heal a physical wound. According to our model, psychological dysfunction, with all its complex elements of lack of self-esteem and self-efficacy, is caused by the information stored in the nervous system. By means of EMDR, this information is accessed, processed, and adaptively resolved. As explained earlier, asking the client to bring a picture of the original event to consciousness stimulates the physiologically stored information. The eye movements (or other stimuli) activate the information-processing mechanism, and with each set new, adaptive, information is assimilated into the neuro network, transforming the target material until it arrives at a healthy, functional state.

For example, during an EMDR session a client who starts with a picture of her abusive father towering threateningly over her may spontaneously report seeing herself grow in size until she is eye-to-eye with him. As the old information evolves toward a therapeutic and healthful resolution with successive sets, the client may spontaneously state something like "I'm fine; Dad really had a problem." This shifted assessment is an integral part of the new affect and sensory experience, an experience that will now dominate whenever the neuro network is activated by either internal or external stimuli. In other words, as the information transmutes, the changing picture corresponds to shifts of affect and self-assessment, which become a part of the way the experience is now stored.

The client will automatically behave differently now, since the underlying belief is "I'm fine" rather than "There is something wrong with me." For most clients, successful EMDR treatment results in the new, positive, cognition generalizing throughout the entire neuro network. Therefore, any associated memories (e.g., of other threats by the abusive father of the woman in our example) that are accessed subsequent to treatment will result in the emergence of the positive cognition ("I'm fine") along with appropriate affect. The therapeutic resolution is shown in all aspects of the target (images, physical sensations, emotion, and so on) and in past and present associated events and is also manifested in an appropriate change in behavior.

FROZEN IN CHILDHOOD

Clinical observations of EMDR treatment sessions indicate that therapeutic results are often achieved through the progressive emergence of an adult perspective, particularly in cases where the client was previously locked into the emotional responses of a childhood trauma. Many childhood experiences are infused with a sense of powerlessness, lack of choice, lack of control, and inadequacy. Even the best of childhoods have moments, such as when parents go out for the evening, in which the child feels abandoned, powerless, and uncared for. The Accelerated Information Processing model posits that even these normal experiences can be the physiologically stored causal events for many dysfunctions.

The language of the client often includes expressions of such childhood states as powerlessness, lack of choice, fear, and inadequacy. For example, the 50-year-old client who speaks long-distance to her mother and starts reacting with fear, frustration, and anxiety is not reacting to the present-day 75-year-old invalid on the telephone. Rather, the emotions of her childhood are experienced because of the stimulation of the neuro network associated with her mother, a network based on earlier touchstone memories that include intense feelings of fear and lack of safety. Essentially, the client cannot react calmly to her mother until the earlier memories are appropriately processed and relegated to their proper place in the past.

As EMDR activates the information-processing system and maintains it in a dynamic state, the guilt and fear of the child's perspective can be progressively transmuted into the adult perspective of appropriate responsibility, safety, and confidence in one's ability to make choices. Perceptions, such as of one's lack of control, that were perfectly valid in childhood or during a rape or combat situation are no longer true for the adult in the present.

It is important to understand the parallel between childhood experience and that of the trauma victim. In both there are feelings of self-blame and inadequacy and a lack of control, safety, or choices. Presumably, a dysfunctional node is set in place in childhood (during developmental stages), when positive information is not assimilated into the neuro network during the critical period immediately following a disturbing experience (e.g., the child may not receive comforting after an injury). The nature of preexisting nodes, as well as the intensity of subsequent stressors, may determine the formation of pronounced PTSD symptoms. In adult trauma victims the presence of a preexisting dysfunctional node may explain why targeting by means of EMDR the chronic memories of the trauma suffered in adulthood often results in the client's reporting the emergence of early childhood memories with similar affect. Adequate information reprocessing allows the client to recognize appropriate present conditions or circumstances on an emotional, as well as a cognitive, level. What we have seen in a vast number of EMDR clients is their progressive evolution to a state of self-forgiveness in which they have a sense of safety and control in the present.

"TIME-FREE" PSYCHOTHERAPY

Traditional psychotherapy has been time-bound in the sense that its effects occur only after a protracted period of time. This probably occurs because conventional therapy uses verbal (rather than physiologically based) procedures to shift information that is dysfunctionally locked in the nervous system. In the Accelerated Information Processing model the healing of psychological dysfunction is viewed as being comparatively "time-free" because rapid treatment effects can be observed when EMDR is applied, regardless of the number of disturbing events and no matter how long ago they occurred.

As discussed earlier, EMDR treatments can target early childhood memories, later traumas, or current situations for positive therapeutic effect because the neuro network has associative links to all similar events. As the client holds the target in consciousness, the dysfunctional information is stimulated. The information-processing system is activated through sets of eye movements (or other stimuli), and the traumatic event is transmuted to an adaptive resolution with appropriate affect, self-attribution, and overall assessment. Since the information is linked associatively, many similar memories can be affected during the treatment session, and it is possible for the new positive affect and positive cognitions to generalize to all events clustered in the neuro network.

Alternatively, since multiple-rape victims, sexual molestation victims, and Vietnam veterans may have many traumatic events in their history, the clinician can cluster the client's memories into groups that have parallel cues and stimuli, such as memories of seeing comrades wounded in combat or memories of abusive acts by an older brother. The EMDR treatment then actively targets one event that represents the entire cluster, which often allows for a generalization effect throughout all the associated experiences.

The changes during EMDR treatment occur rapidly compared to conventional treatment presumably because (1) the memories can be targeted in clusters, (2) the dysfunctional state-dependent material is accessed directly, (3) focused protocols (which will be explained in future chapters) are employed, and (4) the stimulation of the innate information-processing system apparently transforms the information *directly* on a physiological level.

The ability of EMDR treatment effects to be comparatively free from time restraints is analogous to the ability of individuals to dream through extremely long sequences of events in just 45 minutes of REM sleep. Presumably, similar mechanisms in the dream state and the Accelerated Information Processing state of EMDR allow rapid physiological shifting through cognitive/emotive material. Although this processing effect may be found in many individuals following a dream about a minor disturbance, a conscious, active engagement appears necessary for many kinds of traumatic material to be similarly influenced. During an EMDR treatment the adaptive processing of memories is dynamically maintained; that is, EMDR itself keeps the information-processing mechanism active. This is in sharp contrast to the static recall of events typical of long-term verbal therapies.

In EMDR the history taking, the directed procedure, and the treatment protocols all reflect a model that emphasizes a sharp therapeutic focus. As previously mentioned, the model incorporates the notion of self-healing and spontaneously generated recovery once the proper nodes are accessed and the information-processing system is activated (with the obvious exceptions of chemically or organically based disorders).

There is an analogy here to the medical treatment of disease: Just as the use of modern drugs made us revise our assumptions about the amount of time required to heal various physical ailments, so too does the use of EMDR force us to examine our preconceived notions about the time required to heal psychological wounds. In the area of mental health we already equate physiological changes with rapid improvement. Thus, we no longer demand prolonged treatment for recovery from anxiety, depression, bipolar disorder, or obsessive-compulsive disorder when they are treated with medication.

According to the Accelerated Information Processing model, the EMDR clinician catalyzes the appropriate biochemical balance through the interaction of electrical pulses and organic systems. For instance, the neuronal bursts caused by a focused attention and simultaneous eye movements (or alternative stimulation) may interact with the limbic and cortical systems (see Chapter 12). This interaction may underlie rapid treatment effects. However, full therapeutic treatment involves the use of clinical procedures and protocols that maximize the beneficial effect. Each client history, as discussed in Chapter 4, includes indicators of client readiness and demands unique treatment plans and levels of therapeutic support. EMDR clinicians have found that through use of the structured protocols a few sessions can clear up an area of dysfunction that may have appeared resistant to months of previous therapy.

The clinician's model must be open to the fact that rapid, profound, and multidimensional change in a client can take place and can be maintained over time. For those clinicians trained in a long-term model such as psychoanalysis, this may be difficult to accept. However, let me stress that clinical observations of EMDR sessions have revealed that no pertinent stage of healing is skipped: Symbols become clear, insights occur, lessons are learned, and the various stages of emotional resolution are experienced, albeit in a accelerated fashion.

Regardless of the psychological modality used by the clinician, it is only logical that any therapeutic change must ultimately be based on a physiological shift of information stored in the brain. It might be helpful for clinicians to recognize the comparatively short distance involved in crossing a synapse. Even in long-term psychodynamic therapy, insight occurs during a single moment in time; in the Accelerated Information Processing model insight occurs when two neuro networks connect.

TARGETS

The key to psychological change is the ability to facilitate appropriate information processing. This means making connections between healthier associations. Specific targets are used to gain access to the blocked memory networks. On the basis of clinical observation, it appears that any manifestation of the stored information can be used as a target for the EMDR session. Thus, a dream, a memory, and current behavior are all useful foci inasmuch as they all stimulate the specific neuro network containing the disturbing information. For instance, a Vietnam veteran may have a recurring nightmare of being killed, a memory of being shot, or an anxiety reaction to loud noises, along with a pervading belief about lack of control. All these elements can be combined in an appropriate treatment plan. Once the information-processing system is activated, the dysfunctional elements can be meta-bolized and the presenting complaint resolved through the progressive linking of the target with more adaptive material.

In addition, there are a number of indications of blocked memory networks that may be targeted, including memory lapses, dissociations, and the fact that access is restricted to negative material.

Access Restricted to Negative Material

One indicator of a blocked memory network is when the client is able to retrieve only negative memories even when other, positive, events have been experienced. For example, one client's presenting complaint was that she had felt for 2 years that a "black cloud" was hanging over her head. She had been very close to her father, who had died a terrible death in a nursing home while she had been powerless to do anything. Whenever she tried to think of her father, or whenever anything stimulated a memory of him, the only images that arose were of his suffering in the nursing home. EMDR treatment was aimed at these images. Subsequently, to check on the efficacy of the treatment the client was told to think of her father and was asked, "What do you get?" She reported spontaneously seeing a picture of the two of them at a party. When she was then asked to blank out the picture and to think of her father again, the same type of result occurred. The positive images were linked to a feeling of peace, and the black cloud had vanished.

According to the Accelerated Information Processing model, the negative information is held dysfunctionally in an excitatory form and, as a consequence, is more likely to be stimulated than are other associations. Thus, although many kinds of information are stored in the memory network, access to all but the highly charged negative material is blocked. When the disturbing events have been processed, they resolve adaptively into a more neutral form, with cognitions that verbalize a more appropriate affect (in our example, one such cognition would be "He is at peace now"). The positive memories can then emerge. As a result, any internal or external cue that would elicit information from the targeted memory network will no longer access only the dysfunctional information. For instance, if the client in our example is asked to think about her father or if she hears about someone else's father, she will no longer be limited to thoughts about the events at the nursing home. Once the disturbing memories are adequately processed, cues allow access to other, more positive, aspects of the neuro network.

Memory Lapses

Victims of childhood sexual abuse often report being unable to retrieve many memories of the years during which the molestations occurred. It seems that the highly charged information about the abuse is blocking access to the rest of the childhood memory network. Once the trauma is processed, the client is able to remember many positive events, such as experiences with friends, that occurred during that time. As the full memory network becomes available and happy memories become unblocked, the client's self-concept automatically changes. As a result of the increased range of the client's childhood memories and associations she is able to redefine herself as a person with positive abilities, a history, and a future.

Dissociation

Clients may present themselves as highly symptomatic but with no memory of a traumatic event that may have led to this condition. In these cases, the presenting symptoms appear to be a manifestation of dysfunctionally stored information. There is no presumption, however, as to the nature or factual accuracy of the touchstone event. Clinicians should take great care not to lead or interpret for the client (see the section False Memory in Chapter 11).

It should be recalled that dissociated material may be nothing more than information that is unavailable to awareness because it is stored in state-dependent form in an isolated neuro network. As the information is processed, it can emerge into consciousness. However, an image is only one of many possible manifestations of dysfunctionally stored information, and the actual visual memory of an event may never be retrieved. Nevertheless, clinicians have found that by targeting the present symptoms, or the client's sense of danger, approximately 50% of these clients retrieve visual images of the dissociated event. More importantly, however, the present symptoms may subside even if there is no image retrieval. EMDR sessions have shown that effective processing can occur whether or not the information is released as an image into the client's conscious awareness. Metaphorically speaking, the videotape can be running (i.e., the information can be processing) whether or not the monitor is turned on.

Other forms of dissociation occur in clients who merge with the past experience during abreactions. The overwhelming sensations and emotional reactions experienced as the event is accessed are indicators that the information has been held in dysfunctional form. As the information is successfully processed, clients often exclaim, "Oh, I'm here," adding, "I'm not in Vietnam" or "I'm not in my old house" or "I'm not in danger."

Likewise, a complete lack of appropriate affect, which can also be indicated by the client who uses terms such as "numb" or "blocked" when a traumatic event is accessed indicates information that has been dysfunctionally stored. In these cases clients can retrieve the affect, often at a high level of disturbance, during the initial phases of processing. Any inappropriate dissociative response, either an over- or underreaction to a traumatic event, is considered indicative of a blocked memory network and is therefore an appropriate target for EMDR.

INTEGRATED PSYCHOTHERAPY

As you can see from the previous discussions, many psychological modalities dovetail in EMDR. The present paradigm opens new therapeutic possibilities by theoretically supporting effective treatment applications that integrate key elements of the major psychological modalities.

In a typical 90-minute EMDR session the clinician will observe rapid changes in the client. Clinicians who use a psychodynamic approach are likely to notice free association, catharsis, abreaction, symbolism, and family-of-origin material. Behaviorists will easily observe learning chains, generalization, conditioned responses, associative material, and more. The cognitive therapist will find the progressive shifting of cognitive structures and beliefs. The Gestalt therapist will observe the removal of emotional static, which allows the client to differentiate more easily the figure and ground relationship. The Reichian will observe the shifting of physical sensations linked to the dysfunctional material.

In many ways the situation is reminiscent of the story of the blind men who tried to describe an elephant: The one who touched the tail declared that an elephant was like a rope, the one who felt the leg said an elephant was like a tree, and the one who held the trunk claimed it was like a snake. The conclusion of each was based only on the part he had investigated. Clearly, however, it was all one elephant. What we find in EMDR is an interweaving of much of what appears to be valid in traditional psychotherapy, because whatever is true must dovetail. Essentially, regardless of the terms used, what all psychological modalities have in common is that information is stored physiologically in the brain. When healing is activated, the key elements of most psychological approaches are represented.

However, while the Accelerated Information Processing model offers a unifying theory that can be seen as underlying all psychological modalities, the model opens up new territory by defining pathology as dysfunctionally stored information that can be properly assimilated through a dynamically activated processing system. Thus, the EMDR clinician is offered a new role in helping to facilitate positive treatment effects.

Global diagnoses, such as personality disorder, often serve to chain the client to an immovable mountain. Use of the Accelerated Information Processing model and EMDR suggests that the clinician focus on the characteristics that generate the behaviors responsible for the diagnosis rather than attend primarily to a diagnostic label. Characteristics are viewed as having been produced by earlier experiences, including parental modeling, and as being susceptible to change. Thus, a vast range of experiences in childhood, adolescence, and adulthood can be located on a spectrum of trauma and can become subject to EMDR-activated shifts toward self-healing and resolution.

Each clinician, regardless of orientation, is invited to observe EMDR effects and rediscover everything that is believed to be true of his or her modality. The clinician also is urged, however, to consider the proposed information-processing model rather than prematurely superimpose on EMDR a previously derived theoretical approach.

The Accelerated Information Processing model, refinements of the EMDR procedures, and treatment protocols have evolved in order to explain and maximize treatment effects. Therefore, clinicians are advised to use EMDR (as described in later chapters) and observe its clinical results before attempting to define it (thereby circumscribing it) and make it conform to previously established modalities. This caution may help prevent EMDR's benefits from being confined to the limits of what has so far been achieved. For instance, if EMDR is defined simply as hypnosis, its usefulness will be limited to those effects already available to the hypnotist. If it is viewed solely as desensitization, essential dynamics and applications may be ignored by the therapist. Allowing EMDR to define its own parameters on the basis of its effects means that the boundaries observed in other modalities may be surpassed. Thus, it is crucial for the fullest therapeutic effects that the clinician observe the client's responses without preconceived limitations. In actual practice, EMDR may perhaps best be described as an interactive, interactional, intrapsychic, cognitive, behavioral, body-oriented therapy. Key elements of all these modalities are utilized to treat the client as a whole person.

SUMMARY AND CONCLUSIONS

The Accelerated Information Processing model is offered as a working neurophysiological *hypothesis* because current understanding of brain physiology is not yet sufficient to verify its accuracy. However, because this model is based on observed treatment effects, it can serve as a clinical road map that is both explanatory and predictive, even if it turns out that the neurophysiological details of the hypothesis are incorrect.

The Accelerated Information Processing model states that there is an innate physiological system that is designed to transform disturbing input into an adaptive resolution and a psychologically healthy integration. A trauma may disturb the information-processing system, causing perceptions to be stored in state-dependent form and manifested by pronounced symptoms of PTSD. The blocked information-processing system is thought to be stimulated through a variety of possible physiological factors, including (1) a compelled relaxation response, (2) neuronal bursts that cause a shift in synaptic potential or receptor valence, or (3) some other function of a dual-focus information-processing mechanism. Alternative stimuli such as hand taps and sounds have been found to have a clinical effect similar to that of the eye movements. Essentially, the hypothesis states that the targeted information is metabolized and transmuted along associated memory channels through the progressive stages of self-healing. Transmutation is seen in all elements of the information—images, sensations, and beliefs. As the information moves from dysfunctional to functional form, the negative manifestations of the target become diffuse and the positive manifestations become more vivid. In addition, there is a comparatively high incidence of emergence of previously dissociated material as disparate neuro networks progressively associate with one another until an adaptive resolution is achieved.

Most psychopathologies are assumed to be based on earlier life experiences that are in state-dependent storage. The associative nature of the memory network allows the generalization of positive treatment effects to modify present self-assessment and behavior. Whether the complaint is simple PTSD or a more complex diagnosis, the transmutation to an adaptive adult perspective may be accomplished comparatively rapidly by this focused, physiologically based approach, which apparently unblocks the information-processing system and memory networks.

All of the salient elements of the primary psychological modalities, as well as the indicators of profound psychological change, will be apparent in the integrated EMDR approach. However, clinicians are cautioned to remain flexible and to use the proposed model as a clinical road map to permit the possibility of an expansive psychological change that can be achieved with unusual rapidity. It is necessary, of course, for the clinician to have the appropriate education and qualifications since EMDR is only as effective as the person using it and all one's previous clinical training and skill will be called upon to achieve therapeutic success.

CHAPTER 3

Components of EMDR Treatment and Basic Treatment Effects

> If you have built castles in the air, your work need not be lost; that is where they should be. Now put the foundations under them.
>
> *Henry David Thoreau*

In the first part of this chapter we will explore the importance of a delineated target and define the basic components of the EMDR procedure. These include the image; the negative and positive cognitions; the emotions; the physical sensations; and the emotional and cognitive rating scales, the SUD (Subjective Units of Disturbance) and VOC (Validity of Cognition) Scales. We will then describe the eye movements themselves as well as alternative stimuli. Next, we will review the eight phases of EMDR treatment: history taking and treatment planning, preparation, assessment, desensitization, installation, body scan, closure, and reevaluation. Finally, we will discuss some clinical effects of targeting and typical client experiences during EMDR processing. All these aspects of treatment having been defined in this chapter, the following chapters will place them in the context of client–clinician interaction by giving specific instructions for their use.

BASIC COMPONENTS OF THE EMDR PROCEDURE

Effective EMDR processing depends on effective targeting. If the wrong targets (or the wrong components) are used, positive treatment effects are likely to be minimal. For the sexual abuse survivor, appropriate targets include early childhood memories, recent events that trigger current disturbances, and imaginal events that incorporate appropriate

˛uture behaviors. When treating a relatively uncomplicated case, such as a victim of simple PTSD who has suffered a comparatively recent trauma like a natural disaster, it may be necessary to target only the single memory of the event.

Regardless of the number of clinical aspects that require treatment, each target must be individually circumscribed and fully processed. These targets are the building blocks of EMDR treatment and deserve careful clinical attention. A fully delineated target will help the client and clinician to understand the trauma context and configuration (all the details that make up the trauma and response) and will result in more rapid processing. The most useful parameters for treatment are the picture, the negative and positive cognitions, the emotions and their level of disturbance, and the physical sensations. These aspects of the target must be clearly defined for intitiating, processing, and concluding EMDR treatment. Let us take a close look at each of them.

The Image

The clinician should ask the client to think of the event and then to focus on one image that represents either the entire incident or the most upsetting part of it. Whether or not the image is distinct is of little consequence. Indeed, it is quite common for the client to have only a blurred image or fragmented view of the event. The goal is simply to establish a link between consciousness and where the information is stored in the brain.

The Negative Cognition

The client is next asked to identify a statement that expresses the underlying negative belief or maladaptive self-assessment that goes with the image. This statement is called the "negative cognition." While the term *cognition* has often been used to define all of the conscious representations of experience, in EMDR we use it to signify a belief or assessment. Therefore, the cognition represents the client's current *interpretation* of the self, not merely a description. As an interpretation, the negative cognition answers the question "What are my self-denigrating beliefs about myself in relation to the event?" Negative cognitions include statements such as "I am bad/worthless/unable to succeed." The rape victim who looks back at having been bound and gagged and offers the statement "I was powerless" or "I was afraid" is *not* providing a negative cognition; she is giving a statement of fact, a description. EMDR cannot process this rape victim's statement because the method affects only inappropriate, dysfunctional material; when the description is accurate, there is no observable reprocessing effect. An example of a negative cognition appropriate for the hypothetical rape victim might be "I *am* powerless." This statement indicates how she currently feels about herself when she recalls the rape. When the traumatic memory is stimulated, the dysfunctionally stored affect is felt and the negative cognition serves to convey its meaning. Because the statement "I am powerless" is inappropriate or dysfunctional (since there is no current danger or threat), EMDR can be used to reprocess it.

For sexual abuse survivors, some appropriate negative cognitions may include "I am damaged for life," "I am powerless," and "I don't deserve love and can't have it." Note the following characteristics of these negative cognitions: They are all "I statements," they are expressed in the present tense, and they involve negative self-attributions because of the client's participation (though forced) in the traumatic event. These statements indicate pathology. Like the image, the negative cognitions are links to the dysfunctional material that is in need of processing.

The negative cognition is defined as the negative self-assessment that victims make in the present. When the client brings up the memory of a trauma that may have occurred many years ago, the clinician must ascertain how the level of disturbance is presently experienced. The client may continue to think inappropriately about himself in relation to the event (with feelings of self-blame, incapacity, powerlessness, or self-denigration), demonstrating that the memory has not been resolved. When the rape victim brings up the rape scene and states, "I am powerless," or "I am dirty," or "I am worthless," these are interpretations about the self made in the present. Because they represent inappropriate (objectively untrue) negative beliefs, they are prime targets for EMDR.

I want to emphasize that clinical observation indicates that EMDR does not lead the client to falsify history. Thus, a negative cognition that is actually true will not be changed. That is, clinical observation consistently indicates that EMDR cannot be used to remove a true negative cognition or to instill a false one. This phenomenon was first noticed with an EMDR client who was a rape victim. Her presenting negative cognition was "I am guilty." During the treatment session she reported that this cognition became progressively more, not less, valid. When questioned, the client revealed that she was thinking of the fact that she had lied to the police and prosecutor regarding the actual facts of the case; that is, she *was* guilty—of deception. A new negative cognition then had to be used for treatment.

Once again, a negative cognition is interpretive ("There is something wrong with me") rather than descriptive ("Mother did not love me"). When the latter statement is true, as in the case of a psychotic or sadistic mother, it apparently cannot (and obviously should not) be changed by EMDR: An abusive parent cannot be turned into a nurturing parent. However, the resulting negative self-attribution ("There is something wrong with me") can be addressed and appropriately reprocessed in order to help shift the client's pathology. Although as a child the client may have blamed herself for her mother's lack of love, this was and remains inappropriate and constitutes the true target for the reprocessing. In fact, a common negative cognition, often used with victims of child abuse, is "I am not lovable."

Some clients have difficulty constructing a negative cognition. The clinician may offer such a client a list of alternative negative cognitions to help him understand the concept. However, it is important that these suggestions be presented in an open and nonpressured manner that leaves the choice—or construction of a more useful negative cognition—completely up to the client. It is vital that this cognition stem from the client's own experience and not be an artificial construct of the clinician.

If a client has difficulty putting a negative cognition into words, offer some examples that, in your clinical estimation, seem to be a good fit. Examples include the following:

"I should have done something."
"I'm powerless."
"I'm out of control."
"I am to blame."
"I'm worthless."
"There is something wrong with me."
"I'm a bad person."
"I'm dirty."
"I'll be abandoned."
"I'm not lovable."
"I cannot succeed."

Identifying the negative cognition assists the client to recognize more fully its irrationality, establishes a baseline, and helps to stimulate the dysfunctional information that requires reprocessing. A more extensive list of negative and positive cognitions is presented in Appendix A.

The Positive Cognition

Once the client and clinician have identified the negative cognition associated with the target, the next step in the EMDR session is for the client to identify the desired positive cognition and rate it on the 7-point VOC Scale, where 1 is "completely false" and 7 is "completely true." The VOC rating should be based on how true and how believable the positive cognition feels to the client, not on how true it is objectively. Even while remaining in emotional turmoil, the client is often aware that he *should* believe something positive. Therefore, the clinician should ask the client to report his "gut-level" response. For instance, a rape victim may know that the rape was not her fault but may still feel guilty. Therefore, she may initially give only a 4 on the VOC Scale to the positive cognition "I'm a good person."

The purpose of identifying a desired positive cognition is to set a direction for treatment, to stimulate the appropriate alternative neuro networks, and to offer the therapist and client a baseline (the VOC rating) from which to assess progress. Identifying a positive cognition before beginning the reprocessing also provides a statement that can be used for rapid installation (the installation phase immediately follows desensitization and will be described shortly) if a better one fails to emerge in the course of treatment.

Consistent reports of EMDR sessions show that if a client's positive cognition is inappropriate or impossible, it will disrupt the reprocessing. When disruption occurs, the client is generally trying to incorporate some form of wishful thinking. Unrealistic desired positive cognitions will not be incorporated into the client's system. One sign of this condition is an initial VOC rating of 1 ("completely false"), which usually indicates that the desired belief is impossible to achieve. An example of this is from the case of a client who had been raped by her employer. The client's desired cognition was "I can fight back." This seemed reasonable to her clinician, but the initial VOC rating she gave this statement did not increase during her EMDR treatment session. Observing this, the clinician asked her, "What prevents it from being a 7?" The client replied, "He's six and a half feet tall and weighs three hundred and fifty pounds." Unless the five-foot client had taken martial arts lessons, the statement "I can fight back" (which the client meant in a literal sense) was clearly untrue and was inappropriate as a positive cognition for the EMDR session.

When developing a positive cognition, instruct the client whenever possible to make an "I statement" that incorporates an internal locus of control. Clients often offer initial statements that are beyond their control, such as "He will love me" or "They will give me what I want." Give clients appropriate examples to redirect them from such statements, and point out the impossibility of ensuring the truth of statements like "My children will never get hurt." Appropriate positive cognitions—such as "I can handle the situation," "I can trust myself," or "I can act responsibly"—offer the client a redefinition of her own capacities. Clearly, there is more power to the statement "I am lovable" than to "He will love me." The client has no real control over other people's thoughts and actions. The goal should be that the client will be able to maintain a sense of self-worth and equilibrium regardless of external forces instead of resorting to rationalizations or false hopes for the future.

Sometimes the only positive cognitions that can be reasonably presented are embodied in statements like "It's over," "I did the best I could," or "I now have choices." This is particularly true in the case of perpetrator guilt, where sometimes all that can reasonably be said is "It's in the past" or "I can learn from it." In these cases, an appropriate level of responsibility for past behavior is recognized and the emphasis is placed on present and future action. While clinical reports indicate that EMDR cannot obscure or falsify what is appropriate or true, lessons can be learned, the impact of events can be redirected, and the client can be liberated from the negative affect that prevents positive actions in the future.

Helping the client identify a positive cognition is an important step in recovery. The ability to define an alternative view of the trauma in reasonable language offers hope of escape from the pain of self-denigration. This activity is useful in any form of therapy. However, as the session progresses, the initial positive cognition identified by the client may be superseded by a better one. Indeed, in EMDR it is very common for a more beneficial cognition to emerge as the dysfunctional older material is processed. The clinician should take special care to note a preferable cognition and, when possible, to use the client's own words when stating it. For instance, a client may start with a positive cognition of "I can succeed." During processing he might realize not only that he has already succeeded at many tasks but that it is not necessary to define himself by his job. He may end with the cognition "I am a worthwhile person." This second cognition has greater power than the first and should be incorporated into the installation phase of treatment.

At times, the client will need assistance to formulate positive cognitions. If the client has difficulty putting a positive cognition into words, consider whether any of the following statements might apply to the client's case:

"I did the best I could."
"It's in the past."
"I learned from it."
"I'm in control."
"I'm lovable."
"I'm a good person."
"I now have choices."
"I can succeed."

"I can handle it."
"I'm safe now."

Avoid using the word "not" in the formulation of the positive cognition ("I'm not bad" or "I am not powerless"). The therapeutic intention is to assist clients in a positive redefinition of themselves. The new self-concept should be the most positive self-attribution possible. Using the word "not" fails to indicate a completely positive characteristic. Thus, the sentence "I am powerful" is more therapeutic than "I am not powerless." Likewise, "I am a good person" is more useful than "I am not a bad person." However, there may be exceptions. For instance, an abuse survivor may initially benefit greatly from the positive cognition "I am not responsible for my mother's actions." Subsequent sessions can then focus on more personally enhancing self-statements.

After the dysfunctional older material has been processed, the positive cognition will be intentionally linked or associated with the previously upsetting information during the next phase of treatment, known as "installation." In other words, we are inserting the positive cognition into the memory network that holds the target material. In so doing, it becomes possible for this cognition to generalize through the network into all of the associated experiences. Further, when the processed information is subsequently triggered, it will now emerge into consciousness with the positive cognition dominant. In addition, this linkage will allow all the information regarding positive outcomes to be associated with the previously traumatizing material. This linking of neuro networks is viewed by our model as a primary outcome of successful reprocessing.

The clinician should help the client verbalize a positive cognition that can generalize over the largest range of dysfunctional material and that affords the greatest advantage to associated future activities. Often, briefer, less specific cognitions have a better chance for generalization. For example, if a client is reprocessing a memory of falling off a ladder, the negative cognition might be "I'm a failure" whereas an appropriate positive cognition would be "I can succeed." An inadequate positive cognition would be "I can succeed with ladders," because that statement would allow generalization only to incidents that include ladders. Another inadequate positive cognition arose in the case of a client who was reprocessing a memory of having slipped and fallen in public. She was dissuaded from using the statement "It can happen to anyone once" because such a statement, while compatible with the original event, would not support a positive self-assessment if she fell in public again. Whenever possible, self-empowerment for future events should be incorporated into the positive cognition.

The Emotions and Their Level of Disturbance

The client is asked to hold in mind the picture of the memory and the negative cognition, to name the emotion felt, and to give a SUD Scale rating for how it feels now. The clinician should make sure that the client is not reporting the level of distress he felt at the time of the event. The target for EMDR is dysfunctional information. While many things can happen that are originally upsetting, not all remain actively distressing. Some are spontaneously dealt with through natural information processing and are adaptively resolved. Only when a past event is still unresolved should it be targeted for treatment. In most cases, unresolved material is indicated by a significant level of current emotional disturbance.

By having the client evaluate her levels of emotional disturbance using the SUD Scale, the clinician can determine which memories should be targeted. When making a treatment plan for a client, the clinician can isolate the dominant negative belief, such as the cognition "I will be abandoned," and ask the client to scan earlier memories for any related events that rate 5 or higher on the SUD Scale. These become excellent initial targets for processing.

The clinician should take care to determine which emotion the client is rating. Clients who become confused and report positive emotions on the SUD Scale should be reminded that the scale is used to evaluate only disturbing emotions. A variety of emotions can arise during processing, making it important to have the client name the emotion. Further, a client using the SUD Scale may report no change in the intensity of disturbance when, in fact, the emotion has changed qualitatively. For example, anger may have changed to grief, but the client may give the same SUD rating as before. The clinician needs to know which emotion is being rated in order to give the appropriate responses and support and to ensure that processing is occurring.

The Physical Sensations

Clinical experience indicates that the physical sensations generated when clients concentrate on a traumatic memory are very useful focal points for treatment. These sensations may be associated with emotional tension, such as tight neck muscles or increased heart rate. Other physical sensations may be part of the sensory experience of the target trauma itself, such as the sensation of feeling the grip of the perpetrator's hand. Pronounced physical sensations are also associated with negative cognitions. Therefore, the EMDR session is not considered complete until all physical sensations generated by thoughts of the trauma have been appropriately reprocessed. By the end of the treatment a mental scan of the body by the client should reveal no residual tension or atypical physical sensations.

ACTIVATING THE
INFORMATION-PROCESSING SYSTEM

The client's inherent information-processing system can be activated by the use of directed eye movements or by alternative forms of stimulation such as hand taps or sounds.

Eye Movements

As we will see, there are several different kinds of eye movements available in EMDR. The clinician's job is to make use of the kind that best fits the needs of the client. This includes ensuring client comfort in regard to the eye movements themselves. At no time should the clinician proceed if the client reports eye pain, dryness, or anxiety caused by the procedure itself. For example, some clients report strong associations between the clinician's moving hand and memories of having been hit in the face by a parent. In this instance, the clinician would want to use hand taps or auditory stimuli instead of directed eye movements.

The clinician's objective is to generate eye movement from one side of the client's range of vision to the other. This full bilateral movement is done as rapidly as possible without discomfort. The clinician should use two or more fingers as a focal point. This technique allows the client to track the fingers without having to focus on a small object and without having the negative associations that might be elicited by a single moving index finger (e.g., memories of being reprimanded by an adult). The clinician may also use a pen, ruler, or any other object to direct the client's eye movement. However, two fingers serve very well and appear to be preferred by many clients as affording a more interpersonal experience.

Typically, the clinician holds two fingers upright, palm facing the client, approximately 12 to 14 inches from the client's face. The client is then asked, "Is this comfortable?" If the answer is no, the clinician should determine the placement and distance with which the client is most comfortable. The clinician then demonstrates the direction of the eye movements by slowly moving her fingers horizontally from the extreme right to the extreme left (or the reverse) of the client's visual field, a distance of at least 12 inches (see Figure 7). The clinician should evaluate the client's ability to track the moving fingers by starting slowly and then increasing the rate to obtain the maximum comfortably sustainable speed. Clinicians have reported that the majority of clients prefer a fast speed, although some clients work best with a slower motion. During this testing phase many clinicians ask the client to report any preferences regarding speed, distance, height, and so forth, before concentrating on emotionally disturbing material. After the dysfunctional material has been targeted,

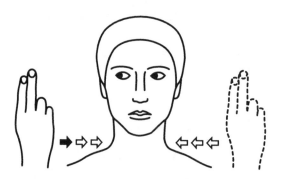

FIGURE 7. Horizontal hand movements used in performing EMDR.

the clinician should listen to the feedback the client gives at the end of each set to assess the amount of processing that has taken place. If the dysfunctional material is shifting readily and the client is relatively comfortable, the speed at which the fingers are moving may be maintained. If either of these conditions is not met, however, the speed as well as the direction (to be discussed shortly) and the number of eye movements within the set may be adjusted.

During this preliminary phase the clinician may find that the client has difficulty in easily following the fingers. This inability can manifest itself as irregular eye movements ("bumpiness"), including stops and starts and darting. When this occurs, the clinician should tell the client, "Push the fingers with your eyes." This statement coaches the client to develop a sense of dynamic connection with the guiding fingers, an exercise that can give him a sense of movement control, thus resulting in smoother tracking.

The clinician can then test the effectiveness of a set of diagonal eye movements by moving her hand across the midline of the client's face from the lower right to upper left (or the opposite), that is, from chin level to contralateral brow level (see Figure 8). Once again, the clinician should evaluate the results regarding ease and speed of movement. If the client tracks more easily in one direction than another, this should be the dominant direction used.

Other possible eye movement sets guide the client's eyes in a vertical, circular, or figure-eight direction. The vertical movements appear to have a calming effect and are particularly helpful in reducing extreme emotional agitation, dizziness, or nausea. This direction has also been found useful when the client is prone to vertigo. If the processing appears stuck (there is no reported change of information after successive sets of eye movements), the clinician should try a variation in the eye movements, starting with a change in direction. Like the vertical movements, the circular and figure-eight eye movements also appear to have a calming effect in many cases.

The duration of the set is also determined by client feedback. The first set consists of 24 bidirectional movements, where a right-to-left-to-right shift equals one movement. This set enables the clinician to assess client comfort, preferred speed, and ability to sustain the eye movements. During this set the client may simply observe his own reactions or concentrate on the safe-place exercise, which will be described in Chapter 5. The same number of movements may be used in the first reprocessing set. After this initial reprocessing set, the clinician should ask, "What do you get now?" This question gives the client the opportunity to report what he is experiencing in terms of imagery, insights, emotions, and physical sensations. If the client shows any indication of increased therapeutic adaptiveness—if he feels better or if new information has emerged—the clinician can repeat the direction, speed, and duration of the set. However, the clinician should be willing to experiment to discover if some variation would be more beneficial. Clinicians have reported that a 24-movement set is generally necessary for the average client to process cognitive material to a new level of adaptation. However, the response of the individual client is the final determinant. Some clients need 36 or more movements per set to process material.

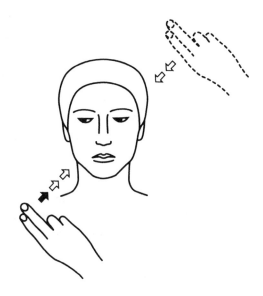

FIGURE 8. Diagonal hand movements used in performing EMDR.

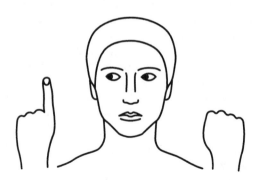

FIGURE 9. Two-handed version of performing EMDR.

Highly emotional responses, which will be covered in Chapter 7, generally demand a great many more eye movements in one set than does purely cognitive material (such as new insights that increase depth of understanding).

On the other hand, some clients are physically incapable of doing more than a few eye movements in a row. These clients may have an inherent weakness in their eye muscles; if so, they should be referred to an eye specialist for examination and possible instruction in performing the appropriate eye exercises (such clients can be trained by starting them with sets of two movements and gradually increasing the number). Other clients may be unable to follow the hand movements owing to a high level of anxiety. Still other clients may show an extreme tracking deficit or may find the tracking movements aversive; they may be treated with the two-handed approach (see Figure 9).

The two-handed approach entails having the therapist position her closed hands on opposite sides of the client's visual field at eye level and then alternately raising her index fingers. The clinician instructs the client to move her eyes from one raised finger to the other. This form of eye movement entails an orienting or attentional response that some clients find much easier to maintain than the tracking movement in the original procedure, and it has often yielded the same therapeutic results. However, the technique does not provide the same flexibility of varying directions when, for example, processing gets stuck.

Significantly, many clinicians have observed that a client may have greater difficulty in maintaining a smooth tracking motion during the earlier stages of processing. It is possible that as anxiety diminishes, the eye movements become more fluid and easier to maintain, which perhaps supports the concept of reciprocal inhibition (see Chapters 1 and 12) as a contributing factor in treatment effects. Consequently, when the clinician has been forced to begin with the two-handed orienting eye movement, it may be useful to switch to the one-handed tracking eye movements once a lower SUD level has been achieved.

Alternative Forms of Stimulation

For those clients who find the eye movements physically or psychologically uncomfortable, the alternative forms of stimulation (hand taps and sounds) can be used and have proved effective. Hand tapping is done by having the client sit with his hands palm upward on his knees. The clinician then (with one or two fingers) rhythmically taps the client's palms, alternating right and left, at the same speed at which sets of eye movements would be conducted. The client need not deliberately fixate each of these hand taps for the therapy to be effective; however, it has been clinically reported that spontaneous sets of rapid eye movements often occur during this procedure.

Auditory stimuli entail having the client keep her eyes open or closed while the clinician alternately snaps fingers next to each ear at a rate comparable to that used with sets of eye movements. While these alternative forms of stimulation preclude the possibility of changing direction, both speed and intensity may be altered. And, of course, they enable the clinician to use the EMDR approach with the blind and visually impaired. However, they do not provide the high level of feedback about the client's attention and connection to the clinician that can be obtained by observing the eye movements.

I have presented only two alternatives to the eye movement technique, but the expectation is that other forms of stimulation (or dual attention) will also prove effective.

THE EIGHT PHASES OF EMDR TREATMENT

EMDR treatment consists of eight essential phases. The number of sessions devoted to each phase and the number of phases included in each session vary greatly from client to client (guidelines are discussed in later chapters.) The first phase involves taking a client history and planning the treatment. This is followed by the preparation phase, in which the clinician introduces the client to EMDR procedures, explains EMDR theory, establishes expectations about treatment effects, and prepares the client for possible between-session disturbance. The third phase, assessment, includes determining the target and baseline response using the SUD and VOC Scales. The fourth phase, desensitization, addresses the client's disturbing emotions. The fifth, or installation, phase focuses on the cognitive restructuring. The sixth phase, which evaluates and addresses residual body tension, is the body scan. Next comes closure, a phase that includes debriefing and is essential for maintaining client equilibrium between sessions. The eighth and final phase is termed reevaluation.

While each phase focuses on different aspects of treatment, it may be useful to remember that many of their effects—an increase in self-efficacy, desensitization of negative affect, shifting of body tension, and a cognitive restructuring—occur simultaneously as the dysfunctional information is processed. These phases will be discussed in detail in Chapters 4 to 8. What is presented here is an overview of the full range of the complex treatment.

Phase One: Client History and Treatment Planning

Effective treatment with EMDR demands knowledge both of how and when to use it. The first phase of EMDR treatment therefore includes an evaluation of the client safety factors that will determine client selection. A major criterion for the suitability of clients for EMDR is their ability to deal with the high levels of disturbance potentially precipitated by the processing of dysfunctional information. Evaluation therefore involves an assessment of personal stability and current life constraints. For example, a client might be facing major deadlines at work and would not want to be distracted by the ongoing processing of traumatic material; in this instance, the clinician might delay processing until such work pressures have eased. In addition, a client should be physically able to withstand intense emotion. The clinician must evaluate potential problems due to age or a preexisting respiratory or cardiac condition.

Once the client has been selected for EMDR treatment, the clinician obtains the information needed to design a treatment plan. This part of the history-taking phase entails an evaluation of the entire clinical picture, including the client's dysfunctional behaviors, symptoms, and characteristics that need to be addressed. The clinician then determines the specific targets that will need to be reprocessed. These targets include the events that initially set the pathology in motion, the present triggers that stimulate the dysfunctional material, and the kinds of positive behaviors and attitudes needed for the future. EMDR should be used to reprocess information only after the clinician has completed a full evaluation of the clinical picture and designed a detailed treatment plan.

Phase Two: Preparation

The preparation phase involves establishing a therapeutic alliance, explaining the EMDR process and its effects, addressing the client's concerns, and initiating relaxation and safety procedures. It is essential that the clinician clearly inform the client of the possibility for emotional disturbance during and after EMDR sessions. Only in this way will the client truly be in a position to give informed consent. Not only does this warning give clients the opportunity to make appropriate choices, but it allows them to prepare their work and social schedules to accommodate any emotional upheaval. Clinicians should also be sure that clients have an audiotape that includes guided relaxation exercises (such as "Letting Go of Stress"; Miller, 1994) and that they practice these exercises before beginning the EMDR reprocessing sessions. The goal is for clients to be proficient in these relaxation techniques and capable of using the tape with confidence so that they can deal with any between-sessions disturbance that may occur.

Before processing begins, clinicians should also use with the client the guided visualization techniques described in Chapter 6 (see the section entitled Phase Seven: Closure). If the client is unable to completely eliminate moderate levels of disturbance with these techniques, the clinician should not continue EMDR. Relaxation techniques like these may be necessary to help the clinician bring to a close an incomplete session and to assist the client in dealing with memories or unpleasant emotions that may emerge after the session. The effective use of these techniques can give clients the confidence to deal with the high levels of disturbing material that may emerge during the session, whereas an inability to handle the disturbing feelings can increase the client's level of fear and make processing even more difficult.

The preparation phase also includes briefing the client on the theory of EMDR and the procedures involved, offering some helpful metaphors to encourage successful processing, and telling the client what he can realistically expect in terms of treatment effects. These aspects, along with sample instructions, will be covered in detail in Chapter 5.

During the preparation phase the clinician should also explore with the client the possibility of secondary gain issues. What does the client have to give up or confront if the pathology is remediated? If there are concerns in this area, they must be addressed before any trauma reprocessing begins. Included in this precaution is the development of an action plan to handle specific situations that may arise, situations such as the client's need to find a new job or a new place to live. If the secondary gains are fed by feelings of low self-esteem or irrational fears, they should become the first target of processing. Until these fears are resolved, no other significant therapeutic effects can be expected or maintained.

Phase Three: Assessment

In the assessment phase the clinician identifies the components of the target and establishes a baseline response before processing begins. Once the memory has been identified, the client is asked to select the image that best represents that memory. Then he chooses a negative cognition that expresses a dysfunctional or maladaptive self-assessment related to his participation in the event. These negative beliefs are actually verbalizations of the disturbing affect and include statements such as "I am useless/worthless/unlovable/dirty/bad." The client then specifies a positive cognition that will later be used to replace the negative cognition during the installation phase (Phase Five). When possible, this statement should incorporate an internal locus of control (e.g., "I am worthwhile/loveable/a good person/in control" or "I can succeed"). The client assesses the validity of the positive cognition using the 7-point VOC Scale.

At this point the image and negative cognition are combined to identify the emotion and the level of disturbance, the latter being measured by the 11-point SUD Scale, described previously. The client is asked to pick a number that indicates the intensity of his emotions when the memory is currently accessed. As reprocessing commences, both the emotions and their intensity will probably change, with the disturbance often becoming temporarily worse.

Next, the client identifies the location of the physical sensations that are stimulated when he concentrates on the event.

Thus, the assessment stage offers a baseline response with respect to the target memory and the specific components necessary to complete processing.

Phase Four: Desensitization

The fourth phase focuses on the client's negative affect, as reflected in the SUD Scale. This phase of treatment encompasses all responses, regardless of whether the client's distress level is increasing, decreasing, or stationary.

During the desensitization phase the clinician repeats the sets, with appropriate variations and changes of focus, if necessary, until the client's SUD level is reduced to 0 or 1 (when "ecologically valid," or appropriate to the individual given his present circumstances). This indicates that the primary dysfunction involving the targeted event has been cleared. However, reprocessing is still incomplete, and the information will need to be addressed further in the crucial remaining phases.

It should be emphasized here that in many cases the sets of eye movements (or alternative forms of stimulation) are not sufficient to complete processing. Clinical reports suggest that at least half the time the processing will stop and the clinician will have to employ various additional strategies and advanced EMDR procedures to restimulate it. These variations are covered in depth in Chapters 7 and 10.

Phase Five: Installation

The fifth phase of treatment is called the installation phase because the focus is on installing and increasing the strength of the positive cognition that the client has identified as the replacement for the original negative cognition. For example, the client might begin with an image of her molestation and the negative cognition "I am powerless." During this fifth phase of treatment the positive cognition "I am now in control" might be installed. The caliber of the treatment effects (i.e., how strongly the client believes the positive cognition) is then measured using the VOC Scale.

The installation phase starts once the client's level of emotion about the target event has dropped to 1 or 0 on the SUD Scale. At this point the clinician asks the client to hold the most appropriate positive cognition in mind along with the target memory. Then the clinician continues the eye movement sets until the client's rating of the positive cognition reaches a level of 6 or 7 on the VOC Scale. Keep in mind that the client should rate the cognition based on how she *feels* at a gut level.

The most appropriate positive cognition might be the one the client identified during the assessment phase of the EMDR treatment session, or it might be one that has emerged spontaneously during the successive sets. Even if a new positive cognition has not emerged, clinicians usually find that the client's VOC rating of the original positive cognition has increased by the end of the desensitization phase. The clinician should continue the sets (with the client simultaneously focusing on the positive cognition and the target event) in order to ensure the greatest possible strengthening of the cognition. While negative images, thoughts, and emotions generally become more diffuse and less valid with each successive set, the positive images, thoughts, and emotions become more vivid and more valid. As long as the client's sense of validity, self-confidence, and certainty is increasing, the sets should be continued.

The VOC rating is extremely valuable in determining what further work must be done to complete the treatment session. For example, if a client reports a VOC rating of less than 7 after two sets, the clinician should question her to determine if the current level of validity is appropriate for her. For instance, a client may say, "I can't give a 7 because I don't believe in extremes" or "I'll have to see my brother to know for sure that I can stand up to him." These are statements of innocuous or appropriate beliefs and indicate no pathology; consequently, the next phase of the treatment session may begin. However, the client may voice a negative belief such as "I don't deserve to be completely happy." Since this type of negative belief will block the complete installation of the positive cognition, it will have to serve as the target of an EMDR treatment. The ultimate goal is the installation of a strong and completely valid positive cognition that will raise the client's sense of self-efficacy and self-esteem.

Linking the positive cognition with the target memory strengthens the associative bond so that if memory of the original incident is triggered, its return to consciousness will now be accompanied by the new, strongly linked positive cognition, such as "It's over; I'm safe now." As the client concentrates on the positive cognition, it is infused into the target memory network, where it can generalize to associated material. As discussed earlier, the positive cognition is chosen on the basis of its ability to generalize and reshape the perspective of the greatest amount of dysfunctional material, as well as to empower the client for present and future occurrences. Metaphorically, the negative and positive cognitions give color to past and present incidents (as if the client were seeing through dark or rose-colored glasses) so that the positive cognition acts as a dye of a different hue that permeates the memory network.

Clearly, the installation and strengthening of the positive cognition is a crucial component of the EMDR treatment session. The very existence of negative cognitions is an indication that the traumatic event is a powerfully defining factor in the person's life, one that has not yet been adequately assimilated into an adaptive framework. Unresolved traumas are typified by negative perspectives on issues of self-control and empowerment, perspectives that may be manifested in many forms throughout a person's life. Fully processed traumatic information, by contrast, is typified by access to a memory that incorporates an adaptive perspective complete with positive cognition and appropriate affect. The installation phase of the EMDR treatment session focuses on the strength of the client's positive self-assessment, which is pivotal for positive therapeutic effect.

Phase Six: Body Scan

After the positive cognition has been fully installed, the client is asked to hold in mind both the target event and the positive cognition and to scan her body mentally from top to bottom. She is asked to identify any residual tension in the form of body sensation. These body sensations are then targeted for successive sets. In many cases the tension will simply resolve, but in some cases additional dysfunctional information will be revealed. As mentioned previously, there appears to be a physical resonance to dysfunctional material, which may be related to the way it is stored physiologically. Identifying residual physical sensation and targeting it in this sixth phase of EMDR treatment can help to resolve any remaining unprocessed information. This is an important phase and can reveal areas of tension or resistance that were previously hidden.

Phase Seven: Closure

The client must be returned to a state of emotional equilibrium by the end of each session, whether or not the reprocessing is complete. (Techniques to close the session are reviewed in Chapter 9.) In addition, it is vital that the client be given the proper instructions at the end of each session. That is, the clinician must remind the client that the disturbing images, thoughts, or emotions that may arise between sessions are evidence of additional processing, which is a positive sign. The client is instructed to keep a log or journal of the negative thoughts, situations, dreams, and memories that may occur. This instruction allows the client to cognitively distance herself from emotional disturbance through the act of writing. Specifically, the client is told to "take a snapshot" of any disturbances so that they can be used as targets for the next session. The use of the log and the visualization techniques taught by the clinician or via a relaxation tape (explained in Chapters 5 and 9) are extremely important for maintaining client stability between sessions. Unless the clinician appropriately debriefs his EMDR client, there is a danger of decompensation or, in an extreme case, suicide, which can occur when the client gives her disturbing emotions too much significance or views them as indications that she is permanently damaged. The clinician should provide the client with realistic expectations about the negative (and positive) responses that may surface both during and after treatment. This information increases the likelihood that the client will maintain a sense of equilibrium in the face of possible disturbance engendered by the stimulation of the dysfunctional material. There may be a domino effect that stimulates other negative memories as the information processing continues. A further review of this material and a sample treatment will be presented in Chapter 6.

Phase Eight: Reevaluation

Reevaluation, the eighth phase of treatment, should be implemented at the beginning of each new session. The clinician has the client reaccess previously reprocessed targets and reviews the client's responses to determine if treatment effects have been maintained. The clinician should ask how the client feels about the previously targeted material and should examine the log reports to see if there are any reverberations of the already processed information that need to be targeted or otherwise addressed. The clinician may decide to target new material but should do so only after the previously treated traumas have been completely integrated.

Integration is determined in terms of intrapsychic factors as well as systems concerns. The reprocessed traumas may have resulted in new behaviors on the part of the client, requiring the clinician to address problems that arise in the family or social system. The reevaluation phase guides the clinician through the various EMDR protocols and the full treatment plan. Successful treatment can only be determined after sufficient reevaluation of reprocessing and behavioral effects.

STANDARD EMDR PROTOCOL

While the standard EMDR procedure takes place during each reprocessing session, the standard EMDR protocol guides the overall treatment of the client. Each reprocessing session must be directed at a particular target. The generic divisions of the targets are defined in the standard protocol as (1) the past experiences that have set the groundwork for the pathology, (2) the present situations or triggers that currently stimulate the disturbance, and (3) the templates necessary for appropriate future action. All of the specialized EMDR protocols (e.g., those regarding phobias or somatic disorders) are interfaced with this standard format.

CHOOSING A TARGET

Choosing a target is straightforward when treating a single-event trauma victim. However, when treating a multiple-trauma victim, the clinician should cluster the traumatic incidents into groups of similar events and then choose as the target a representative incident for each group. Reprocessing the representative incident will usually result in a generalization, allowing the positive treatment effects to spread to all of the associated incidents. Asking clients to designate their ten most disturbing memories allows them to sort through and consolidate their past experience into manageable targets. By assessing the SUD level of every event and arranging them in order of increasing disturbance, the clinician and client can jointly decide which memory should be the initial target for the EMDR treatment.

The decision about whether to begin in the first session at the high end or the low end of the distress continuum will depend on clinician preference and assessment of the client. Some clinicians feel that starting with an event that has a low rather than a high SUD level enables clients to experience the shifting and resolution of material with less distress; the consequent feeling of accomplishment, in turn, gives them confidence to work on more disturbing material. While this is a reasonable strategy, clinicians have found in many cases that a low-SUD target event changes rapidly into more distressing associations or re-membered incidents, perhaps causing the client to be dismayed and to feel ill-prepared to continue treatment. This possibility underscores the importance of proper client preparation.

In my own practice, I prefer (if the client consents) to target the most upsetting incidents first. My rationale is that by preparing the client for the worst eventuality and highest level of distress, there are no surprises later. In addition, clients often feel a sense of great accomplish-ment by the end of the session. Not only can they justly feel that they have relived the worst, but they may discover that the worst is not as bad as they had anticipated. Moreover, they have resolved the most trau-matic memory, which means that subsequent sessions can only be easier. This reprocessing will often result in a generalization effect (a general decrease in associated disturbance), reported as a great reduction of fear and anxiety in the ensuing week.

As noted earlier, some clients experience high levels of emotional disturbance between sessions, particularly if the reprocessing was incom-plete and they have undergone many highly distressing related traumas. The initial target, therefore, should be assessed on the basis of client readiness and stability (see Chapter 4). EMDR should not be used with clients who are unable to contain high levels of emotional disturbance or who are not in an appropriate therapeutic relationship with the clinician.

In attempting to resolve a trauma, the clinician should target all of the following: (1) the memory of the actual event; (2) any flashbacks, since they might be different from the actual traumatic incident; (3) any nightmare images; and (4) any triggers, such as certain loud noises, that bring back feelings of fear and confusion associated with the earlier trauma. Triggers are any stimuli that elicit the dysfunctional images, cognitions, emotions, or sensations, either as full flashbacks or as partial arousal of the dysfunctional material. Clinicians must treat each trigger separately; owing to second-order conditioning, each may have become independently disturbing because of the previous paired asso-ciation. Therefore, for complete resolution of a trauma each of the four elements should be targeted in turn.

Appropriate targets for the EMDR session include any manifestation of the dysfunctional information. For example, one important and often useful treatment focal point is a recurring nightmare. Clinical observation has shown that when a nightmare image is targeted, therapeutic effects are achieved even when the client is initially unsure of the dream's actual meaning. The symbolic overlay of the dream is often removed by EMDR to reveal the life experiences that were driving the discomfort. The Accelerated Information Processing model proposes that the REM dream state is a period when unconscious material arises to be processed. Nightmare images appear to be correlated with the client's level of affect and cognitive assessment. When disturbance is too high, the REM state itself is disrupted, and the disquieting material remains unassimilated.

When the nightmare image is targeted during an EMDR session, it is treated as a direct link to the network in which the underlying traumatic material is stored. It is this link that makes the material available for therapeutic resolution. For instance, a female sexual abuse victim recounting a nightmare of being chased by a monster through a cave may have no understanding of the significance of this dream but may nevertheless have overwhelming feelings of fear and danger. When the image is targeted with EMDR, the client might report seeing it spontaneously shift with successive sets to reveal her stepfather–perpetrator chasing her through her childhood home. This new image is then available for further processing. In other cases the dream image may simply dissipate without obvious references or insights.

Regardless of the level of insight derived from the experience, once the dream image or recurrent nightmare scene is targeted and processed, the dream generally does not recur. Some clinicians have clients report (as part of their logs) any disturbing dreams they may have had in order to use them as targets in subsequent sessions. Dreams that are not disturbing, or were resolved before awakening (e.g., winning a fight), probably were successfully processed and are not targeted.

PATTERNS OF RESPONSE

Clinical observation indicates that approximately 40% of the time clients experience a continual, progressive shift toward a resolution of the target event. The kinds of shifts reported by clients indicate that processing affects all aspects of the traumatic memory and can progress in a variety of ways. At the end of each set, the client may report a change of the target memory or a shift to a different memory. Clients report that new memories appear momentarily during the set, that they emerge and remain during the entire set, or that they surface only as the set concludes. The client may report merely visual images of the event or may give a full-blown description, including thoughts, voices, smells, emotions, and body sensations. The client may experience these elements as merely a shadow of the original or in a full-force abreaction.

In order to explore the types of changes that indicate processing, it is useful to return to the concept that memory networks are associatively linked channels of information. A targeted memory may be one of a number of incidents stored in a particular channel. As the eye movements begin and the information starts processing through the channel, new memories can rise to consciousness. These new memories may appear to the client in flashes (as though the event were suddenly caught in a spotlight), they may appear as a collage of many events all at once, or they may come to consciousness as body sensations. No matter how the information subjectively emerges, as long as processing has continued, the client should simply be directed for the next set with the global statement "Think of it." In other words, the clinician needs to address the targeted memory in whatever form it arises.

In working with EMDR clients over the years, some general patterns of association have become clear. The following list shows the kinds of client responses that may emerge when the information is processing. Clinicians should take careful note of these responses, since they indicate that the clinician can continue the procedure without needing to engage in any advanced EMDR intervention (see Chapter 7). That is, as long as clients are making new associations, the sets may be continued.

The variety of possible associations to a given target is indicated in Figure 10. The first six types of associative channels entail the linkage

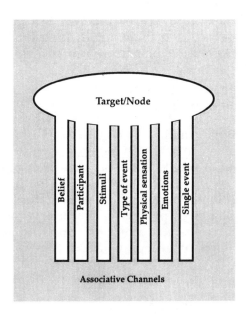

FIGURE 10. Target/node and possible types of associative channels.

of various discrete events that are bound by a common thread whereas the seventh channel indicates shifts of information (e.g., image, insights) confined to the single targeted event.

After a set, a new event may arise that is linked associatively with the initial targeted event. There is no way of knowing before processing begins what the association will be. However, each type of association is linked by one of a variety of dominant threads. No particular pattern of association is considered preferable to another from a therapeutic standpoint, as each type of associative response will achieve a resolution of the material that is unique to the individual client.

In the following paragraphs we will first review patterns that emerge when the client reports a variety of memories. Then we will turn to the kind of processing patterns observed when the client retains only one memory in consciousness throughout the treatment session.

Multimemory Associative Processing

The Belief Inherent in the Trauma

Emerging memories may be linked by the dominant belief inherent in the traumatic target event. For example, a memory of a car accident may be associated with the memory of a sexual assault because they share the cognition "I am powerless." In turn, processing could reveal either of these incidents as the pivotal memory that causes the client extreme anxiety when feelings of powerlessness in the workplace are targeted. Clinicians can often recognize important dysfunctional beliefs by determining what these associated memories have in common. This discovery can be helpful in delineating a more thorough treatment plan, but clinicians should usually postpone discussion of the material with the client until after the eye movement part of the treatment session is concluded.

Remember, associations are always based on the client's experience. No memory will emerge that is not in some way associated with the target. However, the clinician should allow the client to come naturally to a realization of the meaning of the connection (the negative cognition thread), rather than superimposing it or pushing the client to identify it during the early phases of processing. Regardless of whether clients recognize the connections between their negative cognition and their memories, cognitive restructuring will take place during EMDR's installation phase.

The Major Participant or Perpetrator

Targeted memories may be linked with new memories by the perpetrator they have in common. For example, a client's molestation by his father may become associated with a beating his father gave him and with his father's abandonment of him on another occasion. Processing these associations will help the client resolve his "unfinished business" with his abusive parent. Often the abusive parent has set in motion the problems that a client has with authority, lack of self-esteem, and so on. Once the memories connected with a parent are processed, clients often spontaneously begin reacting to present situations differently (e.g., by asserting themselves in the workplace).

The Pronounced Stimuli

The emerging memories may be linked by the primary stimuli inherent in the events. For example, when processing the memory of an earthquake, a Vietnam vet may suddenly recall a combat experience if the sounds of falling objects or loud rumbling dominated both events. Although it is often difficult to separate the emotion (such as fear) or cognition (such as "I am powerless") from the external trigger, there can be a train of associations primarily linked by a sensory cue. The cue is revealed as the connective link during processing because there is a dysfunctional aspect to the client's reaction to the stimulus. That the reaction is dysfunctional is shown by the high level of emotion and the negative cognition it comprises.

The Specific Event

Emerging memories may be linked to the targeted memory by the nature of the event itself. For example, when a rape is targeted in a victim of multiple assaults, a sequence of memories of other rapes may emerge. Naturally, these memories carry the same negative cognition and emotion as the targeted rape, but the dominant thread is the rape itself. It is also possible for dissociated memories of childhood molestation to emerge when the primary target is some other form of sexual abuse. Be aware that a multiple-molestation or multiple-rape victim may feel overwhelmed when many memories of additional assaults emerge during a session. Take special care with these clients to foster feelings of safety, and reassure them that they can rest when they need to. Procedural steps on how to do this are covered in Chapter 5, and additional information on working with this population is presented in Chapter 11.

The Dominant Physical Sensations

Remember that the physical sensations experienced at the time of the event are stored in the nervous system and may constitute the dominant thread of the associative sequence. For example, one client had a physically abusive childhood: The mother used to tie the child's hands to a bed and beat her with a broomstick. As the client processed this memory, the dominant physical sensations she experienced were pressure around her hands and wrists. The next memory to come to consciousness was of a molestation that included the physical sensation of her father forcing her hands around his penis. This memory was followed by one of a rapist holding her hands together during the attack. The final memory to emerge was of awakening after an operation and of being tied down to a gurney in a hospital room and screaming but without understanding why. These sequential memories revealed to the client that the reason for her terror in the hospital was the sense of violation and danger associated with the sensation of pressure around her wrists.

The Dominant Emotions

The emerging memories may be linked by the primary emotion inherent in the event. For example, processing a memory of a failed business venture that generates emotions of despair may be followed by a memory of abandonment by a parent, an event associated with the same emotion. While a cognition may be found that could appropriately link the two events, what is primary for the client is the overwhelming emotion; it is not necessary for the client to engage in a cognitive evaluation of the memories.

Once again, the clinician must be attuned to the amount of emotional distress the client is undergoing during processing. The client who is processing a chain of memories that are stimulating intense despair or the multiple-rape victim who is mentally sequencing through all of the rape experiences of her life could feel as if a locomotive were bearing down on her. As will be more fully explored in the following chapters, the clinician must immediately honor any indication by the client that she needs to stop. This response not only reinforces the client's ability to say no and maintain a sense of control but demonstrates that the client is the final judge of when to rest during the intense processing. However, clinicians should note that when a rape victim, for example, says "Stop" during processing, she may be verbalizing what she said, or wanted to say, to the perpetrator because those are the thoughts, experienced at the time of the event, that are now surfacing. When directed at the perpetrator, words like "No" and "Stop" should be targeted with the sets. When spoken directly to the clinician, they mean the sets should be terminated until the client is willing to proceed. In order to avoid confusion between the two, the client should be encouraged to use a hand gesture that signals a desire to stop. When in doubt, the clinician should stop the set and ask the client.

Single-Memory Processing Effects

While processing is often indicated by a sequential emergence of new memories, as discussed in the previous section, the clinician should note that sometimes new memories surface only temporarily during the set and then shift back to the initial target memory. In other cases no new memories emerge consciously and the target incident is the only one that is consistently maintained. In still other cases the target may shift to another memory that remains in consciousness during most of the session. In all these instances (where a single event continues to occur in consecutive sets) the clinician should assess the target for other indicators of successful processing.

One indicator of processing is when the client describes a change or shift in any of five distinct aspects of the memory: image, sounds, cognition, emotion, or physical sensations. Although all aspects of the incident are shifting simultaneously (e.g., a substantial shift in cognition correlates with a shift in physical sensations and emotion), the client may find that one aspect dominates his consciousness. He should be encouraged to verbalize whatever aspect stands out. When change is evident, the clinician should take care not to pull the client out of the process by asking about aspects that are not spontaneously reported.

The following are the kinds of changes or shifts that the clinician can expect to see during EMDR processing.

Changes in Image

As already indicated, the image of the target event can change to an image of a different but associated event or it can shift to a different aspect of the same event. However, the image can also change its content or appearance. In a content change, a leering face can change to a smiling one, a weapon can disappear, and so forth. The image can change in appearance by a shift in perspective or the expansion of a scene to include more details. For example, a client retrieved the memory of a meeting in which he had been humiliated, but all he could see initially was the look on the face of the colleague who insulted him. As processing continued, the scene expanded, as if blinders had been removed. In the broader scene, the client saw other people—with more positive and supportive expressions. It is interesting to note in this example that this more self-affirming information had always been stored in the client's nervous system. However, it was not previously available when the memory was accessed, presumably because the image of the coworker's face was associated with a particular level of the dominant affect (anxiety and humiliation). As dysfunctional information is processed, a greater access is afforded throughout the associational network. After treatment, the client in this example was able to retrieve not only the look on the face of the person who humiliated him but also other, more positive, details, since anxiety was no longer dominant; when asked to retrieve the memory, he now spontaneously saw the larger scene.

Successful processing is also apparent when the client reports other shifts in the appearance of the image. The picture can become larger, smaller, or blurred; it can turn gray or move closer or further away; or it can disappear completely. The exact nature of the change cannot be predicted. Clients who must give a detailed account of the incident to the police or in court must be warned that after treatment a picture of the event may not be retrievable. Some clients become confused or disturbed when the picture begins to disappear. Often they say, "I must be doing something wrong; I can't get the picture back." Clinicians should reassure them that any change is natural as long as the processing continues and that if they lose the picture, they should just think of the incident, regardless of what comes to mind.

Some clients may become disturbed when the picture begins to disappear because they fear they will lose good memories or will completely forget that the incident occurred. These clients should be reassured that the target event will not be forgotten and that good memories or emotions are never lost in EMDR treatment. They should be told that the dysfunctional information is being "digested" and converted to a more useful form and that all that is being shifted is the way the information is stored in the nervous system, so that the upsetting picture and emotions will no longer dominate.

Any change in image reported by the client is indicative of information processing, and the subjective nature of the shift need not be questioned by the clinician. In other words, it makes no difference how large or small the picture has become or how blurry it appears. Clinicians will know processing has occurred if they detect any indicator of change. Even the statement "It looks different" is sufficient. Clinicians should avoid questioning the client about such changes. Attempts to get a detailed description of the content of the picture or the nature of an unspecified shift can interrupt and undermine the processing effects.

Changes in Sounds

The client may report that the voices of people in the target memory are becoming quieter or have completely disappeared. In one instance a client reported that the target event included hearing her baby screaming; she reported after a few sets that the sound had disappeared completely. Likewise, the sound of gunfire and explosions may increase or decrease in volume as processing continues.

Clients commonly report shifts in the auditory component of target memories when processing interactions with perpetrators, parents, or others in a variety of social settings. When processing an uncomfortable confrontation at work, a client may report that the remembered dialogue has shifted, that he has spontaneously begun to use new, more assertive, language while his coworker is making more deferential statements. During the sets clients often begin verbally asserting themselves with an abusive parent. The clinician should encourage the client to repeat these assertive statements, internally or out loud, until they are confidently and strongly felt. This verbalization has often resulted in major breakthroughs for clients who have been frozen in a childlike role with respect to their parents and other authority figures.

Clients report that the words that were spoken or thought at the time of the event may spontaneously arise along with the image. Clients raised with English as a second language in the household may begin to speak in their native language when early memories are processed. If the client begins to speak in a foreign language, simply direct him as usual ("Just think of that") and continue the sets. Although clients may speak in their childhood language, they can still understand directions in English.

Changes in Cognitions

The client's level of insight often increases from one set to another. As shown in the transcript in Chapter 2 in which the client had to deal with an incompetent coworker, the client's cognitions can become more therapeutically adaptive as the information is processed. However, until the information is completely processed, the cognitions will not be fully appropriate. Metaphorically, the train has not reached its destination until the last stop. Along the way, at pauses between sets, there will still be some dysfunctional material to be processed, and the clinician should resist the temptation to explore or probe a particular information plateau unless processing is stuck. As long as shifts are being reported, the clinician should simply direct the client to think of the cognition just verbalized during the previous set.

Occasionally, a client may give what is termed a "polar" response, which is a dramatic shift from a negative to a positive cognition at an early point in processing. This is interpreted in information-processing terms to be a shift in neuro networks from a configuration of "no" to an associated configuration of "yes." In other words, a client may start with the cognition "There is something wrong with me" in relation to social situations and after a single set may start thinking, "I'm fine." When such an about-face occurs, we assume that the client has reached the end of a channel. The clinician should then bring the client back to the original node (the target memory) and continue processing. There may or may not be additional dysfunctional channels.

Changes in Emotions

As the memory is processed, the associated emotions may lessen in intensity. Remember, however, that the emotional level can increase dramatically before the memory reaches an adaptive resolution. As long as the client is reporting a different level of emotion, either higher or lower, the information is assumed to be processing. When emotion is the dominant presenting element of the memory, clinicians can use the SUD Scale to assess the degree of change.

While the SUD Scale is helpful, remember that it may be an insufficient measure in some cases. Many clients report a shift in the type of emotion (e.g., from grief to anger) as well as shifts in its intensity. When the client feels a different emotion, the SUD level may increase (anxiety at a SUD level of 3 can shift to sadness at a SUD level of 7), decrease, or remain the same. The clinician should be alert to any new emotion that arises during the session in order to meet the client's needs. For instance, the kind of verbal and nonverbal support that would be reassuring to a client experiencing extreme anger is dramatically different from the support needed if the client begins to experience sorrow or despair.

The client will often report a progressive shift toward more ecologically valid, or appropriate, emotions. This shift will manifest itself as movement through different "layers" of emotion (e.g., from guilt to rage to sorrow to acceptance). Once again, each client reacts uniquely, and sometimes the experience of sorrow comes earlier. At times there will not be any expression of a particular emotional state and no specific emotion or level of expression should be demanded of the client. While some clients abreact with a high emotional intensity, others process in a straightforward manner, with little overt display.

Changes in Physical Sensation

When a memory is being processed, most clients experience some manifestation of the information on a somatic level. The body sensations may be connected to emotions experienced during processing (e.g., a high pulse rate and tight stomach associated with fear). Or the body sensations may be those that were experienced during the original event (as in the example of the client who had been bound to a bed as a child and who felt pressure on her wrists while processing that memory). Finally, the body sensations may be a nonspecific physical resonance of the dysfunctional cognition (this will be explained in Chapter 6).

Processing can be manifested somatically through a release of the physical sensations; that is, the client experiences them with decreasing intensity with each set. These changes can appear simply as a reduction in pulse rate or as what is termed a retracing of the experience itself. As an instance of the latter, a client whose mother punished him by burning his hand on the kitchen stove initially reexperienced the burning sensation as if it were occurring in the present. But with each set he felt this sensation lessen in intensity. Remember, however, that while the client may feel only vague physical sensations of the experience at the start of the EMDR session, these sensations can suddenly increase in intensity at any time.

The physical sensations felt by the client are viewed in EMDR simply as a manifestation of the information being processed. Conceptually, since the physical sensations present during the trauma are also locked in the nervous system, the stimulation of the information can be experienced by the client in the part of the body where the sensations were originally felt (through the afferent/efferent nervous system). This stimulation, as with any other painful sensation, may seem to be in the part of the body that hurts, but the pain center is, of course, in the brain.

While explained conceptually here in terms of sensation stored in the neuro network, the actual reexperiencing of the memory (as in an abreaction) can in the absence of preparation be frightening for both client and clinician. A client who experiences distress through the restimulation of the pain of physical assault should be comforted and reminded during the set that he is in no present danger. However, if the clinician is not comfortable with the possibility that the client might feel strong emotions and high levels of physical sensations, she should not use EMDR. This caveat is especially important since the client can certainly be traumatized further if the clinician shows fear or aversion to his reactions during processing.

Processing of information can also be indicated by shifts in the location of body sensations. For instance, a client may initially indicate a tightness in the stomach, but with each set the sensations may seem to move upward (to the chest, throat, or head). The clinician should merely direct the client to think of the new location without attempting to ascertain what the sensation feels like or ascribing a meaning to it. A significant number of clients consistently report that a sensation feels as if it is located in the head. This experience should be treated by the clinician not as a metaphoric construct but as an actual physical sensation. Clinicians should direct clients to focus their attention on wherever the sensation currently resides and not ask them about sensations reported in past sets. Additionally, if the client reports dizziness, pain, or nausea or if no movement in the sensation is reported after two sets, the clinician should change the direction of the eye movement. This change will generally cause the physical sensations to shift in some manner.

While physical sensations during EMDR processing are considered an appropriate target for subsequent sets, the clinician must use common sense. Some physical sensations might actually be the result of problems in the present moment. A heart attack or stroke, after all, could conceivably occur during an EMDR session, just as it could happen during choir practice. Caution is always advised, particularly when working with elderly clients.

As noted earlier, when eye pain is reported, the eye movements should be stopped and the client should be referred to a eye specialist and provided with a description of the kinds of eye movements he will be asked to make during EMDR sessions. At no time should eye movement be continued when the client reports eye pain. (For a discussion of eye muscle weakness, refer to the section on eye movements earlier in this chapter.) Alternative stimuli can easily be substituted.

DIFFERENTIAL EFFECTS

Keep in mind that the aforementioned changes are intended to convey a general idea of what can be expected. Because EMDR is not a regimented approach, no two treatment sessions will be the same. Each client should be treated as a unique individual with needs that vary from moment to moment. Clinicians must be vigilant so that they can alter the procedures at any time to accommodate the needs of the client; they must refrain from viewing EMDR as a race to achieve treatment effects. While the following chapters are offered to assist the clinical implementation of the EMDR treatment model, therapists must be sure to use all their rapport-building skills and clinical resources to support the client. The effectiveness of EMDR depends as much on the quality of the journey as on the designated destination.

SUPERVISED PRACTICE

Instructors may wish to supervise students in exercises that allow them to practice eliciting and developing negative and positive cognitions in a variety of role-play situations. This is a difficult part of the EMDR therapy for many clinicians. A list of generic cognitions is included in Appendix A to assist the clinician's (and client's) learning process. It may also be useful to supervise students in the use of the various types of eye movements and alternative forms of stimulation. This is suggested before the clinician attempts to use the method in an actual reprocessing session.

SUMMARY AND CONCLUSIONS

EMDR treatment effects are based on the ability to target and access dysfunctional material. The initially targeted manifestations of this material include the image, the negative cognition, and the physical sensations associated with the event. Baseline measures include an identification of the stimulated emotion, a SUD rating indicating the intensity of the disturbance, and a VOC rating of how true the client believes the desired positive cognition to be. Processing of the target material is initiated by having the client focus on the appropriate stimuli (eye movements, hand taps, or sounds) while simultaneously concentrating on the aligned elements of the target (image, cognition, and physical sensation). Processing takes place during successive stimulation sets, which alternate with discussions with the client to determine the next appropriate target.

The purpose of the entire eight-phase EMDR treatment is to facilitate accelerated information processing. The first phase determines whether the client is an appropriate candidate for EMDR and includes treatment planning. The second phase prepares the client for any disturbance that may arise during or between sessions. The third, or assessment, phase focuses on ascertaining a target and determining its components and measures. During the following three phases the clinician conducts the stimulation sets. The fourth, or desensitization, phase focuses on the disturbance, which is judged by the SUD Scale. When this is completed, the installation phase begins, a phase that concentrates on installing and strengthening the positive cognition (as measured on the VOC Scale). In the sixth phase the remainder of the reprocessing is accomplished by targeting any material revealed by a body scan. The seventh phase is closure, which returns the client to emotional equilibrium and during which the client is reminded about the potential for between-session processing. During debriefing, the client is also asked to record any attendant disturbance in a log and to use a variety of relaxation techniques to maintain a relative state of calm. Appropriate client selection, thorough preparation, careful application of the method, and adequate debriefing are vital for client safety because unexpected unresolved material can surface during or between EMDR sessions. The eighth and final phase, reevaluation, determines the quality of the treatment effects and guides the clinician through the extended protocols.

The application of EMDR to the treatment of the traumatic memories responsible for pathological symptoms involves grouping the events and then targeting not only a significant representational memory for each cluster but also nightmare images, flashback scenes, and present triggers. The activation of the client's innate self-healing processing system should be done with minimal clinical intrusion. As the processing proceeds, clinical effects are judged by the client's reports of new memories that conform to patterns of associated memory networks linked by similar cues (such as beliefs, participants, or sensations). When a single memory is maintained during the entire session, clinical results are assessed by the quality of the changes in the image, the sounds, the cognitions, the emotions, and the physical sensations. While treatment is straightforward about half the time, the remaining cases demand more complex clinical involvement (see Chapter 7). However, clinical attention and focus are mandatory at all times because of the magnitude and variety of the treatment effects. Specific instructions to guide the treatment process will be offered in the next chapters.

CHAPTER 4

Phase One

CLIENT HISTORY

> The curious paradox is that when I accept myself just as I
> am, then I can change.
>
> *Carl Rogers*

In this chapter we will look at the first phase of EMDR treatment, which entails history taking—to determine whether a given client will benefit from EMDR—and treatment planning. EMDR processing can be very disturbing to the client both during and after sessions. The first section of this chapter offers an understanding of the nature and intensity of the disturbances that may arise. This should assist clinicians to assess the client's readiness. It is imperative that the clinician make informed decisions regarding the client's ability to maintain a sense of stability and to perform certain therapeutic tasks in the face of high levels of emotion.

The next section, on client safety factors, will delineate the areas of inquiry used to select clients for EMDR treatment. Experience has shown that this information should be supplemented with supervised practice. It appears that most clinicians appreciate the magnitude of the changes EMDR brings about only after they have personally experienced it. For those clients deemed appropriate for EMDR treatment, the clinician will then take a detailed history in order to outline a treatment plan and identify the specific information needed to address the presenting problems. To illustrate the clinician–client interaction, this chapter will conclude with a transcript of an actual history-taking session.

CLIENT READINESS

EMDR is not appropriate for every client. The clinician needs to obtain a careful, detailed client history to assess the suitability of clients for

EMDR treatment and to gauge their psychological needs during and after sessions. It is important to remember that each session will be different and each client's needs and responses unique. In order to make an informed decision the therapist must be sensitive to the kinds of experiences clients undergo during the information processing that may occur both inside and outside the office once EMDR has been initiated.

Stimulating the information that constitutes the client's target memory brings its various components to consciousness. Dissociated information can readily surface, as can many of the emotions and physical sensations experienced at the time of the event. This can be extremely distressful for the client. If properly handled by the clinician, the accelerated processing that EMDR activates will resolve this information far more rapidly than conventional therapies. However, the clinician must assess the client's readiness and ability to uncover and withstand the information in order to ascertain whether or not the client can be guided through the disturbance that may emerge as the memory is treated.

An important characteristic of EMDR is that the information processing may continue *after* the session, although at a slower rate. Therefore, the client may experience some discomfort between sessions as new memories are stimulated in or below consciousness. A helpful metaphor is that of a row of falling dominoes: As each memory is stimulated and processed, it may set off an associated memory. Moreover, as each memory is stimulated, it may release disturbing images and emotions. For treatment to be successful, the client must be able to handle whatever emotions—despair, helplessness, vulnerability, and so forth—are associated with the memory.

There is no way to predict exactly how a client will process a particular event. Responses can range from a mild emotional reaction to a full-blown abreaction. In EMDR we define abreaction simply as the reexperiencing of the stimulated memory at a high level of disturbance. Images, thoughts, emotions, and physical sensations may be brought to consciousness as EMDR processes the information. During an abreaction the emotions and physical sensations are particularly strong, perhaps almost as strong as they were during the original event. EMDR does not, however, generate full flashbacks, since the client is coached to have a dual focus by maintaining an awareness of the disturbing past event while staying in the safety of the present. This is aided by the dual tasks of concentrating on the target and following the clinician's fingers.

Because of their great intensity the physical sensations may be frightening to the client. For instance, one client had been playing cowboys and Indians as a young child when her friends captured her, tied a rope around her neck, and hung her from a tree. Luckily, one of the mothers ran out and cut her down with only moments to spare. As her EMDR treatment began, the client began to emit choking sounds, turned color, and clearly was having great difficulty breathing. In this case processing was successfully completed, but clinicians should keep in mind the possibility of such a violent client response when determining safety factors.

Even if the target memory appears minor, it can quickly shift to a highly charged memory. In the flooding treatments used in behavioral therapy, client and clinician expect the target memory to be greatly disturbing and are prepared for the consequences. The hallmark of EMDR treatment is accelerated processing, with its potential for a rapid uncovering of previously unsuspected material, some of which may be extremely distressing. Therefore, client readiness should be carefully assessed.

CLIENT SAFETY FACTORS

The following factors are crucial in maintaining client safety and should be carefully assessed to determine which clients are appropriate for EMDR.

Level of Rapport

Clients should be able to feel comfortable with the possibility of experiencing a high level of vulnerability, a lack of control, and any physical sensations from the event that may be inherent in the target memory. This means that clients must be willing to tell their therapist the truth about what they are experiencing. While it is not necessary for them to reveal the details of their trauma, they must be willing to experience in the presence of the clinician whatever emotions emerge and to report accurately the nature and intensity of these emotions. Sometimes—because of insufficient trust, a high susceptibility to demand characteristics, or a desire to avoid further painful material—a client will inaccurately report a low level of distress and inappropriately or prematurely terminate the session. When this happens, the client is more likely to experience discomfort between sessions and may be forced to deal with abreaction-level material without the appropriate clinical support. Clients are reported to be at greater risk for suicidal ideation and suicide attempts when they feel greatly disturbed but withhold this information from the clinician. While this will be true with any form of therapy, the potential for additional between-sessions disturbance during EMDR treatment underscores the need for a strong therapeutic alliance, specific truth-telling agreements, and a therapist who can convey a message of safety, flexibility, and unconditional regard.

Clients with severe abuse backgrounds should be given careful consideration before proceeding with treatment, because they generally have difficulty around issues of safety and trust. Until the client feels comfortable with the clinician in the common interactions of traditional therapy, EMDR should not be used.

Emotional Disturbance

Clients should be able to withstand and deal with the high levels of emotional disturbance that may arise during or between EMDR sessions. In order to help test this capacity before the traumatic material is specifically targeted, it is strongly recommended that the clinician discover during the history-taking sessions whether or not the client is capable of responding to self-control and relaxation techniques. The clinician should try a variety of these techniques with the client in the office and only proceed with EMDR if the client can successfully be guided to dissipate a moderate level of disturbance.

When targeted material has been incompletely processed during any session, proper debriefing (as defined in Chapter 6) is imperative, and guided visualization techniques or hypnosis are used to assist the client to regain emotional balance. Because the clinician will not be able to predict the level of between-sessions disturbance, it is useful to train clients in these self-control techniques before undertaking EMDR treatment. I also recommend the use of audiotapes that can be used between sessions (such as "Letting Go of Stress"; Miller, 1994). Some of these relaxation techniques will be described in Chapter 9 and can be used to bring closure to otherwise incomplete sessions. They should also be used by clients on a daily basis and to provide relief if spontaneous processing between sessions is causing emotional disturbance.

If the client is unable to use such self-control techniques, EMDR treatment should not be attempted. Clinicians should experiment with alternative methods until the client is able to reduce significant levels of disturbance. Inability to reduce disturbance can justifiably add to the client's fear when dysfunctional material is accessed, and can severely hamper positive treatment effects.

Stability

It is vital that the client be assessed for personal stability. Suicidal ideation is not uncommon after EMDR treatment with certain clients, such as severely disturbed victims of multiple sexual molestations. Clinicians must appropriately debrief such clients (see Chapter 6), and the initial assessment should include the client's capacity to remember the debriefing instructions and ability to ask for assistance if needed.

The level of environmental stability is also significant. For example, clinicians should not attempt to reprocess unrelated traumas if clients are currently undergoing major life pressures (such as family/social crises or financial/career problems) and are unable to handle the additional disturbance engendered by reprocessing.

Of course, clinicians will have to determine whether the earlier traumas are indeed unrelated to the client's present life conditions. Clients who are constantly in a state of crisis may be driven by earlier life experiences that need to be resolved before they can obtain relief from their present problems. It is important to determine which traumatic memories are directly responsible for present dysfunction, and therefore should be processed now with EMDR, and which are incidental to the present crisis, and can be set aside while today's problems are addressed with appropriate plans of action.

Life Supports

Clients must have life supports, including friends and family members who can nurture them through any between-sessions disturbance. If clients are isolated or are primary caretakers without a supportive network of their own, clinicians should proceed with caution. Clinicians should determine whether their clients are able to sustain themselves psychologically or can be sufficiently comforted by them over the telephone if they need help.

General Physical Health

The client should be healthy enough to withstand the physical rigors of memory reprocessing. In the earlier example of the choking memory, the client was in her 30s when treated and strong enough to withstand possible physical consequences. However, had she been 70 years old with a heart condition, we would have had serious concern about her ability to withstand the physical onslaught. In fact, some World War II veterans are currently undergoing EMDR treatment on an inpatient basis because of this concern.

The potential effects of aroused emotion on women who are pregnant should also be taken into account. While to date there have been no reports of serious physical side effects, it is always better to use caution. When any physical problem, including a respiratory or cardiac condition, is part of the clinical picture, a physician should be consulted regarding the possible negative effects of high levels of emotional responses.

Office Consultation versus Inpatient Treatment

Memories should be assessed to distinguish those that may be targeted at the office from those that may require inpatient hospital support. During one reprocessing of a near-death experience, the client stopped breathing; fortunately, the clinician, a psychiatric nurse, had made provisions for resuscitation. In another case a client was being seen in an inpatient setting by a psychiatrist. During the reprocessing of a memory of electrical torture, he began writhing and convulsing in bed almost as if he were being shocked again. The psychiatrist was able to work with him to complete the processing, but clearly the experience would have been much more traumatic for both of them had it not occurred in a protected environment. Clinicians should always assess the need for appropriate restraint, medical attention, or medication when treating clients with schizophrenia, active drug or alcohol addictions, near-death memories, or physical impairments or when in doubt about suicidal tendencies, personal stability, or appropriate life supports. If there is any question of clients becoming a danger to themselves or others, inpatient work should be strongly considered.

Neurological Impairment

There have been no reports of client harm for those suffering from neurological impairment. However, since the Accelerated Information Processing model posits certain underlying physiological processes, clinicians should be sensitive to any history of neurological abnormalities or organic brain damage. It has been reported (Rothbaum, 1992) that clients recently addicted to cocaine received no benefit from EMDR treatment that used eye movements; it is unclear whether alternative stimulation would have had a positive effect (the marker for this deficit appears to be a metabolic abnormality of the orbitofrontal cortex). No contraindications for the use of EMDR have been reported so far with clients suffering from attention-deficit/hyperactivity disorder.

Clinicians have reported a tendency for less treatment generalization to occur with some clients who have organic brain damage and, consequently, a need to target a greater than usual number of memories to achieve full therapeutic effect. While EMDR has been used successfully with clients evincing a range of neurological complaints, caution should be observed when attempting treatment of this population. That is, there may be some form of brain damage that would cause either no response or extreme discomfort during EMDR sessions. A physician consultation should always be sought if the clinician suspects that a physical condition, including neurological impairment, might present a problem. Clinicians attempting EMDR with such individuals should also be thoroughly experienced with a wide range of EMDR treatment effects in order to recognize any abnormal response, in which case the session should be terminated.

Epilepsy

While a number of clients with epilepsy have been successfully treated with EMDR, caution should be observed as a matter of course, as with any client who is neurologically impaired.

I have seen only two reports of clients experiencing seizures (both small) during EMDR sessions. In one instance, the memory being reprocessed was seizure related; the client regained consciousness within 5 minutes, washed her face, and went on with the session without further incident. (This was the only seizure suffered by the client in over a dozen sessions.) Another client suffered a small seizure during an EMDR session but after concluding treatment was never troubled by seizures again. Clients with epilepsy should be informed of the possibility of a seizure during EMDR before treatment is begun.

Also noteworthy is the case of a client with epilepsy who had been successfully treated for PTSD and who attempted the eye movements on her own whenever she had an "aura" or other sign of an oncoming seizure. She discovered that the eye movements enabled her to avoid the attacks.

Eye Problems

There has been a report of a client sustaining severe ocular damage that resulted in blindness because of eye movement treatment. This occurred at the hands of a clinician who was untrained in the use of EMDR. Apparently, even though the client reported consistent eye pain, the clinician, who had no knowledge of EMDR treatment effects, continued to administer the eye movement sets. *Under no circumstances should EMDR be continued if the client reports eye pain.* If this occurs, the clinician should refer the client to an eye specialist who should be informed of the kinds of eye movements required by EMDR treatment. The specialist should assess the physical capacity of the client for these kinds of movements and render judgment about the advisability of their use.

Some clients may be unable to maintain continued eye movement sets because of eye muscle weakness. They too should be sent to an eye specialist for examination and, when appropriate, instructed in eye exercises to increase the muscle strength necessary for continuous eye movement.

Clients who wear contact lenses should bring their lens cases to treatment sessions so that the lenses can be removed if any sign of dryness or irritation occurs. With many clients it may be preferable to avoid using EMDR when they are wearing contacts.

When eye movements cannot be used, the clinician can use alternate forms of stimulation, such as hand taps or sounds (as described in Chapter 3).

Drug and Alcohol Abuse

Clients with a substance abuse history should have in place appropriate supports, such as a 12-step program, before initiating EMDR treatment. Clinicians have reported that while some clients easily abandon substance abuse or cravings during treatment, others have a greater desire to resume the activity, presumably because of the stimulation of disturbing psychological material. Whether the resumption of chemical abuse represents an attempt to medicate against the stressful material that is emerging or stimulation of the old desire is unclear. In any case, clinicians should take special care with this population by briefing clients about potential problems and by setting up safeguards against potential resumption or exacerbation of abuse behaviors.

As noted earlier, stimulation other than by eye movements may be the most effective choice with recent crack cocaine addicts. In addition, there is a report of a client who was a daily abuser of amphetamines for the previous 25 years becoming highly agitated from an EMDR session in a way that necessitated hospitalization. Clinicians should proceed with caution with long-term amphetamine abusers.

Legal Requirements

If a crime victim, witness, or police officer is being treated for a critical incident, it is essential to establish whether a legal deposition or any specific kind of trial testimony is, or may be, required of the individual. During EMDR treatment the image of the event may fade, blur, or completely disappear. Although the client will still be able to tell what occurred, she might not be able to provide a vivid, detailed description of the event. In other cases the client may be able to give a more detailed description and may actually see the picture more clearly after EMDR treatment. However, there is no way of knowing beforehand how a client will process a particular event.

Consequently, informed consent should be used with all pertinent parties when legal proceedings are under way (or might be contemplated). Clinicians should explain that (1) after EMDR treatment the client may be unable to access a vivid picture of the event; (2) the client may no longer recount the incident with extreme emotion (which may be a problem if a very emotional witness is needed on the stand); and (3) while EMDR is not hypnosis (see Chapter 12), it has not yet been fully defined forensically and may eventually be regarded by the court as comparable to hypnosis. For example, molestation victims who have been treated clinically with hypnosis in certain states may lose their right to sue the perpetrator. In addition, hypnotically derived testimony is not admissible in court. At the time of this writing there have been only two tests of EMDR in the courts (see Chapter 11); therefore, the clinician should be cautious and obtain informed consent. It has been suggested that having videotaped interviews with the client prior to treatment may be useful for forensic purposes. For instance, such tapes can verify that a child molestation victim accurately identified the perpetrator and significant events before EMDR was used. However, these tapes may not be sufficient to hold up in court in a given case. A number of clients have chosen not to undergo EMDR treatment until their court cases have concluded.

Systems Control

As with any form of psychotherapy, EMDR treatment influences not only clients but their families and friends as well. As the dysfunctional information is processed and new self-assessments are engendered, the client's behavior changes. As clients become open to new choices, they should be educated with skills training. For instance, they may need to be taught how to deal with problem people or new situations through instruction in assertiveness, dating skills, or career-related matters. Early in treatment, clinicians should arrange for appropriate peer support and training groups for the client. EMDR clients can process material at a surprisingly fast rate, and they must be prepared to handle the resistance they may encounter from colleagues, family members, or friends. For example, if clients insist on remaining in a dangerous environment where new assertiveness would be detrimental (which might be the case for a battered wife who is still living with her alcoholic husband), they should be briefed about potential problems and offered alternative strategies for self-expression.

Clients in dysfunctional social relationships (where, for example, they might be taken advantage of if they appear to be in a vulnerable state) should be cautioned to avoid them immediately after trauma processing. For this reason, treating clients in penal institutions may be contraindicated in many instances because of the peer pressures inherent in the system.

Secondary Gains

Special care must be taken to assess the possible positive consequences, needs, or identity issues that are served by the presenting complaint.

Clients may have organized their existence around their pathology, and this possibility must be addressed, at least cognitively, before any changes can be expected from EMDR treatment. Essentially, the clinician must identify what the client will need to confront or give up if treatment is started or succeeds and must determine if the client has the stability and resources to handle the change.

A prime example of this problem can be found in certain Vietnam veterans. Over 20 years ago our 18-year-old boys were sent to war. They were forced into horrendous circumstances, including a drug culture. Instead of being embraced and nurtured when they returned home, they were often despised and ostracized. Having suffered flashbacks, nightmares, and intrusive thoughts for the last 25 years, they are now offered EMDR treatment along with the claim "We will take away your flashbacks, nightmares, intrusive thoughts—and your disability check." A veteran's fear (which he might reject on a conscious level) of becoming homeless because of loss of income is quite understandable. Unless this issue is addressed, his dysfunction is liable to remain unresolved. The clinician should address this concern (and others) by means of appropriate action plans before attempting to treat the trauma of clients who are receiving compensation or special caretaking because of their emotional disability.

Fear of loss of social identity may also be an issue. A number of veterans have said, "Who am I if I'm not a wounded Vietnam vet?" Combat veterans may be afraid of losing the sense of comradeship that goes along with being a suffering member of their treatment group. They may also be afraid that as their emotional pain lessens, they will stop honoring their dead. Exploring these concerns before starting to work on the trauma is highly recommended. The factors directly related to combat veterans will be more fully explored in Chapter 11.

The fear of loss of identification with a peer group is also pertinent to some molestation victims. They may become afraid of healing because they recognize that as their pain eases, they no longer feel as strong an affiliation with other survivors. Finally, those clients who have been in a treatment group for many years may have established their identity and social structure around treating their dysfunction; such individuals need to become affiliated with the group in a different way if treatment is to be successful.

Timing

The emotional responses of clients and the intensity of their between-sessions disturbance are highly variable. There is no way to predict accurately these reactions before processing begins. It is important, therefore, to assess the client's (and the clinician's) current life situation in order to reduce potential problems. For example, if the client is scheduled to make a very important presentation at work, EMDR should not be used because she may be too distracted or disturbed to function at peak effectiveness.

Further, since there is no way of knowing how much residual dysfunctional material may remain at the end of a session or how much associated processing will continue spontaneously, care must be taken to prevent high levels of distress if the client lacks psychological support. If, for example, the client is about to take an out-of-town trip or if the clinician is scheduled for a 2-week vacation, the reprocessing of a major trauma should not be started.

Clinicians should explain to clients that EMDR may entail emotionally intense work and that no important appointments or long work hours ought to be scheduled immediately following a treatment session. The client's work schedule must be amenable to these postsession requirements. If this is not possible, trauma work is contraindicated.

Clinicians should provide adequate time during each session to process the presenting traumatic memory and conduct the required closure. It is recommended that the initial history taking be done in separate 50-minute (or longer) sessions and that subsequent EMDR work on traumas be carried out in 90-minute sessions. Although long by conventional standards, even a 90-minute session may provide only adequate time for implementing Phases Three through Seven and fully processing a particular trauma. At least a 90-minute session can allow the most distressing aspects of the memory to be adequately addressed. If a single trauma is rapidly treated, more than one memory may be addressed in that session.

As mentioned earlier, if the trauma is insufficiently processed, the client is likely to be left with a relatively high level of disturbance that may continue, or even increase, between sessions. Regardless of the length of the session, under no circumstances should a client leave the office during (or immediately after) an unresolved abreaction. Although some clinicians and clients have been forced to adhere to the more usual 50-minute client hour, this is not recommended. Under these circumstances, EMDR should be done with the understanding that it will increase the likelihood of the client's remaining in a relatively high level of distress at the end of the session and during the processing that continues between sessions. Maintaining the traditional 50-minute hour also generally more than doubles the number of sessions needed for full remediation of clients' complaints. For this reason, a number of insurance companies are offering reimbursement for double sessions. On the other hand, using the longer treatment session may force some clients to postpone starting EMDR treatment until they are in a better financial position.

Since some disorientation may occur immediately after treatment, the clinician should assess the client's ability to leave the office and drive safely. Sufficient time must be left at the conclusion of the session to debrief clients and allow them, if necessary, to regain any loss of equilibrium. Even under the best of conditions, there is the possibility that a trauma will be insufficiently processed after a 90-minute session. Some traumas will take a number of sessions to defuse. Always use caution if a client remains in distress, and assess what special needs he might have in returning to work or going home. The appointment time should be geared to the specific needs of the client. For instance, clients with a great deal of responsibility at work should be seen at the end of the day, or at the end of the week, rather than at the beginning, because they may feel unfit to return to a high-pressure situation.

Medication Needs

At times, a client may already be stabilized on prescribed medication or may be assessed as needing such medication to maintain emotional stability between sessions. So far, no medications appear to completely block EMDR processing, although the benzodiazepines have been reported to reduce treatment efficacy. A client who is on any medication for emotional distress should be carefully monitored so that the drug can be reduced or discontinued at the appropriate time. Presumably, as the dysfunctional psychological material is processed, the attendant anxiety or depression is alleviated, thus reducing the need for medication to treat the problem.

Clinicians should process the presenting traumas again after the client is no longer taking the medication. Clinicians have reported that if a client is asked to reaccess the treated memory after medication has been discontinued, it can return with approximately 50% of its original associated disturbance. For instance, an initial combat trauma that was given a rating of 10 on the SUD Scale may decline to a posttreatment level of 0 while the client is on medication, but once medication has ceased, the memory may elicit a rating of 5. This regression reveals the presence of some residual dysfunction in state-dependent form, a problem that contrasts with the stable treatment effects typically found with nonmedicated patients. Therefore, the need for medication should be assessed carefully, with the understanding that its presence will likely increase the time required for successful treatment.

Dissociative Disorders

Using EMDR with dissociative disorders, especially dissociative identity disorder, or DID (known prior to the DSM-IV as multiple personality disorder, or MPD), is strongly discouraged without supervised training in dissociative disorders and the appropriate EMDR protocols. In addition, the more advanced procedures of EMDR (described in Chapter 11) will be required because of the tendency of clients in this clinical population to remain stuck in the activated memory (see the EMDR Dissociative Disorders Task Force guidelines in Appendix B). While dissociative disorders constitute a separate section in the DSM-IV, EMDR specialists regard DID as a complex form of PTSD (Spiegel, 1984, 1993) in which the victimization was so great that, for survival, the global memory was compartmentalized to hold different aspects of the pain and disturbance; thus, the alter personalities are conceptualized as neuro network configurations that serve as memory compartments (Braun, 1988). When EMDR (or other treatments, such as hypnotic abreaction) has successfully resolved the traumatic material, the need for the compartmentalization lessens, amnestic barriers between the alters dissolve, and "co-consciousness" emerges.

Clinicians report that a comparatively rapid spontaneous integration of alters is observed when EMDR is properly utilized with DID. However, clients are at great risk if the pathology is misdiagnosed or if treatment is attempted by a clinician who lacks appropriate training in dissociative disorders. If a client with DID is treated without the appropriate safeguards, the processing of traumatic memories may result in the client's getting stuck at a high level of disturbance. Furthermore, although the material may appear to come to a successful conclusion during a session, its activation may cause a high level of disturbance by "affect bridging" (in the rest of the memory system), an effect that can result in the need for hospitalization or emergency care between sessions. In addition, there have been reports of a significant number of incidents of DID alters spontaneously emerging with the initiation of EMDR treatment, a phenomenon that may be due to the active stimulation of the associated neuro networks.

Because many clinicians are not educated in the treatment of dissociative disorders and greatly underestimate their prevalence, the appropriate safeguards must be stressed. To the surprise of many, a recent study by Ross (1991) indicated that a full 10% of the assessed clinical population of a representative city suffered from a dissociative disorder. A common characteristic of clients with DID is a history of many previous diagnoses, because they are not easily identified (Kluft, 1985; Putnam, 1989). Therefore, the clinician intending to initiate EMDR should first administer the Dissociative Experiences Scale (Bernstein & Putnam, 1986; Carlson & Putnam, 1993) and do a thorough clinical assessment with every client. A brief summary will be given here of several of the primary indicators of DID. Note that while most clinicians associate DID with memory lapses, well-organized multiples can successfully fill in a narrative history and may be unaware that dissociative episodes have occurred (Putnam, 1989).

Within a standard mental status exam the following clinical signs should suggest to the interviewer that the client may have a dissociative disorder: (1) intractable, unexplained somatic symptoms, (2) sleep problems, (3) flashbacks, (4) derealization and depersonalization, (5) Schneiderian symptoms (e.g., voices, unexplainable feelings), (6) memory lapses, (7) multiple psychiatric hospitalizations, and (8) multiple diagnoses with little treatment progress (Kluft, 1987a, 1987b; Putnam, 1989; Ross, 1991). Although dissociative disorders have been underdiagnosed, care must also be taken not to overdiagnose. The EMDR Dissociative Disorders Task Force's recommended guidelines in Appendix B offers further diagnostic assistance. When in doubt, the clinician is strongly advised to refer the client to an expert in dissociative disorders for a thorough evaluation.

TREATMENT PLANNING

As in any form of psychotherapy, the purpose of history-taking sessions is to identify the complete clinical picture before attempting to treat the client. While the initial stage of history taking in EMDR determines the suitability of the client for trauma processing, the second stage identifies the potential targets with as much specificity as possible. A useful metaphor is to imagine the presenting pathology to be a board screwed down on top of the client. The clinician's job is to remove the board in order to give the client room to grow. Rather than hammering away at the board, it is more appropriate to attempt to identify the screws that need to be targeted. Thus, in a manner of speaking, EMDR serves as a power tool to remove these screws more rapidly.

Even if two clients enter therapy with the identical complaint, their treatment needs may vary greatly. Clinicians must determine which problems should be remediated by education, problem solving, or stress management techniques and which are based on dysfunctional information that needs processing. While EMDR may be used to increase the assimilation of new skills, any existing dysfunctional patterns should be generally addressed first.

For instance, if a client requests help because of an abusive marriage, the history-taking process will need to ascertain the primary focus of the EMDR intervention. If the client's husband recently became abusive following a car accident, the appropriate treatment plan clearly will differ from the one needed if the client has had a long history of abusive relationships that included a domineering father. While in the first example the client may require the reprocessing of the abusive events that have just occurred in the marriage, the existence of a normal relationship before the husband was injured in a way that caused a personality change allows the clinician to concentrate on present factors, stimuli, and problem solving.

In the second example, the client's history of abusive relationships indicates characterological elements that need to be specifically addressed. This observation is not new in the area of psychotherapy in general. However, in this case the EMDR treatment plan is based, among other things, on a conclusion from the clinical observation of thousands of reprocessing sessions, namely, that earlier abuse experiences are often directly responsible for dysfunctional relationships in the present. The association between present dysfunction and earlier incidents (explored in Chapter 2 in the context of the Accelerated Information Processing model) is consistently demonstrated by client reports during EMDR sessions that attempt to target the present situations. In order to treat clients with current dysfunctional relationships who have a history of early or serial abuse, their pervasive characteristics (including predispositions and behaviors associated with negative beliefs) must be identified. Along with the abuses that have occurred in the current relationship, the earlier touchstone events (i.e., early, pivotal self-defining incidents) will generally have to be targeted and reprocessed before substantial and pervasive present behavioral changes can be expected.

While some single-event PTSD victims may be treated with EMDR by merely targeting the traumatic memory, most clients will need a more comprehensive treatment. This treatment should entail sequential targeting of the early, critical touchstone experiences, the present situations that stimulate the dysfunction, and alternative behaviors that can be used in the future to meet the goals of therapy. The clinician should attempt to delineate the presenting complaint and its antecedents with as much specificity as possible. While the following list is not exhaustive, it provides the clinician with some basic guidelines. Clinicians should take care to ascertain the following:

1. *Symptoms.* What are the prevalent dysfunctional behaviors, emotions, and negative cognitions? What are the specific symptoms, such as flashbacks, intrusive thoughts, and panic attacks? What are the current triggers and their frequency, timing, locations, and other characteristics?

Let us use as an example the case of the client who was currently involved in a marriage that was the most recent in a series of abusive relationships. The clinician determined that the primary pathology was defined by the client's feelings of shame and powerlessness, along with the cognition "I am worthless," all of which were contributing to her continuing attraction to abusive partners and to her inability to assert herself. History taking revealed that feelings of panic and memories of childhood beatings occurred when the client's husband acted coldly, when her boss became angry, when she had to assert herself with a storekeeper, and so forth.

2. *Duration.* How long has the pathology been apparent? How has it changed over time? What alterations have occurred in the factors contributing to the pathology?

In our sample case, the client's pathology had existed since childhood, but the panic attacks had increased in number and intensity in recent years. Since having a baby, the client felt more vulnerable and out of control.

3. *Initial cause.* What was the original occurrence or most disturbing primary event, modeling, lesson, and so forth, that represents the genesis of the dysfunction? What were the circumstances—including interactional, social, or family systems factors—at the time of the first event?

In our sample case, the client was the youngest of three children. She was beaten by her father for minor infractions and was bullied by her siblings. The first panic attack she was able to recall occurred when she ran to her mother for assistance and was pushed aside. Her mother believed her siblings' story and yelled at her, "Wait until your father gets home."

4. *Additional past occurrences.* What other incidents have been instrumental in influencing or reinforcing the pathology? What other significant variables exist? Who are the major participants? What categories of participants, maladaptive responses, negative cognitions, and so on, are apparent? How could the events be clustered or grouped to maximize the generalization of treatment effects? Clients can be asked to identify their ten most disturbing memories. These will generally help to define the types of negative cognitions and experiences that will have to be addressed.

The client in our sample case was negatively influenced by multiple abuses and beatings throughout her childhood; by her dyslexia, which resulted in humiliations at school; by a date rape, which occurred during her adolescence; and by her experiences with a series of abusive boyfriends. It was possible to cluster the different kinds of abuse and humiliation. Parents, siblings, three teachers, and the abusive boyfriends were targeted as the major perpetrators, and the following negative cognitions were identified: "I am worthless," "I am dirty," "I am not in control," and "I cannot succeed." Such cognitions surfaced at work, in social relationships, and when the client was involved with authority figures.

5. *Other complaints.* What other difficulties are encountered? What other dysfunctions may be masked by the primary presentation?

In the sample case, work-related difficulties and inadequate parenting by the client of a daughter had to be addressed.

6. *Present constraints.* How is the client currently affected? What dysfunctional emotions or behaviors are elicited? What actions is the client unable to take? What systems issues (such as dysfunctional family or social structure) need to be addressed?

The client in our example was unhappy in her home and work environment and had pervasive feelings of failure and low self-worth. She could not assert herself, leave her present situation, or offer appropriate support to her daughter. Furthermore, it was clear that neither her parents nor her husband would welcome the behaviors that would result from an increase in her self-esteem.

7. *Desired state.* How would the client prefer to be acting, appearing, feeling, and believing? What, specifically, is preventing this? What are the potential consequences of successful treatment?

Although the client in our example wanted to be more assertive and to have an increased sense of self-worth, she was constantly bombarded by memories of earlier abuse and by the negative emotions triggered by her husband and her boss. While some of her feelings were appropriate to present situations, their intensity was compounded by childhood events; thus, her feelings often overwhelmed her to the point of inaction. The potential consequences of successful treatment included the client's concluding that she might need to divorce her husband and find a higher-paying job to support herself and her child. Understandably, the prospect of standing up for herself triggered the negative cognition "I cannot succeed." Of course, any existing secondary gain issues would have to be addressed first.

Overall, the clinician is attempting in planning treatment to discover parallels between the client's past and present in order to identify patterns of responses. Having delineated the present stimuli, dysfunctional cognitions, emotions, and behaviors, the clinician must isolate specific targets, which can range from a client's earliest memories to the latest disturbing experience. Treatment plans entail targeting (1) the early memories that set the groundwork for the dysfunction, (2) present triggers that stimulate the material, and (3) desired future responses (the standard protocol is discussed in Chapters 3 and 8).

HISTORY-TAKING TRANSCRIPT

The following transcript includes sections of a history-taking session that involved treatment planning. The client is a sexual abuse victim who was in therapy to alleviate the sequelae of the molestation. The annotations indicate the therapist's purpose in asking particular questions and the answers the therapist intends to pursue in future sessions.

THERAPIST: What brings you here?

CLIENT: I've had nightmares and sleep disturbance for really as long as I can remember, I don't really remember not having it, and I attribute that to sexual abuse by my uncle when I was around 5 years old. I think it's a combination of that and my dad being what I call emotionally incestuous. He never touched me or anything like that but made really inappropriate sexual comments, stuff like that. And my mother, during my childhood, always ran a lot of rage. You ever watch these training films for child abuse? And you know when the parent who's about to hit the kid starts escalating? It was that level of escalation, short of hitting, on a daily basis. So it's like the triple whammy. It's all that altogether. I did a lot of therapy, I've done a lot of meditation, and I've done really tons of stuff. You know, 5 years ago I woke up terrified six nights a week, and I would say now it's more like a sleep disturbance. And I have really bad nightmares when I get stressed.

[The therapist identifies the primary complaint as a sleep disturbance. Primary targets will include the client's father, mother, and uncle.]

THERAPIST: How often?

[Therapist attempts to establish the frequency as a baseline.]

CLIENT: I was trying to think, because I figured you would ask me that. It depends on my stress level. Maybe a few times a month.

THERAPIST: How many? Four, three?

CLIENT: Around that.

THERAPIST: Okay. To what do you attribute the partial resolution so that 5 years ago it was six nights a week and now it's only three times a month?

CLIENT: I think it's a combination of everything I've done. I do a lot of meditation, draw, writing, therapy, and I think there was a sense 5 years ago of the trauma being unconscious and therefore being more powerful. And I think at this point I am, well, maybe I am more powerful. I am more conscious of how the trauma affects me and how it affects my relationships with other people, so I think that's what's brought down the charge.

THERAPIST: What brought about more consciousness?

CLIENT: It was repressed for 15 years, from 5 to 20. I was on vacation, and _____. In the wake of that I remembered; the memory came back. And even for a couple of years into my own therapy, I wasn't real sure it had happened, because when you're five it's like a dream, you know. And after a couple of years I told my parents and found out that he's sexually abused most of the women in my family.

[In this interchange (and in a deleted subsequent portion) the therapist explores parameters and limitations of memory recall and attempts to determine whether conditions warrant a formal report.]

THERAPIST: Tell me a bit about what you remember as far as the molestation.

[Therapist identifies one of the primary targets.]

CLIENT: The memories are very dreamlike. What I remember is a birthday party and him like climbing on top of me on all fours with my pants down. I was in a car accident about 4 months ago, and I've been getting a lot of body work done, particularly around this area of my buttocks and hips. During a couple of sessions I had more memories of being held down and inserting something in my buttocks. I don't think it was a penis. It was like a finger or an object, or something like that.

THERAPIST: Okay. Any other memories?

CLIENT: No.

THERAPIST: So the one memory then, at the birthday party with him climbing on you, holding you down, and inserting something.

CLIENT: It was two separate memories. The birthday party was one, and then being held down and putting something in me was like another one. It's like two separate fragments.

THERAPIST: Okay. Do you have any idea where that took place?

[Therapist checks for clarity.]

CLIENT: My house, the first one. I remember that really clearly. My house where I grew up.

THERAPIST: So the birthday party occurred in your house? And the other memory?

CLIENT: I don't know.

THERAPIST: Okay. How old was he?

CLIENT: Probably in his thirties.

THERAPIST: And you were five? Okay. So we are looking at someone in his sixties, around there?

[Therapist defines parameters regarding present safety for future work.]

CLIENT: Yes.

THERAPIST: Okay. When you say that you believe the nightmares stem from that, could you be a little bit more specific?

CLIENT: Well, it s always men attacking me sexually.

THERAPIST: Okay. So are they the same dream, the same men?

[Therapist attempts to define targets of dream imagery.]

CLIENT: No, different, but with the same theme.

THERAPIST: Do you have vivid recollections of them?

[Therapist seeks to identify targets for processing.]

CLIENT: The most recent one that I had was actually not my uncle but my father. And the dream—this was a really bad one—he was masturbating and using me as a fantasy to jack off. I was screaming in the dream for him not to do that.

THERAPIST: Okay.

CLIENT: It's usually being threatened, waking up and someone's in the room who's going to hurt me, someone breaking into the apartment.

THERAPIST: Okay.

CLIENT: One I had as a kid that was particularly terrifying is a bunch of men coming in the door with guns threatening me. One was my dad. My dad worked where the garage was and that he had an evil double who was masquerading as him. And that was terrifying to me as a kid.

THERAPIST: Okay. Besides the nightmares that go on, how else do you feel you might be affected now?

[Therapist elicits other complaints.]

CLIENT: Well, I have this real hypervigilance. You know, it's really hard to calm down. I have a lot of trouble in my relationships with men.

THERAPIST: In what way?

CLIENT: All ways. I've recently realized that I tend to choose men who are kind of sociopathic, like my dad. Very charismatic, very charming, very attractive, who really don't bond. They have an affair with somebody else, they lie to me about it. Usually men who are very angry and hostile and emotionally abusive, I would say.

THERAPIST: Are you in a relationship with one right now?

CLIENT: No! (*laughs*)

THERAPIST: When was the last one?

[Therapist searches for a relationship that can be used as a target.]

CLIENT: I had a breakup around 6 months ago. It was an 8-month relationship and it was very serious and it was all that I just described. He said he had fallen in love with someone else, and he was very cruel. That was really devastating for me, and I am really just over it now.

THERAPIST: Okay. What about the relationship with your father now?

CLIENT: Boy, it's difficult, because with my uncle I can more or less cut him off. My dad was the person in my family who nurtured me, probably more than anybody else. It's always been really hard for me to individuate from my dad, and—how can I say it?—there is still a lot of warmth and nurturing. A few years ago I just really set a limit on his sexual comments and told him I couldn't spend time with him if he did that, and he stopped.

[Present relationship with father will be targeted.]

THERAPIST: You said that the men reminded you of your father in terms of being sociopathic. How did that manifest for you? What about your dad specifically?

CLIENT: Well, after 25 years he left my mother, leaving a note and running off to Europe with his girlfriend and never really seemed to find anything wrong with that. Interestingly enough, my mom got into therapy a couple of years before that and started to change. Started to really come into her own and drop the rage. My relationship with my mother is healthier than it's ever been. We process stuff and we work through stuff. She's still my mother, she still drives me crazy but it's a working relationship that I have with her.

THERAPIST: Okay. What memory do you have of your father that would represent your feeling of disturbance about him?

CLIENT: One of the first things that pops into my head was walking out the door to go to a party and my dad looked at me and he said, "You have too much makeup on," and I had no makeup on. There was a sense of him saying, "Don't grow up, don't be a woman, don't be sexual, don't be with somebody else."

[This memory will be targeted.]

THERAPIST: Okay.

CLIENT: I really hadn't thought of that in about 15 years.

THERAPIST: Okay. What about in relation to mom?

CLIENT: The memory is of me, literally on my knees, with her screaming at me and me saying, "What do you want me to do?" and she couldn't answer.

[This memory will be targeted.]

THERAPIST: Okay. What other relationships or memories do you have that come up that reinforce the feeling of your not being good enough or your being powerless?

[Issues of self-worth and control will be targeted and used for negative and positive cognitions.]

CLIENT: Does it have to be family? Can it be anybody in my life?

THERAPIST: Kind of the top ten on the hit parade.

[In this case the therapeutic issues appear clear; in other cases the therapist might ask for the ten most disturbing memories without suggesting a specific cognitive theme.]

CLIENT: One is a man who I slept with a few years ago. We were about to have sex, and he told me in bed that I just didn't turn him on. That devastated me. I don't know that it would devastate me as much now, but at the time it really did.

[This memory will be targeted.]

THERAPIST: You were how old?

CLIENT: Twenty-three maybe. It's during the last year and a half that I'm really getting to the core of some of this stuff.

THERAPIST: What else has reinforced it?

CLIENT: The breakup with this man 6 months ago, and it's not like any particular instance but of him really treating me like I was yesterday's garbage.

THERAPIST: Is there any memory there that would represent it?

CLIENT: Of me saying, "You've deceived me," and he said, "Yeah, you'd like to think that." And there was just so much hostility in his voice.

[This may be targeted depending on the level of disturbance at a later stage of treatment.]

THERAPIST: Okay. Are there more ways that's been reinforced?

CLIENT: Yes. There's another belief I have, too. Making an appointment to come here brought up all kinds of stuff, like what would it be like to lose my nightmares? You know, I identify with my nightmares. I identify with my trauma and my mood, and one belief I have is that I am damaged for life. And that on some level, my choice of profession, you know, and my relationships with men—all that revolves around my wound and trauma.

THERAPIST: And what would happen if you weren't damaged for life?

[Therapist investigates secondary gains and goals. "I'm damaged for life" will also be targeted as a negative cognition.]

CLIENT: You know, I have glimpses of that. I guess a glimpse that I have is being more—I know it's very general—just being more joyful. Feeling like I deserve love and the good things that I have in my life already. Being able to have more good things. Like a stable, healthy relationship.

[These statements will be used therapeutically and transformed into positive cognitions.]

THERAPIST: Are there any specific memories that you have where you feel you were taught that you didn't deserve love and you didn't deserve good things?

[These will be targeted negative cognitions.]

CLIENT: Yeah. The big thing that I got from my mom is I had to be beautiful. So I remember . . . if I was looking at this today . . . see this little thing on my pants here? That would be an hour's rage. That if I didn't look perfect, if I wasn't beautiful, if I was fat, she just raged at me as a kid for gaining five pounds. And I was a thin kid. I don't understand why I don't have an eating disorder. All the other women in my family do.

[Mother's reaction will be targeted.]

THERAPIST: What's the best realization that you feel you've gotten out of all the years of therapy that you had?

CLIENT: It's just realizing that there is a reason I don't have good relationships with men. It never made sense to me. I'm a nice person. Why am I having bad relationships? I have wonderful friendships. How I'm really repeating these patterns that have to do with my uncle, have to do with my mom, have to do with my father, and really watching how I do that. Pulling myself out when it looks like that's going to start happening. I've been dating a lot, and I kind of stumbled a couple of times. I dated one guy who was like that pattern, and it cycled very quickly. It was just a few weeks or something.

THERAPIST: You've mentioned feelings or thoughts regarding not being good enough or being powerless or being damaged for life. The feeling about having to be perfect—is that still there for you?

[Therapist summarizes client's negative cognitions and seeks more information.]

CLIENT: It's better. It's still there.

THERAPIST: What memory do you have that's connected with that specifically? Is that raging at the five pounds?

CLIENT: Yeah.

THERAPIST: Okay. Any other beliefs that you could say have run you, like the need to be perfect but not being good enough, needing to be beautiful? Anything else?

CLIENT: That really the only thing that is important about me is how I look.

THERAPIST: And what memory goes along with that?

[Therapist elicits a memory in order to target the negative cognition.]

CLIENT: Everything. Well, it's recent memories, actually. My mom came out for a visit, and it was her constant attention to what I was eating. She took me shopping, and she concentrated her comments on what a nice figure I had, more than anything else. Are you looking for like one specific thing, like how?

THERAPIST: Yes, let's say that there were a lot of messages that you had in childhood and beyond that were saying who you were or what you were being judged by was your appearance. If you cluster them, if you were going to say, "Okay, there were a lot," would you say you got that message more from your mother or more from your father?

CLIENT: Both.

THERAPIST: From both. Okay.

CLIENT: More from my mom, like, "You have to be beautiful." But you see with my dad it was more subtle. With my dad I had to kind of be the wife to get nurturing from him. I had to be kind of sexualized to get nurturing from my dad, and I had to be beautiful to get any strokes from my mom.

THERAPIST: Okay. So what memories do you have in regards to the need to be sexualized to get nurturing?

CLIENT: I remember the both of them just standing there and saying, "Oh, you are just so beautiful." I was 10 years old or something like that. I've looked at pictures of when I was 10 years old, and I was not beautiful. I was really gawky and . . . but, you know, that's what it was for them. And as an adolescent my dad going on and on, on the phone, about how sexy I was. And how people, men in particular, were probably nice to me because I was pretty. I probably got out of that traffic ticket because I was pretty.

[The memories of the parents' reactions will be used as targets.]

THERAPIST: In regards to the dreams, what was the last dream?

CLIENT: The last dream was the masturbation dream with my dad.

THERAPIST: And before that?

CLIENT: It was another one with my dad. Actually, the last couple have been a little more empowered, terrifying. I was dating somebody, and he was unavailable. I was supposed to spend the night with him and he was unavailable and I wound up in the same room with my dad to sleep. There was a double bed, and there were flowers there or something. The other part of the dream I remember is telling him I think I wanted to sleep in my own bed.

THERAPIST: Okay. You said that the dreams come up more when you are stressed. What is it that gets you stressed?

[Therapist attempts to identify present stimuli.]

CLIENT: I was dating somebody, and it started to break up during the last month. We both realized that it wasn't going to go anywhere, and I started getting the dreams then. If I see anything on TV that has to do with someone being traumatized, that brings it out.

THERAPIST: Any kind of trauma in particular?

CLIENT: Sexual trauma.

THERAPIST: Okay. Anything else?

CLIENT: I think that's pretty much it.

THERAPIST: Breaking up a relationship or sexual trauma on TV?

CLIENT: Yeah.

THERAPIST: How would you describe your job right now?

[Therapist examines alternative complaints and systems issues.]

CLIENT: My job. Well, I'm working. I work at _____, and I like it.

THERAPIST: Okay. Anything else?

CLIENT: Not that I can think of.

THERAPIST: If we proceed with the EMDR work, how will you know that we are done? What's going to make you decide that you are finished?

[The goals the client states may constitute behavioral measures for later assessment.]

CLIENT: To be able to sleep deeply and peacefully and to really break up that concept that I'm damaged for life and that I don't deserve love and I can't have it. To be in a healthy relationship.

THERAPIST: Anything else?

CLIENT: More joy in life.

THERAPIST: Anything else?

CLIENT: No.

THERAPIST: When you say, "I don't deserve love and I can't have it," when did that come up for you?

[Therapist searches for a target for the negative cognition.]

CLIENT: I don't think there are times when it flares in particular. Probably when I'm very stressed out and I am working a lot and not getting enough back. Certainly during this last breakup.

THERAPIST: Is there anything else about the men that you choose besides the fact that they give the signs of not being able to bond?

[Therapist explores additional problems.]

CLIENT: I pay too much attention to looks. I mean, if they are good-looking, I'll go out with them. I ignore the rest. Another thing, too, is that I always know right at the beginning that it is a mistake. My intuition is really good; that's really intact. It's following it which has been a challenge for me.

THERAPIST: Give me a run-through.

CLIENT: With this last relationship, I remember telling a friend, "You know, I'm getting together with this guy, but I know he's trouble. I'm not going to get involved with him." And I end up in a 8-month relationship. Not only did I think it, I said it out loud to another person. I mean, what could be clearer?

THERAPIST: So what happened between that statement and the time you went out with him?

CLIENT: He came on like gangbusters. He was really seductive, and the sex was really good. And I just did what I do; I just gave up my power. I just really go along with this to get this nurturing.

THERAPIST: What does "give up your power" mean?

CLIENT: It means I don't act on what my perceptions are. It's like the inside and the outside lose any kind of congruency. It's like I have the perception and then I ignore it, and I go along with the other person's plan, the other person's agenda.

THERAPIST: What about abilities to set boundaries in terms of saying, "No, I'd prefer not to" or "I want to do that instead" or asserting a desire to do something? How are you at that?

[Therapist searches for behaviors to be targeted.]

CLIENT: Sometimes good, sometimes bad.

THERAPIST: Well, let's say in relationships.

CLIENT: In relationships sometimes I'll wind up having sex with a man when I know it doesn't feel right. I'll just push through the sense it doesn't feel right.

[Therapist identifies this as a behavior to be targeted.]

THERAPIST: What do you gain by that?

CLIENT: Nothing. But it's following an old pattern; it's what's most familiar. Just ignoring, you know. I mean growing up surrounded by these abusive people, what could I do but to ignore my perceptions? It was too painful, and I couldn't do anything about it, anyway.

THERAPIST: What else other than having sex even when it doesn't feel good?

CLIENT: I'm really caretaking, and sometimes I'll just give and give and give, rather than saying, "It's your problem; you deal with it."

[Therapist identifies this behavior as a potential target if it is still problematic at a later stage of therapy.]

THERAPIST: How about self-nurturing?

[Therapist is checking for overt signs of self-destructiveness or instability.]

CLIENT: I do a lot of that. I've had this back injury, but I really like to exercise a lot and hike and take lots of hot baths. The only area I really don't take good care of myself is I don't cook. It's part of a lifestyle thing. I'm just busy.

This transcript indicates that the client is suffering from sleep disturbances and low self-esteem. The associated negative cognitions reveal feelings of worthlessness and lack of control. The client's negative self-assessments appear to be the result of a possible early molestation, as well as of dysfunctional parent–child relationships. These difficulties have been partly responsible for a series of self-destructive and abusive relationships in adulthood.

Incidents directly relating to the client's negative self-assessments will be reprocessed during the initial phase of therapy. These include the earlier childhood incidents involving her mother and father, as well as a number of more recent interactions that reinforced her feelings of being worthless and damaged. Part of the processing will include the introduction of new, positive, relationship behaviors. Specific nightmares directly related to feelings of fear and equivocal emotions relating to men in her life will also be targeted.

A similar therapeutic assessment, conducted on the basis of a history taken at a depth equivalent to that revealed by the foregoing transcript, would be needed if the client had presented an eating disorder or substance abuse issue that needed to be directly addressed. However, with the information already available, an EMDR session targeting the molestation scenes she described can proceed after the screening for dissociative disorder, administration of any desired objective psychometrics, and completion of the preparation phase, including instruction in performing the relaxation exercises.

SUPERVISED PRACTICE

Instructors may wish to supervise students in practice history-taking exercises and review the consequent treatment plans. Appropriate client selection is such a vital part of treatment and client safety that instructors are encouraged to test the students' knowledge of the indicators for caution and exclusion. The client checklists in Appendix A may be helpful for this purpose.

SUMMARY AND CONCLUSIONS

EMDR is a highly interactive therapeutic approach that demands clinician sensitivity and flexibility. It is essential that client selection be conducted properly because of the nature of the unresolved, dissociated material that may spontaneously emerge during treatment and the intensity of the emotional experience that may be generated. Therefore, clinicians should use EMDR only with clients who have sufficient stability and appropriate life conditions to handle possible abreactive responses and the distressing processing that may continue between therapeutic sessions.

Client safety requires that the clinician assess such therapeutic factors as the clinical relationship; life conditions, including legal and relationship needs; issues of stabilization, including hospitalization and medication needs; dual diagnoses; physical constraints; and the client's ability to utilize the relaxation procedures. Adequate screening for dissociative disorders must also be done before attempting EMDR (see Appendix B).

EMDR is never implemented in the absence of an adequate client history, a clinical relationship that includes rapport and client comfort, and a treatment plan. The treatment plan should identify specific targets, including aspects of secondary gain, which should be sequentially addressed. Essentially, the clinician should ascertain the past memories that set the pathology in motion, the present people and situations that stimulate the dysfunction, and the components necessary for an adaptive, desirable template for appropriate future action. Unless the symptoms, contributing factors, and baseline of dysfunction are adequately assessed, clinical effectiveness will be limited. EMDR is not one-session therapy, and the clinician should have a clear picture of the client's problem areas and the sequence in which they should be targeted. Finally, EMDR should only be used by trained, qualified, licensed clinicians or closely supervised interns with prepared clients who have given adequate informed consent.

CHAPTER 5

• • •

Phases Two and Three

PREPARATION AND ASSESSMENT

It does not matter how slowly you go as long as you do not stop.

Confucius

After the clinician has taken a thorough client history and completed treatment planning, she needs to set the stage for the reprocessing. Client preparation involves establishing a safe therapeutic relationship with the client, explaining in detail the process and its effects, and addressing the client's concerns and potential emotional needs. Assessment determines the components of the target memory and the baseline measures of the client's reactions to the process.

This chapter supplements the information about the individual components of EMDR therapy already described in Chapter 3 and explores how to work with these components. For both phases covered in this chapter we begin with a discussion of the clinical perspective and the type of information clinicians have found useful to communicate to clients. Next, sample wording is suggested for some specific instructions the clinician will give the client. We then review possible client reactions and alternative clinical strategies to assist with client comfort.

PHASE TWO: PREPARATION

The preparation phase sets the therapeutic framework and appropriate level of expectation for the client. Preparing the client to handle the disturbance that may arise in EMDR processing is crucial. Before starting the preparation phase clinicians must lay the proper groundwork (as defined in Chapter 4); that is, they must take an appropriate client history, determine that the client is suitable for EMDR, prepare a treatment plan, and formulate an action plan to address any secondary gain issues that might prevent treatment effects.

Having done this, the clinician must complete certain steps before beginning to use the eye movements (or other stimuli) on any disturbing material. As discussed in Chapter 1, avoidance behavior is considered both part of the pathology and the reason it is maintained. The steps discussed in the following sections will let the client access the traumatic material for processing and will set a therapeutic framework that will promote the exposure necessary for desensitization and complete reprocessing.

Adopting a Clinical Stance

Inasmuch as EMDR is a highly interactive, client-centered procedure, it demands flexibility on the part of the clinician. Throughout the procedure the clinician must be finely attuned to the needs and particular characteristics of the client and prepared to adjust and change direction, if necessary.

The clinician's attitude should be one of respect and accommodation regarding the client's need for safety and reassurance. The clinician's job is to facilitate the client's self-healing process. Any nonspecific aids to this end (including ways to facilitate therapeutic bonding and communicate unconditional support and regard) will increase therapeutic effectiveness. As with any treatment modality, EMDR should interface with clinical skills, not substitute for them.

Forming a Bond with the Client

The clinician must establish a relationship with the client that includes a firm therapeutic alliance, a recognition of common goals, and an understanding of the need for honest communication. Unless the client and clinician have established a sufficient level of trust, EMDR should not be used. Clients must feel that they will be protected during processing and that, ultimately, they are in control. This can be done only if an atmosphere of safety and confidence is established during the initial sessions. Attaining this level of rapport may take many months with some clients; for others, it will be a matter of one or two sessions. Regardless of how long bonding takes, EMDR processing should not be attempted without it, or the client may break off treatment during an abreaction, refuse to continue EMDR, and perhaps terminate therapy altogether.

The clinician should make sure that the client understands the importance, during and between sessions, of the "truth telling" agreements. If the client falsely informs the clinician that the emotional disturbance is reduced (in order to "do it right," to please the therapist, or perhaps to end the treatment), there is a good chance that between-sessions disturbance will increase, and the client may be at risk without the proper support. Because of the desire of many clients to please the therapist, it is important to convey to the client that the clinician desires an accurate report, regardless of its nature, even if the client wishes to stop. The clinician should say something like the following:

> **"All you need to do is tell me the truth about what you are experiencing so I can make the proper choices. There is no way for you to do EMDR wrong. Just give me accurate feedback about what is happening. Also, you are the one in control. If you need to stop, just let me know. Just tell me what is happening for you."**

Explaining the Theory

The clinician should provide clients with a general understanding of EMDR theory in language they can understand. For most clients a brief description, such as the following statement, will be sufficient: "When a trauma occurs, it appears to get locked in the nervous system." In addition, clients should be informed that this "locked information" often gets triggered by a variety of reminders and is responsible for their frequent feelings of helplessness, hopelessness, fear, and so forth.

Clients seem to respond very well to this description because their own experience is often one of feeling that something is locked inside them. For instance, client language often conveys feelings of being "stuck" or "imprisoned." Offering clients this explanation also helps remove the sense of shame and guilt they often feel at having been unable to shake their symptoms. Placing the blame on the nervous system, rather than on the client, is often a liberating step in its own right.

The clinician should tell the client that the eye movements appear to allow the information to be unlocked and processed, perhaps in a way similar to what occurs during rapid eye movement (REM) sleep, and that using the eye movements while awake permits the negative information to be discharged from the nervous system in a more focused way. Clinicians might use an explanation such as the following:

> **"Often, when something traumatic happens, it seems to get locked in the nervous system with the original picture, sounds, thoughts, feelings, and so on. Since the experience is locked there, it continues to be triggered whenever a reminder comes up. It can be the basis for a lot of discomfort and sometimes a lot of negative emotions, such as fear and helplessness, that we can't seem to control. These are really the emotions connected with the old experience that are being triggered.**

"The eye movements we use in EMDR seem to unlock the nervous system and allow your brain to process the experience. That may be what is happening in REM, or dream, sleep: The eye movements may be involved in processing the unconscious material. The important thing to remember is that it is your own brain that will be doing the healing and that you are the one in control."

Testing the Eye Movements

It is useful for clinicians to test the client's ability to make the eye movements before targeting any disturbing material. Using finger movements according to the guidelines in Chapter 3, clinicians should ask the client to follow the movements and to give feedback on how comfortable this is to do. Clinicians can experiment to find the most comfortable distance from the client's eyes at which to hold their fingers and can then determine whether the client is able to execute eye movements in various directions. The direction the client finds easiest is often the most successful during the processing phase.

Clinicians should also experiment with different speeds of eye movement in each direction. Most clients seem to prefer a rapid rate. Clinicians should make notes if they observe any difficulties during these exercises or if the client reports any problems, including headaches, with any particular direction (this direction should be avoided during actual processing). If the client is unable to follow the clinician's fingers in a tracking motion, the clinician should experiment with the two-handed approach and with hand taps (described in Chapter 3).

This is a good time to tell the client that if she needs to stop during processing, she can hold up her hand as a signal, or turn her head. This gives the client a greater sense of control and is an important element for client comfort and safety. If a client gives either of these signals, the clinician should stop immediately, find out what the difficulty is, and meet the client's needs before resuming. Ignoring the client's signal will be antitherapeutic and can cause a permanent breach of trust.

This testing phase provides the opportunity to experiment with the eye movements, assess any difficulties, and determine the preferred signaling method. The clinician might, for example, give the following instructions:

"Let's just experiment with the kinds of eye movements we use. If you find them uncomfortable, just hold your hand up like this [demonstrate] or turn your head away to let me know. Remember, I just need accurate feedback about what you are experiencing.

"As I hold my fingers up [demonstrate], just focus on them. Is this a comfortable distance? [adjust for client comfort] Good, now just follow my fingers with your eyes."

Creating a Safe Place

In Chapter 4 the clinician was instructed to use a number of relaxation techniques with prospective EMDR clients during the history-taking phase and to plan to use EMDR only with those clients who responded favorably. These self-control techniques are explained in Chapter 9. However, I will include here one exercise that can be particularly helpful to reassure the client that he can quickly recover his emotional stability during any disturbance. The exercise is especially useful for a client who cannot relax because he feels a need to remain vigilant, a need that may have been conditioned during episodes of sexual abuse or in combat. PTSD subjects in a recent study of EMDR (Wilson et al., in press) reported that this exercise was particularly helpful for them; we now suggest that it be used with everyone. It also serves to set up an initial positive association with the use of the eye movements.

The eight-step "safe place" exercise, to be described shortly, is a variation of one of the guided visualizations included on the stress tape "Letting Go of Stress" (Miller, 1994). If the clinician provides this tape (or a similar one) to the client during the history-taking session, she will be able to practice daily before EMDR processing begins. This can increase the effectiveness of the exercise as a self-control technique.

The objective is for clients to create a safe place in their imagination before processing. This emotional oasis can be used for a temporary rest during processing, as an aid to closing down the disturbance in order to end the session, and as a way to deal with disturbing material that may arise between sessions. The clinician should allow the client complete leeway in identifying a personal refuge and should carefully assess the client's reaction to it. Some clients try to use an image that is popularly associated with a feeling of calm but is just the opposite for them because it is too closely associated with a traumatic event. For example, a client may try to imagine a beautiful beach and ignore the anxiety generated by the memory of being assaulted near the ocean as a child. Obviously, in this case another safe place should be found.

The eight-step exercise is as follows:

Step 1: *Image.* The clinician and client identify an image of a safe place that the client can easily evoke and that creates a personal feeling of calm and safety.

Step 2: *Emotions and sensations.* The clinician asks the client to focus on the image, feel the emotions, and identify the location of the pleasing physical sensations.

Step 3: *Enhancement.* The clinician may use soothing hypnotic tones to enhance the imagery and affect. He should take care to convey a sense of safety and security for the client, who is asked to report when she feels the emotions.

Step 4: *Eye movements.* The positive response is further expanded by including a series of eye movements. The clinician should use the direction and speed of movement that the client has identified as most comfortable and should say, **"Bring up the image of a place that feels safe and calm. Concentrate on where you feel the pleasant sensations in your body and allow yourself to enjoy them. Now concentrate on those sensations and follow my fingers with your eyes."** At the end of the set the clinician asks the client, **"How do you feel now?"** If the client feels better, the clinician should do four to six more sets. If the client's positive emotions have not increased, the clinician should try alternative directions of eye movements until the client reports improvement.

Step 5: *Cue word.* The client is then asked to identify a single word that fits the picture (e.g., "relax," "beach," "mountain," "trees") and to rehearse it mentally as pleasant sensations and a sense of emotional security are noticed and enhanced by the clinician's directions. This procedure is repeated four to six times, along with additional eye movements.

Step 6: *Self-cuing.* The client is then instructed to repeat the procedure on her own, bringing up the image and the word and experiencing the positive feelings (both emotions and physical sensations), without any eye movements. When the client has successfully repeated the exercise independently, the clinician points out how the client can use it to relax during times of stress.

Step 7: *Cuing with disturbance.* To emphasize the preceding point, the clinician asks the client to bring up a minor annoyance and notice the accompanying negative feelings. The clinician then guides the client through the exercise until the negative feelings dissipate.

Step 8: *Self-cuing with disturbance.* The clinician then asks the client to bring up a disturbing thought once again and to follow the exercise, this time without the clinician's assistance, to its relaxing conclusion.

Once this exercise has been completed, the clinician should instruct the client to practice it at home every day by calling up the positive feelings and the associated word and image while she uses a relaxation tape or performs some other relaxation exercise (such as those reviewed in Chapter 9). Clients can then use the technique for simple relaxation and stress reduction. Finally, before any EMDR session the clinician should say to the client, **"Remember, this safe place is always available to you. Just let me know if you need to return to it at any time."** The clinician should occasionally use the eye movements to reinforce the safe place. This also maintains a positive association with the eye movements themselves.

Describing the Model

The clinician should remind the client that just as positive feelings are available to him, so too are negative feelings of old memories stored in his nervous system. When the client brings up the safe place, he experiences the pleasant feelings; when he brings up the old memories, he will experience the disturbing feelings.

It may be useful to explain to clients that the brain has stored the disturbing event in a memory network in a way that isolates it and prevents it from connecting with more useful, adaptive information and that when EMDR processing begins, the appropriate connections are made. In addition, in order to explain how other disturbing material from the past can emerge unexpectedly and how resolution can take place, the clinician can sketch a diagram that shows how memory networks can link up. For example, the clinician can draw a diagram similar to Figure 11 and can then give an explanation such as the following:

> **"Disturbing events can be stored in the brain in an isolated memory network. This prevents learning from taking place. The old material just keeps getting triggered over and over again. In another part of your brain, in a separate network, is most of the information you need to resolve it. It's just prevented from linking up to the old stuff. Once we start processing with EMDR, the two**

FIGURE 11. Separate target and adaptive networks.

networks can link up. New information can come to mind and resolve the old problems."

The clinician then indicates, in a diagram similar to Figure 12, how the two networks are linked.

Clients should also be told that when this disturbing material is unlocked and allowed to process, the reservoir of negative emotions is drained along with it. This explanation often gives the client the courage to persist through the intense emotions that arise during treatment. The client should be told that, regardless of how disturbing the emotions might be as they come up, "nothing negative is being put in." Instead, it is being let out. The client may be able to see that, rather than "dying a thousand deaths" every day, she can help to be liberated by one processing experience. The client needs to know that the unpleasant sensations that may arise during treatment are simply a sign of the old material leaving the nervous system.

It may be helpful to use the analogy of driving through a dimly lit tunnel. If the driver wishes to speed through the tunnel, he'll have to keep his foot on the accelerator. If he takes his foot off the accelerator, the car will slow down and merely coast. In EMDR the eye movements (or other stimuli) appear to be like the accelerator. If the set is allowed to continue, the processing can be accelerated and the unpleasant sensations or emotions can be passed through rapidly. If the eye movements are stopped prematurely, however, the unpleasant sensations will be experienced longer. Of course, clients should be reassured that if they wish to stop for a moment, all they need to do is give the signal.

The clinician's description of the EMDR model should include the reassurance that, although unpleasant sensations and emotions may arise during EMDR treatment, they are caused merely by the processing of the old memories and present no current danger. It is useful in allaying the client's apprehension to say something like "Just because you feel fear does not mean there is a real tiger in the room." The clinician must state this in a manner that is nurturing and reassuring

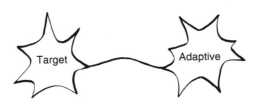

FIGURE 12. Connected target and adaptive networks.

and in no way dismissive. The level of fear and vulnerability that may surface for the client can be extremely high, and this experience should not be minimized or trivialized. However, clinicians need to bolster their clients' ability to withstand, as well as observe, their emotions without attempting to block or escape them. To warn the client that avoidance is counterproductive, the clinician might say the following:

> **"Although unpleasant pictures, sensations, or emotions may come up as we do the eye movements, you can stop the process whenever you want simply by raising your hand like this [demonstrate]. It is best to allow the eye movements to continue as long as possible, but if things feel too rough, we can stop and you can rest. The idea is that if you want to drive through a dark tunnel quickly, you keep your foot on the accelerator. If you take your foot off, your car slows down and coasts. So, to get through unpleasant emotions, keeping the eyes moving will get us through more quickly.**
>
> **"As we do the sets of eye movements, try to remember that we are only processing old stuff. It may feel real, but it's just the old memories locked in the nervous system. Just because you feel fear, does not mean there is a real tiger in the room. The idea is to let the brain become unlocked, and let the information process through."**

Setting Expectations

It is useful to assure the client that nothing will be imposed upon him during treatment, that the memories will be processed as a function of his own self-healing capacity, and that he will remain in control and can rest at any time simply by using the stop signal. It cannot be too heavily stressed that if the client raises his hand for "stop," the clinician should *stop immediately*. Because most trauma victims feel they are personally inadequate and have no control in their lives, the client's fears and negative self-assessments are likely to be reinforced if the clinician persists after being told to stop. Regardless of the clinician's intention, such a breach of trust can undermine treatment benefits. Regardless of the level of support being provided, the clinician cannot possibly know the amount of pain being experienced by the client at any given moment in the treatment. Therefore, it is crucial that the client have the power to take a break on command.

The initial description of what can be expected in the treatment phase provides reassurance for the client. The emphasis should be on safety and joint participation. It is often useful to state to the client that while emotions and recalled experiences may arise, they should be seen as merely transient, that it is as if the client is on a train and the experiences are merely the scenery passing by. This explanation helps promote a sense of safety in that it connotes movement away from the pain and suggests that, regardless of how real the experience may seem, there is no real danger since the client is protected (i.e., he is inside the train). Also implicit in this metaphor is the notion that even as the scenery is noticed through the train's window, it is already passing by.

The intent is to impress upon clients the idea that they should observe the experience rather than give significance to it. The objective is to allow the experience to process, permitting sensations and emotions to flow through consciousness without being afraid of the fear, which can cause a retraumatization. The client should be told, in essence, "Just let whatever happens, happen."

The clinician should tell the client that while he is asked to start by concentrating on an image, he will probably find it impossible to maintain this image. The idea is simply to begin by focusing on the designated target and then to allow the processing to occur during the eye movements. The clinician should remember that the dominant belief system of the client may emerge: For example, the client who has always viewed himself as a failure can make statements such as the following: "I must be doing something wrong; my eyes aren't moving" or "I can't keep the picture" or "I'm thinking of something else." The client should be reassured that he is doing the exercise correctly.

The clinician should tell the client that the set of eye movements will continue for a while and that she will then be asked for feedback; that is, she should then describe whatever new or relevant information has emerged. However, as with all EMDR instructions, the clinician should avoid placing demands on the client about her performance, expected treatment results, or the amount of time the processing should take. As much as possible, the client should be placed in a state of mind where she is willing to allow the processing to take its own course, rather than attempting to make anything specific happen. If the client tries to force anything to occur, the processing is likely to stop. To return to our metaphor, it is as if we are letting the train lay down its own track as it goes along. Both clinician and client must try to stay out of the way as much as possible. The clinician might, for example, say the following to the client:

> **"As we process the information and digest the old events, pictures, sensations, or emotions may arise, but your job is just to notice them, just to let them happen. Imagine that you are on a train and the scenery is passing by. Just notice the scenery without**

trying to grab hold of it or make it significant. Remember, if you need to take a rest, just hold up your hand.

"We will start by asking you to focus on a target. Then I will ask you to follow my fingers with your eyes. After we do that for a while, we will stop and talk about anything that comes up. You can't keep a picture steady while the eye movements are going on, so don't try. When we talk, you just need to give me feedback on what is happening. Sometimes things will change and sometimes they won't. I may ask if something else comes up; sometimes it will and sometimes it won't. There are no 'supposed to's' in this process. So just tell me what is happening, without judging whether it should be happening or not. Just let whatever happens, happen. Any questions?"

Addressing Client Fears

Whenever giving instructions, the clinician should be sensitive to nonverbal signals of confusion from the client and should answer questions as they arise. Case examples should be given when necessary to illustrate certain points. For instance, to explain how old memories impinge on daily life, the client may be told of the woman who would feel terror every time her employer got angry, because her father used to look at her in exactly the same way before beating her.

It is important that the client understand the instructions, because the clinician will use the same analogies during processing to reassure or calm the client when disturbing material comes up. That is, it is easier to remind a disturbed client to treat the material as "scenery passing by" than to try to introduce the metaphor for the first time while the client is strongly reexperiencing a memory. Please note that the sample instructions included here are only suggested; adjust the language and illustrations to the needs of the individual client.

All of the client's questions and doubts should be addressed, including fears of going crazy, of not being able to handle the treatment experience, or of "not making it back." The clinician should assure the client that although these fears are normal, these kinds of negative effects have never been observed with EMDR. Sometimes the client will want to talk to someone else who has had EMDR treatment, read an article about it, or otherwise obtain corroboration (see Appendix C for clinician resources) before continuing treatment. *EMDR should not be implemented until the client is ready.*

If the client declares an unwillingness to proceed with processing in general or with any particular memory, that wish must be respected. If the clinician resorts to high-level demand characteristics to impose treatment, for instance, intimating that EMDR is the only way to heal and that the client "should" engage in the treatment, negative results are likely to occur. The client may remain anxious during the entire session, break off treatment during an abreaction, or dissociate in order to escape the ordeal. If EMDR is not agreed on by the client and viewed as an enterprise of joint participation, treatment should not proceed.

Sometimes a client is unwilling to concentrate on a particular memory because of shame or guilt. The clinician should reassure the client that because the processing is happening internally, she need not divulge the details of the memory; merely reporting the fact that she is withholding something is sufficient.

This reassurance has been particularly helpful to rape victims who are humiliated by their experiences, molestation victims who have been threatened and warned not to tell, and combat veterans who are wracked with guilt. With all such clients, processing can proceed satisfactorily, even in the absence of specific details. Often, however, once the material is sufficiently resolved, the client may reveal more about a specific event. These revelations should not be discouraged, since it will be very therapeutic for some clients to receive a response of unconditional support from the clinician. However, for other clients, this is unnecessary for resolution, and they should not be prodded to divulge details.

The ability to process traumatic memories without the client providing a clear picture of the event can also be very helpful to the clinician. Some clinicians have been vicariously traumatized (McCann & Pearlman, 1990) by vivid client imagery. When a clinician has been bombarded by highly detailed accounts of traumatic episodes, self-administered eye movements can be used to minimize the negative effects. Self-administered eye movements are contraindicated for personal therapy but can be very useful for rapid reduction of minor stress. This will be explained in Chapter 9.

PHASE THREE: ASSESSMENT

During the assessment phase the clinician determines the components of the target memory and establishes baseline measures for the client's reactions to the process.

Once the client has identified the memory to be treated, the clinician asks the client, **"What happens when you think of the incident?"** or **"When you think of the incident, what do you get?"** The client's response will provide a baseline on how he is currently encoding the information. By the end of the treatment, the same questions should elicit a very different response.

The client is invited to reveal whatever she desires and to state any relevant parts of the memory. However, this aspect of the treatment session need not be emphasized; as discussed earlier, successful EMDR treatment does not require that the clinician be aware of all the details of the memory. Remember, the client should not be pressured to reveal more details than he can comfortably handle. The clinician may need to explain to the client that although other therapies he may have undergone required him to reveal all the explicit details, this is not necessary for EMDR and that, instead of most of the session being used to discuss what occurred, the time is spent in processing the disturbing information. Therapeutic processing will start at an accelerated rate with the beginning of the eye movements and will be done by the client's internal information-processing system rather than as a result of interaction with or interpretation by the clinician. The client must feel comfortable and safe in the presence of the clinician in order to experience or reveal anything she feels is important. On no account should the therapist make the client feel that her revelations are unwelcome or distasteful.

Selecting the Picture

After the client has described any relevant elements of the traumatic incident, the clinician should ask him to designate a single image as the initial focus for treatment. While the image does not have to be vivid, it allows primary access to the memory network by representing a single event rather than an abstract thought (such as the general idea of molestation or military combat). While the client often cannot maintain the image after the eye movements begin, it provides the initial link to the neurologically stored information.

Specifically, the clinician asks the client, **"What picture represents the entire incident?"** If there are many choices or if the client becomes confused, the clinician assists by asking, **"What picture represents the most traumatic part of the incident?"** When a picture is unavailable, the clinician merely invites the client to **"think of the incident."**

Remember, the image is only one manifestation of the disturbing information regarding the event that has been dysfunctionally stored. Although the image may be initially dissociated, indistinct, or blurry or may become diffused and unavailable after subsequent processing, merely thinking of the incident causes the accessing and stimulation of the targeted information. In addition, some clients do not think or remember events in terms of imagery. This assessment phase delineates the most dominant manifestations of the incident (whether they be images, physical sensations, emotions, etc.) as the access points to the targeted information. When simply asked to think of the incident, the client stimulates her own subjective connections.

Identifying the Negative Cognition

The next step is to identify the negative cognition, that is, the negative self-statement associated with the event. Although the event may have occurred in the distant past, its evocation is likely to cause feelings of dysfunction and distress that feed the client's negative self-beliefs. The client is asked to isolate the present self-limiting or self-denigrating belief about himself or his participation in the event. In other words, when the stored information is stimulated, a variety of emotions emerge that color the client's present perceptions, and these emotions should be verbalized in the negative cognition.

The client may have difficulty stating his negative cognition. He may be embarrassed, anxious, or unclear about what is meant by belief. It may help to explain to the client that these self-limiting assessments are irrational and that there is likely to be a split between what the client *knows* to be true and what he *feels*. Explaining that emotional responses arise independently of logic and mature awareness is often necessary to reduce the client's embarrassment so that he can state his negative self-belief. At times, it helps if the clinician tells the client, "State what you think of yourself in your worst moments, even if you know it isn't true." However, for most clients a simple understanding of the concept of irrational negative beliefs is all that is necessary.

Specifically, the clinician asks the client, **"What words best go with the picture that express your negative belief about yourself or the experience?"** When the client cannot specify a negative self-statement, the clinician should offer a list of suggestions, such as "I'm worthless/powerless/not lovable," "I should have done something," "I will be abandoned," or "I can never succeed." It is important for the clinician to use verbal and nonverbal cues that give the client complete permission to choose or reject these suggestions. The clinician might also write out a list of negative cognitions (reviewed in Chapter 3 and Appendix A) and hand it to the client as a set of alternatives. If these strategies are not successful, the clinician can ask, after inviting the client to hold the memory in mind, **"What thoughts do you have about yourself?"** The clinician can then assist the client to formulate an appropriate negative cognition.

When the thoughts, emotions, or situation appear to be too confusing or complex, it is appropriate to continue without the negative cognition. However, if at all possible, one should be specified. The assessment phase itself, along with a simple negative self-statement that the client perceives to be even slightly irrational, can greatly assist the therapeutic process. In addition, pinpointing the appropriate negative cognition seems to allow that stratum of dysfunctional material to be more fully accessed for subsequent reprocessing.

The clinician should make sure that the negative cognition is self-referential, is stated in the present tense, and is a belief rather than a description of circumstances. For instance, "I am powerless" is a good negative cognition; "I was not in control" is not because it is merely an accurate description of the event as it occurred. The clinician should explain to the client that because EMDR cannot modify anything that is factually true, it will not work to use EMDR on a statement such as "I was powerless," which is a truthful description of a past condition and cannot be changed.

In addition to formulating a statement in the present tense, the clinician must take care to avoid simple statements of emotion. For example, while a statement such as "I am afraid" aptly describes the emotion currently felt, it is not therapeutically useful for EMDR. The therapeutic goal is to identify a self-denigrating or self-limiting statement that is inaccurate by consensually derived standards of reality in the present. The appropriate negative cognition would therefore be "I am powerless" or, at least, "I am in danger" (if the primary problem is fear), which is an irrational cognition, since the traumatic event actually occurred long ago.

If there is a valid present reason for fear—if the rapist is still stalking the victim, for example—EMDR will not shift the information verbalized by the statement, because it is not dysfunctional. And since clinical reports indicate that EMDR will not eliminate any healthy responses (such as arousal necessary as an impetus to correct action), an alternate target will have to be found. In the case of real danger, the client and clinician will have to work through the appropriate real-life possibilities and then attempt to reduce the excessive fear by focusing on a negative cognition such as "I am powerless." This excessive fear needs to be reduced because it may paralyze the client and prevent appropriate action. In one case, after processing excessive fear about a man who had raped her, a client decided to move to a new town because she could not get police protection. Later it became clear how appropriate this solution was: The rapist was arrested only after he murdered his next victim.

The clinician should take care not to accept cognitions that merely verbalize sad or unfortunate childhood experiences. Remember, accurate descriptions, regardless of the nature of the tragedy, will not be changed by EMDR. A statement such as "Father didn't love me," "I didn't stand a chance," or "It was unfair" should be adapted into an appropriate negative cognition by asking questions such as **"How does that make you feel about yourself?"** Typically, this will elicit appropriate negative cognitions in the form of denigrating self-statements such as "There is something wrong with me" or "I am not lovable." For a negative cognition to be most effective, it should be stated in the client's own words and be accompanied by the significant associated affect.

Even if the clinician is capable of formulating a more elegant statement, he should allow the client to use words and expressions that are familiar to her and that elicit feelings that are congruent with the statement.

As with the positive cognition, the negative cognition should represent a general statement about the self rather than about the specifics of the event. For example, the client will be able to process more material about a childhood experience if she uses the general negative cognition "I am a failure" rather than the more specific "I fail in baseball games."

Developing a Positive Cognition

Once the negative cognition is identified, the positive cognition should be developed. The positive cognition is a verbalization of the desired state (a self-belief that is a distillation of the positive affect) and is generally a 180-degree shift from the negative cognition. It is an empowering self-assessment incorporating the same theme or personal issue as the negative cognition. This self-assessment should be put in positive terms that indicate how the client would prefer to think about himself currently, even though the disturbing event did happen.

Specifically, the clinician asks the client, **"What would you like to believe about the event or yourself?"** When possible, the positive cognition should include a self-referencing internal locus of control, thereby reinforcing the client's ability to enhance and incorporate a new feeling of self-worth and to make effective choices, all of which are aspects of the optimal EMDR treatment outcome.

The positive cognition makes possible a generalization of the positive self-assessment throughout the neuro network, which, through principles of association, will presumably influence not only the client's perceptions of past events but his current assessments and expectations for the future. The positive cognition should be the most powerful statement the client can conceive, even though it may be hard for him to believe at the present time. In order to greatly increase the possibilities for high self-esteem, it is important that the word "not" generally be avoided in the positive cognition. For example, statements like "I will not fail" or "I am not incompetent" do not offer the client a sufficiently positive evaluation, nor do they stimulate and directly link to the appropriate positive information stored in the client's brain as strongly as do statements such as "I can succeed" and "I am competent." When possible, the positive cognition should incorporate a new self-assessment with implications for a positive future.

Exceptions to this guideline may be made when the overriding feeling of fear in regard to a traumatic incident is the primary manifestation of the dysfunction. In this case an appropriate positive cognition might simply place the incident firmly in the past, since the constant intrusions and current state of fear are the most troublesome aspects of the event. A useful generic positive cognition in this case might be "It's over; I'm safe now." In addition, as reviewed in Chapter 3, perpetrator guilt may be dealt with by statements such as "I did the best I could," "I learned from it," and "I can now make other choices."

Once again, it is vital that clinicians determine the appropriateness of the client's positive cognition. Whenever possible, the clinician should ensure that the positive cognition is a valid self-assessment or belief regarding the targeted memory. Statements indicating wishful thinking or an attempt to rewrite history, such as "I can trust everyone" or "It never happened" will disrupt treatment effects. Any attempt to utilize an untrue positive cognition will stop the processing. Clinical reports have consistently indicated that EMDR will not allow the client to incorporate into his belief system anything that is inappropriate or invalid. Because of this, clinicians should view with suspicion any positive cognition that uses words like "always" and "never." For example, statements such as "I will always succeed" and "I will never fail" are inappropriate.

The clinician may have optimal positive cognitions in mind only to have them rejected by the client as too unrealistic given her present psychological condition. The clinician should be sensitive enough to accept a statement that seems right to the client and most closely approximates a positive therapeutic direction. One client who was a victim of sexual molestation by her father wanted to use "I was an abused child" as her positive cognition because it felt diametrically opposed to her negative cognition of "I am a whore." While the first statement was obviously descriptive and not currently applicable or overtly empowering, it was clearly the first step toward relieving the client's guilt about having participated in the molestation. Likewise, a client may at first only be able to accept a positive cognition of "I can learn to trust myself" before fully adopting the stance "I can trust my own judgment." Remember that once EMDR treatment is initiated, a more suitable positive cognition may emerge or may be suggested by the clinician, depending on client readiness. It is crucial, however, for the client to feel in control of the situation; imposing negative or positive cognitions on him, regardless of how eloquent they are, is likely to have a detrimental effect.

Rating the Validity of Cognition

Once the client has developed the positive cognition, the VOC level for that cognition is ascertained to provide a baseline and ensure that the positive cognition is actually possible (and not a product of wishful thinking). The clinician asks the client, **"When you think of the incident and repeat the words [clinician states the positive cognition], how true do they feel, from 1 (completely false) to 7 (completely true)?"**

Sometimes it is necessary to explain further: **"Remember, sometimes we know something with our head, but it feels differently in our gut. In this case, what is the gut-level feeling of the truth of [clinician states the positive cognition], from 1 (completely false) to 7 (completely true)?"**

If the client reports that the desired cognition is no more than a 1, the clinician should assess the statement for flaws in logic, applicability, or ecological validity (appropriateness and validity within the client's present environment). While some EMDR clients will successfully assimilate positive cognitions that are initially assessed at a 1 or 2, such a low rating is often an indication of unsuitability.

As discussed earlier, the assessment phase has many positive therapeutic effects built into it. However, if the client begins to abreact during this phase, the clinician should not force the assessment to continue but should instead initiate reprocessing. This is why the clinician should provide the relevant instructions, theory, and metaphors to the client before the assessment phase begins. We expect that the client will get progressively more stimulated as the assessment phase progresses. The EMDR components (and the order in which they are used) are specifically designed to access the dysfunctional information. Once this is done, the client's level of distress increases accordingly, and the clinician should be prepared to engage the client in the actual reprocessing to help alleviate the disturbance. Therefore, while discomfort can arise even when identifying the cognitions, the clinician should remain cognizant of the fact that when measurements are taken of emotions and physical sensations, the order of the measurements is designed to stimulate the target material as well. Once activation is accomplished, the sets of eye movements should be started immediately after a final reminder to the client about the EMDR procedure and expectations.

Naming the Emotion

In order to complete the assessment of baseline measures and stimulate the dysfunctional material, the client is next asked to bring up the image of the event and hold it in mind, along with the negative cognition. Specifically, the clinician says, **"When you concentrate on the picture and repeat the words [clinician states the negative cognition], what emotion comes up?"**

This convergence of the image and negative cognition will generally stimulate the dysfunctional material to a greater intensity than either of the two alone. Clients are asked to name the specific emotion or emotions that arise; this prevents confusion in case they subsequently describe the reprocessing experience by primarily using the SUD Scale (i.e.,by simply reporting a number after each set). Such a response might lead the clinician to conclude that nothing has changed, when actually the emotion might have shifted from guilt to rage to sorrow. The clinician should also keep in mind that the SUD rating can rise dramatically when new layers of emotion emerge.

Estimating the Subjective Units of Disturbance

After the client has named the emotion he is feeling, the SUD Scale rating should be determined. Specifically, the clinician should ask, **"From 0 (neutral or calm) to 10 (the worst you can think of), how does it feel?"**

If there are a number of different emotions felt, the SUD rating is given only on the total disturbance, not on each separate emotion. Getting this rating gives a baseline reading not only to the clinician but to the client as well. Even if the client's traumatic memory is not fully processed in one session, the SUD level at the end of the session will generally have decreased. This can give the client a sense of accomplishment, which is one of the goals of every therapy session.

Identifying Body Sensations

Next, the clinician asks the client, **"Where do you feel it in your body?"** Clinical experience with EMDR has shown that the responses of the body to a trauma are often an important aspect of treatment. This question assumes that there is, typically, physical resonance to dysfunctional material. Although it asks the client to determine where that body sensation is located, it is not necessary to ask for a description of the sensation. In fact, doing so will actually stall the procedure by including irrelevant details.

A client who has difficulty assessing the location of the body sensations should be coached (instructions will be provided shortly). One of the benefits to the client of identifying the location of the body sensations is that it provides the client with an alternative to the reliance on verbalization inherent in most traditional therapies. That is, focusing on the body sensation stimulated during successive sets frees the client from the need to concentrate on painful thoughts or gory pictures.

Identifying the location of body sensations during successive sets is often necessary in order to assess the effects of EMDR processing, and it also lays the groundwork for the next phase of the procedure. However, the clinician should be aware that many clients may need sensation-awareness training because they have learned to separate themselves psychologically from their bodies, either as a result of continuing disturbance or in the belief that their needs will not be fulfilled.

Clinicians can assist some clients in locating body sensations by referring them to their SUD score: **"You reported an 8 SUDs. Where do you feel the 8 in your body?"** If the client is still unable to respond, the clinician should gently offer additional help, such as the following simple, nonintrusive instruction:

> **"Close your eyes and notice how your body feels. Now I will ask you to think of something, and when I do, just notice what changes in your body. Okay, notice your body. Now, think of (or bring up the picture of) the memory. Tell me what changes. Now add the words [the clinician states the negative cognition]. Tell me what changes."**

Most clients will be able to notice the tightening of a muscle or an increase in heart rate or breathing. No matter how small a change the client notices, this body sensation should be targeted. This, in turn, will often increase the client's awareness of other sensations.

The clinician should also stay alert to any response by the client that denies body awareness while simultaneously revealing a physical sensation. For instance, when a client says "I feel numb," "I feel blocked," or "I feel separated," this indicates a specific set of sensations that have taken on a particular emotional connotation mistakenly indicating a lack of feeling. In response to such verbalization the clinician should ask the client to locate the sensations ("Where do you feel blocked?") and then focus attention on them.

A few clients will be unable to identify a body location despite coaching, and the clinician will have to adjust subsequent instructions accordingly by asking the client to concentrate on the other components of the target. One of the therapeutic goals, however, will be to enable the client to gain greater access to physical sensations and emotions. Frequently, this aim can be more easily achieved during reprocessing or after a number of the more formidable memories have been treated.

IMPORTANCE OF THE COMPONENTS

At this point the client should be sufficiently prepared and the clinician should have enough baseline information to commence with EMDR processing. The next four phases of treatment (desensitization, installation, body scan, and closure) will be described in Chapter 6. Before continuing, however, remember that the clinician must pay careful attention to all components of EMDR procedures, since each component may prove therapeutically effective. There are a number of reasons for this, including the following:

1. The use of negative and positive cognitions is a necessary element for the most effective case formulation. In addition, identifying and verbalizing the negative cognition gives the client an opportunity to begin to observe the irrationality of his present beliefs, while the positive cognition offers him an alternative that serves as a light at the end of the tunnel. This factor may inspire the client with courage and commitment to treatment born of the belief that an alternative is indeed possible.

2. The use of the SUD and VOC scales provides the client with quantitative data for a progress report, even in an uncompleted session. The sense of accomplishment on the part of the client—and the sense of accountability on the part of the clinician—allows for the progressive evaluation of new blocks and goals.

3. The use of the physical sensations as a focal point for processing allows clients who are inhibited because of the negative content of their thoughts to concentrate on a factor that offers no negative personal connotations. Further, it allows clients who have a tendency to become bogged down because of overanalysis to focus on a factor that eliminates their need to buffer negative affect.

4. Identifying the components of the trauma (image, cognition, and so on), the sequential bringing to mind and blanking out of the traumatic imagery, the use of metaphors and hand signals—all are geared to convince the client that she is larger than the pathology and can effectively remain an observer of its previously overwhelming effects. This stance offers the client a greater ability to achieve the sense of understanding, accomplishment, and control that is an essential outcome of any successful therapeutic intervention. In addition, the sequential, small doses of exposure while the client maintains a sense of control can aid the deconditioning process.

5. The eye movements themselves allow an apparent titration of the negative affect of the target memory while simultaneously giving the client a task he can accomplish effectively and, consequently, a sense of self-efficacy. Even if research someday shows that other stimuli are just as effective as the eye movements, the paired movement of the clinician's hand and the client's eyes may establish a sense of teamwork that can offer support during times of high disturbance. In addition, the use of eye movements gives the clinician a good indication of client attention to the task, which may be an important benefit when treatment is carried out with highly traumatized clients who might otherwise dissociate into the material and stare fixedly into space. The clinical attention to monitoring and maintaining the client's dual attention may

be responsible for the comparative ease with which clients handle EMDR processing, as opposed to the intensity of hypnotically induced abreactions. Clinical comparisons of the two states have indicated that EMDR processing is much less disturbing to the client, just as comparisons with flooding have indicated that EMDR is easier on both client and clinician (Lipke, 1992, 1994, Appendix D).

SUPERVISED PRACTICE

Instructors may wish to supervise exercises involving the preparation and assessment phases. Specific attention should be given to using the eye movements with the safe-place exercise and developing the negative and positive cognitions. Checklists are provided in Appendix A.

SUMMARY AND CONCLUSIONS

The second and third phases of EMDR treatment are a vital part of the overall methodology. The clinical preparation for EMDR treatment includes the establishment of rapport and adequate bonding to give clients a sense of safety and foster their ability to tell the clinician accurately and with sufficient information what they are experiencing once processing starts. The preparation phase also provides the client with information about treatment effects. After explaining EMDR theory to clients and setting their expectations (using instructions and metaphors in terms they can understand), clinicians should carefully address all client concerns. The safe-place exercise is an important element of the preparation phase that will increase the likelihood of successful processing.

In Phase Three, the clinician should ascertain baseline measures on the client's current state (image, cognitions, somatic responses, SUD and VOC scales) before beginning accelerated processing. The specific instructions given here to elicit baseline measures and access the target material for processing are suggestions only. Clinicians should have sufficient understanding of all aspects of EMDR treatment to enhance the instructions and metaphors if a particular client needs more assistance in following the directions.

Clinicians should notice that most of this chapter is devoted to preparing the client. This is an essential phase of EMDR treatment because it sets up therapeutic conditions conducive to feelings of client safety, which encourage exposure to the memory instead of the avoidance that can maintain or exacerbate the negative effects of the initial trauma.

The assessment phase includes accessing the memory, which stimulates the information stored at the time of the trauma. Clinicians must remain cognizant of the fact that client distress may therefore increase during this phase. The stimulation and initial processing have already begun, even before the eye movements are used on the disturbing material. Once again, EMDR is not limited to eye movements but includes a variety of components, all of which interact to increase treatment efficacy.

The ultimate goal of therapy is to increase the client's sense of self-esteem and self-efficacy. This can best be accomplished if the clinician enhances these abilities at every phase of treatment. The client should always feel empowered and in control of the treatment session. EMDR is a client-centered approach in which the clinician acts as a facilitator of the client's self-healing process.

The next four phases of EMDR treatment, including the accelerated processing of the target memory and closure, will be covered in detail in Chapter 6.

Phases Four to Seven

DESENSITIZATION, INSTALLATION, BODY SCAN, AND CLOSURE

> The great thing in this world is not so much where we
> are but in which direction we are moving.
> *Oliver Wendell Holmes*

This chapter discusses the desensitization, installation, body scan, and closure phases of EMDR. The first three entail the accelerated processing of the target memory; the closure phase describes procedures and information that should be used to debrief clients at the end of every EMDR session. For each phase we review the conceptual material (which should be augmented by the pertinent information in Chapter 3) and the clinical intention, along with suggested wording for client instructions.

The desensitization, installation, and body scan phases all involve the accelerated processing of information. This chapter begins with a description of the interactions that are applicable to all three phases. Following this, instructions for each individual phase, along with pertinent process information, will be presented.

The present chapter offers some general guidelines for effective processing. Clinical strategies for restimulating the system if processing appears blocked will be covered in the next chapter, and advanced methods for more disturbed clients will be covered in Chapter 10. The material covered in this chapter should first be reviewed in a practice session using a low-level disturbance before more advanced material is targeted.

ACCELERATED PROCESSING OF THE MEMORY

After the clinician has carefully prepared the client and assessed the baseline information about the target, the stage is set for the accelerated reprocessing. As soon as the final step in the assessment phase is complete (identifying the location of the body sensation connected to the traumatic event), the clinician should review with the client how EMDR works and stress the importance of not purposely discarding any information. The latter point is particularly necessary with clients who are working on an identified adult trauma. These clients may find a childhood memory emerging during processing but may ignore it as not being part of the problem. Actually, this early memory may be the root cause of the client's high level of distress and should therefore be the focal point of the next set. It is critical to remind the client to notice whatever comes up during processing and to report it accurately. Because time has elapsed since the explanation of the treatment was initially given to the client in the preparation phase, some additional reminders may be in order. The clinician should be alert to any signs of confusion or hesitation in the client. A reminder may be worded as follows:

> **"Now remember, it is your own brain that is doing the healing and you are the one in control. I will ask you to mentally focus on the target and to follow my fingers with your eyes. Just let whatever happens, happen, and we will talk at the end of the set. Just tell me what comes up, and don't discard anything as unimportant. Any new information that comes to mind is connected in some way. If you want to stop, just raise your hand."**

The clinician should then ask the client to keep the image in mind, along with the negative cognition and an awareness of the body sensation. For example, the clinician might say, **"Bring up the picture and the words [clinician repeats the negative cognition] and notice where you feel it in your body. Now, follow my fingers with your eyes."** Metaphorically, this is the equivalent of directing three laser beams at the dysfunctionally stored material. Simultaneously holding all three elements in mind will usually intensify the level of response. This is done only to establish an initial link to the dysfunctional memory; as soon as the eye movements begin, new images, thoughts, and feelings will emerge. For instance, after the first set, the negative cognition is generally not used again during processing (exceptions will be discussed in Chapter 7). Similarly, the client should not try to hold on to the image she started with. Its purpose is merely to serve as an initial focal point for entering the memory network.

Immediately after the material is accessed, the clinician initiates the sets of eye movements. The first set should number around 24 and should be done horizontally (a set of 24 movements has been found clinically to produce a marked processing effect in many clients). The initial set is used to determine whether the horizontal direction is effective for the client (see Chapter 3 for a complete discussion of the number, direction, and speed of the eye movements). Clinicians should gently reinforce the client's effort by softly saying "Good" during the set. This often reassures clients who are not sure they are doing it right.

At the end of the set the clinician says, **"Rest/let it go/blank it out, and take a deep breath."** To "blank it out" clients are coached simply to draw a curtain over the material. While doing this, they are not coached to close their eyes because this could contribute to dissociation or trance-like states. This refocusing period serves to interrupt the intensity of focus and concentration and gives the client permission to rest, reorient, and prepare to verbalize the new information plateau. Being able to set the disturbance temporarily aside also tacitly teaches the client that she is larger than the pathology and can be in control of her own experience. Alternating eye movements and instructions also provides the client with small doses of exposure to the target and enables the clinician to assess progress.

In order to increase a sense of bonding, the clinician might want to inhale and exhale along with the client at the end of the set, after the instruction to take a deep breath. Such nonspecific adjuncts to treatment play an important role in the positive therapeutic effects derived from any method. It is important to maintain a sense of bonding and teamwork throughout the entire session.

When the client appears ready, the clinician reestablishes contact by asking, **"What do you get now?"** or **"What came up for you?"** This allows the clinician to get a readout from the client on any aspects of the event that have shifted and on the current state of the targeted material. The client will generally reveal new information, images, emotions, or dominant sensations. The clinician can then judge if any reprocessing has taken place. If the client says he gets nothing, the clinician should direct him to think of the incident again by asking, **"When you think of the incident, what do you get?"**

The intention here is to be as nondemanding as possible regarding any particular aspect of the event so that the client can easily state what is most salient and so that processing can continue between sets. For some clients the focus will be a change in the image, for others a new insight or shift in perspective, and for still others a marked shift in body sensations. For that reason, the clinician should not say "What do you see?" or "What are you feeling?" when trying to prompt a response.

The interval between sets is extremely important for many clients because it provides the opportunity to put words to an internal experience and allows them to understand the changes more readily. The accelerated processing can occur so rapidly during the sets that the client is unable to understand it fully until she can verbalize it. Regardless of what the client says, the clinician should listen with compassion and unconditional support.

Since reprocessing will manifest itself differently in each individual, the general statement "What do you get now?" allows clients to report whatever appears dominant regarding a change in thought, feeling, image, emotion, body sensation, new incident, and so forth. If a significant change in any of the information is indicated, the same direction of eye movement should be used for the next set. If there is no change, a different direction of eye movement should be tried. As noted earlier, if the processing still fails to occur or if information that has started to change seems to get stuck and does not move after two or three different directions have been attempted, the clinician will need to consult the more advanced material covered in Chapter 7 before proceeding.

An apparent lack of treatment effect may also mean that the client is simply not amenable to processing in the office. However, even if there has been little or no obvious processing, a closure and debriefing should be done, as explained later in this chapter.

For most clients, some type of change will occur. Regardless of the kind of experience reported, any change in material generally indicates that processing is continuing. As long as this is so, the clinician should refrain from making interpretive remarks. The clinician can confirm the client's experience by such nonverbal means as smiles or nods or by comments such as "Good" or "Uh-huh." Rather than attempting cognitive restructuring or going off on a tangential explication of issues that will become irrelevant once the problem is resolved, the clinician can achieve the most effective treatment by asking the client to concentrate on the new material for a new set. The intention in EMDR is to stimulate the dysfunctional material, activate the processing mechanism, and allow information to flow along its natural course to adaptive resolution. To best accomplish this the client must be allowed to remain within the experience, that is, in touch with the sensory manifestations of the information.

The use of active listening—with the clinician stating, "What I hear you say is . . ." and then repeating or paraphrasing the client's words—should *not* be used in EMDR. Although this technique is used widely in other forms of psychotherapy, where therapeutic gains rely largely on verbal reassessments, it is antithetical to EMDR treatment effects. When the clinician repeats the client's words, even a slight shift in intonation can change the meaning. The client is forced to step out of his experience sufficiently to interpret the clinician's words, compare the clinician's statement to what is actually being felt, and then verbalize the comparison. This form of cognitive interpretation, which takes the client out of the emotional and sensory experience, can interrupt the processing. The clinician should not attempt to repeat or summarize, even if the client has spoken for 5 minutes after the set; the client is aware of his own key points and does not need them repeated. Asking the client to keep his attention on what he just said (or, if the client is confused, to the last thing he said) is preferable to the clinician's trying to paraphrase or reiterate the client's words.

Another approach that can hinder rapid EMDR treatment is a clinician-imposed attempt to explore the meaning of any symbols, memories, thoughts, feelings, and so on, that arise for the client during the sets. Clients continually report new insights and understandings that evolve naturally as the processing continues. For instance, when a new memory emerges, it is assumed that there is an associative link to the earlier material. Therefore, rather than asking the client "What do you think that means?" or "Why do you think that came up?" the clinician should merely direct the client to pay attention to the new memory during the next set. Clients will generally volunteer pertinent cognitive interpretations, or these can be discussed after the processing is completed. The clinician's attempts to interpret each plateau can have a detrimental effect on treatment by distracting the client from the stimulated experience and replacing it with a cognitive digression. Keep in mind that cognitive interpretation is the hallmark of many forms of traditional therapy, all of which have had only limited success in the treatment of trauma. In EMDR, a new cognition should be the manifestation of a new plateau of processed information, not a clinician-imposed construct.

When the client has revealed a shift in any part of the information, her attention should again be focused with the instruction **"Think of that"** and a new set should be initiated. At this point the clinician should use the client's nonverbal cues (e.g., widening or narrowing of the eyes, changes in pupil size or mouth tension, etc.) to determine the length of the new set. The intention is to bring the client to a new plateau of processing with every set. The clinician should stay alert to the client's responses to ascertain any new awareness or any lessening of suffering. Keep in mind that the new information will register on the client's face before she is cognitively aware of it. Therefore, to enable the client to get an internal grasp of it, the clinician should continue the set for a few seconds after noticing the new facial expression. These cues are best demonstrated in a practice session.

If pronounced emotion is evident, the clinician should continue the set until it is apparent that new plateaus of information have been reached. The clinician's attention to nonverbal cues in the client's attempt to reach a more therapeutic plateau is particularly important for abreactive responses, which will be dealt with more fully in the next chapter. If the shifts in information are primarily cognitive rather than emotive, the clinician should experiment to determine if the client responds better with sets of 36 or 48 movements. (For some clients, a set of less then 24 movements appears to give better results.) However, the clinician should not concentrate on counting the movements but should simply get a sense of the set's approximate length; the clinician's attention should be on the facial expressions and other body cues of the client.

While a SUD level should not be requested after each set, a good guideline is that the equivalent of a change at least one SUD (on the 11-point scale) should be evident in the client's responses after each set. Remember, however, that increases in distress can also indicate processing. That is, new emotions or new associations can temporarily increase the disturbance as the processing proceeds. Appropriately administering the sets in response to the client's nonverbal cues can often be crucial in achieving therapeutic effect. This is why I strongly recommend that the reader engage in practice and be instructed and supervised by a trained EMDR clinician before proceeding with a client. The following sections will augment this instruction.

Clinical reports have supported the need to alter the characteristics of the eye movement sets for best therapeutic results. Therefore, if headache, dizziness, or nausea is reported, the client should be asked to concentrate only on the disturbing body sensation while the direction of the set is changed. This procedure often allows the physical sensations to dissipate. The direction of the eye movement should also be changed if no shift in information is manifested. It has been observed clinically that some clients only process if eye movement sets are done in a certain direction, whereas others either process equally with all directions or process only if the direction is changed at different times during the treatment.

Likewise, the length and speed of the set must be changed to accommodate individual differences. Clinical reports have consistently shown this to be the case, and possible explanations are explored in Chapter 12. Changing the direction, length, and speed of the set may cause different kinds of effects for different clients. When applying EMDR, perhaps 40% of the time the proper application of the eye movements alone causes a consistent reprocessing of the dysfunctional information to an adaptive resolution. When the information does not shift after repeated changes of the sets, other alterations (discussed in the following chapters) must be made.

PHASE FOUR: DESENSITIZATION

For purposes of standardization, the fourth phase, which concentrates on reducing the client's disturbance (when possible) to 0 or 1 on the

SUD Scale, is called the desensitization phase. However, while this term is used to designate one phase of the EMDR procedure, it should not be viewed too narrowly. Rather, desensitization, or removal of disturbance, is actually a by-product of the reprocessing, as is the positive restructuring of the cognition; both continue throughout the entire treatment.

For desensitization to occur, it is necessary to process the dysfunctional material that is stored in all of the channels associated with the target event. When an event is reprocessed, a variety of channels of association may be revealed in consciousness. Each initial target is considered a physiological node to which other past experiences are linked. It is assumed that the disturbance inherent within any target node is fueled by the various channels of association.

Processing of the information in these channels can be evinced through the observed shifting of the manifestations of the information (image, affect, thoughts, sounds, sensations, or beliefs) while the client remains focused on the target memory. For some clients, the shifts can occur through awareness of other linked events or through a progression of insights. For many clients, treatment sessions will include a variety of these different forms of association. The clinician should be sure to give the proper reassurances, when necessary, for client comfort but, at the same time, should try to allow the processing to continue without undue interference.

The clinician should keep in mind as a clinical heuristic the notion of a target node with ancillary channels (see Figure 13). Each new awareness of a shift is a sign of a domino effect of progressive processing through the channel. The sets should be applied to each new sign of progressive awareness until all the channels are "cleaned out."

As each channel is accessed, there emerges a set of lawfully linked associations. (These associations were explored in Chapter 2.) For instance, some channels will include a shifting of manifestations of the target incident, others will include a shifting of awareness through different incidents that are linked by the dominant emotions, still others will be manifested solely by shifting beliefs, and yet others will manifest new insights linked with other memories that serve as either examples or counterexamples. In the last instance, a client may begin to accept the fact that she was not responsible for being abandoned by her mother and may remember scenes of happiness with her parents or other family members; these memories may be interspersed with others that incorporate the theme of abandonment.

Between each set the clinician should listen carefully to the client in order to identify the next focus for processing. Depending on the client's response, the clinician will direct attention to the latest statement, to some alternative aspect of the experience, or to a new target.

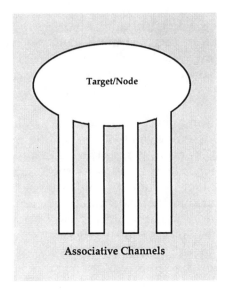

FIGURE 13. A graphic representation of the progression of EMDR treatment through the memory network.

The following examples illustrate dysfunctional information in associated channels that needs to be addressed. In all cases, once the chain of association is exhausted, the client should be asked to return to the original target for additional sets. This will reveal if new channels need to be processed. When all channels are treated, the installation phase (described later in this chapter) can begin.

Associative Processing

Clients report their experiences in terms of changing imagery, sounds, sensations, emotions, tastes, or smells. If tastes or smells emerge, they should be targeted immediately for successive sets. If these sets cause them to fade without leading to another association, the original target should be reaccessed.

Imagery

Most often, clients describe processing in terms of changing images. Regardless of whether these are new memories or alterations of a single event, the emerging material should become the focus of concentration for a new set. Again, the clinician should not encourage any particular way of reporting (e.g., by asking, "What do you see?") because the client may be most attentive to new thoughts or other sensory stimuli. The following are generally observed client patterns involving shifts in imagery and the appropriate clinical response:

New Memory. When the client reports that a new memory has come to consciousness during the previous set, that memory becomes the focus in the next set. If several memories are reported, the client should be instructed to concentrate on the one he finds most disturbing. If all the memories are reported to be at the same level of disturbance, then the focus should be directed to the last one to appear.

Some clients offer a seemingly endless stream of associated distinct memories. It may be useful to ask these clients to return to the original memory after each shift. However, this should be done only if 10 to 15 new memories are revealed sequentially after each set, a situation not uncommon with war veterans. (Further research is needed to determine if a generalization effect occurs in such cases.)

In all cases, the clinician should note for subsequent targeting any transient memory reported during processing that appears particularly relevant or disturbing. Such memories may surface briefly and vanish in one set. However, retargeting generally should not occur until after the presenting memory has been completely processed. (This subsequent targeting will be covered more fully in Chapter 8.) When possible, the client should be allowed to take the lead by targeting the content of her progressive consciousness as the information changes within each channel. However, it is important to return to the original target for further processing after a line of association has ended.

Image Changes. At times, clients will report a shift in the presenting image (even though the incident remains the same) or an image without any specific incident attached, such as a person's face. If a negative image emerges (e.g., mother scowling), it should be targeted with the next set. If a neutral or positive image emerges (e.g., mother sitting in the living room or mother smiling happily), a set or two may be added to see if it will be strengthened, but the original image should be readdressed as soon as possible, especially if it has occurred early in the session. If this situation occurs later in the processing session, the sets should be continued on the positive image until the strengthening ceases. If the client states that two images have emerged, one negative and one positive (such as mother scowling and mother smiling), the negative one should be targeted. This guideline is based on the assumption that positive associations will take care of themselves, whereas negative ones must be processed. In order to ensure the lowest level of disturbance for the client (e.g., if the treatment is not completed within a single session), as many of the negative associations as possible should be processed. Once again, the dysfunctional channels must be "cleaned out" before the positive associations can be permanently strengthened.

Incident Unfolds. When a trauma occurs, it becomes locked in the nervous system in its originally disturbing form; clients often state that the information feels "stuck" or always present. This is evident in many clients who when asked to bring the memory of a particular incident to mind find that the most disturbing part of the incident is the only one available. For instance, when a woman who had been in a boating accident was asked to think of the incident, what emerged was the scene of going under for the third time. Understandably, this was the most terrifying moment of the entire event, one that defined her subsequent stress reactions. However, since the woman was currently sitting in the clinician's office, she clearly was not in danger of drowning. Metaphorically, it as if the entire incident is being played on a VCR that has been put on "pause." When the scene is targeted for processing and the sets begin, it is not unusual for the incident to start unfolding, frame by frame, as if the VCR had returned to "play." For example, the aforementioned client reported seeing someone jump in the water and remembered being grabbed and rescued, resting in the boat, being taken to shore, and so on. Very often, the incident will even continue to include the client's subsequent experience (e.g., in the hospital) and any disturbing family reactions. The client should focus on each scene in separate sets, until resolution is achieved.

The actual aftermath of the initially identified traumatic event can often be as disturbing as the trauma itself. For example, some rape victims have reported feeling grossly violated by hospital attendants and police during the subsequent investigation. When the targeted incident has not spontaneously moved to this portion of the event, it may be appropriate for the clinician to elicit these channels, particularly if these aspects were reported to be troubling during the initial history-taking session.

Appearance Changes. Some clients will focus on a profoundly disturbing aspect of an event that is represented by a single image. These images are often reported as intrusive thoughts, flashback scenes, or recurrent nightmare images. During reprocessing, the appearance of the image itself may change. As long as changes in appearance are being reported (such as getting darker, brighter, bigger, or smaller or being seen from a different angle), the sets should be repeated with the changed image as their focus. Even if the picture is described as "blurry," the client should be asked simply to concentrate on it.

At times, the client will report that the image disappears although some disturbance remains. When this occurs, the client should be told,

"Just think of the incident" (and concentrate on the physical sensations). This allows the information about the event to be stimulated so that reprocessing can be completed. It is important that the clinician continue the sets until the disturbance is resolved and not assume that the disappearance of the image signifies therapeutic success.

The client may have to be reassured that he can retain an accurate memory of the event or of an individual even though a particular image has disappeared during reprocessing. This is especially important for the client who is grieving for a loved one, in which case he should be reassured that other images will still be available once reprocessing is complete. The clinician should remember, however, that since the disappearance of the pivotal image is a common occurrence, the legal ramifications must be carefully evaluated before EMDR is used (a topic covered in Chapter 4).

Sounds and Thoughts

The clinician should be sensitive to any evidence that the target information is being processed. While many clients report shifts in images, the auditory and cognitive changes are no less significant. Thus, the focus can change with a sequence of new thoughts, thoughts that were experienced at the time of the event can emerge, or insights can unfold without visual references. As long as the thoughts occur spontaneously and progressively, the client is simply encouraged to note them for use in subsequent sets. Once again, after an auditory or cognitive channel of association has been successfully processed, the client should be invited to reaccess the original target.

Negative Statements. When a new negative statement or idea emerges, the clinician should ask the client where she feels it in her body. This should be done before a new set is begun. This can reduce the emphasis on the self-denigrating aspects of the statement. Generally, a new thought will emerge, and the sequence of question (**"Where do you feel it in your body?"**) and set should be repeated.

The clinician should look for a progressive lessening of the negative associations. If the same negative thoughts persist, the client may be stuck (see Chapter 7) or "looping" and the clinician may need to use the proactive version of EMDR, called the "cognitive interweave" (see Chapter 10). Generally, looping is said to be occurring when the same negative statements and a high level of disturbance are generated and recycled over a 15-minute period and none of the suggested alternatives in the next chapter have worked. New clinicians should disengage with such a client and then resume with the proactive version of EMDR, but only after they have had sufficient practice and supervision.

Mismatches. A mismatch occurs when the client deliberately tries to bring something to consciousness that is inconsistent with the current level of affect. We assume that processing can take place when the eye movements are done in concert with a conscious focus on the aligned components of the dysfunctional material (image, thought, physical sensation). After the clinician has coached the client to formulate a negative cognition that verbalizes the level of affect associated with a target event and has asked the client to maintain awareness of the physical sensations that are associated with the target, all these elements (image, cognition, sensation) are held in consciousness. They can be thought of as the equivalent of three laser beams directed at the physiologically stored dysfunctional material. If while experiencing a high level of distress because of a trauma-induced sense of powerlessness, the client attempts to comfort himself by adding an affirmation, such as "I am powerful," the mismatch between the affect and the affirmation will generally cause processing to cease.

If the client unexpectedly reports after a set that she is thinking of something pleasant, the clinician should determine if the client is deliberately attempting to evoke a sense of relief by the addition of a less distressing thought by asking the client, **"Are you doing or saying anything deliberately?"** If this is the case, the client should be invited to drop the mismatched statement and, once again, instructed as follows: **"Just let it happen, without judging or trying to force anything to happen."**

Please note, however, that positive statements can spontaneously arise in direct response to the negative cognition, and these should not be discouraged. For instance, without any deliberate attempt on the part of the client, the words "I am fine" can emerge in response to the negative cognition "I am terrible." At times, the two statements will alternate spontaneously throughout a set. However, this alternation does not cause processing to cease. It is only problematic when the client consciously attempts to orchestrate processing by inserting a positive statement prematurely.

Positive Thoughts. If a new positive thought emerges early in the treatment, the clinician should instruct the client to concentrate on it when another set is initiated. However, unless a significant change then occurs, the client should be directed to return to the original target. If the positive thought is strengthened, additional sets should be administered. It is especially important to focus on and strengthen new positive thoughts that are particularly adaptive for the client before returning to the target. When both negative and positive thoughts emerge simultaneously, the client should be directed to concentrate on the negative one. Once again, the negative statement is associated with more dysfunctional material that must be metabolized, whereas the positive thought is connected to appropriate material that is progressing spontaneously toward integration. All the negative associations should be reprocessed before concentrating on a full integration. Therefore, if positive thoughts emerge during the later stages of processing, particularly during the installation phase, the sets should be continued.

Insights. If insights become progressively more adaptive, the client is requested to maintain awareness of her latest thoughts during the next set. Regardless of what the client says, the clinician should merely say, **"Think of that,"** and not attempt to repeat or explicate it. Allowing processing to progress unimpeded can be extremely difficult for many clinicians, especially when the client's statements appear to have flaws in logic or to reveal imperfect understanding. However, it is important for the clinician to remember that the processing entails a transmutation of the dysfunctional material and a gradual linkup with appropriate, useful self-enhancing information. Each statement is a verbalization of the specific plateau of information and stage of processing. Until the end of the EMDR treatment, each statement will be less than fully adaptive but will set the stage for the next plateau.

If we remember the metaphor of a train progressing to each new stop, it becomes clear that the client's view cannot be completely functional until the "last stop" of fully adaptive information is reached. Challenging the client or attempting to explicate his statements is equivalent to asking him to get off the train. In EMDR we are attempting to stimulate the dysfunctional material and process it in an accelerated manner with additional sets. The clinician should intentionally intervene only if processing becomes blocked. (The appropriate timing and interventions for blocked processing will be discussed in the next chapter.) Even if a client has just given a lengthy discourse on the newly revealed information, the simple instruction "Think of it" allows him to concentrate on the most pertinent element of what was just reported. If the client asks for instructions, the clinician should advise him to hold in mind the last pertinent point made.

Sensation and Affect

Clients often report processing effects in terms of emerging and changing physical sensations or emotions. EMDR processing may release into the client's conscious awareness not only the physical sensations associated with a variety of emotions but the physical sensations stored at the time of the traumatic event. For example, the rape victim may feel the hands of the rapist and the accident victim may feel the crash of the car. Special care must be taken when a client experiences painful affect or physical sensations associated with trauma. Instructions for working with clients in abreactions that include high levels of disturbance will be reviewed in the next chapter. However, regardless of the level of disturbance, as long as the material is shifting, the usual processing instructions apply.

New Emotions. When an incident is processed, a variety of emotions may sequentially emerge. Whenever the client mentions a new emotion, the clinician should ask, **"Where do you feel it in your body?"** and should then begin another set. Specific emotions or a combination of several emotions can arise and be dispelled within a single set, or they can remain for the entire session. Because these emotions can be intense, it is important to remind the client that they are manifestations of old material, that, for instance, just because one is experiencing fear does not mean there is actual danger. The clinician should not be surprised if a low level of one emotion transmutes into a high level of another. For instance, sorrow rated as 3 on the SUD Scale can easily turn into a level of anger rated 8 on that scale. The new emotion should be targeted without reference to the previous one. For instance, asking "Are you also feeling sad?" may only delay processing.

It is preferable that the accelerated processing of emotions be done in the office, but at times the client will continue to experience the emotion in "real time" or a variety of emotions will spontaneously emerge sometime after the session. The client should be given adequate debriefing (discussed later in this chapter) about EMDR, regardless of its apparent effect. This is important because even when an incident appears to be completely processed, new emotions may emerge. For instance, after the successful reprocessing of an incest memory, a client returned the following week in intense grief and reported, "I have been grieving for the death of my father. I never mourned him before."

When a client describes feeling numb or dissociated, the clinician should first ask him to locate the feeling in his body and then continue the sets. The clinician should be verbally supportive and should reassure the client during the sets by reminding him of the therapeutic process. This can be a very frightening time for the client. Saying things like **"That's it; just remember it's the old stuff"** can be very helpful.

Remember, however, that the client should be appropriately screened for dissociative disorder before starting EMDR. If this has been adequately done, feelings of dissociation are viewed as the next layer of emotion that needs to be processed. Feelings of dissociation in PTSD clients are not uncommon, because many clients dissociated at the time of the trauma. However, the clinician should make sure that he has not pushed the client too far, that is, into trying to dissociate to escape the perceived ordeal of the EMDR session itself.

When in doubt, stop and ask the client how she feels about continuing the session before proceeding.

Shifting Sensations. If the body sensations shift, the client should be directed to focus on the new location during additional sets. Although it is tempting, the clinician should not request an appraisal or description of the sensation because this does not provide useful information. In addition, if the sensation shifts, the clinician should refrain from asking about the status of a sensation previously reported (e.g., "Do you still feel it in your stomach?"). The body scan will take care of all remnants of physical sensation at the end of the session. To facilitate processing, the clinician should in general ask the client as few questions as possible.

Assessment

Each line of association should be assessed to ascertain whether there appears to be a progression, a sequential processing, that is therapeutically relevant. The dominant tendency is for the client to report new or shifting information that is progressively less disturbing. However, even if disturbance increases, reprocessing can be occurring owing to the fact that another aspect of the memory is being experienced as it is metabolized.

Clinicians can assume that a channel has been cleared out when the client has become progressively less disturbed, when the associations appear to have reached a reasonable stopping point, and when nothing new or significant emerges after two sets of eye movements in different directions. The clinician should be sensitive to the fact that a new image or statement coming to the client's consciousness may simply be at the same plateau of information as the previous image or statement. For example, if a client begins to access positive feelings about his mother and reports scenes of different parties or luncheons they attended together, these released memories, though pleasant, are not indicative of a new plateau.

As the sets of therapeutically enhanced associations cease, the client should be asked to retarget the original incident: **"Think of the incident. What do you get?"** Then a new set is initiated, even if the response appears positive or clients believe there is nothing left to process. Often, the new set will open up an otherwise unexpected channel. Any new channels should be processed according to the foregoing guidelines. At the end of each channel the clinician should ask the client to return to the original target.

If after retargeting the original incident and completing a set on it no new associations are given and no new emotions, sensations, or images are revealed, the clinician should recheck the client's SUD level. If the client reports a zero, the target is considered desensitized and the installation phase can begin. Once again, however, the distinction between these phases is somewhat arbitrary, because the entire EMDR treatment is considered a reprocessing and the desensitization and enhancement of positive responses are considered simultaneous by-products.

While it is necessary to process all channels of revealed dysfunctional information before the installation phase begins, the clinician should remain conscious of time. Arriving at the end of any given channel will leave the client feeling less disturbed, but retargeting the original information may open another channel with yet more disturbing material. Therefore, if there are only a few minutes left in the session, a new channel should not be opened. The clinician may wish to go directly to the closure phase if there is insufficient time to finish the processing. The idea is to leave the client at the end of each session feeling empowered and possessing a sense of accomplishment.

If the client reports a low SUD level (but more than zero) that does not shift with changes of direction in two eye movement sets, an additional assessment is made. The clinician asks, **"What emotion are you feeling?"** At times, clients will have become confused and will give a SUD level to report a feeling of calm or well-being. If so, they should be reminded to assess only disturbing emotions. If, however, the client reports low-grade negative emotions, the clinician should ask, **"What prevents it from being a zero?"**

A response revealing a blocking belief such as "If I'm too happy, I'll be sorry" will need to be addressed by a full EMDR treatment on a corresponding memory. If the client's response appears appropriate to the situation (e.g., "I'm feeling sadness because my uncle died"), the installation phase may then be carried out.

The clinician should be careful not to accept prematurely a client's statement that seems to limit further progress. For instance, if a client is working on a public speaking phobia, it might be tempting to leave him with a low grade of anxiety, especially if the client states, "I guess I'll always be a little anxious in order to do a good job." This kind of statement may be merely a belief that is consistent with that plateau of processing. Unfortunately, some clinicians may accept this kind of statement and truncate the treatment because it parallels their own belief system; however, some people can indeed make wonderful speeches feeling anticipation and excitement, rather than anxiety, as the source of arousal. Therefore, the clinician should acknowledge the client's statement and do at least two additional sets of different eye movements before accepting the limitation as an accurate statement. Stopping the sets prematurely may leave important unexplored areas or unwarranted levels of disturbance. Limitations should be accepted only if they appear reasonable and if two additional sets prove unproductive. SUD levels higher than a 1 should be carefully examined to determine their ecological validity before proceeding to the installation phase.

PHASE FIVE: INSTALLATION

After desensitization has been achieved—with the SUD rating at 0 or 1—the installation phase begins. Installation concentrates primarily on the full integration of a positive self-assessment with the targeted information. This phase is used to enhance the positive cognition and to link it specifically with the original target issue or event. Since all of the information should have shifted during reprocessing, the positive cognition is checked for both applicability and current validity. The clinician asks the client to evaluate the positive cognition she chose during the assessment phase; that is, the clinician says, **"How does [clinician repeats positive cognition] sound?"**

By this point in the session the client should have progressed dramatically in the way she feels about the original event. Because of a variety of new insights she may have far surpassed her own expectations and may now view the event in a much more positive light than originally imagined. In other words, the positive cognition she desired at the start of treatment may not be positive enough now. For instance, feelings of failure and guilt in response to an early tragedy might have led a client initially to choose the cognition "I learned from it." At the end of treatment, however, the client may come to realize that she in fact did very well at the time of the event, and the more appropriate positive cognition may now be "I am a worthwhile person."

After the clinician repeats the original desired cognition, the client should be encouraged to accept or change it or to substitute a better one. The clinician should also note whether a more therapeutic or enhanced positive cognition has emerged during processing. If so, the clinician should offer the new positive cognition to the client in a tone that easily permits its rejection.

It is crucial that the client choose the positive cognition that is most meaningful for her. However, it is the clinician's job to assist in the therapeutic process. Just as the clinician's expertise in case formulation is needed to help frame the initial negative and positive cognition, so too is that expertise necessary to help the clinician create a new positive cognition that sums up the processing experience and is particularly useful and acceptable to the client. When offering a potential positive cognition that was not initially voiced by the client, the clinician should be careful to frame it as a tentative suggestion only. No demand characteristics should be used since the primary goal is the client's sense of self-efficacy. If the client accepts the suggestion, the installation can proceed after checking her VOC rating on the new cognition.

If the client accepts the original positive cognition, the clinician should ask for a VOC rating to see if it has improved: **"How do the words feel, from 1 (completely false) to 7 (completely true)?"** If the VOC has not increased, the positive cognition should be reexamined. That is, with the information now processed, the client's increased sense of self-efficacy should be reflected in a strengthening of the cognition. If it is not, there is a good chance that the proposed positive cognition is inappropriate, and a substitute will need to be found.

After the VOC is checked, the chosen positive cognition is linked with the previously traumatic event. By instructing the client to **"think of the event,"** either the original image or the current manifestation will emerge. The instruction is a general one because the original image may have disappeared or been replaced by one that is now more pertinent. The client is then asked to hold the image in mind (if there is no image, the client is asked to "just think of it") while mentally repeating the positive cognition. That is, the clinician says, **"Think of the event, and hold it together with the words [clinician repeats the positive cognition],"** and then leads the client in a new set. Afterward, the clinician checks the VOC again, and the sets are repeated, with the event and the positive cognition linked, until the VOC reaches 7, or "completely true." Once the client rates the positive cognition as a 7, the sets are repeated until the cognition's validity and sense of appropriateness have reached maximum. The increase in validity may continue well past the arbitrary level of 7 on the VOC Scale, since the client is often initially unaware of how positive and right a cognition can actually feel. It is often useful to coach the client in determining if the statement feels "stronger" or "more solid." The guideline for the installation phase is that if the information continues to move further along the information-processing track, the sets should be repeated. The greater the client's sense of validity of the positive cognition, the greater the potential for improved self-esteem and a generalized self-enhancement.

If with repeated application of different directions of eye movements the client reports that the VOC level does not rise above a 5 or 6, he is asked, **"What prevents it from being a 7?"** The client will generally be able to report the blocking belief, which might be as benign as "I'll have to go through it to be certain it can be true" or as dysfunctional as "I don't deserve to be healthy." When an innocuous, nonproblematic statement is made, the clinician should proceed to the next phase, the body scan. When a dysfunctional blocking belief is revealed, the clinician will need to target it with a full EMDR treatment on the associated memory that is driving the negative self-assessment.

Typically, until the early memories that cause the blocking dysfunction are reprocessed, a completely successful treatment of the original target trauma cannot be attained. Once the early blocking memory is reprocessed with desensitization, installation, and body scan, the clinician should reevaluate the original target memory and complete the installation. Generally, however, because of time limitations, the clinician should wait until the following session to inaugurate treatment on a new early memory. When this is the case, the clinician should move to the closure phase (skipping the body scan) and administer an especially careful debriefing. Any uncompleted session is liable to increase the level of between-sessions disturbance, and no treatment is considered successful without completing the body scan.

PHASE SIX: BODY SCAN

The Accelerated Information Processing model that guides EMDR practice posits that the dysfunctional material may have a discernible physical resonance (i.e., physical sensations that correspond to cognitive processes) that can itself be targeted. Therefore, the sixth phase of treatment, which concludes the accelerated reprocessing, concentrates primarily on body tension.

Once the positive cognition reaches at least a 7 on the VOC Scale (or perhaps a 6 if ecologically valid) and does not increase in strength with additional sets, the client is asked to hold both the image and the cognition in mind while mentally scanning her entire body to identify any lingering feelings of tension or tightness or any unusual sensation. The clinician might, for example, say the following:

> **"Close your eyes and keep in mind the original memory and the positive cognition. Then bring your attention to the different parts of your body, starting with your head and working downward. Any place you find any tension, tightness, or unusual sensation, tell me."**

If the client reports any unusual physical sensations, they are targeted with further sets. These sensations may disappear uneventfully with a few successive sets. On the other hand, focusing on body sensations at this point can open other channels of information that must be processed. These can include anger or grief that the pathology has existed for such a long time. The body scan can also highlight major areas of resistance stemming from the client's fears of who he will be or what he must confront if he lets go of his pathology. In addition, the body scan may reveal other associated networks containing dysfunctional material.

The importance of the body scan in the complete reprocessing of the targeted event and associated material cannot be overemphasized. Its importance is clearly illustrated in a case of a woman who was being treated for performance anxiety and who had successfully reprocessed a memory of having frozen during a presentation. When asked to do a body scan, she reported a strange sensation at the small of her back, which she rationalized as having been caused by sitting so long during the session. When the sensation in her back was targeted with successive sets, however, the client suddenly exclaimed at the image that arose of being molested by her uncle, who held her down on the bed with his hand at the small of her back. Although this association was anticipated neither by the clinician nor the client, it supports the hypothesis that material stimulated by EMDR is lawfully associated. In other words, dysfunctional material associated with the presenting complaint of performance anxiety (i.e., the client's memory of freezing during a presentation) could logically be linked to a molestation where she would have felt anxiety and distress at having to "perform." While previously unrevealed, this kind of antecedent is often revealed to be the cause of a seemingly innocuous presenting complaint. The clinician should not automatically assume that traumatic material is at the root of a presenting complaint but should be prepared for the possibility that it will emerge spontaneously. This underscores the need for the proper therapeutic alliance and for flexibility in clinical considerations, such as the scheduling of extra time for processing sessions.

The body scan phase of treatment is completed when the client, holding in mind the target event and the positive cognition, can mentally scan the body and find no residual tension. If a positive or comfortable sensation is reported, sets can be done to strengthen it.

PHASE SEVEN: CLOSURE

While the clinician should be scrupulous in attempting to clear the channels of dysfunctional information, sufficient time to do so must be allotted. Although a 90-minute session will be sufficient to process successfully most traumatic material involving a single memory, this may not always be the case. This is why the clinician should always reserve time to close the session with proper instructions, leaving the client in a positive frame of mind and able to safely return home.

The clinician should never allow the client to leave the office in a high level of disturbance or in the middle of an abreaction. Therefore, if only a few minutes of the session are left, a new channel should *not* be targeted and a body scan should *not* be done. A client may be feeling fairly calm after the successful reprocessing of a single channel and may have reached therapeutic insight regarding one chain of associations. The client may also feel a sense of well-being at reaching a VOC level of 7 regarding a new positive attribution. However, targeting a new channel or the tension revealed in a body scan can set off a new chain of associations that will require more than a few minutes to process. Therefore, the clinician should always use good judgment regarding the time requirements necessary to enable the client to leave the office in a stable state.

Visualization

If at the end of the allotted time for the session the client is evincing any signs of disturbance or is abreacting, the clinician should utilize hypnosis or a guided visualization to return her to a state of comfort. Clinicians who are unfamiliar with these techniques should learn them before using EMDR. The safe-place exercise described in Chapter 5 may be used with most EMDR clients, since clinicians have consistently reported positive effects from it. In addition, clinicians can use segments of the audiotapes listed in the reference section (Miller, 1994) and the closure exercises reviewed in Chapter 9 for this purpose.

As noted before, clinicians should use a relaxation process, such as the safe-place exercise, with the client in an early session, before processing begins, a precaution that can give the client confidence about her ability to stop the accelerated processing and bring the disturbance under control. It is easier to use a previously successful relaxation method with a client during the closure phase than to experiment with new ones.

Safety Assessment

After using guided imagery, the clinician should assess the client for any dissociation that would prevent him from returning to the here and now or hamper his ability to negotiate the streets or drive a car. It may sometimes be necessary for a client to remain in the waiting room for some period of time until the clinician determines that there is no potential for danger.

While most clients can be assisted in closing down the incomplete processing of a targeted event to a level that will be manageable until the next session, in a small number of cases it will be necessary either to see the client later in the day in order to complete the reprocessing or to schedule an appointment for later in the week.

While a week is generally recommended between sessions to give the client a chance to integrate the material that has been processed and to identify new targets, some clients will need to be seen more often. This is the case if many new disturbing memories are emerging or if the client is in great distress because of an incomplete session. This is a good time to assess the client's potential for high-level disturbance and to schedule a telephone appointment to check on his progress, if necessary.

The clinician should keep in mind the cautions and guidelines covered in earlier chapters and rely on her own assessment of the client and level of disturbance; there is no substitute for the clinical judgment of a licensed clinician.

Debriefing and Log

It is important to give a debriefing to each client at the end of each session. However, it is especially important to give a thorough, detailed debriefing if the material has not been fully processed, for there is greater likelihood in this case that the client will continue the processing between sessions at a higher level of disturbance. In order to lessen the client's disturbance, the clinician should tell him that the target will be reaccessed at the next session.

It is important to remind the client at the end of each session to keep a log of any memories, dreams, thoughts, and situations that are in any way disturbing. By keeping such a journal the client will be able to report to the clinician any obvious targets that should be treated. In addition, the clinician may be able to use the journal entries to identify any dysfunctional patterns of behavior that should be targeted.

The client should be told that it is important for him not to proceed too rapidly and that further disturbance is part of the processing. While this is actually the case, this statement also incorporates a paradoxical intervention (Fisch, Weakland, & Segal, 1982) that helps the client to accept any disturbance as part of the healing process. Thus, the client can be happy if no disturbance arises or if some arises. The client's ability to simply "let whatever happens, happen" is an important aspect of the between-sessions condition.

If the debriefing is not properly done, the client may feel fine after a session and assume that she is finished. However, if disturbance then arises between sessions, she may view herself as "damaged goods." Unless appropriate debriefings are given to ensure realistic expectations, clients who have low self-esteem to begin with will look at this as another sign of their failure, and suicidal ideation can arise.

It is vital that the client understand that, regardless of the nature of the disturbance, it simply represents the continuation of the EMDR domino effect. Sometimes images and memories may emerge and sometimes only disturbing emotions. Regardless of the nature of the distress, the client should just jot it down—without making it significant—and then use a relaxation exercise. If the client has any questions, he should call the clinician. A proper debriefing will result in fewer emergency calls (possibly fewer than the clinician has previously experienced). A properly prepared client can observe, rather than succumb to, the distress.

Another reason for requesting that the client keep a log is that it gives him another way to distance himself from the between-session disturbances. By observing his own distress, the client is again tacitly taught that he is larger than the pathology. He is asked to "take a snapshot" of the disturbance by jotting down a short description of what triggered it and of any specific thoughts, emotions, physical sensations, or images that came to mind at the time. This gives him the opportunity to observe his own patterns and responses. In addition, instead of using statements such as "I was afraid," the client is asked simply to identify the components of the fear. This begins to educate him that emotions such as fear, shame, and anger are actually primarily physical sensations that can be described and that can be changed. This educational process is further implemented by asking the client to use a relaxation audiotape or safe-place exercise after writing the information into his log.

It is not necessary for the client to write a great deal in the log; what is needed is only enough information to allow him to bring the circumstances of the disturbance to mind for discussion and possible targeting during the next session. The log can include dreams, past events, present situations, or fears of the future. In order to balance the ledger it is useful to ask the client to note anything pleasant that arises as well. Positive insights are also useful for treatment planning and direction.

Although the clinician may have a list of the client's traumas derived from the history-taking sessions, no new traumatic memories should be targeted until the major reverberations from the old ones have died down. In other words, if the client experiences a number of nightmares obviously linked to the event just processed, the clinician should target them during the next session. If a number of associated images emerge or if the client reports a new perspective on the original target that needs further attention, the clinician should help the client process this before a new trauma is treated. It is important to leave the client in a state of psychological equilibrium. If ramifications of the original target are still disturbing, these should be addressed before processing new trauma material that may cause additional distress. However, if another disturbing memory has just arisen or is now being fixated, it should be addressed as part of the domino effect. The log should be the immediate indicator of the target for the next session.

During the initial stages of EMDR therapy the emphasis is on treating the most dysfunctional memories, which have set the groundwork for the pathology. Along with the history taking, the log reveals the most pertinent targets, including disturbing memories, dreams, and associated incidents. Further uses of the log are reviewed in Chapter 8, which covers the reevaluation phase, the eighth and final phase of treatment. Chapter 8 guides the clinician through the extended application of the EMDR three-stage standard protocol and discusses its appropriate placement in an overall treatment plan.

Some clients will show little or no change from reprocessing in the treatment setting. Nevertheless, the clinician should give the client the appropriate debriefing and the instructions for keeping a log, even if no obvious reprocessing has been accomplished. It is not unusual for a client to be comparatively resistant to in-session treatment but to process the material later. This unexpected processing can be highly disturbing to clients, and clinicians should take care to ensure their safety regardless of the amount of change observed during the session.

Clients should be encouraged to use a stress-control tape daily as an aid to relaxation and as a tool to deal with any disturbing thoughts or emotions that might arise. A guided visualization or relaxation exercise can be a stronger aid for most clients than attempts at unassisted cognitive or behavioral modification. If commercial tapes are not available or acceptable, the clinician can audiotape one of the closure techniques given in Chapter 9 for the client's home use.

Naturally, the client must be told to be prepared for any shift in emotions or, conversely, for no change at all. The clinician should attempt to instill in the client a sense of acceptance and objectivity ("Just let it happen and merely observe") so that changes are neither sought nor forced between sessions. For many clients the time between sessions is a period of additional insights; for others it may be a time of chaotic feelings and emotions. While the clinician may hope for signs of successful processing by way of new insights or behaviors, if the client is given false or undue expectations, any therapeutic benefit is likely to be undermined. The general tone used is summed up in the following example of what the clinician might say to the client:

"**Things may come up or they may not. If they do, great. Write them down, and they can be a target for next time. If you get any new memories, dreams, or situations that disturb you, just take a good snapshot. It isn't necessary to give a lot of detail. Just put down enough to remind you so we can target it next time. The same thing goes for any positive dreams or situations. If negative feelings do come up, try not to make them significant. Remember, it's still just the old stuff. Just write it down for next time. Then use the tape or safe-place exercise to let as much of the disturbance go as possible. Even if nothing comes up, make sure to use the tape every day and give me a call if you need to.**"

While this concludes an individual EMDR session, EMDR treatment is not complete without attention to the reevaluation phase discussed in Chapter 8. EMDR is not a one-session therapy, and the clinician should treat a client only when arrangements have been made for appropriate follow-up and assessment of potential needs. Even if the client appears to have successfully reprocessed a single-event trauma that was the stated reason for seeking therapy, another session should be scheduled for the following week. Without a follow-up appointment, the client will be more apt to feel like a failure if new aspects of the memory arise that need to be treated; he may feel too discouraged to seek further assistance. Therefore, the clinician should frame the next appointment as an integral part of treatment. Most clients can readily accept the need to complete EMDR's eight phases if the clinician compares it to the need to finish a prescribed bottle of antibiotics.

SUPERVISED PRACTICE

Before clients are treated, clinicians are advised to work with a trained EMDR instructor in supervised small groups to practice the information covered to this point by targeting old memories whose level of disturbance is expressed as a 5 on the SUD Scale. Once the clinician is comfortable treating this level of disturbance, practice should be done using the following chapters as a guide for treating more disturbing memories, for instance, those that are rated as a 7 or higher on the SUD Scale. Once treatment has begun, more disturbing memories have a tendency to start processing and to then become stuck or to produce an abreaction response. Of course, the clinician should remember that targets that seem quite innocuous at first can rapidly shift into more disturbing material and should therefore ensure that the appropriate clinical safeguards are taken.

SUMMARY AND CONCLUSIONS

The phases of accelerated reprocessing are the desensitization, installation, and body scan phases. Although these designations offer useful divisions, a lessening of disturbance, a restructuring of positive attributions, and a decrease in body tension are part of the whole reprocessing effect.

During the desensitization phase the clinician gives attention to "cleaning out" the channels of dysfunctional information associated with the target. The assessment tool is the 0-to-10 SUD Scale. At the end of this phase the client should be able to concentrate on the target event with a SUD score of only 0 or 1.

The installation phase links the most adaptive positive cognition to the original target and aims for a validity rating of 6 or 7 (or more if it continues to strengthen) on the VOC Scale. It is important that the clinician's assessment of the client's level of validity take into consideration his current life circumstances, that is, that it be ecologically valid. Any blocking beliefs revealed during this phase will need to be addressed with a separate treatment directed at the memories that laid the groundwork for the dysfunction.

The body scan asks the client to assess mentally the presence of any residual physical sensations while the target event and the positive cognition are held in consciousness. The sensations will be processed with additional sets, which may reveal other channels of dysfunctional information, including fears, anger, sadness, or resistance to change. A completed treatment includes a body scan that reveals no tension or associated sensations.

At the end of the session the clinician should make an adequate assessment of the client's safety, including his ability to leave the office and to handle any emotional disturbance that may subsequently arise. It is essential that adequate debriefing take place regarding the use of a log and relaxation tape, both of which allow the client to observe, rather than be caught up in, any new material that emerges, both within and between sessions. If clients become too overwhelmed or lose their sense of being ultimately in control of the process, they may terminate treatment prematurely. In addition to the safe-place exercise described in the previous chapter, appropriate closure exercises are described in Chapter 9. The final phase of treatment, the reevaluation phase, places the individual reprocessing session in the context of the overall treatment plan (the reevaluation phase is covered in Chapter 8).

Clinicians new to EMDR should use the material in this book in a supervised practicum with a trained EMDR instructor. Initial use should be on circumscribed old memories rated at no higher than a 5 on the SUD Scale. Events of higher disturbance than this often need a greater amount of clinical intervention (see Chapter 7) and should not be attempted until clinicians are comfortable with the basic components of EMDR. For information on authorized EMDR trainings, including graduate school programs, and the availability of training consultants, consult Appendix C. Many facets of EMDR treatment, including cues for the appropriate timing of successive sets, can only be conveyed in person; the better qualified the instructor, the better prepared the clinician will be.

This chapter covers the standard clinician–client interaction and the fundamental EMDR procedure. Advanced methods and variations are addressed in the following chapters. Various clinical aids, including a list of negative and positive cognitions, are found in Appendix A.

• • •

CHAPTER 7

Working with Abreaction and Blocks

Our work is to keep our hearts open in hell.
Stephen Levine

This chapter presents strategies for reprocessing sessions with especially challenging clients. As these approaches are incorporated into phases four through six, I have placed this chapter here, rather than proceeding with our exploration of the final phase of the EMDR treatment–reevaluation.

As discussed in the previous chapter, some EMDR clients report a consistent reprocessing effect while focusing on a single picture, whereas others report a variety of other associations stemming from the original target. At the end of each set, the clinician must guide the client by instructing her either to maintain awareness of the emerging material or to shift her attention to something different. In addition, the clinician may need to help the client determine what aspect of the target to focus on during the next set or to help her formulate a new target.

The choices the clinician will be called on to make are decided moment by moment as the effects of each set are observed. Approximately 40% of the time the alignment of the standard components (image, cognition, body sensation), together with the eye movements, will allow full processing to take place. In the remainder of cases, a number of alternative procedural strategies are necessary for therapeutic effectiveness.

The challenges to which this chapter is devoted include clients who are abreacting with a high level of disturbance and situations in which the processing stops prematurely. Each EMDR therapy session is unique in the kinds of subjective experiences displayed by the client. However, clinical observations over thousands of treatment sessions indicate that certain generalizations can be made regarding successful therapeutic interventions.

This chapter begins with a discussion of procedural strategies that are useful during abreactive responses. As defined previously, abreactions are the reexperiencing of stimulated material at a high level of disturbance. The section on abreaction covers a number of important clinical considerations and the decision points necessary for adequate processing. The second half of the chapter includes instructions for dealing with clients whose processing has stopped despite successive sets of multidirectioned eye movements.

Clients with high levels of disturbance should not be treated until the clinician is familiar with the strategies described in this chapter. More advanced methods will be covered in Chapter 10, but these should not be attempted until the clinician has adequately practiced and is comfortable with the material presented here. Suggestions for appropriate practice sessions will be offered at the end of the chapter.

ABREACTION

An abreaction is considered a normal potential part of the integrative emotional and cognitive processing of any given target. Clinicians should not view abreaction as either mandatory or unnecessary but should accept it, if present, as an integral part of the client's subjective response during the processing of the dysfunctional information.

The clinician should remember (and should remind the client in appropriate language) that the targeted memories are considered to be information packages, which are stored in the nervous system with the original perceptions and are held intact in state-specific form. When memories are stimulated, the client may notice both the sensory cues that were originally perceived and the thoughts that were occurring at the time of the event. In addition, the physical sensations and emotions that are part of the information about the targeted incident may also be stimulated. Clients may experience these with an intensity that can range anywhere from a duplication of the original experience to a mere shadow of it.

The focus of the EMDR session is the targeting and accessing of the stored dysfunctional information. Because the information is stimulated, the original unmetabolized perceptions will be brought to some degree of consciousness. When these are experienced at a high level of disturbance, an abreaction is said to have occurred. However, since we make no assumptions about the level of intensity necessary for sufficiently processing a targeted memory, the client should not be encouraged to force an abreaction or to suppress one. The clinician's ongoing message to clients should simply be "Let whatever happens, happen." Attempting to force the client to conform to any clinical standard will be detrimental to full therapeutic efficacy.

It is important to note the specific way that EMDR defines abreaction because the term has different meanings for different clinicians. While abreaction as EMDR defines it includes a high level of disturbance, it does not include the element of dissociation usually seen in hypnotic abreactions. When properly used, EMDR does not bring on full flashbacks, because the client is coached to have a dual focus, namely, an awareness of the past and a feeling of safety in the present. In addition, unlike hypnosis, the EMDR abreaction does not continue moment by moment in a "real time" reliving of the event. (Even in cases of induced time distortion the hypnosis client will generally go through each instant of the event sequentially.) However, the consensus of clinicians trained in both clinical hypnosis and EMDR is that the EMDR abreaction moves four to five times more rapidly than in hypnosis, with the client appearing to jump from one key element of the event to another. Since the processing appears accelerated in EMDR, these sessions can resolve traumas comparatively quickly.

Clinicians must take great care during the abreaction to maintain the client's sense of safety. The clinician must also be comfortable with displays of intense emotion. Any fear or distaste the clinician might have for the client's response is likely to be communicated by tone of voice and nonverbal signals. The client's need for unconditional regard and support is evident throughout EMDR work, but it is especially important during times of abreactions.

It is essential for the clinician to remember that stimulating target memories allows the emotions that were locked in at the time of the event to surface. For example, while the client may be 40 years old at the time of treatment, the emotions felt may well be those of a child. Thus, the helpless terror of a 4-year-old during a molestation or physical assault may be reexperienced in all its original intensity. A client who has tried to deny, wall off, or suppress these powerful emotions for 35 years must be made to feel that it is safe to experience them in the clinician's presence. This is especially important since feelings of self-denigration and self-blame, which are often inherent in the earlier experience, may be stimulated during EMDR. It is the clinician's job to help the client to process old material without fear of rejection or negative judgments.

Any clinician who finds strong emotional responses distasteful should not use EMDR, regardless of how innocuous the clinical presentation may seem. The cause of many apparently straightforward present disturbances is one or more quite traumatic earlier life events. Therefore, regardless of the clinician's expectation, targeting the present dysfunction may cause the client to shift spontaneously to an earlier memory at full abreactive intensity. If the clinician has not prepared her for this, the client may try to suppress her emotional response, which may cause retraumatization.

Guidelines for Facilitating Abreaction

The guidelines in this section can help clinicians facilitate client progress through an abreaction. Some will be familiar to clinicians already skilled in abreactive work with other methods, whereas others are specific to EMDR processing. For clinical balance and client comfort, it is useful to keep in mind the following fourteen points:

1. *EMDR is not causing the client's distress; it is simply releasing it.* The targeted event has been the source of continuous dysfunction in the client's life. It is the root of the presenting complaint, and the negative emotions inherent within the experience have been triggered repeatedly (either consciously or below the conscious threshold) since the event occurred. An abreaction during EMDR processing is a sign that the dysfunctional material is being metabolized.

2. *An abreaction has a beginning, middle, and end.* Clinical observations have indicated that EMDR allows processing of abreactions to occur at an accelerated rate, indeed, much more rapidly than hypnotically induced abreactions. While the client may be experiencing high levels of disturbance, the abreaction will certainly not last as long as the original experience; the client's distress should begin to subside dramatically within the first 20 minutes. In most instances, the traumatic memory will be substantially processed within a 90-minute session.

3. *In most instances, the abreaction is occurring as the information is being processed.* Therefore, as the abreaction is successfully completed, the source of the dysfunction is simultaneously resolved. EMDR abreactions are not the same as reactions to flooding, which must be repeated a number of times for therapeutic effect (Keane & Kaloupek, 1982). While the clinician may have seen clients become extremely disturbed during conventional therapies whenever a childhood trauma or recent assault was discussed, those emotions were signs of the triggered disturbance and indicated the dysfunction; in contrast, an abreaction induced by EMDR is a sign of the transformation of the disturbing material and should therefore be viewed as a sign of emerging health. This is not to say that one abreactive session will necessarily resolve the entire trauma. But if the information is processing, that extreme level of distress will generally not reemerge in subsequent sessions.

4. *The clinician should maintain a position of detached compassion in relation to the client.* If the clinician becomes immersed in the disturbing emotions or horror of the traumatic event, she may overlook important decision points and interventions. The client relies on the clinician to provide emotional stability and a sense of safety during the abreaction. On the other hand, the client also needs compassion; he will not be well

served if the clinician shows cold indifference to his evinced level of suffering.

Finding the balance necessary for optimal clinical support in the face of pronounced distress may be difficult for clinicians who are used to more cognitive interventions. It may be useful for these clinicians to recall a time when they offered support to a family member who was in pain. In order to help, they had to be understanding and compassionate while simultaneously using sound judgment. Some clinicians versed in hypnosis or guided imagery prepare themselves for intense sessions by visualizing the client surrounded by a "healing light" and themselves surrounded by a protective "golden bubble." For other clinicians, remembering the preceding three points of this list can help maintain a balanced detachment.

5. *To increase the client's sense of safety, follow the "golden rule" of "Do unto others . . ."* That is, the clinician should ask himself what kind of support he would want if he were suddenly flooded with the emotions and physical sensations of childhood terror. The answer will probably reveal the importance of something that conveys an atmosphere of nurturing and trust and makes him feel that it is safe to proceed. On the basis of this assumption, the client should be continually reassured that the clinician is calm, caring, unsurprised by the content of the abreaction, supportive of its manifestation (regardless of how intensely expressed), and responsible for the safety of the situation. This stance allows the client simply to notice the material as it arises in consciousness and to "let whatever happens, happen."

In order to create and maintain this atmosphere, the clinician should reassure the client during each set in a tone of voice that is both soothing and supportive. Using expressions such as "That's it" and "Good," encouraging the client to "just notice," and reminding him during sets that what he is experiencing is "just the scenery" can give the client the courage and reassurance that EMDR is progressing as expected.

Because clients can observe the clinician's reactions with their peripheral vision, the clinician should maintain an expression of calm, sympathetic support throughout the processing. As mentioned previously, any nonverbal indication of fear, disgust, or displeasure on the part of the clinician can be detrimental to the client's sense of safety and may severely limit his ability to complete processing.

6. *Before treatment, clients should be reminded that they are safe in the present.* To allay fears of experiencing the traumatic event, it is important for clients to remember that any disturbance they are experiencing is being caused by the "old stuff" and that they are no longer in danger. Clinicians should remind them that different aspects of the targeted event can be observed and controlled in the same way that a videotape

can be seen and controlled on a TV screen as the VCR operates: It is as if the client is the one who holds the controls of the VCR, for when she signals the clinician by holding up her hand or turning her head away, the clinician will halt the eye movements and the "movie" will stop. The intention is to allow the client to feel the experience fully while still maintaining a sense of control.

It is also helpful for clients to remember the metaphor of the train ride, where the client is the passenger and the "old stuff" is the scenery. Even though the client may experience emotions and physical sensations, as well as images, it is helpful to think of this as just the scenery passing by. The client should remember that even as he notices this scenery, the train has already safely passed.

Another useful metaphor, mentioned previously, likens EMDR to driving a car through a tunnel. To get through the tunnel quickly, we need to keep our foot on the accelerator. The accelerator in EMDR treatment is the eye movement (or other form of stimulation), which seems to speed up the processing of the information. If we take our foot off the accelerator, the car will slow down and it will take longer to get through the tunnel. Therefore, to get through the discomfort, the client should keep her eyes moving as much as possible.

It is important to inform clients that even if they begin to cry, it is useful to keep their eyes open and continue the eye movements so that processing can go on. If they cannot keep their eyes open, the other forms of stimulation can be substituted. However, it is mandatory that clients be told that they can stop the processing at any time by using hand or head signals. As usual, clinicians should honor those signals immediately.

7. *It is vital that the clinician read the client's nonverbal cues to determine whether the disturbing information has reached a new plateau and the set can be ended.* Ideally, the goal of each set is to move the client from one plateau of information to a new plateau with greater therapeutic validity. Clinicians can observe the achievement of a new plateau when the client reveals (nonverbally) either a new insight or a dramatic decrease in level of suffering. The nonverbal indicators may be changes in eye movement, facial tension, body posture, breathing rate, or facial color. Changes of this sort should be pointed out to clinicians during practice sessions supervised by an experienced EMDR instructor.

Although nonverbal cues are good indicators of new plateaus, the clinician should not stop the set immediately. New plateaus appear to manifest themselves physically before clients are able to make the conscious/cognitive connection. Therefore, the clinician should continue the set for 5 to 10 seconds after noticing the change in facial expression in order to allow the information to become integrated. Figuratively speaking, the clinician should allow the client time to climb up and onto the new plateau. Keep in mind, however, that the climb may be too long and arduous to complete during any one set.

8. *Clients' nonverbal cues should also be used to ascertain if the set should be ended before a new plateau is achieved.* While the transmutation of information appears to occur at an accelerated rate during the stimulation sets, clinical observation has indicated that the amount of time between sets is of great importance. The following are reasons for breaking the stimulation into sets, rather than administering one continuous sequence:

a. To provide an opportunity for client feedback, that is, to assess whether processing has actually occurred.
b. To enable the client to integrate the new information on a verbal/conscious level.
c. To allow the client to experience any new revelations shared with and reaffirmed by the clinician.
d. To reorient the client to the sense of present time and consequent safety.
e. To provide the client with a rest so she can endure the physical stimulation of an abreactive response.
f. To reinforce the notion that the client is larger than and in control of the abreaction through his ability to enter and exit the disturbance at will.
g. To allow the client to reassure herself of the clinician's ongoing encouragement.
h. To allow the clinician to judge the need for additional clinical interventions.

The length of the rest period after a set is determined by the needs of the individual client, although this will probably differ from one set to another. The clinician should never reengage the eye movements if the client still needs reassurance and stabilizing. It is also important to remember that processing continues during the rest period, albeit at a slower rate. For this reason, clinicians should watch clients carefully to ascertain whether an abreaction is starting again; if so, the sets should be resumed.

9. *The clinician should reinforce the client's dual focus of attention.* Clinicians should remind clients to remain aware of the information being processed internally while they simultaneously attend to any stimuli presented by the clinician. In this way, clients can allow the information from the past to be accessed and stimulated while remaining conscious of their current safety (and the current task). On a physiological level, this dual focus of attention may alter the stereotypical trauma response and aid in the therapeutic adaptation. On a conscious level, the dual awareness allows the client to maintain a sense of the present along with a connection to the resources of the therapist.

This can increase the client's ability to withstand the emotional turmoil of the abreaction.

In addition to providing verbal reassurances, the clinician can enhance the client's connection to present time by purposely changing the direction and speed of the eye movements. For clients to be able to follow the eye movements during an abreaction, the clinician may have to make slower movements or cover a shorter range. When a client is crying or showing other signs of high emotional disturbance, the clinician may need to alter the eye movements to make it easier for the client to follow the external focal point. Many clients cannot maintain the full bilateral eye movement during strong disturbance and may falter if the clinician attempts to speed up the movements. Take special care not to instill a sense of failure in clients because of their inability to attain the usual speed or range of motion.

In addition, if eye movements become too predictable, the client may anticipate them and perform them mechanically while directing her full attention to the dysfunctional material. This is detrimental to processing and should be avoided by altering the speed of the eye movements during the set. Thus, by following the clinician's lead in slowing down and then speeding up her eye movements, the client is forced to remain conscious of the present environment. Changing the direction of the eye movement randomly from one set to the next (but not within an individual set) can also have this effect. Of course, the clinician should be sure to use only directions of movements that facilitate change for a given client. Remember that some clients will not process at all with certain directions of eye movements. It is important for the client to try to process the maximum amount of information possible during each set while maintaining a state of psychological equilibrium in order to feel encouraged to continue.

10. *During the abreaction, clinicians should treat a sense of dissociation as they would any other layer of emotion that presents itself to be metabolized.* Many clients dissociated at the time of the original trauma and report seeing the event as if they were "up on the ceiling." When this happens during EMDR processing, the clinician should be able to discern the true nature of the apparent dissociation as one of the following possibilities: (a) the old feeling of dissociation that arises from the target memory and that will be metabolized by the sets, (b) a new dissociation that is being triggered because the client has been pushed too far, or (c) a dissociation that is the product of an undiagnosed dissociative disorder.

The latter two antitherapeutic dissociative possibilities have been discussed in Chapters 4 through 6, and pains should have been taken to avoid them. If they still occur, the clinician must stop the reprocessing immediately and take corrective action. If, however, the problem is the old dissociation, the clinician should ask the client to notice the relevant physical sensations and sense of dissociation and should assist her to stay in the present as processing continues. This can be achieved by (a) saying things like "Stay with me" or "You're safe now"; (b) using cadence sounds, such as "Yes, yes," in unison with finger movements to facilitate forceful eye movement; (c) asking the client to pound on the arms of the chair in unison with the eye movement; or (d) asking the client to relate what is occurring in the memory being processed while doing the eye movements.

11. *Clinicians can try to decrease the client's disturbance by inviting him to engage in certain visual manipulations of the target memory.* Emotional distancing strategies that clinicians may use include asking the client to (a) change the memory into a still photo, (b) change the memory into a black-and-white videotape, (c) imagine the child victim holding the hand of her adult self, (d) place a protective glass wall between the self and the event, and (e) place a protective glass wall between the self and the perpetrator, who is placed at a great distance. As the processing continues in this last case, the perpetrator is slowly brought toward the victim, with the glass remaining in place (Wolpe & Abrams, 1991).

However, for several reasons, clinicians should stay alert to the need for additional strategies: First, not all clients are capable of the visual control necessary to make these adjustments; second, visual control can be lost during a set, allowing the level of disturbance to rise again; third, if visual manipulation is used, it will eventually be necessary to return to the original image in order to reprocess any information that may remain in state-dependent form. The purpose of the visual manipulation is to find a vantage point from which the client can observe the memory with a lower level of disturbance. Also inherent in the client's ability to manipulate the memory is the notion that the client is larger than the disturbance and is actually in control. Remember, however, that visual manipulation is used as a transition device. Ultimately, the target information must be fully processed. This situation will be covered more thoroughly in the next section of this chapter, which deals with blocked processing.

12. *To ensure the greatest possible emotional stability, the clinician should encourage clients to make whatever personal arrangements are necessary for the session or afterward.* For instance, many clients choose to (a) have a loved one pick them up after the session or (b) bring with them a special object—such as a book, stuffed animal, or talisman—to give them a greater sense of safety. Pets are not appropriate, however, since they may be disruptive to the processing, particularly if they sense the client's disturbance. It is also not usually helpful to have other people present during the processing session because of the possibility of distraction, therapeutic splitting, or nonsupportive dynamics.

In order to reassure the client during disturbing processing, it is appropriate for the clinician to leave one hand available for the client to grasp if an additional sense of connection or stability is needed. However, it is strongly advised that the clinician not move to take the client's hand or touch him in any way during an abreaction, since such acts may feed into the sense of violation caused by the perpetrator or the trauma itself. Remaining available to a client's expressed desires is quite different from intruding, which can lead to retraumatization.

13. *Clinicians should change to auditory stimuli or hand taps, if appropriate.* In some instances, the client is unable to maintain processing with eyes open due to fear because of an association of hand movement to prior abuse, or because of uncontrollable sobbing. When the client's eyes cannot track, the clinician should attempt to use either rhythmical tones or hand taps. Great care should be taken when using these alternate stimuli during an abreaction because they make it harder to notice whether the client is dissociating. One advantage of the eye movements is that the clinician is able to see when the client is beginning to associate too fully with the internal material because the eyes stop tracking. However, for some clients, the hand taps appear to titrate the intensity of response and thereby enable processing to continue when the disturbance is too high for adequate eye-movement tracking. The importance of nonverbal cues is critical in this case, and the clinician must decide whether processing is continuing from set to set.

14. *When the client is not processing information, despite the use of eye movements, hand taps, or auditory stimuli, the clinician should use strategies designed to deal with "blocking."* A common form of blocking during abreactions is "looping." In this situation, instead of steadily progressing from one plateau to another (or indicating no change), the client is cycling around on the same plateau of information. Looping reveals itself when clients evidence a high level of abreactive distress and report that the same emotions, sensations, images, and so forth, are recurring in successive sets. Sometimes there is a slight decrease of distress, followed by an immediate return to the same round of negative thoughts and emotions. Clinicians should use the various strategies offered in the next section to restimulate processing during blocking. Clients who are looping will generally need the strategies covered in Chapter 10.

If Abreaction Persists

If all of the foregoing suggestions and those covered in the following section on blocked responses have been tried during an abreaction and have met with failure, the clinician new to EMDR should use the safe-place exercise (see Chapter 5) or one of the closure procedures described in Chapter 9 to disengage. The more proactive version of EMDR, which is needed to continue processing, is given in Chapter 10.

However, remember that this book is to be used initially as a textbook with practice sessions supervised by a trained EMDR instructor. The more proactive version of EMDR should be attempted only after the clinician has become practiced and adept in the EMDR variations reviewed in the present chapter.

STRATEGIES FOR BLOCKED PROCESSING

The strategies offered in the rest of this chapter can assist the clinician to restimulate processing that has become stuck. Those listed in the next section, entitled Primary Target, maintain the client's concentration on manifestations of the original target. The suggestions given in the section entitled Ancillary Targets for Blocked Processing focus on contributing factors that may be causing the block. These factors should be explored because continued client distress may indicate the need to reprocess different material before returning to the original target; they should be used if the strategies in the earlier section have been unsuccessful in activating processing. However, the clinician should stay alert to the possibility that alternative strategies from both these sections may be necessary for a given session.

Primary Target

This section offers variations in procedure that the clinician may use to direct a shift in client focus regarding the immediate target when the reprocessing effect appears to have ceased. The clinician should assume that processing has stopped when the information has not reached the appropriate desensitization level but is unchanged after two consecutive sets.

As will be explained shortly, the first two technical variations are a change in the eye movements themselves and a concentration on only the body sensations. If these variations prove ineffective, additional strategies are required. The underlying principle is to "jump-start" the brain by asking the client to deliberately shift consciousness in a way that typically occurs spontaneously when processing is successful. These suggestions are the product of many hours of clinical observation, but the list is not exhaustive. After developing expertise with EMDR, clinicians should feel free to add new variations from their own clinical experience.

Keep in mind that the more proactive version of EMDR will be necessary for some clients, particularly those who dissociate. This version, described in Chapter 10, should be used only after working with the more basic version of EMDR for at least 8 weeks (or approximately 50 sessions) following appropriately supervised practice. To use the proactive version of EMDR effectively, the clinician will need enough practice to become comfortable implementing the information in Chapters 4 though 9 and enough experience to obtain a general sense of the client response baseline. Clinicians not meeting this criteria should terminate the session with appropriate closure if a blocked client does not resume processing after all of the variations in this chapter are tried and should switch to other forms of treatment until they have had supervised practice in using the proactive version.

The following variations are listed in the order of their utility. In all cases of blocked processing, the change in eye movement and attention to body sensation should be tried first.

Altering the Eye Movement

If the client's response remains the same after two eye movement sets, the clinician should change the direction, length, speed, or height of the eye movements, gradually moving up and down in a horizontal plane. Combinations of changes may prove to have the greatest success.

Focusing on Body Sensation

Body sensations may be a manifestation of the affect or physical sensations experienced at the time of the event. Some of the most useful strategies for restarting processing involve attending to various aspects of sensation, as explained in the following paragraphs.

All Sensation. Clinicians should ask clients to drop the image and the thoughts and to focus primarily on their bodies and should direct them to concentrate on the attendant physical sensations while the eye movement sets are systematically altered.

The Primary Sensation. If processing does not resume and the client reports many body sensations, she should be directed during the next set to concentrate on the most pronounced sensation, again without image or cognition.

Unspoken Words. Certain kinds of body tension can indicate the need to voice unspoken words, that is, the cries or statements the client held back during the trauma or in childhood during abuse. When clients appear to be experiencing emotions of anger or betrayal (or physical sensations congruent with these states), the clinician should ask them to say whatever they want out loud or to themselves. This is particularly useful if the client reports tension in the jaw or throat, since cries for help or of anger are often choked back for fear of reprisal.

Once the client is prompted to verbalize these unspoken words and focus on them in the next sets, processing can resume at the former accelerated rate.

The clinician must be careful to maintain a supportive and encouraging demeanor, regardless of the client's words. When intense pockets of rage are tapped, clients may visualize or describe horrendous atrocities toward the perpetrator. Clinicians should assure clients that these feelings are natural and that it is much better to let them out than to keep them bottled up. It is essentially the powerlessness of childhood rage (or the frustration of adult rage) that has finally been tapped. The clinician should communicate that the client's verbalization carries no moral stigma and will do no damage. Therefore, regardless of what the client says to the (imagined) perpetrator (e.g., "I'll cut you up"), the clinician should act as a cheering squad for the verbalization itself. By continuing the sets, the anger and fear that suppressed the no longer unspoken words can be resolved. Obviously, the clinician will need to debrief the client before the end of the session about his present feelings and proposed actions. It is vital that the clinician discourage the client from attempting a confrontation with the perpetrator if the old material has not finished processing.

There are many options for clients to speak these unspoken words out loud or to themselves either during or between sets. If the client verbalizes between sets, her statements should be mentally rehearsed during the next set. They should be repeated with successive sets until they are said firmly and without fear. While it is preferable for the clinician to hear such statements himself to judge their timbre and volume for a sense of resolution, the client may be too inhibited to make a statement out loud. If so, she should be asked to verbalize internally during the set and to use the hand signal that indicates the desire to stop when she is finished. The clinician should extend the set until the hand signal is given. The client should then be asked how she feels, and her response should tell the clinician whether repeated verbalization and more sets are needed. In addition, clinicians can assist clients to state their declarations strongly by asking them first to mouth, then whisper, and then vocalize the statements in a progressively louder voice with each successive set.

This powerful intervention can greatly enhance the clinical treatment. By this means, the abuse victim is often able for the first time to make a declaration of independence from a parent or perpetrator. It is important, however, that the client's statements evolve from the helpless fear of childhood into an adult perspective that includes the appropriate placing of responsibility (i.e., on the perpetrator) and an understanding of present safety. The statements and the sets should continue until the client feels both justification and conviction without fear or self-blame.

Using Movement. As noted before, physical sensations can be a manifestation of affect or simply the sensations experienced at the time of the target event. For instance, during experiences involving fear or anger the client may have inhibited certain body reactions, such as striking out at someone. Therefore, when the client feels tension in any area of the body, indicating, for example, that it was suppressed during the original experience, he should be encouraged to act out the associated movement, such as striking out.

One client whose processing was blocked reported great feelings of anger at her father for humiliating her at her prom, and as she talked of it her hands and arms became very tense. Because it was clear that her hands were curling into fists, she was urged to punch out if she felt so inclined. The sets were repeated as she punched out in front of her and processing resumed.

This manifestation of physical sensation is similar to the unspoken words phenomenon. With both, the principle is to allow the stored information to be adequately processed, which includes a stimulation of the suppressed emotions, statements, and physical actions. Allowing these to be vented during the sets appears to increase the rate of processing. However, clients should feel safe enough within the therapeutic alliance to express anything that emerges, because trying to suppress the material can cause retraumatization. The only restriction is the client's agreement not to injure herself or the therapist during reprocessing. This strategy has proved successful, even with the most explosive veterans in Veterans Affairs Medical Centers.

Pressing the Location. When processing appears stuck and the primary manifestation is a body sensation that will not shift and there are no attendant thoughts or images, it can be useful to have the client physically press his fingers into the location of the sensation. Increased pressure will often cause the emergence of an image or thought about an associated memory, which should then be targeted (Martinez, 1991). The clinician can achieve the same results with many clients by simply asking them to close their eyes and fix their entire attention on the location of the sensation. Whatever image or thought appears should then be targeted. If nothing emerges, it may be useful to return to the original target for processing.

Scanning

Once again, if processing stops, the clinician should specifically instruct the client to change the focal point of the next set. Successful processing will often involve a variety of elements spontaneously coming to consciousness. When blocked material must be artificially stimulated, clients are asked to do deliberately what has been spontaneously generated by other clients. It is presumed that in this way the neurophysiological connections will be made that allow information processing to resume.

Visual Cues. The clinician should ask the client to scan the incident for something that is currently more upsetting than the original target. For instance, when a rape victim is first asked to focus on the most upsetting part of the memory, she might concentrate on seeing the moment of vaginal penetration. In successful reprocessing, other aspects and events during the rape might spontaneously emerge. However, if the reprocessing effect ceases after the initial scene is targeted and only some of its emotional disturbance has eased after successive sets, the clinician should ask the victim to review the entire rape in her mind to see if she notices another aspect of the event that is particularly disturbing now. At this point the client might report more distress about the attempt at oral penetration. Once identified, this scene is brought into focus for a set. Quite often, this will allow reprocessing to continue and the emotional distress to decrease. The clinician may need to invite the client to shift her visual focus to another part of the memory several times before desensitization is complete. Before installation, the dominant manifestation of the event should be elicited and checked for complete processing by asking the client to return to the original target.

Sound Effects. If reprocessing stops, clients should be invited to search for a sound effect that may be particularly disturbing. Take, for instance, the case of the Vietnam veteran who had awakened to find that his men had released a prisoner so that they could shoot him in the back as he ran into the jungle. During reprocessing, the client's SUD level dropped to 5 but seemed stuck there. When he was asked to scan his memory for a sound effect, he noticed that the sound of the M-16 gunfire seemed to increase his anxiety dramatically. When the clinician asked him to focus on the sound of the rifle alone during the next set, the client's SUD level dropped further. The successful intervention having led to the end of a channel, the client was asked, as per the usual procedure, to return to the original target for further processing.

Dialogue. Another aspect of the memory that may not have emerged spontaneously and that may have to be sought is the dialogue that occurred during the event. When clients who are targeting a memory of physical abuse are invited to scan for what was said, they often find that it is the verbal abuse that is now significant. By focusing on the perpetrator's words and their own physical reactions, clients can reactivate the processing during subsequent sets.

Alterations

When strategies in which the client concentrates directly on the perceived memory are unsuccessful, the clinician may ask him to alter his focus of attention or the target itself. For instance, having the client imagine the event or its associated aspects in a different way (see the following paragraphs) during the sets may restimulate processing. Clinicians have not reported problems for clients when the target memory is retrieved after treatment is completed. Clients still know what actually happened, regardless of the alterations they made (whether deliberately or spontaneously) during processing. However, as always, the clinician should eventually ask the client to return to the original target for final reprocessing.

Appearance of Image. Attempting to alter the image itself can allow processing to resume. Some clients in EMDR treatment can successfully restimulate processing by making the image brighter, smaller, or more distant, or by changing it to black and white. Once again, this involves asking the client to do something deliberately that happens spontaneously during EMDR for others. The clinical caution is that clients must have good visualization control to implement this alteration and that the original manifestation of the memory, without the superimposed distortion, should be retargeted to effect full reprocessing. Often the image distortion will shift spontaneously back to its original form during subsequent sets. Whether it is retrieved spontaneously or deliberately, the original image will usually generate much less disturbance once the altered image is sufficiently desensitized.

No Action. Another strategy of visual alteration is to request the client to visualize the perpetrator (or other person causing distress) but not his actions. This usually reduces the disturbance and allows processing to resume.

Even when successful processing has been achieved, focusing on the perpetrator but not his actions produces a more complete generalization, particularly with children (see Chapter 11). Perhaps because there are comparatively few associated experiences in the neuro network of a child, asking children to imagine the perpetrator the way he was usually dressed, without focusing on any particular action, produces a rapid generalization effect. This is especially true if the most salient memories have already been processed. For instance, a 5-year-old abuse victim revealed only three traumatic events, all of which were successfully reprocessed. However, she had many more memories, since the abuse had occurred over many months. Because the perpetrator habitually wore a red gown and mask when violating her, the child was asked to envision him simply standing in that attire. She did so while approximately seven eye movement sets were administered. After a single treatment her presenting complaints of bed-wetting and nightmares ceased.

Hierarchy. Another visual alteration is the creation and use of a treatment hierarchy, a procedure that achieved psychological repute by its use in systematic desensitization (Wolpe, 1991). Essentially, clients are asked to make the target event less disturbing by imagining an alteration of it in terms of time or distance (e.g., "Imagine the spider two blocks away rather than on your arm").

Thus, an abuse victim can imagine a glass wall between himself and the perpetrator, or the perpetrator can be made to appear more distant and only gradually brought back to the original location. While initial processing can be successful with these manipulations, be sure to return eventually to the original target so that it can be completely processed without distortion.

Redirecting to Image. When different events have emerged during processing in a particular channel, one specific event may appear to cause a high level of disturbance. In subsequent sets the client may start concentrating on thoughts or feelings about that specific event. Processing continues until the client's feelings or thoughts reach a state of mild disturbance and then will not shift any further. When this occurs, redirect the client's attention to the image of the last significantly disturbing event that emerged. This can reintensify the experience, and processing can resume.

Redirecting to Negative Cognition. As indicated in the last example, an incident may appear initially disturbing, but may then become less upsetting as subsequent tangential thoughts emerge. If processing appears stuck, it may be useful to reintroduce the original negative cognition in conjunction with the image of the last disturbing event. This can restimulate the dysfunctional material and allow it to continue processing.

Adding a Positive Statement. When the processing becomes stuck at a low level of disturbance, the clinician may invite the client to add the statement "It's over" during a set. This often gives the client a greater sense of safety and allows processing to resume. In addition, the clinician can invite the client to introduce the positive cognition during the set. This may prompt spontaneous insights about secondary gain issues, or it may bring up fears about adopting the positive cognition, which must be addressed. In other instances, the SUD level will automatically drop without bringing up additional cognitive material. The positive cognition should be used only with material that is stuck at a low level of disturbance. An attempt to introduce it prematurely, when there is a high level of disturbance, can backfire, leaving the client feeling worse and believing that the positive cognition is not true and probably never will be. Clinical observation indicates that under the usual circumstances EMDR will not allow a false statement to be considered true; in this case, however, the processing itself is stuck and the dominant feelings will generate beliefs on that plateau.

Checking the Positive Cognition. Because clinical reports have indicated that EMDR does not appear to allow the assimilation of untrue, unrealistic, or ecologically invalid material, the clinician should reassess the appropriateness of the positive cognition if a client is not processing appropriately during the installation phase. This reassessment is mandatory if the client begins to become agitated during the sets that focus on the positive cognition. Another reason for increased agitation at this point in processing may be the stimulation of a blocking belief. The investigation of this factor is covered later in this chapter in the section entitled Ancillary Targets.

Return to Target

If the associations appear to stop in a given channel, the clinician should direct the client to return to the target for additional sets. In addition, the final stage of any session includes a return to the target with sets performed to (1) ascertain if there are additional channels of dysfunctional information, (2) inaugurate the installation phase, and (3) complete the session with the body scan.

Since all proposed interventions are exploratory, the clinician should take care to offer each as a possibility rather than as a surefire solution. An open-minded clinical stance is mandatory because each client processes as a unique individual. There is no guarantee that any particular suggestion will be acceptable or appropriate. In addition, when properly applied, EMDR will not allow anything to be incorporated into the client's schema that is contradictory or inappropriate to that client's ecologically valid beliefs. If this is tried, the client will either become more anxious or openly reject the material. It is crucial that clients not be placed in a conflict between their inner perceptions of truth and the demand characteristics of the clinician.

Ancillary Targets

The strategies discussed in this section require an even higher level of clinical acumen and experience in identifying the appropriate target.

As noted earlier, EMDR can only interface with clinical skills, not substitute for them. When a client has not been able to resume processing by shifting focus regarding the target event, there is the possibility that other factors are contributing to the disturbance.

The clinician must identify the problem areas and deal with them by offering the proper reassurances and, when necessary, reprocessing the residual blocks. Sometimes returning to the original target will have to be postponed to another session while in other cases only a few moments will be needed before returning to it. In either situation the client should be reassured that redefining the focus of an EMDR session is part of the overall clinical strategy, just as a long-distance runner would make adjustments for new terrain along a course. The clinician may need to do a closure exercise with clients to be able to discuss any problems that arise and may need to arrange an action plan.

Feeder Memories

Feeder memories are untapped earlier memories that are contributing to the current dysfunction and blocking processing of it. Let us start our discussion of feeder memories by reviewing some background material. The initial history-taking session is used to identify long-standing patterns of client dysfunction and the original events that set them in motion. The suggested EMDR protocol for most presenting complaints (explained in detail in the next chapter) has three stages: first, targeting the original material; second, targeting the present stimuli that elicit the current dysfunction; and, third, incorporating a positive template that will initiate the accelerated learning of healthy new behaviors for appropriate future action. I arrived at this protocol because when I experimented in 1987 with first targeting clients' current dysfunction, I discovered that most people spontaneously remembered earlier experiences during the sets and that those who stayed fixated on the present situation often became more anxious and their processing remained stuck.

Applying the underlying principle that processing can be unblocked by having the client do something deliberately that has already emerged spontaneously during successful processing, I asked those first EMDR clients to scan for an earlier memory that incorporated the negative cognition. Once such a memory was identified and successfully treated, I found that the current dysfunction was much less disturbing and much more amenable to processing than before. Asking the client to find an earlier memory by means of the negative cognition has become an important strategy to unblock processing. It should be one of the first options considered by the clinician when it is necessary to process a client's memories from adulthood.

The client may have no idea that an earlier dysfunction is related to his current experience. In these cases, if the negative reaction to present stimuli is targeted first, the client's disturbance may actually increase and none of the variations previously suggested in this chapter will reduce it. Here's an example:

A client desired an EMDR session to allow her to feel calmer at work, where she had been experiencing great distress whenever her boss got angry with her. After first confirming that her distress was inappropriate (she was not in danger of being fired), the clinician targeted her situation at work. The client reported high levels of anxiety, along with an annoying but unidentifiable sensation in her foot. Despite a targeting of various sensations and the use of several strategies for blocked processing, the client's high level of disturbance remained unchanged. Finally, the clinician asked her to focus on the negative cognition "I am in danger" while scanning her childhood to identify another occasion when anger meant danger. After a few moments she reported a vivid memory of her father angrily throwing her against the refrigerator door. When this memory was targeted, processing began in earnest (the sensation in her foot, where her father had injured her, first increased and then disappeared). Once processing of this memory was completed, the client found the present situation with her boss less disturbing and was able to process it more easily.

While many clinicians will undoubtedly suspect that a client's inappropriate reaction to anger as an adult originated in childhood, at times the genesis of the dysfunction may not be so obvious. The theoretical assumption of EMDR treatment is that any current dysfunctional reaction (with the exception of organically or chemically based pathologies) is always the result of a previous experience, although, of course, not necessarily one from childhood. Obviously, a recent traumatic event (e.g., a natural disaster or car accident) that appears to be the primary complaint should be immediately targeted. However, feeder memories may block processing. While clinicians with a strict behavioral orientation may continue to apply EMDR exclusively to current dysfunctions (and with excellent initial results in many cases), it remains important to scan for a feeder memory when reprocessing appears blocked.

The negative effects of feeder memories can also be seen when a seemingly successful reprocessing of a current situation once again appears disturbing when subsequently retargeted. Because it can be very disturbing and disheartening to have to scan for a feeder memory when processing is blocked or to reprocess a memory that seemed to be successfully treated, the clinician is encouraged to use the standard EMDR protocols and initially treat the earlier memories whenever possible. However, the problem of feeder memories can also arise during the second stage of the protocol (targeting the present stimuli) when early events different from those targeted in the first stage of the protocol prove to be the unexpected source of disturbance.

Clients should be allowed to take the lead in ascertaining the earliest memory. One client wanted to use EMDR to target his anxiety about an anticipated inspection visit by a government agency. The first step the clinician took was to determine if the anxiety was based on consensual reality, since, as noted earlier, EMDR will not remove any emotions that are either appropriate to the situation or an impetus to appropriate action. In other words, if the client was anxious because he was ill-prepared, his justifiable disturbance would not have been amenable to change with EMDR. After determining that the client was fully prepared for the inspection, the clinician began treatment with the negative cognition "I am a failure." This cognition was chosen because the client's anxiety was obviously linked to anticipation of being found inadequate by the inspectors. The client reported a continued feeling of disturbance, which he rated as 8 on the SUD Scale, regardless of the number of EMDR variations used. The clinician then asked him to identify a memory from childhood that had taught him the lesson "I will fail." The client stated that nothing from childhood came to mind but that he did remember a relevant incident in graduate school. After this incident and the negative cognition were targeted in one set, the client remarked, "Oh, there was that time in first grade." Processing that memory led to the client's recognition that he had not failed after all in the childhood incident (he discovered that he had passed the test when the exam papers were returned) and that he had actually been rewarded for the success. When the upcoming inspection visit was retargeted, the client's SUD level was greatly reduced and the remaining distress was easily reprocessed.

As exemplified in these cases, the clinician should instruct clients to locate the earliest available memory to which the negative cognition applies. Scanning childhood memories while thinking of the negative cognition will often reveal the original material needed for effective processing. Clinical skill is necessary, however, because the original negative cognition designated by the client may not actually be the one linked to the earlier memory. For instance, the original negative cognition of the office worker who was unduly upset by her boss's anger might have been chosen to focus on her situation as an adult and been verbalized as "I can't succeed." It would then be the clinician's task to formulate the link between the client's feeling of fear and a possible childhood message.

Another way to access feeder memories is to ask the client to focus on the dominant emotion and physical sensation, to verbalize it, and then to scan for an earlier memory. For example, while the presenting complaint of a client who had a fear of flying was being reprocessed by targeting an actual plane trip, the client's emotion changed and processing ceased. His new emotion and the associated sensations were quite strong. The client offered the negative cognition "I feel inadequate." He was then asked to close his eyes, focus on the physical sensations and the words, and then scan for a time in his childhood when he felt strongly that way. He remembered a time when his mother lamented that he had been born. After reprocessing this memory, his fear of flying, which was associated with a number of contributory control issues, was largely resolved.

When working with blocks due to undiscovered feeder memories, clinicians should be willing to explore a variety of possibilities. Fortunately, EMDR processing effects are so rapid that false avenues are quickly revealed. Keep in mind that feeder memories are an extremely important element in the successful processing of adult targets, whether these are memories or present situations.

Blocking Beliefs

When processing of the initial target is unsuccessful, the clinician should look for negative beliefs that are blocking progress. As indicated in the previous chapter, this can be done by asking the client "What prevents your SUD score from being a zero?" (if the client is in the desensitization phase) or "What prevents your VOC score from being a 7?" (if the client is in the installation phase). Often, clients can identify another negative cognition that should be targeted and are able, after scanning, to designate the appropriate early memory associated with it. Until that identified negative cognition (the "blocking belief") is targeted and reprocessed, progress on the initial target will be halted.

A case in point is a Vietnam veteran who was in treatment for PTSD symptoms. He reported panic attacks three to four times a week, flashbacks every time a plane went overhead, high levels of general anxiety, and relationship avoidance. After assessing the case, the clinician suggested the positive cognition "I can be comfortably in control"; the clinician felt that the client's need for control was high inasmuch as his panic emerged whenever he felt it slipping. The client accepted the positive cognition. Then the negative cognition "I am out of control" was introduced. When the clinician asked the client to target an event that represented this cognition, he described the time his wife had him committed to a mental hospital after the war, a memory that he rated as 10 on the SUD Scale (and was able to process down to 0). However, when the clinician asked him to designate a VOC for the suggested positive cognition, the client responded, "I am not worthy of being comfortably in control." This statement is considered a blocking belief because it prevents the continued processing and resolution of the control issue. Therefore, the clinician asked the client to identify the memory that represented his feelings of lack of worth. The veteran spoke then of a failed sexual encounter with a woman he cared for deeply. That memory was processed from 8 to 0 on the SUD Scale without incident. However, before the VOC could be ascertained, the client spontaneously remarked, "I should probably talk to her about it, but I'll probably fail the way I have with everything else." This was also identified as a negative cognition blocking further resolution, and the client was asked to identify the pivotal memory related to feeling like a failure. The client then revealed a tragic story of being falsely accused of dereliction of duty and causing the death of some soldiers while he was actually performing a heroic act. That memory, with its attendant negative cognition "I'm a failure" was success- fully processed, allowing the positive cognition "I can be comfortably in control" to rise to a 7 on the VOC Scale. The client's PTSD symptoms subsequently declined steadily as he engaged in a number of self-help activities. Within 3 months he was successfully employed and involved in an intimate relationship.

Blocking beliefs may not always be verbalized by clients as clearly as in this case. When processing has ceased, despite a number of variations, the client should be asked to close her eyes, think of the situation, and verbalize any thoughts that emerge. The clinician should carefully assess the client's stream of consciousness for negative self-attributions that are inherent in her musings. Exploring possible interpretations and applica- ble negative cognitions with the client can often reveal a blocking belief, which can then be addressed. When the memory representing the blocking belief has been successfully reprocessed, the client should reac- cess the initial target memory for completion. This should proceed smoothly if the blocks have been sufficiently processed.

Fears

Processing of targeted information also can be blocked by the client's fear of the outcome or of the process itself. First and foremost, the clinician must be sure that the client (1) feels safe and supported in the therapeutic relationship and (2) is not altering or inhibiting the emo- tional or cognitive processing effects.

Fear of the clinical outcome is most likely related to secondary gain issues, such as who or what the client will be forced to confront if therapy is successful. As explained in Chapter 4, all secondary gain issues must be addressed before pronounced therapeutic effects can be achieved. Fear of the process itself can be most easily recognized when the client mentions some element of EMDR or the therapeutic relationship that is problematic for him. For instance, a client may voice a concern about discovering the cause of his disturbance, or about the possibility that his level of distress will alienate the therapist. Regardless of the cause of the block, it must be explored and the client's fears allayed before EMDR resumes. Once the fear is cognitively debriefed, any remnants of the fear itself can be targeted (with the client's permission).

In addition to the client's statements, other indicators of fears that are blocking processing include the following: (1) pronounced tension independent of processed material, such as when a client is upset by the sight of the clinician's moving fingers; (2) consistent stopping during the middle of eye movement sets; (3) difficulty performing the eye movements themselves; and (4) reluctance to engage in EMDR even though previous experiences and clinical outcomes with it have been positive.

The clinician should explicitly explore any of these hesitancies, when present, by specifically questioning the client about the factors causing the problem or preventing a resolution. Any of the indicators just mentioned may be caused by a variety of factors; therefore, the clinician should be exploratory, never adamant. Naturally, the clinician must take care to reassure clients that they are not the problem, that there are simply other conditions that have to be met for therapeutic progress. It may be useful to convey to the client that in one sense all fears are normal because there are understandable reasons for them; the clinical aim is to identify and reprocess those fears that are no longer useful.

Clinicians should be alert to both verbal and nonverbal indicators of fear. Remember that all fears need to be debriefed and the client calmed before processing on the original target can be resumed. During processing, the client may state any of a number of fears, some of which are discussed in the following paragraphs.

Fear of Going Crazy. If the feelings that arise during an EMDR session are extremely intense and confusing, the client may become afraid of being permanently overwhelmed. Clients should be reassured that their emotions are part of their old experiences, which are being metabolized, and that there are no reported cases of EMDR clients going crazy because of the processing. Clients should be reminded of the metaphor of the train ride, of their prerogative to signal the clinician to stop, and of their ability to return to a safe place. They should be encouraged merely to notice the sensations and emotions rather than to judge them or fear them. Clients should be reminded that abreactive responses can be passed through most rapidly if the eye movements are continued, just as one can drive through a tunnel most rapidly by keeping the foot firmly on the accelerator. Once the client feels reassured and gives permission to continue, the clinician should target any residual fear with successive sets until it declines. Then clinician and client should return to the original target.

Fear of Losing the Good Memories. The rapid change in an image during EMDR can sometimes alarm clients. Some respond by saying, "I must be doing something wrong; I can't get the image." Others fear that they will lose all memories of the person or situation associated with the target. For instance, a client being treated for excessive grief over the loss of a loved one may target a tragic circumstance or his loved one in intense suffering. When targeted, these images may become dimmer or more blurry, and the client may fear that if processing is continued, his ability to recall his loved one will be lost.

The client should be assured that there have been no reported cases of EMDR clients losing their memories of good experiences or of people they cared for. In fact, clinical observation indicates that when negative images are processed, positive ones become even more accessible. In addition, the negative event will be remembered even if no image is present, since memory involves more than imagery and is based on a variety of sensory and cognitive factors. EMDR does not cause amnesia. However, an image may fade, just as distant memories do. EMDR simply allows the memory to take its place in the past.

The client can be further reassured by asking him to remember another, more positive, incident involving the loved one and to note that this memory has not changed. Once the client is convinced, processing can resume.

Fear of Change. The fear of change can be the most difficult of all to address clinically because secondary gain issues must be ascertained and reprocessed before the original targets can be reengaged. The clinical difficulty lies in the fact that secondary gain issues may entail a variety of possible, indeed probable, aspects of the expected therapeutic process or outcome, including fears of

- Success
- Failure
- The unknown
- Loss of control
- Loss of identity
- Who or what will need to be confronted if therapy is successful
- Letting go of therapy or the therapist
- Betrayal of parental injunctions
- Disloyalty to parents by becoming unlike them

The major therapeutic difficulty these fears pose is the fact that they may be grounded in old dysfunctional material that should be processed with EMDR but that spread an insidious web that makes the client reluctant to cooperate in the attainment of the therapeutic goal.

The clinician must attempt to identify the dysfunctional beliefs behind the fear of change. Then client and clinician should cognitively explore the areas of resistance. Clinicians should ask clients questions such as "What would happen if you were successful?" and should employ cognitive restructuring, metaphor, and so forth, to debrief them. The clinician should then arrange a hierarchy of negative beliefs that block the client's ability to change; for example, the first fear to be listed might be fear of separation from the therapist, the second one might be fear of failure, and so on. Those fears that can be dealt with by an action plan are addressed first. (For instance, a fear of separating from the therapist can be reasonably handled by appropriate agreements regarding continued therapeutic support.) After identifying the pivotal memories that have contributed to the other negative beliefs, the clinician should seek the client's permission to process them. The importance of identifying these aspects and defusing them in order to attain treatment effects cannot be overemphasized.

It is often those clients who have been engaged in long-term traditional therapy who are the most susceptible to fear of change. One such client, who had been involved in psychodynamic therapy for 25 years, terminated his first EMDR session, which targeted a memory of a parental abuse, by saying, "I can feel it leaving me, and I don't want it to go. I feel there might be a lot more to learn." Such clients often can be recognized by pronounced noncompliance with homework assignments, oververbalization of experiences, and attempts to rigidly control the therapeutic process. Unless their fear of therapeutic change is addressed successfully, the clinical outcome may be negligible.

Clinicians should not assume that long-term or noncooperative clients are the only ones with fears of change. They should always be alert to the possible emergence of these fears during the successful processing of any client. It is not uncommon for fear of change to emerge at some point after a number of major traumatic events have been successfully addressed. Once the most troubling material has been dealt with, the client becomes more aware of the actual environmental factors currently present in his life. Fears of change may emerge as he tries to adjust his behaviors to his new sense of awareness or as he becomes aware of the need to integrate his new sense of self into an apparently dysfunctional family, workplace, or social system. The client may specifically identify these fears in his log report, or the fears may emerge during subsequent processing of new targets. In addition, it is quite possible that any client may report the fear of change as a negative cognition during the installation phase of any session.

If the client reports that the fear of change has emerged during a session, it is possible not only to debrief the fear cognitively but also to target the fear itself by asking "Where do you feel it in your body?" At times, the fear will dissipate without the need to target the original material associated with it. If the client spontaneously remembers the origin of the fear, the memory should, of course, be processed before returning to the initial target. If the fear itself becomes weakened without the original material emerging, the processing can be completed, but the target should be checked the following week for an increase in disturbance. If the therapeutic effect has not been maintained, the fear of change may not have been adequately processed. In this case, the negative cognition associated with the fear should be explored, the present situation analyzed to identify and deal with any appropriate concerns, and the origin of the dysfunction targeted. In all cases, the clinician should view and treat the fear of change and any secondary gain issues as part of the pathology. Remember, however, that some fears are reality based, such as a PTSD-disabled veteran's fear of losing his disability check. These fears must be addressed with an action plan because clinical reports indicate that EMDR will not eliminate anything that is actually true.

Wellsprings of Disturbance

The wellspring phenomenon indicates the presence of a large number of blocked emotions that can be resistant to full processing during standard EMDR treatment. This condition may occur in a variety of individuals who ordinarily would be loath to seek clinical help. These clients may be induced to seek therapy by significant others, but they have no real desire of their own to "get in touch with" their feelings. Included in this group are those who have been forced into therapy by a spouse in order to "save the marriage." An example is the husband who described during an intake interview a terrible legal situation in which his ex-wife was causing continuous disruption and financial difficulties but who nevertheless assigned the situation a SUD rating of only 3. The clinical picture indicated that the husband could not consciously connect with any higher level of disturbance because of early experiences that gave him the message that he was not allowed to feel, that his feelings would be disregarded, and that it was is some way unmanly to have feelings. To consciously experience disturbance at a 7 or 8 SUD level, which would have been appropriate to the situation and more congruent with his testiness and irritable actions at home, this man would require something on the level of a bomb attack during combat.

If sufficient clinical rapport and permission can be established with such clients, the first targets should be the early memories associated with the negative beliefs that block their ability to feel emotions. When these are sufficiently processed, the current experiences will be easier to assimilate. If permission to treat the full clinical picture is not forthcoming and the client insists on dealing only with present circumstances, the clinician can use EMDR to obtain some behavioral shifts and to lessen general tension; however, the SUD level may remain unchanged during the session.

The theoretical assumption is that the negative beliefs are causing the suppression of a high level of disturbance and that these dysfunctional emotions act as a wellspring that continues to feed the present pathology. When the current situations are targeted, the emotions will surface to the maximum level permitted consciously (which such clients are likely to rate as 2 or 3 on the SUD Scale), and the processing will be experienced only at this tolerable range.

The wellspring phenomenon can be recognized clinically when there is a change in the client's insight, imagery, and body sensations, but a continued low level of disturbance is reported. For some clients, no processing effects at all will be evidenced and other treatments should be inaugurated. Clients with this kind of history can be very difficult to work with, and even if full clinical permission is given and early memories are accessed, there may be a need for the proactive EMDR strategies discussed in Chapter 10. (These special populations will be extensively explored in a forthcoming volume on the advanced clinical applications of EMDR.)

SUPERVISED PRACTICE

The strategies presented in this chapter can best be practiced by working in small-group exercises with an intact trauma at a level of disturbance between 7 and 8 on the SUD Scale. Before clinicians try working with clients in the isolation of their office, they should be supervised by qualified EMDR instructors through at least three practica experiences with high-level disturbance.

Clinicians should become thoroughly familiar with the information and protocols covered in the next two chapters and should be comfortable with the standard procedures and strategies. Generally, clinicians should work with EMDR for approximately 50 sessions before attempting the more advanced material in Chapter 10.

SUMMARY AND CONCLUSIONS

Strategic variations of EMDR are needed for the successful processing of especially challenging cases. These can include abreactions and situations in which processing has become stuck.

In EMDR, abreaction is defined as a state in which stimulated material is experienced at a high level of disturbance. Because abreaction is a natural part of processing and integration, clinicians using EMDR must be comfortable with high levels of emotion in their clients. To assure clients that it is safe to have these experiences during a session, clinicians should follow a "golden rule" philosophy, while keeping clients in a dual focus of attention, that is, where they are aware of being in the safety of the present time while they simultaneously direct their attention to the dysfunctional material. The clinician should note the clients' nonverbal signals to ascertain their achievement of information plateaus and to guide successive sets. Processing should continue during periods of dissociation as long as appropriate screening and clinical cautions have been observed. However, variations on standard practice may be needed for abreactive work.

While simple treatment effects may be observed with a minimum of clinical intrusion in about 40% of cases, the clinician's more active assistance will be required in the remainder. When progressive treatment effects are absent for two successive sets, clinicians should first change the direction, length, and speed of the sets. If these attempts are unsuccessful, they should try to open blocked processing by changing the client's focus. This is done by evaluating and redirecting the client's attention to the preparatory material or to the target.

If the client becomes stuck, the clinician asks him to do deliberately what has occurred spontaneously in other clients. This is an open-ended list of possibilities, since clinicians can creatively add more strategies based on their own client observations.

When changing the client's focus of attention to another aspect of the target or to a different memory does not cause processing to resume, the clinician should look at ancillary factors that may be causing the block, such as feeder memories, blocking beliefs, or a need to maintain secondary gains. It is important to remember that EMDR does not function in the absence of clinical skills but, rather, dovetails with them. Inexperienced clinicians should make sure they receive adequate supervision and have consultants available to assist in case formulation and to direct EMDR strategies. Clinicians should combine the material in this and the following chapter to guide them in their next practicum on a target that is rated a 7 or 8 on the SUD Scale. It should be understood, however, that the more proactive version of EMDR (described in Chapter 10) will be necessary for certain clients.

CHAPTER 8

Phase Eight: Reevaluation and Use of the EMDR Standard Protocol

We do not err because truth is difficult to see. It is visible at a glance. We err because this is more comfortable.
Alexander Solzhenitsyn

The final, or reevaluation, phase is vital to EMDR treatment. During this phase, which should open each session after the first, the clinician assesses how well the previously targeted material has been resolved and determines if the client requires any new processing. New targeting may be required for a number of reasons. First, the rapid treatment effects can have immediate repercussions intrapsychically and interactionally. Behavior change resulting from the alleviation of suffering can have unforeseen ramifications for some clients within their family system or social environment. As a result, additional targets may arise. Second, other targets may have been uncovered, those that remained hidden because of the overwhelming nature of the original complaint. To help the client work through the various levels of dysfunction, the clinician should follow the general EMDR protocol, targeting past and current issues and preparing the client for alternative ways of dealing with whatever future issues may arise.

In EMDR therapy each session should always be integrated into a full treatment plan. The reevaluation phase is essential because every human being is a complex individual incorporated into a complex social system. Any profound treatment effect can have significant impact on the person's associated intrapsychic factors and behaviors. These, in turn, will have an impact on the individuals with whom the client interacts, necessitating attention to interpersonal systems issues.

The number of reevaluations will vary from one client to another. A client with a single trauma may require only one reprocessing session, followed by a revaluation phase of one or two follow-up sessions to review the treatment outcome and the log. For multiple-event and long-term trauma survivors, a comprehensive reevaluation will involve targeting, reaccessing, and review over many months of consecutive sessions. Each subsequent reevaluation of the previous sessions' work will guide the clinician through the three stages of the standard EMDR protocol. The final reevaluation will generally conclude with an extensive follow-up period.

The standard three-stage EMDR protocol targets areas of dysfunction from both the past and present and then focuses on alternatives for the future. For example, a survivor of childhood physical abuse will first need to reprocess a large number of early memories. In addition, the people and situations in his life that currently stimulate feelings of intimidation and fear must be targeted. Finally, new ways of socially interacting and standing up for himself will also be targeted. The EMDR treatment may take many months, as will the follow-up reevaluation needed to ensure the client's social integration.

As noted previously, even when working with a single-event trauma, responsible EMDR treatment includes adequate history taking and follow-up, in addition to the reprocessing session(s). Clients should not be treated in a single session, because reprocessed material causes new internal and external interactions. The reevaluation phase requires the clinician to pay close attention to how well the processed information has become integrated within the client and how well the client has become integrated within a healthy social system. The clinician will select subsequent targets based on these findings.

This chapter explores the standard EMDR protocol and the reevaluations that guide the clinical treatment for most trauma victims. The EMDR protocol provides the fundamental blueprint for the treatment of most clients. It delineates the sequence of targets for reprocessing and assessment and should be fully implemented before concluding therapy. Clients with more extensive complaints are treated with a number of additional protocols, which will be covered in the next chapter.

PHASE EIGHT: REEVALUATION

The term *reevaluation* reflects the need for the precise clinical attention and follow-up that frame any EMDR treatment session that targets disturbing material. The clinician actively integrates the targeting sessions within an overall treatment plan. Regardless of how simple or complicated a case may be, adequate clinical attention must be paid to four factors, which are addressed in the following questions:

1. Has the individual target been resolved?
2. Has associated material been activated that must be addressed?
3. Have all the necessary targets been reprocessed to allow the client to feel at peace with the past, empowered in the present, and able to make choices for the future?
4. Has an adequate assimilation been made within a healthy social system?

In the following pages these four factors will be discussed as they are reflected in the standard EMDR protocol. I will first provide an overview of the three-stage protocol and then a detailed description of the various aspects of treatment.

THE STANDARD EMDR PROTOCOL

Success with EMDR requires the careful use of all three stages of the standard EMDR protocol. These three stages call for the clinician to assess the appropriate targets and outcomes in relation to the client's past, present, and future.

Working on the Past

The first stage of the EMDR protocol focuses on the question "What earlier events have set the groundwork for the presenting dysfunction?" In Phase One the clinician takes a client history and delineates the pathological condition. Treatment (Phases Two through Seven) targets and reprocesses the traumatic and disturbing memories that are the cause of the client's present symptoms. For a single-trauma victim the cause will be self-evident. For the multiple-trauma victim the clinician should determine during the history-taking sessions the ten most disturbing memories. These should be reprocessed first (after any secondary gain issues have been addressed). The most disturbing memories may have similar or different themes and content and may involve the same or different perpetrators. Regardless, each should be identified, assessed for SUD level, and processed individually (and organized, if appropriate, into groups with similar themes). The fact that these memories are the most disturbing to the client is sufficient reason to process them first. Generally, they are revealed as important nodes with associations to several pertinent areas of dysfunction. It is possible that as the memories with the highest level of disturbance are reprocessed, the treatment effects will generalize and the others will become less troublesome. Even if this is the case, however, the other memories should be targeted to clear out any dysfunction that may remain.

In addition, the other disturbing memories discussed during the history taking should be divided into clusters of similar events. One representative event from each cluster should be identified and reprocessed. This will often allow a generalization effect to reduce disturbance in all of the associated memories. Clustering events into similar occurrences (as described in Chapter 3) can help leverage clinical time. It also allows both client and clinician to determine patterns of responses and negative cognitions that may have a continued detrimental effect in present time.

As treatment progresses, other events may surface that need to be targeted. A clinical rule of thumb is that all negative associative material for one distinct traumatic target should be processed before moving on to another. The reevaluation phase that begins each subsequent EMDR session determines the appropriate target.

The aim of the first stage of the EMDR protocol is to reprocess the dysfunctional residue from the past so that the client can be freed to live in the present. Any inappropriate fears or behaviors are considered products of the past which need to be targeted. The clinician should assess clinical outcomes for each target and recycle through treated material to make sure that all dysfunction has been reprocessed and that the treatment effects are being maintained.

Single-Target Outcome

The clinician should reevaluate the successful reprocessing of any memory both at the beginning of the session following the one in which the reprocessing took place and once again later in therapy. After the full EMDR procedure, including the installation and body scan, has been implemented, the clinician can assume that the target memory has reached adaptive resolution. Therefore, in the following session the clinician should ask the client to reaccess the memory to see how disturbing it is. Based on the results, the clinician will do one of the following: continue reprocessing that target, move to another target, begin another stage of the protocol, or enter the final follow-up period necessary to conclude EMDR therapy.

After asking the client to think of the previously targeted event, the clinician should ask him to judge once again the quality of the memory that comes up and the level of disturbance evoked (using the SUD Scale). Because the client is asked to retrieve the memory as a whole, successful reprocessing will generally result in the emergence of a picture indicative of a resolution. If this picture is still highlighted by disturbing elements or vividly fixated on the most horrific moment of the trauma, more reprocessing is probably necessary. In addition, if the SUD rating indicates a level of emotional disturbance that is inappropriate to the circumstances, the memory should be retargeted. A number of new emotions may emerge that demand clinical attention.

It is also useful to ascertain the VOC level of the positive cognition to determine if the client has any unresolved doubts about it. In addition, the clinician might ask the client to think about the event and to voice any thoughts that come up about it. This can indicate whether there are additional cognitive distortions that need to be addressed. A variety of new perspectives may prove to be problematic and may require further attention.

In general, returning to the targeted memory after a period of disengagement is a good test of the treatment effects. Therefore, if there is time during the initial reprocessing session, the client should be asked to retarget the memory immediately after the debriefing (as described in Chapter 6). Not only is the debriefing an essential part of client care, but it also helps the client disengage from the disturbing material. Asking clients to reaccess the memory thus allows a restimulation of the neuro network to ascertain how the material is now being stored. As this may indicate the need for further reprocessing, the clinician should attempt reaccessing only if there is sufficient time to resolve whatever might come up.

Regardless of the outcome, the memory should also be reevaluated at the next session to determine if it has other elements that need resolution. A certain amount of real time is needed to check for the full integration of the processed information within the client. It is also vital to retarget the memory if the client was on medication at the time it was originally processed. Clinical observations have indicated the need to reprocess the memory again to deal with any information still held in state-dependent form. For example, there may be aspects of a client's memory that will only emerge when he is feeling anxious. If this client first processed the memory while on antianxiety medication, it will be necessary to reprocess the same memory later, once he is no longer taking the medication and is able to feel anxiety.

Another useful measure of clinical outcome is the Impact of Event Scale (Horowitz, 1979; Horowitz, Wilmer, & Alvarez, 1979). While this measure was designed for research purposes, it is very useful in clinical practice. The victim of a single-event trauma may be asked to fill out the questionnaire during the history-taking session. This is helpful for establishing a good baseline of client responses regarding intrusion or avoidance symptoms. The week after the targeting session the client should complete the questionnaire again. The new score can indicate the extent of resolution or point to other associated material to be resolved.

For instance, a client who had been molested by her grandfather was troubled by intrusive thoughts and nightmares of the event. The Impact of Event Scale revealed a high score on all intrusion and avoidance symptoms. The client's memories of her grandfather were targeted during two EMDR reprocessing sessions, and the client reported feeling a sense of peace and forgave her grandfather for his "ignorance." However, the following session revealed that the Impact of Event Scale item related to intrusive thoughts was rated at a moderate level, although the rest of the items were low or at zero. When questioned, the client revealed that she had been thinking about her grandmother, who had not believed she was molested. The client's memory of her grandmother disbelieving her was subsequently targeted, and the issue was resolved.

Recycling through Multiple Targets

After the initially identified targets and emerging associated memories have been reprocessed, the clinician should recycle through the material to make sure that the treatment effects have been maintained. This reevaluation, described in detail shortly, is necessary before moving on to the second two stages of the protocol.

It is also useful to repeat the reassessment of the pivotal memories sometime before termination of therapy. Keep in mind that the information will continue processing between sessions and that new avenues of perception or emotions that should be addressed may be revealed. However, in the course of ongoing therapy, material unrelated to the previous targets may have appeared more disturbing, and these newly opened avenues of the original target may have been overlooked. Retargeting such material can determine whether any necessary processing or exploration is still incomplete and is a safeguard for thorough clinical treatment.

After the pronounced complaints appear to have been resolved and before therapy is terminated, the clinician should ask the client to reaccess a number of the targets. The purpose is to recycle through the earlier material and current issues that the client came to therapy to resolve in order to identify and reprocess any troubling material that may remain. This will help prevent the client from uncovering disturbing material on his own later. While the client may have attained all the clinical goals identified during the initial history-taking session, retargeting will help ensure maintenance of the treatment effects.

Specifically, the clinician should reevaluate the previous work with the client and reaccess, assess, and appropriately reprocess (if necessary) the kinds of memories discussed in the following paragraphs.

Primary Events. The primary events are those that have greatest significance to the client or that have been identified as representing certain crucial areas of dysfunction. These usually consist of no more than 20 memories that the clinician should retarget to assess the magnitude and constancy of the treatment effects and to determine if other significant aspects of the memory appear to be unresolved.

Past Events. The clinician should ask the client to hold the most important negative cognitions in mind and ascertain if there are any other memories that are still disturbing. Any memory that emerges should be examined for significant differences of content or context from the memories already treated that may give the negative cognition a new meaning. For instance, the client may have started with the negative cognition "I'm different," which was reprocessed for incidents involving social discomfort. However, she may have a memory involving herself acting insensitively that is still disturbing and that gives the cognition a different meaning, namely, "I'm a terrible person." Whether or not differences in the meaning of the cognition emerge, the memory should be appropriately reprocessed as long as disturbance is evinced.

Progressions. While processing an identified target, the client may disclose another memory that comes momentarily to consciousness during or between sets. Additional sets may cause yet another memory to emerge or the initially targeted one to resurface. The clinician should, of course, follow the client's emerging consciousness and reprocess appropriately. However, the clinician should note any memories that emerge in passing that appear particularly salient to the clinical picture. Memories that appear fleetingly in relation to one issue may be central to another dysfunctional cognition or configuration. The clinician should use professional judgment in identifying and returning to these memories at an appropriate juncture in the therapy.

Clusters. During the initial history-taking sessions the clinician will have developed a series of clusters by appropriately grouping similar incidents. He will then ask the client to choose for reprocessing one incident that represents a particular cluster. Clinical reports have verified that generalization will usually occur, causing a reprocessing effect throughout the entire cluster of incidents. The clinician should verify this by asking the client to scan through the incidents in each separate cluster to identify any other memories that have not been resolved. Let us say, for instance, that a sexual abuse victim has identified a cluster of incidents around being raped by her brother. Although the client may have been assaulted many times by her brother, a convenient cluster might be the times she was raped in the basement while hearing other family members walking around in the house above her. When returning to this cluster of incidents for reassessment, the client may discover that one incident remains unresolved because an additional humiliation (being watched by her brother's friend) was involved with the rape. In other words, incidents that contain additional factors (or significant variants) may require individual targeting for complete resolution.

Participants. The significant people in the client's life should be identified and individually targeted to determine if any disturbing memories or issues regarding them remain. This is particularly important in childhood abuse, a situation in which all family members should be targeted in order to identify any contributing elements to continuing issues of low self-esteem, lack of feelings of self-efficacy, and so forth. While only one member of the family may have sexually abused the client, the state of traumatization might lead to a heightened vulnerability to any deliberate or unintentional critical messages from others. When an individual family member is targeted and the client responds with a significant amount of disturbance, that person should be targeted to access any key memories that have remained dysfunctionally stored.

Working on the past is the first stage of the standard EMDR protocol. When a reevaluation of the past events that have been identified as the most troubling indicates that they have been sufficiently resolved, the clinician should change the emphasis to present stimuli. This is the second stage of the standard protocol.

Working on the Present

The second stage of the EMDR protocol focuses on the question "What present stimuli continue to elicit the disturbing dysfunctional material?" This stage targets the current conditions, situations, and people that evoke pathological or disturbing reactions and behaviors. Human behavior is not random; patterns of reaction and behavior established in the past are frequently triggered in the present. Good history taking delineates the current dysfunction and establishes a baseline of inappropriate responses. However, the initial history-taking sessions must be continually supplemented by ongoing assessment and clinical observation, because processing primary trauma during the initial stage of the protocol is often the only way that underlying problems can be fully seen. Often, resolution of the pronounced symptoms (such as nightmares, intrusive thoughts, and flashbacks) that have been preoccupying the client will allow the clinician to make a more thorough evaluation of the client's current life conditions.

Once early events have been processed, the clinician should reevaluate the client's current responses and check them against the information gleaned during the history taking. The common pattern seen in EMDR is that fears and anxieties will have greatly decreased as a result of trauma reprocessing. Not only will associated early memories be less troublesome, but there is often a generalization to present-day situations. For example, a molestation victim may find that as a result of targeting the memories of early assaults he is no longer afraid to be alone at night, and an accident victim may find that she is no longer afraid to drive. These changes occur automatically, that is, without directly targeting the present-day situations.

It is important to check for the client's current reactions because although some stimuli will be automatically affected, others will have to be specifically reprocessed. As discussed in Chapter 3, owing to the effects of second-order conditioning, some current situations will have become independent sources of disturbance as a result of having been frequently paired with negative emotions in the past. Any present condition or interaction that causes disturbance should be individually targeted and reprocessed. In most instances, this will be comparatively easy, because the earlier source of dysfunction has already been treated. However, the clinician should be prepared for the emergence of other memories that may be unexpected sources of disturbance. In addition, if the disturbance about the present-day situation does not diminish, the clinician may need to search for feeder memories. (The use of the client's log in this stage of treatment will be discussed more fully later in this chapter.)

It is important to check treatment effects by recycling through any present-day situations that were targeted. The clinician should ask the client to reaccess any present stimuli that were previously identified as disturbing and should make the appropriate reevaluation. She should also ask the client to scan his current family, social, and work environment for any undue disturbance. The clinician should address any necessary client education (e.g., on assertiveness) and then have the client reprocess the stimuli.

Using the Log to Report Systems Issues

It is important for clients to keep a log after each EMDR session in order for the clinician to ascertain what else needs to be targeted. Asking a client to reaccess a particular target allows the clinician to determine how well the client has integrated the material within himself. What the log does is to enable the clinician to see how well the client's new pattern of reaction has been integrated with his current environment. This reevaluation gives the clinician the opportunity to review the quality of the client's internal and behavioral responses within his social system.

Since human beings are not machines, we would not anticipate that successful EMDR clients would now be totally unresponsive to the traumatic events that led to their dysfunction or current unpleasant circumstances. For instance, the Vietnam veteran who was able to let go of the guilt he felt about a prisoner's death still maintained a degree of sadness he rated as 2 on the SUD Scale because, as he said, "A man died." Likewise, certain levels of disturbing emotions may be viewed as appropriate responses to current situations.

Remember that EMDR will not remove any disturbance experienced by the client that is fitting or that serves as an incentive to appropriate action. For example, a client may be living or working in a situation that would be considered unpleasant, unjust, or unfair by any standard of consensus reality. When his log reports a high level of disturbance, the clinician must assess the entire situation in order to judge the appropriateness of the client's response to it. Even if the client's situation is untenable, the clinician should help him determine what is the most appropriate action he can take within the system and should ensure that he can do so without the accompanying sense of self-denigration and worthlessness he may have felt during past experiences of victimization. Thus, log reports are vital to evaluate the client's current responses to the actual situation.

The clinician must explore the consensus-reality validity of the client's situation, along with any real-world conflicts, to determine how the client's current responses should be addressed. They might be dealt with by means of reprocessing, education, family therapy, or self-control techniques to help the client accept the unchangeable—and sometimes unfair—facts of daily life. Indeed, an important aspect of mental health is the ability to stop focusing on the "unfairness" of something and accept the simple fact that "it is."

As previously discussed, log reports are vital for determining if there are aspects of targeted material that remain dysfunctional or if previously unanticipated issues need to be addressed. The client's present condition can be most fully explored if she uses the log to report on any disturbances. Accurate log reports are necessary for comprehensive EMDR treatment because they can reveal patterns of responses that need to be addressed by identifying other core dysfunctional memories, before directly targeting the present disturbing condition.

At times the clinician will notice that the disturbances recorded in the log reveal troublesome negative cognitions. However, occasionally these negative cognitions may seem justified to the client because of his earlier life experiences. In these cases the clinician must be attuned to the necessity for cognitive investigation and appropriate education. The clinician should sensitively explore with the client the possibility that even if the dysfunctional beliefs were appropriate previously, society may have changed so as to make them obsolete now. Since the client has been locked in the life experiences and messages from his past, there has been little opportunity for the evolution of his social consciousness.

This scenario may apply especially to issues of relationships and gender identity. For instance, a female client may need to learn that holding a powerful position in business is compatible with femininity and a male client may need to learn that experiencing emotions and taking care of the children are not threats to his masculinity. Also, systems issues may need to be addressed so the client can cope with any peer pressure from old dysfunctional relationships.

Often, the clinician may need to explain the basics of systems dynamics to the client, showing her how her newfound sense of self-efficacy or new attitudes may not be welcomed by the people in her life. For instance, the client will discover that not everyone is emotionally stable, responsible, compassionate, tolerant, fair, or trustworthy. She may need to learn that as an adult she has choices about relationships and work that were not previously available to her, choices that include simply withdrawing from an unpleasant and unchangeable situation. The clinician must make the appropriate evaluation to determine if the client needs to do specific work on new behaviors so that such choices can be made.

Working on the Future

Once the dysfunctional events of the past have been identified and reprocessed and the present disturbance has been targeted and reprocessed, the clinician should focus on the client's ability to make new choices in the future. This is done by the identification and reprocessing of anticipatory fears as well as by targeting a "positive template" that will incorporate appropriate future behaviors. This third stage of the EMDR protocol includes adequate education, modeling, and imagining in conjunction with EMDR targeting to allow the client to respond differently in the future. The clinician should help the client assimilate new information and provide her with experiences to help ensure future successes. The third stage of the EMDR standard protocol is a vital aspect of treatment.

Significant People

When the client has reprocessed memories about a significant person, the clinician should ask him to imagine encountering that person in the future. The client's reaction should be assessed to determine if additional processing is needed. For instance, a client who has processed memories of childhood molestations by a brother should be asked to imagine seeing him at a future family gathering. This is particularly important if such a future encounter is likely to occur. If the client describes feeling fear, the consensus reality of the situation should be explored. For instance, if the brother is violent or likely to attempt a verbal or physical assault, the client's reactions may be appropriate. However, if the client reports the brother as passive or repentant, there is good reason to assume that the client's fear is the result of unresolved material, which should be targeted. If the fear is inappropriate, the clinician should reevaluate the clusters of events involving the brother for any unresolved issues. Any remaining dysfunctional memories should be accessed and reprocessed. Other fears the client has about asserting herself or setting boundaries in general may need to be explored and appropriately targeted. Whether the fears are warranted or not, the clinician should discuss with the client appropriate adaptive behaviors and help her assimilate the information through the use of a positive template (to be discussed later in this chapter).

Significant Situations

As noted earlier, it is important for the client to imagine himself in significant situations in the future to determine if he has any other areas of disturbance that have gone undetected. Any inappropriate anticipatory fear is considered to be driven by earlier unresolved dysfunctional memories. It may be useful to have the client imagine a videotape of how situations from his current life would evolve one or more years into the future. Any disturbance can be assessed for the appropriate clinical interventions, including education about successful interpersonal strategies, modeling of appropriate behaviors, or reprocessing of dysfunctional memories. As mentioned earlier, it is also useful to ask clients to imagine specific situations or encounters with significant people who have been disturbing in the past. This can allow the clinician to pinpoint and address areas of difficulty.

Incorporating a Positive Template

The evolution of a healthy self-image is dependent on the interaction between intrapsychic responses and external reinforcement. The clinician must therefore take care to monitor both factors in order to see whether specific therapeutic interventions are indicated. These include targeting inappropriate responses for subsequent treatment or specifically addressing systemic issues.

The concept of successful integration is inherent in each aspect of EMDR treatment. During each session the clinician should attempt to identify the positive cognition that, when installed, will not only best serve to shift the client's perspective on past events but will empower him most fully in present situations and possible future ones. Once installed, the positive cognition appears to generalize to the associated memories and to positively orient the cognitive processes in regard to subsequent associations. It appears that a client's beliefs about his individual worth, efficacy, and relation to others are verbalizations of his sense of personal identity. Thus, we expect to see adequately processed targeted material integrated within an overall positive schema and a sense of self that spans past, present, and future.

While the installation phase is a part of each EMDR treatment session, the overall EMDR treatment protocol calls for specific targeting of (1) early memories that have set the groundwork for the present dysfunction, (2) present stimuli that elicit the dysfunctional material, and (3) a positive template to guide appropriate future action. While an EMDR treatment that concentrates on the client's responses to present stimuli includes the installation of a positive cognition to allow a different perspective, the treatment is not complete until there is a specific incorporation of an alternative behavioral response pattern. Such patterns represent what we refer to as a positive template.

In effect, the incorporation of a positive template for appropriate future action is an expansion of the installation phase. The clinician and client explore how the client would most like to be perceiving, feeling, acting, and believing from now on. It is important for the clinician to monitor the client's projections into the future because they may incorporate inappropriate goals or fears of failure due to lack of experience or poor early modeling.

For example, even after all the memories of a molestation victim have been reprocessed, she is not necessarily ready to start dating. The clinician may have to provide education about assertiveness, social customs, sexual safety, and so on before this stage of the protocol can be completed. The clinician will have to address (either in the therapy session or through referral to a self-help group) the deficits in the client's early life experiences and the information that should have been integrated during the appropriate developmental stages. Further, the clinician will have to reevaluate the client's successful integration of any treatment effects through the log reports.

The molestation or abuse victim is often unable to learn about appropriate social interactions because of the feelings of low self-esteem, fear, and isolation that were part of his early upbringing. In addition, many of his social skills are likely to be missing because of inappropriate parenting and lack of good modeling. It becomes the job of the clinician to help such clients learn aspects of social and family interaction that were not acquired in childhood. This is an important phase of treatment because it helps the client to become actively integrated within the social fabric.

The incorporation of a positive template is an aspect of EMDR that includes visualization work similar to the kind done by some Olympic athletes during training. Imagining positive outcomes seems to assist the learning process. In the case of a molestation victim, the clinician can review dating and assertiveness skills and then ask the client to try them out in a role play and in her imagination. Essentially, once the client has received the appropriate education, she is asked to imagine the optimal behavioral responses, along with an enhancing positive cognition. The clinician then leads her in successive sets to assist her in assimilating the information and incorporating it into a positive template for future action.

Initially, a molestation or other abuse victim may find just the prospect of holding someone's hand disturbing. In this case, she should be assisted in imagining the whole sequence of meeting someone, dating, and progressing through evolving sexual experiences. The clinician should ask her to imagine a given situation and then help her reprocess the resulting disturbance. Next, she is asked to visualize the images again while feeling positively. This is supported with additional sets. The incorporation of these positive templates allows the client to achieve some sense of comfort and experience with new situations in the safety of the office. After the entire imagined dating sequence from an initial meeting to a sexual experience has been targeted, the client should be encouraged to begin social exploration. Once she has done this, there is a greater likelihood of actual positive experiences, because these internalized positive templates will be triggered by future external cues in the real world. Obviously, the clinician will need feedback about these real-world experiences to determine if a client needs additional assistance.

The same type of sequencing should be done with abuse victims who decide to look for a better job. First, the clinician or a job counselor should educate him about job hunting. Then, a series of positive templates should be incorporated involving the steps necessary for him to take and the personal encounters he is likely to have when job hunting. Of course, the client should continue to keep a log in order to identify for reprocessing any difficulties he encounters in real-life situations. Once again, processing imagined encounters to incorporate a positive template for the future will generally result in fewer disturbances in the real world. It is much better for the client if the primary areas of disturbance are identified and dealt with in the clinician's office rather than encountered for the first time when he is on his own.

Remember that the positive cognition is installed (during the sessions that target memory work) only after the dysfunctional material has been reprocessed. Likewise, the incorporation of a detailed positive template should not generally be attempted until both the earlier memories that caused the dysfunctional reactions and the present stimuli are considered to be successfully reprocessed. Since new and more adaptive positive cognitions are possible once the memories are processed, more adaptive actions can be envisioned by the client. The clinician should use EMDR to metabolize the dysfunctional material that drives the maladaptive behavior and to assist the client in imagining more life-enhancing responses and in formulating appropriate behaviors in his mind. Sets can then be used to integrate the imagined future responses before clients are invited to actualize them in real life.

This third and last stage of the standard EMDR protocol allows the clinician to monitor the client's responses in order to help her work through in the office any internal resistance or obvious problems she is likely to encounter before she tries out her new actions in the real world. Using the sets with the imagined actions and behaviors inaugurates the processing of a condition that can be described as "What would happen if I am successful?" The clinician must be attuned to any sense of fear or resistance the client may feel as the positive template is processed. These can be explored to see if they include any false expectations or cognitive distortions. Once the appropriate cognitive explanation has taken place, any residual tension can be reprocessed.

Specifically, clients are asked to notice any negative feelings, beliefs, or disturbing sensations that arise when the positive template is imagined. These are then targeted directly by the sets. If a negative belief emerges, it is advisable to take the following steps before attempting to incorporate the positive template: (1) explore its meaning and appropriateness; (2) isolate any pertinent early memories that may be driving it; and (3) direct treatment to the applicable representational memory, including the installation of an appropriate positive cognition. In many cases, however, a simple discussion of the situation, along with appropriate information and modeling, may be all that is necessary to dispel the client's negative feelings. In any case, the final step should be to have the client experience the assimilation of the positive template with a feeling of well-being and self-efficacy. Naturally, it is necessary to reevaluate treatment effects through the log reports and behavioral monitoring.

CONCLUDING THERAPY

Follow-Up

The final aspect of reevaluation involves decisions about the advisability of concluding the therapy. The client should reduce his therapy sessions while continuing to keep his log for follow-up. After the log reports suggest that weekly sessions are unwarranted, the clinician may schedule an appointment for 2 weeks later, then 1 month, and then 3 months. During this time the log is vital to identify any previously undisclosed patterns that need attention. It also assists the client in remaining more self-aware, which can encourage him to continue using the stress-control tapes and other techniques for ongoing psychological maintenance.

The need for extensive follow-up is especially important for clients with long-term abuse histories, for the negative beliefs resulting from the abuse are likely to lead to circumstances in adult life that constantly reinforce feelings of worthlessness and powerlessness. For instance, it is likely that the client's job performance will be mediocre and that she will anticipate failure and disapproval.

If the client has been successfully treated with EMDR, the early memories of abuse will have been sufficiently metabolized to permit a cognition such as "I'm fine. Mom and Dad really had a problem. I can succeed." The present stimuli can then be reprocessed so that negative reactions in social and work situations can now be replaced by appropriate responses that encourage a new sense of empowerment. A positive template for a variety of social situations can be incorporated to make up for any educational deficits (in assertiveness, boundary setting, and so forth) due to inappropriate modeling and the self-denigration caused by the negative beliefs inherent in the abuse background.

In addition to the incorporation of specific positive templates, automatic changes in the client can apparently occur with EMDR. Thus, one of the anticipated consequences of appropriate reprocessing is a ripple effect. That is, new behaviors spontaneously arise owing to the new sense of identity that emerges when the negative messages of the client's early memories are transformed. Thus, clinicians can expect that the job performance of abuse clients will begin to improve and that this improvement will result in even greater job success.

The clinician should remember that any new client actions will be met with new external responses, which in turn will stimulate other neuro networks in the client that also contain positive or negative beliefs. One hopes, of course, that the client will begin to receive positive reinforcement for her new actions, but in the course of receiving compliments, promotions, or commendations the client may experience fear or anxiety. This may be caused by the activation of a neuro network that contains a dysfunctional belief such as "If I am too successful, I will be abandoned." Such a belief may have been incorporated from the observation of a real-life situation, book, or movie. Regardless of its genesis, this belief was not previously examined because the client had never before achieved sufficient positive results (and the consequent praise) to activate it. Nevertheless, negative emotions stimulated by situations that would normally be expected to evoke satisfaction should alert the clinician to the need for processing.

It is crucial that the client understand the clinician's need to continue monitoring her in order to reevaluate her reactions and determine if clinical intervention is called for. The memories that set the node points for the negative beliefs should be identified and processed and the appropriate positive cognition installed.

Terminating Therapy

While the client's log can highlight disturbing feelings indicative of dysfunction, it can also reveal disturbances that are merely the result of the vicissitudes of life. When the log begins to report minor and random arousal as the primary complaint, the client should consider whether therapy is still a necessity for emotional healing or simply an option for personal growth (which can be an independent, lifelong adventure). With some clients it will be important to discuss appropriate current goals and expectations.

In many cases the client must learn the limitations inherent in being human, regardless of how well adjusted or "self-actualized" she is. For example, many victims of PTSD believe that if their symptoms were successfully handled, they would never be unhappy again. While it would be unfair to prematurely short-circuit their personal goals, clients may need to be cautioned that life entails a series of shocks to the nervous system that trigger both appropriate and inappropriate reactions, depending on a number of factors, including chemical and hormonal balance, fatigue level, and convergence of stimuli. Instead of beating themselves up when anger, hurt, or fear arises, it would be more useful for them to determine if the arousal is an appropriate impetus for action and, if so, to take the necessary steps to address the disturbing situation and any body tension that may remain.

Some clients will need to be debriefed about the difference between "cannot" and "prefer not." For instance, a client who had been unable to fly in an airplane since childhood successfully reprocessed his fears in a few EMDR sessions. At that point, situations that previously would have induced a panic reaction were retargeted. When it was time to incorporate a positive template, the client remarked that it was difficult to tell the difference between what he felt and what normal people might reasonably feel. For example, he had to be reassured that most people would not enjoy sitting in the middle seat of an airplane and that his dislike of it was perfectly normal. He learned that this kind of reaction should not and need not be expected to change. The important thing was to recognize that he could sit in the middle seat if he had to.

Once areas of dysfunction have been reprocessed, the client is experiencing success and joy in the present, she has the necessary education to make new choices in the future, and the log reveals no new problem areas as therapy is tapered off, it is time to terminate the therapeutic process. It is nonetheless important for the client to feel that the door is always open if the need arises. She should be informed that if another area of concern arises or if she observes patterns of dysfunctional responses that do not respond to self-help techniques, then additional therapy is always available. The appropriate level of expectation is vital in order to continue therapeutic gains.

In one instance, a client who had been successfully treated 6 years earlier for a severe case of PTSD caused by Vietnam combat reentered therapy. The initial dysfunction had not returned, he had started a successful and lucrative job, and he was now happily married. However, his current presenting complaint was a series of molestation memories and attendant disturbance that had recently arisen. In his earlier therapy there had been no signs of sexual dysfunction or other indications of an abuse history, but the client had recently seen his mother in a particular body position at a motel and had begun to remember scenes of a childhood molestation involving his father and another woman. Conversations with his brother seemed to confirm his suspicions, which were accompanied by more molestation images. The client's disturbance now became extreme, because the emerging scenes entailed a lot of blood and seemed to indicate that a murder had been committed in his presence. These scenes were appropriately targeted and reprocessed in three EMDR sessions. During the reprocessing the image became more distinct and appeared to involve not a murder but a woman menstruating. While a molestation did seem to be involved, the disturbance was handled without difficulty and the client was again discharged after a reminder that the therapist's door would always be open.

This case exemplifies a number of operational principles for the clinician:

1. *Do not assume that every possible unconscious dysfunction has been resolved within a given number of EMDR sessions.* Clients may arrive at a state of health and equilibrium appropriate for their current stage of life and personal development without having unearthed every possible source of disturbance. While clinicians have reported that EMDR seems to release "repressed" or dissociated material more often than other modalities (Lipke, 1992b), the successful targeting of all disturbance necessary to remediate the presenting problems does not mean that other issues will not arise in the future.

2. *It is necessary to communicate to clients that other material may arise and that this is not evidence of failure on their part but, rather, a natural unfolding process.* It may be helpful to speak metaphorically, to say, for example, "Targeting any new material that surfaces is like peeling an artichoke." (I prefer "artichoke" to "onion" because at the center of an artichoke is a heart.) This gives clients the sense that their essential health is always stable and intact within them and the message that the

unfolding of a new target simply offers them the opportunity to acquire additional refinement and information. The client should be instructed that other issues may naturally arise as she more fully integrates changes and new life experiences. Providing this information allows new material to be dealt with at the appropriate level of client readiness, which appears to accelerate the overall treatment outcome.

3. *It is necessary to instill in clients a sense of self-empowerment and confidence in their ability to exercise post-therapy self-monitoring.* The client should be asked to consider that an important aspect of continued mental health for any individual is the ability to identify a feeling of self-satisfaction and joy as a baseline response and to remain as alert as possible to the arousal of any states of internal suffering. Identifying the source of the disturbance will allow the client to decide what kind of intervention is needed. Before clinical assistance is deemed appropriate, the client should attempt a variety of personal interventions. In many instances, the solution to the disturbance may be as simple as taking appropriate action or using guided imagery, meditation, or self-hypnosis. In addition, the self-administered eye movement procedure (presented in Chapter 9) may be used by clients at this stage of therapy.

SUPERVISED PRACTICE

Clinicians should use the information in Chapters 5, 6, and 7 during supervised practice before implementing the information in this chapter and the protocols given in Chapter 9. The more advanced material offered in Chapter 10 should not be used by clinicians until they have become comfortable at this level of practice and have acquired the appropriate baseline of experience. This should take from 6 to 8 weeks. As mentioned earlier, during this practice period some clients may be found to "loop" (maintain the same level of disturbance) even when the alternatives described in these chapters are used. For this group the more proactive version of EMDR described in Chapter 10 is needed. Therefore, clinicians-in-training who are dealing with this kind of client should use the closure exercises offered in Chapter 9 and should refrain from reinaugurating treatment until they have been adequately supervised on the more advanced material.

SUMMARY AND CONCLUSIONS

Phase eight of EMDR treatment is called the reevaluation phase. During this phase determinations are made regarding clients' assimilation of the reprocessed information and their integration into a healthy social structure. The reevaluation phase takes place at the beginning of each session subsequent to reprocessing, when the clinician has the client reaccess the earlier targeted material and reviews the log. This phase guides the clinician through a three-stage protocol that targets both the past events that laid the groundwork for the dysfunction and the present conditions that stimulate the disturbance and installs a positive template for the future that helps incorporate appropriate actions. The reevaluation of previous work indicates when a new stage of the protocol should be entered or when therapy should be concluded. Appropriate follow-ups are a crucial aspect of EMDR therapy.

Treatment effects are reevaluated by assessing the quality of the image that represents the targeted event, the SUD level, the cognitions, the VOC level, the log, and the client's reaction to projections of the future. Before the client completes therapy, the material covered in the history taking and subsequent reprocessing sessions should be reevaluated. All pertinent memories, present stimuli, and future anticipated events should be targeted. A positive template for appropriate future action should be created to incorporate new adaptive behaviors and to process any cognitive distortions. It is possible that the clinician will need to educate the client about new behaviors or attitudes in order to address deficits caused by inappropriate parenting and life experiences.

Reevaluation of the clinical work includes the client's reports regarding real-life occurrences. The log is necessary to ascertain potential targets and is crucial for full clinical effectiveness. Disturbances should be evaluated for appropriateness to the circumstances, new distortions, or systems issues that may need to be addressed. The clinician should coach the client about realistic expectations, self-care techniques, and the availability of future clinical intervention, if the latter becomes necessary. The final reevaluation may include extensive follow-ups before deciding that it is appropriate to conclude therapy.

CHAPTER 9

Protocols and Procedures
for Special Situations

You can outdistance that which is running after you, but
you cannot outdistance that which is running inside you.
African proverb

The standard EMDR procedure is applied to various clinical problems by means of a number of specific protocols. So far, we have explored the basic principles of EMDR clinical work, the standard procedure, and the standard three-stage protocol used for most trauma survivors. The three-stage protocol, described in detail in the previous chapter, directs comprehensive attention to all dysfunctional material manifested by the client's responses to past occurrences, present stimuli, and future projections.

This chapter provides an outline to review the standard procedure and then describes additional protocols and procedures. Any of these protocols and procedures may be applicable to an individual client (e.g., a trauma survivor may need treatment that combines the protocols for specific traumas, phobias, and illness, a treatment that is positioned appropriately within the standard three-stage protocol described in the last chapter). In addition, the chapter provides instructions for clinicians who may also want to teach their clients how to use the eye movements on themselves at the conclusion of therapy.

These additional protocols demonstrate how to apply EMDR to various clinical problems and provide the guidelines needed to serve most clients. Information on the use of these protocols with selected, and perhaps more highly disturbed, clinical populations is covered in Chapter 11. However, the clinician should first use these additional protocols with the circumscribed targets of more intact clients during the 2-month practice period.

The following outline is a reminder of the basic procedural steps of EMDR. The selection of targets will be based on the client's feedback and the three stages defined in the standard protocol.

THE 11-STEP STANDARD PROCEDURE

The EMDR methodology requires a carefully defined treatment plan and suitable therapeutic framework. After taking a client history (Phase One) and preparing the client (Phase Two), the clinician may begin the assessment, identify the appropriate components, and proceed with an individual treatment session by completing the procedure described in detail in the preceding chapters. This standard procedure involves attention to the following steps:

1. Image: Have the client access an image that represents the entire event, generally depicting the most traumatic part of the incident. If none is available, the client simply thinks of the incident.
2. Negative cognition: Develop the negative self-statement that conveys an underlying limiting self-belief or assessment. It should begin with "I am" and incorporate words that go with the image.
3. Positive cognition: Create a desirable positive self-statement that, when possible, incorporates an internal locus of control.
4. Validity of Cognition (VOC) level: Determine a client rating of the gut-level validity of the positive cognition (where 1 equals "completely false" and 7 equals "completely true").
5. Emotion: Identify the name of the disturbing emotion that arises when the image and the negative cognition are linked.
6. Subjective Units of Disturbance (SUD) level: Determine a client rating of the degree of disturbance that arises when the memory is stimulated (where 0 equals "neutral" or "calm" and 10 equals "the worst disturbance imaginable").
7. Location of body sensation: Identify where the physical sensations are felt when the disturbing information is accessed.
8. Desensitization: Inaugurate the process whereby all associated channels are cleared and the targeted event has a SUD rating of 0 or 1 (a higher score is acceptable only if ecologically valid).
9. Installation: Infuse the positive cognition.
   a. Check the appropriateness and VOC of the original or new positive cognition.
   b. Link the positive cognition with the target event.
   c. Attain a VOC of 7 or greater (unless otherwise ecologically valid).
10. Body scan: Have the client mentally scan for any residual physical sensation while holding the target event and positive cognition in mind.
11. Closure: End the treatment session in a way that gives the client feelings of self-efficacy and accomplishment as well as reasonable expectations.

    a. Visualization: Use guided imagery to dispel any disturbance that still remains.

    b. Debriefing: Give posttreatment instructions to clients regarding potential ongoing processing, keeping a log, and using a relaxation tape and other self-control procedures.

The client keeps a log regarding any between-sessions disturbance in order to facilitate the reevaluation phase, which opens the next session and serves to define the next target. In using the standard three-stage protocol, clinical attention is directed first to reprocessing the past event that caused the dysfunction, then to working on the present stimuli that elicit the disturbance, and finally to establishing a positive template for future action.

PROTOCOL FOR A SINGLE TRAUMATIC EVENT

While the standard three-stage protocol guides the clinician through the overall stages of therapy, the single-event protocol identifies the specific targets involved in the reprocessing of the individual traumatic event. Although this protocol should be incorporated into the standard three-stage protocol for most clients, it may be sufficient in cases in which a single memory is causing intrusive symptoms. It must be underscored, however, that victims of PTSD will undoubtedly need the full three-stage protocol that was reviewed in the previous chapter in order to address all of their symptoms. For instance, while the protocol for a single traumatic event focuses primarily on intrusive symptoms, avoidance symptoms will also have to be addressed by the inclusion of positive templates (the third stage of the standard protocol).

For single traumatic events, the standard procedure should be applied to the following targets (assuming they are are available):

1. Memory or image of the actual traumatic event.
2. Flashback scene (which may differ from the recalled image that represents the trauma).
3. Dream image, or most traumatic scene in a recurring nightmare.
4. Present stimuli that trigger the disturbing memory or reaction (such as the sound of a car backfiring or being touched in a certain way).

PROTOCOL FOR CURRENT ANXIETY AND BEHAVIOR

Most trauma clients will report a number of anxieties and behaviors that are currently disturbing them. Some clients have anxieties that are not related to major trauma. The following protocol helps the clinician focus on these problems.

For current anxiety and behavior, the clinician assists the client to specify (1) the anxiety to be treated, (2) the initial cause and memory (if available), and (3) the desired response.

The components are used and measurements are taken as the targets are reprocessed in the following order:

1. Initial memory.
2. Most recent or most representative example of a present situation that causes anxiety.
3. Future projection of a desired emotional and behavioral response.

In all cases the client's log reports will guide the clinician's reevaluation of the treatment effect by reporting any disturbances that arise in subsequent weeks when the client encounters the target situation in the real world. As usual, it is vital that the clinician then target these as soon as possible after they emerge.

PROTOCOL FOR RECENT TRAUMATIC EVENTS

The standard protocol for most trauma involves focusing on the traumatic memory itself. Older memories generally can be treated by concentrating on one part of the event. The target is accessed by asking the client to identify a picture that represents either the entire incident or the most upsetting part of it. Targeting this one moment of the incident usually results in the whole memory being reprocessed as other aspects of the memory come fleetingly to consciousness or as the pivotal picture changes in some way. Thus, the reprocessing effect has become generalized to the entire memory.

However, I discovered that a different approach was needed when people came for EMDR treatment just a few weeks after the 1989 San Francisco Bay Area earthquake. At that time I found that concentrating on one part of the memory had no effect on any other part of the incident. For example, when a client reprocessed the most traumatic part of the memory, such as the chimney collapsing and nearly burying him, this did not cause him to feel better when he thought of other parts of the event. It appeared that, on some level of information processing, the memory had not had sufficient time to consolidate into an integrated whole. This is an interesting phenomenon and may ultimately shed some light on the activation and physiological mechanisms of memory itself.

Clearly, the memory of a recent traumatic event is consolidated on some level, since the client can give a serial description of the experience, but on a crucial stratum of information association the various aspects of memory are not integrally linked. On the basis of clinical observation, I estimate that the period required for consolidation is approximately 2 to 3 months. Presumably, future research will define this period more precisely. The clinician can tell that consolidation of a recent traumatic memory is complete when successful treatment requires only the standard application of the 11-step procedure, rather than the more extended protocol. The latter is as follows:

1. Obtain a narrative history of the event.
2. Target the most disturbing aspect of the memory (if necessary).
3. Target the remainder of the narrative in chronological order.
4. Have client visualize the entire sequence of the event with eyes closed and reprocess it as disturbance arises. Repeat until the entire event can be visualized from start to finish without distress.
5. Have client visualize the event from start to finish with eyes open, and install positive cognition.
6. Conclude with body scan.
7. Process present stimuli, if necessary.

When working with a recent memory, the clinician should ask the client to describe the event in narrative form. As the client recites the history, the clinician should take note of each separate aspect of the event (e.g., "I felt myself rocking, then I heard the dresser falling, then I saw the books dropping . . ."). Each of these experiences should be treated as a separate target and given the standard EMDR procedure, including a cognitive installation for each segment. The body scan, however, should not be used until the final segment of the memory has been treated and all of the targets have been addressed, for only then can one expect all associated body tension to disappear.

Specifically, the client is asked to identify any part of the memory that is so disturbing that it might divert attention when trying to target another part of the incident. This might occur when, for example, a flood victim lost hold of a loved one in the rising water, when a beam almost fell on an earthquake victim, or when a rape victim felt the gun against her face. Whatever part of the memory is particularly upsetting should be targeted first.

If there is no one part that is particularly distracting, the clinician should target the part that occurred first. Since the most common reaction to a recent trauma is fear, the clinician can suggest the negative cognition "I am in danger" and the positive cognition "It's over; I'm safe now." Of course, the clinician should suggest these cognitions in a manner that allows clients to select another that better

fits their personal experience. As the client concentrates on the first (or most distressing) part of the memory, the clinician implements the standard EMDR procedure up through the installation of the positive cognition.

After each of the reported aspects has been treated, the clinician should ask the client to close her eyes and visualize the experience as one might run a videotape through a VCR. This part of the protocol should not be confused with the hypnotic exercise that calls for a dissociation of emotions as a movie is projected on a distant screen. The reprocessing of a target calls for the client to have a full association to the material. The client is asked merely to play the entire incident in her mind as if it were a videotape, so that she can assess her emotional reaction to the whole event and stop it at will. Most clients can scan visual content more easily if their eyes are closed, and this may be suggested. Therefore, the client is instructed that any time emotional, cognitive, or somatic disturbance arises during this "video presentation," she should stop, open her eyes, and so inform the clinician. At that point, the EMDR procedure, including the negative and positive cognitions, is implemented with regard to that part of the memory of the event. It is not unusual for various aspects of the memory that were not previously remembered to surface as disturbing. Metaphorically, the first round of reprocessing flattens the mountains so that clients can more easily see the hills.

After all of these relatively minor disturbances have been addressed, the clinician should ask the client to "run through the videotape" again with eyes closed. Once again, any newly revealed aspects of the memory that are distressing should be reprocessed.

If there are no further disturbances, the client should "run through the videotape" with her eyes open, holding in mind the positive cognition while the clinician administers a long set. The clinician should specifically ask the client to scan the videotape mentally—even though the images will not be clear—and to give the stop signal when she is finished. After this, the body scan can be done.

In addition to working on the actual memory, the clinician should be prepared to address any present stimuli that may be reported to cause a startle response (such as a truck rumbling by), nightmares, and other reminders of the event (such as seeing a crack in the sidewalk) that the client still finds disturbing. While the protocol appears lengthy, it can usually be accomplished in less than three sessions, since each aspect is generally dealt with very rapidly. However, clinicians should not place time restraints on clients, since their responses are unique and therefore unpredictable.

It is particularly important to remain flexible regarding the time necessary for treatment because there is no way of knowing with what earlier material the identified target (the recent traumatic event) is actually linked. For clients whose earlier history contains unresolved events that are associated with lack of safety and control, a longer treatment may be required. Since during processing it is not unusual for some survivors of natural disaster to recall earlier memories of physical or sexual assault, clients must be informed about the possible lengthiness of treatment. In addition, as always, the clinician should take the appropriate steps to ensure client safety, even when the presenting complaint appears to be an isolated and recent trauma.

This protocol is generally applicable to events that are up to 2 or 3 months old. If the event is more than 3 months old, the clinician should first use the single-trauma protocol. However, he should be prepared to switch to the extended protocol if the entire incident is not appropriately reprocessed.

PROTOCOL FOR PHOBIAS

Many trauma clients have phobias, and these require separate treatment. For other clients, the initial experience of fear has taken on traumatic proportions. In addition, phobic clients may be continually traumatized by the "fear of fear" and of the ongoing phobic experience (e.g., the ever-present danger of encountering a feared object, such as a dog). Many clients have organized their lives around avoiding the feared object or event. Therefore, it is important that the clinician do the appropriate clinical work to help the client fully assimilate newly acquired fearless behaviors.

For the purposes of EMDR intervention, phobias may be divided into two classes, which I have designated as "simple" and "process." A simple phobia is defined as fear of an object (e.g., a spider) that is circumscribed and independent of the client's actions. The fear is generated by the sight of the object and is independent of further participation. A process phobia, on the other hand, is defined as fear of a situation in which the client must actively participate. For instance, a phobia of flying requires the participation of the client: In order to be in the feared situation the client must purchase tickets, drive to the airport, and get in the airplane. Therefore, when targeting a process phobia, the clinician must address all the pertinent aspects of the phobia, including decision making and anticipatory anxiety.

Simple Phobias

The protocol for treating simple phobias (such as fear of spiders or snakes) is as follows:

1. Teach self-control procedures to handle the fear of fear.
2. Target and reprocess the following:
   a. Any ancillary events that contribute to the phobia
   b. The first time the fear was experienced
   c. The most disturbing experiences
   d. The most recent time it was experienced
   e. Any associated present stimuli
   f. The physical sensations or other manifestations of fear, including hyperventilation
3. Incorporate a positive template for fear-free future action.

Process Phobias

The protocol for treating process phobias (such as fear of flying or public speaking) is to add to the simple-phobia protocol the following steps:

1. Arrange contract for action.
2. Run mental videotape of full sequence and reprocess disturbance.
3. Complete reprocessing of targets revealed between sessions.

The use of self-control techniques is particularly important with phobic clients. Many phobias entail a fear of fear. Clients may report that they have avoided the activity so long that they no longer know if they actually still fear it. Rather, they are afraid of being overwhelmed by the fear itself if it arises. This is a very appropriate attitude if the client has never been able to deal with fear adequately. In order to address this problem, the clinician should teach the client a number of self-control procedures, some of which are listed later in this chapter. The client should practice these techniques in the office until she has achieved a degree of self-mastery and feels she can handle a certain level of anxiety and fear with a measure of confidence.

Most clients will need to learn how to identify the physical sensations that accompany the cognition "I am afraid." Concentrating only on the global sense of the emotion can be overwhelming for clients. If, instead, a client can learn that the physical sensations he equates with fear are simply sensations felt in his stomach and chest, for example, and that they are amenable to change, he will gain a greater capacity for controlling them. The ability to identify these sensations also implicitly allows the client to perceive himself as larger than the fear, since he can cognitively separate himself from it and place it under his control.

While the protocols for both simple and process phobias are straightforward, the clinician must first explore the client's history in order to identify any secondary gains issues that may exist. For instance, a client had reported a fear of snakes as her presenting complaint. However, during the history taking it became clear that there were a number of factors contributing to the phobia, including boundary issues, lack of assertiveness, and low self-esteem. An inquiry into the client's marital relationship revealed that her husband was domineering and got his way on most issues; in addition, he was a camping fanatic. Thus, it appeared that the client's snake phobia conveniently provided her with an acceptable excuse to stay home rather than accompany her husband on overnight excursions. (The same factors would apply in the case of a process phobia in which the wife is afraid of flying, thereby keeping her traveling salesman husband from insisting that she accompany him on his cross-country trips.) Clearly, until secondary gain issues are handled, phobias will not be amenable to treatment.

As with all treatments, the client should be reassured that there will be no pressure to perform or to conform to any outside standard. Clients should also be made to understand that giving up the fear does not mean they must engage in any particular activity: Relinquishing a fear of snakes does not force one to take up camping; losing a fear of heights does not mean that one must go skydiving. The clinician should make it clear to the phobic client that the right to choose is his and that his actions need not be motivated—or mandated—by either the fear or its absence.

In all cases the clinician must explore the genesis of the fear, because it may be rooted in an event that is apparently quite separate from the actual phobic response. For instance, one client reported a fear of driving a car. Every time she was confronted with an unanticipated situation while driving, she experienced a panic attack. History taking revealed that before her first phobic response she had been an exchange student in Europe. Since she did not know anyone well, she had been delighted to be invited to a party by a fellow student. Unfortunately, after drinking some punch she had begun to feel ill and had left the party. Once back in her room, she began to experience hallucinations, apparently because someone had spiked the punch with LSD. Frightened and alone and feeling completely out of control, the client had spent a terrifying night until the hallucinations subsided. Subsequently, while driving a car she had experienced a similar sense of loss of control during a near accident and had panicked. This feeling of panic evidently generalized to any experience of loss of control when behind the wheel of a car, even relatively minor ones. Obviously, before attempting to focus on the phobic response, it was necessary for the clinician to target the earlier experience of terror during the LSD hallucinations.

Once the appropriate antecedents of a phobia are reprocessed, a full EMDR treatment, including installation and body scan, should be carried out on each event in the following order: The first memory is targeted first, because it is assumed to include the stimuli pertinent to the genesis of the fear. The most frightening incidents are targeted second because they are assumed to include exacerbating stimuli. The most recent memory is targeted third because it is assumed to include stimuli that have become potent because of second-order conditioning. Additional stimuli should be processed separately, as there are various independent situations that can trigger the fear. For instance, in the case of a process phobia of flying, one client may become afraid only when a personal trip is imminent, another may be fearful whenever a family member has to travel, and still another not only may fear these situations but also may become fearful when hearing a plane overhead. Triggers should be appropriately reprocessed before attempting to incorporate any positive template for the future. For generalized phobias, such as claustrophobia, a representative incident of each anxiety-producing situation should be targeted (e.g., elevators, traffic jams, theater seats, etc.).

If symptoms of fear, including hyperventilation, arise during the treatment session, the clinician should target those physical sensations with successive sets. The clinician should speak soothingly to clients as the fear arises, encouraging them as follows: "Just notice the sensations; don't force them one way or another." Continuing the set through the fear, even in the case of a full-blown panic attack, may dissipate the disturbing emotion and reprocess the client's fear of fear. After the fear has subsided, the clinician should review a self-control technique (e.g., a safe-place exercise) with the client. This can reaffirm the client's ability to handle any fear that might arise.

With a simple phobia, a positive template is incorporated by using a single image, for instance, imagining being in the presence of a snake while feeling calm and relaxed. This projection should be reprocessed until it reaches a 6 or 7 on the VOC Scale. Often, clients will stop at a VOC level of 6 because they feel a need to experience the feared object firsthand to be fully convinced that they are not afraid of it. Regardless of the client's anticipatory state, he should be cautioned to maintain a log of any negative responses, which will be used as targets for future treatment. The log entry should constitute a good snapshot of what occurred, including images, thoughts, and physical sensations. For the claustrophobic client, a positive template should be installed for every trigger.

In the case of a process phobia, it is necessary to address the issue of anticipatory anxiety, as well as any cues that have become fear evoking owing to second-order conditioning. For instance, once clients who are afraid of flying are able to imagine themselves riding without fear in an airplane, a contract is made to have them actually take a flight within the month. The client is then asked to close her eyes and imagine a videotape of the time between the present session and the successful completion of her return plane trip. Each disturbing aspect of the process (choosing a destination, calling the airline, packing, driving to the airport, and so on) is reprocessed as a separate target. The process is repeated until the entire mental videotape can be viewed without fear.

The client must also report any fear or anxiety that arises as she takes the actions necessary to fulfill the contract. She should use the self-control techniques she has learned and keep an accurate record of each stimulus and her response to it for future processing. In all cases the clinician should assist the client to view her fearful reactions as feedback rather than failure. It may be useful to emphasize for the client that some moments of fear are to be expected in the ensuing weeks and that it is only necessary for her to identify these moments for targeting. This may lower the expectation of treatment effects sufficiently so that the client will not become unduly discouraged if fear momentarily emerges. The client should be encouraged to enter the situation that exposes her to the stimulus as an adventure of exploration, not merely as a prelude to successful resolution.

It is also possible that the primary phobic response will completely disappear when EMDR is applied only to the genesis event. However, the full treatment protocol should be implemented, when possible, to prevent future reactivation of the phobia. If the phobic response has gone into remission, the other targets can easily be addressed in a follow-up session.

PROTOCOL FOR EXCESSIVE GRIEF

The loss of a loved one is often a traumatic experience. The amount of suffering may be intense and will last for varying amounts of time. Under normal circumstances people eventually overcome their grief over the loss. However, this process of adjustment can suffer impediments, as indicated by a high level of suffering, self-denigration, and lack of remediation over time. Using EMDR to overcome these impediments may prove difficult for clinicians who are concerned that such a fast-acting intervention may not allow people the necessary period of time to "learn from their grief." However, as we have noted, EMDR does not eliminate or even dilute healthy, appropriate emotions, including grief. Rather, it can allow clients to mourn with a greater sense of inner peace.

With excessively grief-stricken clients the following should be targeted and reprocessed, as necessary:

1. Actual events, including the loved one's suffering or death.

2. Intrusive images.
3. Nightmare images.
4. Present triggers.
5. Issues of personal responsibility, mortality, or previous unresolved losses.

The EMDR protocol for excessive grief is similar to the standard protocol for trauma. Many clients report that their feelings of grief, sadness, and guilt are linked to intrusive memories, dreams, or fantasies of the loved one that seem to block their access to any pleasant memories or associations (see Access Restricted to Negative Material in Chapter 2). These negative images should be targeted and appropriately reprocessed. For example, a mother whose daughter had committed suicide in a mental institution blamed herself for her child's death. Any reminders of her daughter elicited terrible images of her child's suffering during the mental breakdown, along with concomitant feelings of guilt and powerlessness. After the negative images had been processed, the images that emerged when the clinician said, "Think of your daughter," were of happy childhood scenes of play and a ballet. Similarly, two youngsters whose father had committed suicide both reported their inability to produce anything but negative memories of him. When they were asked to think of their father, their only images were of his death (these were fantasies, since they had not been present) and of his sitting in front of the TV in an alcoholic stupor (which they had witnessed repeatedly in the months before his death). When these images were processed, positive memories of shared fishing trips emerged. The use of EMDR allows clients to continue the period of adjustment and loss but without the knife-sharp edge of intense pain.

Often, targeting the appropriate level of responsibility and any concerns clients have regarding their own present safety is crucially involved in the treatment of excessive grief (Solomon & Shapiro, in press). Because these factors are likely to be masked by intense sadness and emotional pain, they may become apparent only during processing. It is important, therefore, that the clinician maintain a respectful, nurturing attitude when clients reveal these previously hidden aspects of their suffering. For example, a negative emotional response may be the result of guilt engendered by the client's memories of being harsh or unkind toward the loved one. These incidents should be targeted for reprocessing.

The client's suffering because of the loved one's death may be compounded by a reactivation of earlier experiences of unresolved emotional loss. Such losses should be processed as they emerge. In addition, because the target situation is the death of a loved one, it is crucial that the client be carefully questioned (for appropriate targeting) about any distress that she may have experienced between sessions, particularly thoughts about personal injury or the mortality of other family members.

The use of EMDR should allow the grieving client to accept her painful personal loss and enable her to think back on various aspects of her life with the loved one with a wide range of feelings, including, hopefully, an appreciation of the positive experiences they shared. EMDR appears to restimulate the blocked system that is symptomatic of pathological grief, to accelerate the processing of dysfunctional information, and to allow appropriate, healthy insights and emotions to emerge.

It cannot be stressed too much, however, that EMDR does not eliminate or neutralize appropriate emotions and does not forestall personal growth. Thus, when EMDR is used, a grief-stricken client will naturally—and in her own way—move toward acceptance of her loss while simultaneously resolving impediments to recovery.

Even after a given treatment session, information processing and the enhancement of various stages of recovery will continue. Therefore, the clinician need not feel obliged to decide for the client how long she should suffer before implementing EMDR. He should feel free to use it at any time, especially since no clinical model can predict with certainty the optimal recovery time for a given client and since no clinician can fully appreciate the pain she is experiencing. Further, setting an arbitrary time limit before EMDR can be tried (e.g., "You should grieve at least 3 months/1 year/2 years") is antithetical to the notion of the ecological validity of the client's self-healing process. As is true for all other clinical populations, if the felt emotion (and its intensity) is appropriate for the grieving client, it will remain despite the application of EMDR.

One case of excessive grief involved a woman whose infant son had died. Just prior to his death she had nursed him through the night while telephoning and begging her physician to admit him to the hospital. The doctor continued to reassure her and insist that she keep the child at home. Holding her son to her breast, she rocked him through the night until they both fell asleep. When the mother awoke the next morning, the baby was lying dead against her chest. Her feelings of pain over this death were immense, and she sought relief from an EMDR therapist. After the 90-minute treatment session, she said, "I can feel him in my heart. I'm grateful for the time we had together. He's in a better place." Such a dramatic release from suffering after a very brief period of therapy directly addresses the question of how long the clinician should withhold therapy from a client. The answer, I believe, is to leave the decision to the client.

PROTOCOL FOR ILLNESS AND SOMATIC DISORDERS

The following protocol is included to underscore the fact that victims of physical illness may also be suffering from psychological trauma. While trauma responses, such as PTSD, are easily diagnosed in clients who have suffered rape or battlefield stress, many clinicians do not recognize that the assault on the psyche of the client may be just as severe—or even more severe—when the perpetrator is perceived to be the client's own body. Whether the psychological effects are debilitating because of the pain and fatigue born of chronic illness or because of the impact of a catastrophic disease such as cancer or AIDS, such clients must be treated with the same nurturing concern afforded the rape or wartime victim. Indeed, in many instances, the psychological and social issues that must be addressed are similar.

In brief, the EMDR protocol for working with illness and somatic disorders is as follows:

1. Create an action plan to address real needs.
2. Identify and reprocess relevant memories, present situations, and fears of the future dealing with
   a. personal and physical constraints
   b. social issues
   c. medical experiences
3. Run "videotape" of the next 1 to 5 years.
4. Use Simonton-type imagery with appropriate cognitive groundwork.
5. Identify suitable positive cognition.
6. Link image and positive cognition.
7. Assign homework with the self-use procedure.
8. Use log and self-care procedures.

This protocol addresses both psychological and physical factors related to somatic complaints. However, it should not be a substitute for appropriate medical care but an adjunct to it. Although the protocol will be discussed in the context of treating a cancer patient, it can easily be amended to apply to the psychological (and possibly physical) concomitants of any illness, physical complaint, or somatic disorder.

For many clients with somatic complaints, addressing the psychological dimensions will cause partial or complete remission of the physical symptoms. When primarily organic processes are involved, the psychological issues may be viewed as exacerbating the physical condition. While physical symptomatology may not remit, the clinical emphasis is on improving the person's quality of life. Very often, it is the client's psychological tension or self-identification as a helpless victim that can be the most debilitating factor.

A perfect example of the psychological determinants of the quality of a person's life in the face of debilitating conditions is seen in the life of Ronald A. Martinez, who served as one of the EMDR Institute's first educational associates. When Ron was a 15-year-old sports fanatic, he made a simple dive into a swimming pool—and became a permanent quadriplegic. One day many months later he made the choice between remaining an invalid on the dole, which his friends told him was a completely acceptable option, and making something of his life (Martinez, 1992). He chose the latter and became a loving and extraordinary clinician who inspired thousands of people. Ron remains the exemplar of a principle that has become central to EMDR therapy: "It's not what happens to you but how you deal with it that matters."

Obviously, in the case of a permanent disability, the clinician will have to address issues of finances, career, relationship changes, and so on. EMDR will not eliminate the fears or anxieties related to issues that should be addressed by means of education or action. Only after devising a plan of action and addressing the client's most pressing needs should the clinician deal with the psychological ramifications of the disability. If this is not done, realistic fears may interfere with the client's ability to focus on and reprocess the dysfunctional material. Once a practical plan has been developed, the clinician can use EMDR to target any dysfunctional fears or doubts that the client may have about implementing it. However, an exception to this strategy is when the primary presentation is pronounced, intrusive symptomatology. In this case the primary intrusions should be addressed before targeting the rest of the symptoms, because the fears engendered by the intrusive symptomatology can hamper the client's ability to think logically and effectively enough to construct appropriate action plans.

With cancer, as with most presenting pathologies, the EMDR model requires a search for the relevant memories, present factors, and fears of the future. EMDR must be used on all identified problem areas. A detailed client history may reveal patterns of self-sacrifice and difficulty in dealing with anger. With any illness, the issues of secondary gain engendered by these kinds of patterns must be addressed. For instance, practically everyone has had the experience of backing out of a social obligation by using the excuse of not feeling well. This is one of the few generic excuses met with sympathy rather than hurt feelings. The clinician should pay careful attention to the client's ability to draw appropriate boundaries, voice appropriate needs, and take appropriate levels of responsibility. Some clients can permit themselves to cease nurturing others only when they are physically unable to do so. For other clients, illness is the only way they can receive nurturing because of either earlier modeling or actual present-life circumstances.

The clinician should take care to assess present factors, which may include a no-win situation that is generating feelings of helplessness and hopelessness. In addition, it is important to address the systems issues in relation to the disease. Not unlike the rape victim, the victim of a catastrophic illness must confront the reactions of family and friends. It is not unusual for the presumed support system to fail, because friends are negatively affected by the client's disease. In some cases, they are so distressed at the thought of losing the person or at thoughts about their own mortality that they actually abandon the client. In other cases, friends may deal with the situation by minimizing the possibility of death or by exerting strong pressure on the client to maintain an optimistic facade. The full clinical picture must take into account these possible reactions and the client's emotions. It is not unusual for feelings of guilt and helplessness to dominate the client's consciousness to the point where she is unable to establish appropriate boundaries and personal stability without clinical assistance.

Besides addressing social issues, the clinician should assess the impact of medical procedures and professionals on the client's psychological stability. Memories of distressing medical experiences can be detrimental to client comfort. For instance, a cancer patient sought treatment with EMDR because her only hope appeared to be a new experimental treatment for her metastasized cancer. The problem was her inability to decide whether the possible benefits of the treatment outweighed the possible adverse effects on her quality of life, because of intrusive thoughts related to an earlier negative reaction to chemotherapy. EMDR was used to metabolize the earlier memories and instill a feeling of control and ability to choose. When the client decided to undergo the experimental cancer treatment, EMDR was also used to reprocess the inappropriate fear and to provide her with a variety of coping skills to be used during treatment. After undergoing the chemotherapy, the client reported that her state of mind during the medical procedure allowed her to experience it with ease. She also noted that the experimental medical procedure had produced the fewest negative side effects of any cancer treatment she had undergone.

The clinician should also take care to assess and address the negative consequences of any insensitive remarks that may have been made to the client by medical personnel. The unfortunate tendency of some physicians to use fear to motivate clients to comply with treatment regimens can have a highly negative effect on client stability. Any disturbing events of this nature should be targeted at the initial stage of the protocol.

It is vital that the clinician address the client's future and pose (and perhaps target) questions such as "Who am I without the cancer?" and "What do I have to change or confront?" If they apply, the memories that laid the groundwork for feelings of low self-esteem and powerlessness must be metabolized. Issues concerning parents, family, significant others, career, identity crises, and present disturbances must also be addressed. Family therapy may be necessary to allow family members to adjust to a new image of a mortal parent or spouse and to concomitant feelings of anger, betrayal, and grief.

The clinician should work with family members to reprocess any of their responses that are distressing to the client, thus enabling the family to provide the greatest support. If the client is forced to focus continuously on the dysfunctional responses of the family, his sense of helplessness and lack of control will be intensified. If family members are not available for treatment, EMDR should be used to help the client adjust to his family as they are, not as he wishes them to be.

Ultimately, the client must explore the question "Do I want to live?" along with any negative concomitant emotions that arise. Reprocessing of inappropriate fears and expectations can help the client arrive at an affirmative answer.

In order to process any residual dysfunction most effectively, it is useful to have the client envision himself in a healthy state 1 and 5 years from now. The client is asked to "run a videotape," along with a positive cognition, of the next 1 to 5 years of his life. Whenever the client notices undue disturbance or doubts, the eye movements should be initiated.

While the following section addresses ways to bolster the immune system in order to facilitate the healing process, premature death may be inevitable for some clients. It is important, therefore, to couch this material in a way that invites a possible healing but also concentrates on the quality of life of the client who may, in fact, be dying. Ultimately, if the client must accept death from the illness, the clinician should use EMDR to target his ability to reconcile with his family and friends, put his estate in order, and cope with his fears of death itself. An imagined videotape of the future can be played for this purpose as well. EMDR has also been used in the hospital to assist clients who are suffering from intractable pain to let go of the guilt they feel about wanting to die and be released from their pain.

In attending to the psychological dimensions or the disease process itself, it is vital that the clinician help the client to feel empowered, not guilt-laden. When discussing the possibility of mobilizing resources to assist in the healing process, the clinician must take care that the client does not infer that he is responsible for his illness. Such a misperception can leave a client feeling that if he is not cured, it is his fault. This is devastating to treatment and should be avoided at all costs.

The client must be made to understand that he is not responsible for the disease because his susceptibility to stressors that inhibit the immune system may be genetic and the early modeling that encouraged some types of reactions and any contributing psychological characteristics were foisted on him long before he had any choice in the matter. The concept of a potential healing process must be explored in a way that does not contribute to additional tension or self-denigration. It is important to convey to the client that just because he is attempting to catalyze his own healing does not mean that he is to blame for the disease.

An excellent resource on bolstering the immune system and mobilizing all resources to combat the cancer disease process is a book called *Getting Well Again* (Simonton & Creighton, 1982). Back in the 1970s when working as a psychologist and radiologist team, the Simontons received referrals primarily of terminally ill patients. They were intrigued by the question of differential survival rates among these patients, and their analysis revealed that these rates were often correlated with the patients' attitude and mental imagery. The Simontons suggested helping patients to formulate a mental image of the immune system as a powerful entity capable in some way of defeating the weak cancer cells. In many instances, a positive effect on quality of life and longevity was reported as a result of enhanced mental attitude and these imagery exercises. Many researchers in the burgeoning field of psychoneuroimmunology have supported the Simontons' early findings (Cousins, 1989; Pelletier, 1977; Rossi, 1986; Siegel, 1989; Solomon & Temoshok, 1987).

In order to assist the client in creating a positive image, I suggest a good cognitive groundwork. Assure the client that cancer cells are the weakest in the system. That is why chemotherapy and radiation therapy work; they kill off the cancer cells while the stronger, healthier cells survive. Often, EMDR may be used at this point to work on some problematic statements that may have been made by medical personnel regarding the cancer's potency. In addition, clients often report distress when remembering the look on their doctor's face as they received the diagnosis, a look they associate with the delivery of a death sentence. It is unfortunate that there are still physicians who are ignorant of the findings of psychoneuroimmunology.

One drawback to the imagery advocated by the Simontons is that it entails picturing the immune system as an overpowering force in a warlike state, for example, as wolves or as artillery whose job is to destroy the cancer cells, which are pictured as a weaker enemy. While this type of imagery was excellent for some clients, it was extremely troubling for others because of their pacifist views. It is important, therefore, that the imagery used by clients be geared to their psychological makeup and personal beliefs. A destructive, warlike force may be appropriate for some, whereas an image of the heart of Jesus or another spiritual icon sending in a healing light would be a better choice for others. Once again, with EMDR it is important to employ a client-centered approach, which allows clients to choose the images and cognitions that work best for them. The objective is to provide a dynamic image of the cancer cells being destroyed and leaving the body.

Once an appropriate image has been selected, the ease of application, along with the choice of an appropriate cognition, should be addressed. One client who worked with the Simontons had developed an image of electricity coming through the top of his head and moving through his entire body killing all the cancer cells. However, when applying for EMDR treatment, he reported that he had used the imagery only rarely and, in addition, that the electricity often got "stuck" in certain parts of his body and would not proceed the entire way through. The EMDR clinician first asked the client to formulate a positive cognition to go with the picture. He chose "My immune system heals me." He was then instructed to hold simultaneously in mind the picture of the electricity and the positive cognition; then the eye movements were added until the cognition became stronger. He was next instructed to close his eyes and imagine the electricity moving throughout his body. Whenever it got stuck he was to open his eyes, and the eye movements were used until the electricity began moving freely again. EMDR was used repeatedly in the office, targeting the linked cognition and image, until the client could easily access both of them with an attendant sense of power. Imagery homework was then assigned that instructed the client to use the imagery, cognition, and eye movements (the self-directed use of eye movements is discussed later in this chapter) at least three times a day. The client decided that he would rehearse the imagery every time he urinated, thus reinforcing his positive cognition with the thought that the cancer cells were being washed out of his system. That is, he simultaneously used the imagery, the eye movements, and the thought "It will take away all the poison."

When possible, the image and positive cognition should be linked continuously when the eye movements are used. If that is not possible—for instance, if the image is a moving picture and the client has difficulty maintaining a focused attention—the eye movements should be used with the positive cognition at the opening and close of the image-viewing process.

The clinician should instruct the client in the self-directed use of eye movements to ensure continuous processing during the imagery homework. While it is usually inadvisable for clients to use the eye movement sets at home during early stages of therapy because of potential abreactions, an exception is made with this protocol because the imagery and cognition that will be targeted at home have already been treated by repeated eye movement sets in the clinician's office.

Therefore, any dysfunctional material in the channels associated with the target will already have been reprocessed before the client uses the eye movements at home. The client should record in his log any doubts, resistance, pertinent memories, or current upsets that may arise during the self-directed use of the eye movements. EMDR should be used to address not only the fear, but all of the ongoing traumatizing experiences related to the cancer, including feelings of body betrayal; the real or perceived callousness or indifference of medical personnel, family, and friends; and negative emotions related to hospital stays, medical tests, operations, and so forth.

Once again, it should be emphasized that most victims of severe illness are likely to be suffering from PTSD as well. While this concomitant is quite apparent with rape or molestation victims, it may also occur when the perceived perpetrator is the victim's own body or immune system. Because the resulting sense of powerlessness and self-disgust can be quite paralyzing, the clinician must be careful to frame the work in terms of self-healing, a focus that helps to restore the client's sense of power and choice.

Relaxation and pain-control techniques, such as those given later in this chapter in the section Self-Control/Closure Procedures, can be very helpful in producing a sense of self-efficacy. In addition to having psychological benefits, the "light stream" technique described in that section is particularly useful with acute pain (S. Levine, personal communication, 1982; Levine, 1991). The eye movement sets themselves have also been reported to be useful for pain management (Hekmat, Groth, & Rogers, 1994). Encouraging clients to make use of supportive group therapy (Spiegel, Kraemer, Bloom, & Gottheil, 1989) and one or more alternative health-care approaches, such as massage or nutrition, to promote a sense of self-nurturing and to mobilize psychological resources and a greater sense of control may also be beneficial. Self-care and the logging of doubts and fears are ongoing processes, and any client concerns or restrictions should be targeted by the clinician.

EMDR treatment may be considered essentially complete when clients are able to envision themselves as healthy and cancer free and a body scan reveals no negative sensations. Although the image of good health is strengthened by EMDR, it must of course be done with realistic goals. In other words, EMDR can help empower the client to do whatever it takes to attain a positive quality of life that is enhanced by a sense of control and self-efficacy, and through the present EMDR protocol the body may be mobilized to do what it can to enhance the healing process. Ultimately, however, the client needs to reconcile himself to the outcome of his illness, whatever that turns out to be. He must be convinced that although reaching for something does not ensure that it can be grasped, nothing can be accomplished without the attempt.

SELF-DIRECTED USE OF EYE MOVEMENT SETS FOR STRESS REDUCTION

Caveats and Suggestions

It is difficult, if not impossible, to engage in intense, complete personal therapy without a clinician's assistance. This section presents the ways in which the eye movement sets can be used by clients as self-directed techniques for stress reduction, not as techniques for the self-implementation of the full EMDR procedure for therapy purposes. As we have seen, EMDR is much more than just eye movements, and the various clinical choice points—which are obvious to a trained clinician—are not necessarily discernible to clients, even if they are clinicians themselves.

In addition, it is not recommended that clients be taught the self-directed use of eye movements in the early stages of therapy. There is no way of knowing to what a given target or anxiety response is linked, and even seemingly innocuous disturbances can be rooted in extremely disturbing childhood memories. If the eye movement sets are attempted by clients prematurely, even on apparently minor stressors, high-level abreactions can be stimulated and can cause a retraumatization, since clients will not be able to maintain the sets themselves to reprocess the material. It is not unusual for a client's eyes to stop moving during a typical treatment session; it is the clinician's responsibility to monitor the client's progress and to make sure that the eye movement set is continued for the appropriate amount of time.

If the client engages in the eye movement sets without clinician supervision, even a successful session can result in continued processing that can be disruptive to the clinician's treatment plan. Therefore, the clinician should request that the client avoid self-directed use of the eye movements before consulting with him and refrain from attempting their use with another layperson. However, if the client has reached the end of the overall therapy, the clinician may suggest the eye movement sets for home use, since the client has already processed most of the major channels of information. Even in this case, however, the clinician should urge the client to keep a log of any new disturbing memories or reactions that may arise.

Self-directed use of the eye movements can also be extremely helpful for clinicians who wish to minimize the effects of vicarious traumatization by reprocessing their own response to clients' disturbing stories. The effects of vicarious traumatization, which are well documented in the field of mental health (Figley, 1995; McCann & Pearlman, 1990), can interfere not only with the therapist's ability to maintain a detached clinical perspective, but with her sense of personal safety and satisfaction. It can be extremely beneficial for the clinician to use the eye movements whenever client stories or images of atrocities are particularly disturbing. The sooner the sets are done with this material, the sooner it will be processed, assimilated, and resolved.

Clinicians should, of course, be aware that dissociated material may be activating their high level of disturbance in vicarious traumatization and might emerge as a result of the eye movement sets. If this occurs, they should seek appropriate assistance and not attempt to resolve the problem alone. Attempting self-directed therapy in these instances can also result in retraumatization, since the memory may merely be dissociated once more rather than reprocessed.

Technical Considerations

To aid the self-application of eye movement sets, it may be useful to set a metronome at an appropriate speed to help in maintaining rhythmic movements. The metronome should be used for purposes of auditory input only, as the sweep of the standard metronome is not sufficiently wide to accommodate a full side-to-side movement of the eyes. The metronome should be placed so that the sound is heard with equal volume in both ears in order to maintain bilateral attention. However, this auditory assistance, while helpful for some individuals, may be distracting for others.

The following is a list of suggested strategies for the self-directed use of eye movements (though it is by no means exhaustive):

1. Hold the head straight, look forward, and then move the eyes to the extreme right and observe a distant object. The same movement is then made to the extreme left. Then the eyes are moved back and forth between the two objects.
2. Look alternately at one side of the room (or a point on the wall) and then another.
3. Sit with one hand, palm down, on each thigh (with legs parted) and raise one index finger at a time while the eyes move back and forth between them.
4. Move a lifted hand back and forth across the line of vision.
5. By far the easiest way to maintain the eye movements is to use an externally generated moving focal point. Some individuals have hung a pendulum from the ceiling or used a light bar. A light bar with variable speed and direction has been designed and tested and is now available for personal use by therapists (Neurotek, 1994).

In addition to using the preceding strategies, the client can imagine the therapist's fingers moving across his visual field. This technique is especially helpful because it incorporates a motion with which the client is usually very familiar. It also carries a sense of safety that has been conditioned by the therapeutic relationship. It is important to remember, however, that self-directed use of eye movements should be applied only to minor anxieties, since highly abreactive responses can interrupt the focus needed for continuous eye movement and adequate resolution of the target.

SELF-CONTROL/CLOSURE PROCEDURES

Since it is vital that a client never be allowed to leave the office in the middle of an abreaction, an adequate closure procedure should be established prior to a treatment session. Such a procedure must provide the clinician with a means of ending the processing session so that the client is in a state of relative calm even if the processing has been incomplete. Further, since material can continue to undergo processing between sessions, the client should be equipped with a variety of self-control techniques and a stress-reduction tape in order to handle any disturbing thoughts and emotions that may arise.

In the following paragraphs I will describe some of the many procedures that can be utilized for self-control and closure of an incomplete treatment session. The clinician should initiate one or more of these before EMDR processing begins to determine which works best for the client; the procedure can then be introduced with confidence if disengagement is called for during an abreactive response. Once a technique has proved successful in defusing emotional disturbances, the client can be reminded of this experience if and when subsequent abreactions occur.

Reassuring the client that her disturbance can be reduced by using the technique may encourage her to continue the processing to a successful conclusion. As stated earlier, if the client has always been overwhelmed by fear and anxiety, the "fear of fear" can disrupt the treatment process. Having a successful experience in handling a disturbing emotional state is an important factor in the client's ability to process material during the treatment session and to manage adequately between sessions. Self-control/closure techniques are particularly important when working with patients who are suffering from traumas, phobias, or panic disorders.

While clinician-guided hypnosis may be excellent for ending an incomplete treatment session, it does not provide the client with a sense of self-efficacy and self-reliance between sessions. Therefore, if the clinician has a favorite hypnotic technique, it would be useful to modify it after successful administration for the client's self-use between sessions.

Safe-Place Imagery

Before processing, clinicians should help clients construct a safe place in their imagination. (This procedure is explained in Chapter 5.) The safe place allows the client to access a sense of comfort and equilibrium by focusing on a key image or phrase.

Taped Visualizations

Visualizations are offered on a variety of commercially available stress-reduction tapes (e.g., Emmett Miller's "Letting Go of Stress" by Source Cassette Tapes). These tapes are extremely useful for stress management and are highly recommended for client self-care. Clients should be encouraged to use one or more visualizations each day after the initial history-taking session. The client's favorite visualization may then be implemented in the office by the clinician and used before the first treatment session. If the commercial stress-reduction tapes are not relaxing to the client, the clinician should tape her own for the client's home use.

The Light-Stream Technique

The "light stream" technique is described here in detail because feed-back based on its use during EMDR trainings has indicated it to be effective approximately 90% of the time. This technique is also provided for use by clients for the alleviation of chronic and acute pain and, in fact, is an expanded version of an ancient yoga exercise that has been used successfully with sufferers of chronic physical and emotional pain (S. Levine, personal communication, 1982; Levine, 1991). The clinician should be guided by the client's responses; the second set of questions is asked in order to determine whether it is appropriate to continue.

Before EMDR processing is begun, the client is asked to bring up some disturbing target and to concentrate on the body sensations that accompany the disturbance. Since the use of EMDR includes the identification of body sensations, this is also a good opportunity to see if the client needs education on this skill. If so, the clinician asks the client to concentrate on a blank screen and notice how his body feels by mentally scanning it. Then the clinician asks the client to bring a disturbing target to mind and to notice the resulting changes in his body sensations. The clinician repeats this procedure until the client is easily able to identify body sensations that accompany disturbing material.

Once the client is able to concentrate on his body sensations, the visualization proceeds. The clinician tells the client that this is an imaginal exercise and that there are no right or wrong answers. The clinician then asks the client to concentrate on body sensations: **"Concentrate on the feeling in your body. If the feeling had a shape, what would it be?"** After the client responds (e.g., the client might reply, "Round"), the clinician continues with **"And if it had a size, what would it be?"** (The same client might, for example, reply, "Like an apple.") The clinician continues this line of questioning by asking about the feeling's color, temperature, texture, and sound (e.g., **"If it had a color, what would it be?"**). When clients are asked about the feeling's sound, they are told to simply describe it as "high-pitched or low"; otherwise, they might become frustrated or anxious by trying to make the sound.

After the client has responded to these questions, he is asked, **"Which of your favorite colors might you associate with healing?"** It is important that the clinician accept the client's answer—unless it is the same one he offered for the color of the feeling in the body. In this case, the clinician should ask for another color. Once the client identifies a color, the clinician continues as follows:

> **"Imagine that this favorite colored light is coming in through the top of your head and directing itself at the shape in your body. Let's pretend that the source of this light is the cosmos: The more you use, the more you have available.** *The light directs itself at the shape and penetrates and permeates it, resonating and vibrating in and around it. As it does, what happens to the shape, size, or color?"*

If the client indicates that it is changing in any way, the clinician continues, repeating a version of the italicized portion above and asking for feedback until the shape is completely gone, has become transparent, has assumed the same color as the light, or has undergone some other transformation. Change in the image usually correlates with the disappearance of the upsetting feeling. If no change occurs after the second attempt (the client might say, "Nothing is happening; the light is just bouncing off"), the technique should be discontinued and another one tried.

After the feeling that accompanies the disturbing material dissipates, the clinician may continue in a slow, soothing tone:

> **"As the light continues to direct itself to that area, you can allow the light to come in and gently and easily fill your entire head, easily and gently. Now allow it to descend through your neck, into your shoulders, and down your arms into your hands and out your fingertips. Now allow it to come down your neck and into the trunk of your body, easily and gently. Now allow it to descend**

through your buttocks into your legs, streaming down your legs and flowing out your feet."

Once the clinician perceives that the client is fully relaxed, he gives the client a positive suggestion for peace and calm until the next session. Then he asks the client to become awake and aware on the count of five.

Vertical Eye Movements

To help close an incomplete session, the clinician should direct the client in sets of vertical eye movements (which seem to have a calming effect) and offer soothing comments such as **"We can put it away now,"** or **"It can be put in a box until next time,"** or **"We can let it go for now."** After the client agrees with this statement, the clinician may use the safe-place or the light-stream technique for further calming effects. Alternatively, the clinician may ask the client, "What is the most helpful thing you have learned today?" The client's answer is then reworded as a positive cognition and used with additional vertical eye movements. This can assist the client by increasing her sense of accomplishment as well as by installing a meaningful positive cognition.

DEBRIEFING AND SAFETY ASSESSMENT

Whatever the form of hypnosis, guided imagery, or other procedure used to end a session, the clinician should give the client a thorough debriefing. Explain that regardless of what occurs during the week, the client should use the log and not hesitate to call if there is undue disturbance. An incomplete treatment has a tendency to continue processing between sessions at a level of disturbance that is higher than that following a completed one.

It is also vital that the client make an informed decision about driving a car after sessions. Regardless of the inconvenience, a client who is incapable of driving should not be allowed to leave until alternate arrangements are made for transportation. A client who is highly susceptible to hypnosis can often be helped to reassociate by asking him to become conscious of his feet or to imagine a cord connecting his spinal column to the center of the earth. The clinician should allow sufficient time at the end of each session to assess and provide for the client's needs regarding his ability to function safely. The visualization used to close a trauma session can itself be temporarily disorienting.

SUMMARY AND CONCLUSIONS

Clinicians should be comfortable with the use of the standard 11-part EMDR procedure as the basis for all clinical applications. Flexibility is also important, however, because the clinician may need to modify the procedure during a given client's treatment. Whether variations of the procedure are used or not, the clinician should take care to retarget all pertinent material in order to determine if any additional channels need processing and to properly conclude the session.

The reevaluation phase opens each subsequent treatment session and guides the clinician in the application of specific treatment protocols. Any number of protocols, both standard and specialized, may be necessary for an individual client. The standard three-stage protocol reviewed in Chapter 8 provides the comprehensive targeting necessary for most trauma survivors. This is mandatory when the client shows full PTSD symptomatology. The additional protocols that are covered in this chapter are generally used in conjunction with the standard three-stage protocol.

Applying EMDR to the memory of a major trauma includes targeting all pertinent representations of the event as well as its present stimuli. Addressing a specific dysfunctional behavior also necessitates the incorporation of a positive template for future action.

The 11-part procedure is directed at all targets. Traumas that have occurred within the past 2 months may have to be treated with the protocol for recent events. If the standard protocol is used for events less than 3 months old, clinicians should switch to the protocol for recent events if treatment effects do not generalize to the entire memory.

As with all clinical populations treated with EMDR, phobic clients should be investigated for secondary gain issues and taught self-control procedures to deal with any unforeseen disturbance. The multitarget phobia protocols should both incorporate a positive template and address the anticipatory anxiety confronting victims of process phobias. Log reports are necessary to ascertain currently conditioned stimuli in need of reprocessing.

The treatment of grieving clients indicates that while a period of adjustment and a deep sense of loss naturally accompany the death of a loved one, impediments to healing may cause persistent suffering and block the memory network so that the client recalls only disturbing memories. Clinical observations indicate that EMDR does not cause clients to lose anything that is beneficial to them and that it may be applied at any time during the grieving process to allow healing to proceed more gently.

The protocols for illness or somatic disorders incorporate the use of Simonton imagery, along with the standard three-pronged attention to memories that have caused or contributed to the disturbance, to present situations that exacerbate the condition, and to a future template that includes positive cognitions related to health and well-being. While not intended to take the place of medical treatment, EMDR can have beneficial results when used according to principles espoused by those in the field of psychoneuroimmunology (e.g., Cousins, 1989).

The self-directed use of eye movement sets can relieve minor disturbances but should not be attempted for complete personal therapy. As with any application of EMDR, there is no way of knowing what associations underlie the target, and an abreaction precipitated by disturbing material would prevent the self-directed user from continuing the eye movement sets to completion. However, after the primary therapy has been concluded, such self-directed use can be added to the client's repertoire of self-control techniques. Clinicians can use the self-control procedures to bring closure to incomplete sessions, and clients can use them to dissipate disturbance arising between sessions. The light-stream technique and self-administered eye movements are useful for pain control as well as stress control. A final debriefing and safety assessment is mandatory when these procedures are used to conclude a treatment session.

CHAPTER 10

The Cognitive Interweave

A PROACTIVE STRATEGY FOR WORKING
WITH CHALLENGING CLIENTS

> As you go the way of life, you will see a great chasm.
> Jump. It is not as wide as you think.
> *From a Native American initiation rite*

The cognitive interweave is an EMDR strategy that was developed to handle challenging sessions with highly disturbed clients. These clients often enter into cognitive and emotional loops that are not amenable to the simpler EMDR interventions. To develop a more proactive strategy, I turned to the clinical heuristic provided by the Accelerated Information Processing model. The interventions I developed are strategies to "jump-start" blocked processing by introducing certain material rather than depending on the client to provide all of it. The term *interweave* refers to the fact that this strategy calls for the clinician to offer statements that therapeutically weave together the appropriate neuro networks and associations.

When working with populations characterized by particularly complicated pathologies, the clinician may find a large percentage of clients who require the cognitive interweave. Generally, the clients who need it most are those with personality disorders, dissociative disorders, multiple-abuse histories, and educational deficits. However, because any client in a given session may run into blocks that necessitate the use of the cognitive interweave, the clinician should become comfortable with its use.

While the strategies for blocked processing described in Chapter 7 call for clients to concentrate directly on the emerging material, at times this will not be sufficient to allow the old dysfunctional material to reach resolution. When this happens, the clinician will need to use the cognitive interweave to introduce new information or a new perspective. Remember, however, to use the cognitive interweave selectively so that the client's own processing system can do the work necessary for the full integration of the information.

The cognitive interweave should be used when spontaneous processing is insufficient for the achievement of therapeutic goals. Specifically, clients will need clinician-initiated processing in four situations:

1. *Looping.* Even after successive sets the client remains at a high level of disturbance with repetitive negative thoughts, affect, and imagery. Processing remains blocked even after the clinician has used the EMDR variations described in Chapter 7.

2. *Insufficient information.* The client's educational level or life experiences have not given him the appropriate data to progress cognitively or behaviorally.

3. *Lack of generalization.* The client has achieved a more positive emotional plateau or cognition with respect to one target, but processing does not generalize to ancillary targets.

4. *Time pressures.* During the last third of the clinical session, the client has an abreaction or fails to process an abreaction sufficiently or a target appears that is multifaceted in the number of negative cognitions associated with it (and therefore will require more time than the remainder of the session allows).

This proactive version of EMDR deliberately interlaces clinician-derived or clinician-elicited statements with client-generated material, instead of relying solely on the client's spontaneous processing effects. While extremely useful to the clinician, it should be used sparingly, because the most powerful changes for the client are almost always those that arise from within. Further, when the client sees that the major insights and shifts of consciousness she is experiencing are due to her own internal processes, her sense of self-esteem and self-efficacy is greatly enhanced.

The information in this chapter should be used only after the clinician has become comfortable, through supervised practice, with the material covered earlier in this book. While use of the cognitive interweave is necessary to complete the treatment effects for a significant number of clients, clinicians will generally not be able to discriminate the indicators and appropriate timing for these interventions unless they are at ease using the basic EMDR methodology. After sufficient experience with EMDR, they will understand how far an individual client can process the target material without needing additional clinical intervention and will therefore be able to establish a baseline to indicate when the cognitive interweave is required.

Before using the cognitive interweave the clinician should determine whether blocked processing may be due to an insufficient implementation of any aspect of treatment described in previous chapters. This includes inadequate attention to the need to ensure that the client feels safe with the clinician and understands how processing works (e.g., that it requires that the client notice but not resist or force material to emerge during processing). The clinician should also make sure that there are no secondary gains or current situations that must first be addressed with an action plan and that there are no blocking beliefs to handle. Any of these conditions can result in excessive looping.

In order to understand the use of the cognitive interweave, we need to go back to the fundamental concepts of the Accelerated Information Processing model. This is particularly important because of my previous emphasis on the need for the clinician to allow the client's spontaneous processing to occur without interference. We will now be exploring ways of proactively stimulating blocked processing. In the cognitive interweave, proper timing and targeting are vital for success. We will briefly review the theoretical model as a refresher and as a reminder not to fall back on the old habits of talk therapy. The clinician should intervene only when needed and then as briefly as possible. The neuro network conceptualization guided my introduction of the cognitive interweave into EMDR standard practice, and clinicians can perhaps be aided by continuing to use this metaphor.

FOUNDATION OF THE INTERWEAVE

The Accelerated Information Processing model states that dysfunctional material is held in a neuro network in state-specific form. Therefore, each of these neuro networks is dominated by the emotional and cognitive content of the traumatic event (i.e., by the emotional state and the cognitive state of mind the client was in at the time of the trauma). In the case of trauma from childhood, this condition incorporates and maintains the perspective of the child; that is, it encompasses the state of cognitive and emotional understanding achieved by the child at the time of the event, which is stored in state-specific form. Moreover, it is isolated from any later adaptive interpretations and experiences the client may have had. While pathology can be seen as stemming from the intrusive and pervasive aspects of dysfunctional material from the past, clients obviously seek clinical assistance because of their belief that something needs to change in the present. However, this more adaptive view of the need for change can be seen to result from the accumulation of later information and more functional judgments about the traumatic event, all of which pervade another neuro network—the adult perspective.

The outcome of an EMDR session apparently causes the linkup of the two networks; an assimilation of the painful material into its proper perspective (i.e., that it belongs to the past); and a discharge of the dysfunctional affect, with generalization of the adaptive cognitions through the hitherto isolated material. Thus, after the treatment of a trauma the client is able to bring up earlier memories that are now fully integrated into the more adaptive perspective. Along with this new perspective comes the ability to act in a more appropriate and empowered way.

During the majority of EMDR sessions the adaptive processing of information can be viewed as the spontaneous linkage of appropriate neuro networks. Metaphorically, the train is laying down its own tracks as it moves progressively from one stop (therapeutically adaptive plateau) to another. However, when the processing is blocked, the clinician can use the cognitive interweave as a means of deliberately laying down new tracks to link the appropriate neuro networks. This linkage is accomplished by stimulating nodes that already exist or by infusing new information into the system.

By using the cognitive interweave the clinician attempts to change the client's perspectives and personal referents to the adult or adaptive perspective. Once the client cognitively accepts even the possibility of the adaptive perspective, the clinician adds a set of eye movements to forge the appropriate link between the network containing the targeted dysfunctional material and the network containing the positive perspective. Time permitting, the clinician then allows the client to return to spontaneous processing through successive sets that are performed without the intervention of the cognitive interweave.

RESPONSIBILITY, SAFETY, AND CHOICES

Accurate timing and sequencing of the proactive interventions are necessary for the success of the cognitive interweave. In order to stimulate blocked processing the clinician must try to duplicate as much as possible what would occur spontaneously. During their EMDR sessions clients do not generally jump immediately from intense negative to profound positive affect or cognitions. Rather, there is a transmutation of information as progressively more adaptive material is sequentially integrated. Clinicians will be able to use the cognitive interweave most beneficially if they are aware of the relevant clinical issues and can introduce new adaptive perspectives in a progressive manner that parallels the typical client's natural healing process.

In this section we will use the example of trauma clients, who generally confront three major issues—responsibility, safety, and choice. Thousands of EMDR sessions have indicated that processing these three concerns, generally in this order, is an integral part of successful treatment. During processing, a client may spontaneously move through the three cognitive and emotional plateaus (inappropriate feelings of guilt, perceived lack of safety, and helplessness) to a more mature and balanced view. The clinician can observe this movement with respect to guilt when the client shifts during a session from a negative cognition such as "I am a bad person" or "I should have done something" to a positive cognition such as "I am a good person" or "I did the best I could." In other sessions, feelings of fear and lack of safety may transform a negative cognition such as "I am in danger" into a positive one ("It's over; I'm safe now"). A client's confidence in his ability to make future choices may be reflected in the shift from the cognition "I have no control" to "As an adult, I can now choose" or "I am now in control." When spontaneous changes do not occur, the cognitive interweave introduces the appropriate plateaus. Let us take a look at how this works.

Specifically using the cognitive interweave with the topics of responsibility, safety, and choice, in that order, can vastly accelerate the treatment of early trauma. The initial objectives are to help clients (1) recognize and attribute appropriate responsibility and (2) discard the guilt and self-blame that have undercut their sense of self-esteem and self-efficacy. Once these clinical goals have been achieved, it is easier for clients to recognize that they are no longer threatened and are able to make safe choices in both the present and the future.

For example, a client who was molested by her uncle still felt intense feelings of fear and guilt when she accessed the memory. Although now in her 30s, she felt as she had as a child, when she was unable to leave or get the help she needed. When processing does not cause a spontaneous change in such feelings, the clinician uses the cognitive interweave. Specifically, the clinician tries to elicit the client's awareness of more functional and adaptive perceptions by asking pointed questions (such as "Whose responsibility is it?") or by offering appropriate information to lead the client to the desired response. Thus, in our example, as soon as the client decided, however tentatively, that it was the perpetrator who was to blame (or at least that she was not responsible) for the traumatic incident, the clinician administered additional sets with the direction "Just think of that." This was followed by a spontaneous processing that transmutes the affect from fear and guilt to disgust or anger at the perpetrator.

The following is an excerpt of the transcript of a treatment session in which the client in our example was processing the initial memory of sexual abuse by her uncle. This client also had a sexually inappropriate father who made suggestive comments and remarks to her throughout most of her life, a factor that compounded the problem. The transcript shows the usual EMDR assessment and targeting, which is followed by the use of the cognitive interweave to assist the processing of a block.

THERAPIST: So, there were two memories having to do with your uncle. When you think of him now, which one's more upsetting?

CLIENT: The most vivid one.

THERAPIST: Describe that just a little.

CLIENT: It was just a fragment of memory of him holding me down and putting something, like a finger, in my buttocks.

THERAPIST: Okay. Now if you hold that memory in mind, what negative belief goes along with it, something negative that you're saying about yourself.

CLIENT: I'm bad.

[This cognition represents a common theme among sexual abuse survivors.]

THERAPIST: And if we could just change the belief, what would you like to have instead?

CLIENT: It's not my fault.

THERAPIST: And "I'm fine"?

[The clinician suggests an adjustment to the positive cognition.]

CLIENT: And I'm fine; I'm safe.

THERAPIST: As you hold the memory and the words "I'm fine; I'm safe," from 1, completely false, to 7, completely true, how true do the words feel?

CLIENT: About a 4.

THERAPIST: Okay. If you bring up the picture and you bring up that cognition of "I'm bad," what emotion comes up for you?

CLIENT: Terror.

THERAPIST: Zero to 10—zero is neutral and 10 is the worst you can think of.

CLIENT: About a 9 or 10.

THERAPIST: Where do you feel it in the body?

CLIENT: My lungs.

[The client's processing then became stuck after the initial memory was replaced by thoughts of her more recent difficulties with men. In the next segment of the transcript she is focusing on a time when she was humiliated by a former lover and was unable to express her anger about it.]

THERAPIST: What do you get?

CLIENT: I was blaming myself for choosing somebody like that.

THERAPIST: Okay. Whose responsibility was it that you learned not to be able to express anger? That you learned to choose men like that? Whose is that?

[The therapist uses the cognitive interweave to address the issue of responsibility by asking questions that identify two of the sources of the client's predicament.]

CLIENT: My uncle.

THERAPIST: Just stay with that. (*leads client in a set of eye movements*)

CLIENT: My father's, too.

THERAPIST: (*leads client in a set of eye movements*) What did you get?

CLIENT: My head started feeling a little tight; my heart is still palpitating some.

THERAPIST: Just notice. (*leads client in a set of eye movements*) What do you get now?

CLIENT: Those men were my uncle and my father.

THERAPIST: Just notice. (*leads client in a set of eye movements*) What did you get now?

CLIENT: It's something like my family sacrificing me to be abused.

THERAPIST: Where do you feel it?

CLIENT: I feel it everywhere.

THERAPIST: Just notice. (*leads client in a set of eye movements*) What did you get?

CLIENT: It's like I'm supposed to be the beautiful little china doll or something. Just supposed to look good and nothing else really matters. Sort of horror and anger.

THERAPIST: Just notice. (*leads client in a set of eye movements*) What did you get?

CLIENT: What I got was, it really wasn't my fault and that I'm not a hollow shell.

THERAPIST: Okay. That's good. Stay with that. (*leads client in a set of eye movements*) What did you get?

CLIENT: My heart is starting to palpitate again, and my head is feeling kind of tingly.

THERAPIST: Just stay with that. (*leads client in a set of eye movements*) What did you get?

CLIENT: Anger at all of them for doing that. They still do it.

THERAPIST: They still do it?

CLIENT: They still just really see me for what I look like and not really who I am. There's still a big piece of that.

THERAPIST: And whose responsibility is that?

[Therapist again uses cognitive interweave to address appropriate responsibility.]

CLIENT: It's theirs.

THERAPIST: Think of that. (*leads client in a set of eye movements*)

[Clearly, no child is responsible for her molestation by an adult, and the sequelae of the abuse are directly attributable to the perpetrator. Making this connection on an emotional level is one of the first stages of the healing process. When the processing is blocked or the client is looping, the clinician helps her to make the cognitive connection so that it can be emotionally assimilated as the processing proceeds.

After the clinician in this case study used the cognitive interweave to help the client reach the first plateau of appropriate responsibility, the client began to make additional cognitive connections. The subsequent plateaus of safety and choices emerged spontaneously.]

CLIENT: I don't have to attract men like those men, and I also don't have to be alone. I mean sometimes I think I have to be with abusive men or totally by myself.

[The client makes a spontaneous assertion of her freedom to make choices that ensure her safety.]

THERAPIST: (*leads client in a set of eye movements*) What did you get now?

CLIENT: Just a picture of some of my friends. Just that it's safe to love them. They're not like any of my abusive family members.

THERAPIST: Good. (*leads client in a set of eye movements*)

CLIENT: They love me for who I am, not for what I look like. And, ironically, they are all beautiful. It's comforting.

[The client is aware of the beneficial choices available to her.]

THERAPIST: Stay with that. (*leads client in a set of eye movements*)

[The client then returned to the target memory and began making additional associations about other areas of dysfunction. For instance, her relationships had always been with abusive men. She found herself sexually attracted only to men who had narcissistic qualities and who ended up hurting her. Memories emerged of dreams and nightmares that always included her uncle and father, generally along with other angry or violent men. Because the client's feelings of safety had not fully generalized to the associated material, the clinician used another cognitive interweave (which places the memory in the past) in order to reinforce them.]

CLIENT: It's something about my nightmares. Sometimes I'm afraid to go to sleep or go back to sleep when I wake up.

THERAPIST: Stay with that. (*leads client in a set of eye movements*)

CLIENT: The statement that "It's okay." I can feel the fear around going to sleep as in the past.

THERAPIST: Stay with it. (*leads client in a set of eye movements*)

CLIENT: It's just how everything scared me as a kid. And how I couldn't really be spontaneous.

THERAPIST: Okay. just stay with it. (*leads client in a set of eye movements*)

THERAPIST: What do you get?

CLIENT: I just feel a little calmer.

THERAPIST: What happens if you think the words, "It's over, I'm safe now?"

[The therapist uses cognitive interweave to help the client separate past from present in order to help her recognize that she is no longer a vulnerable child.]

CLIENT: I don't know. I'm not sure.

THERAPIST: Just think about it.

[The client does not have to embrace the statement wholeheartedly at first. Simply attending to the suggestion allows the adaptive information already inherent in her memory system to be stimulated.]

CLIENT: Okay.

THERAPIST: (*leads client in a set of eye movements*) Good. What did you get now?

CLIENT: That he won't do that to me again. I won't let him. He won't do that to me again because I am an adult and I can keep myself safe.

[The client's words indicate a spontaneous emergence of the recognition that she can make adult choices.]

THERAPIST: What do you get?

CLIENT: Sore over here (*points to neck*). And I hate them. And it's not my fault.

THERAPIST: (*leads client in a set of eye movements*) What do you get?

CLIENT: That it's okay to be safe, and it's okay to be loved.

THERAPIST: Good.

CLIENT: And I love my father.

THERAPIST: Stay with that. (*leads client in a set of eye movements*)

[The client's admission of love for her father is ecologically valid. Independence does not mean hatred.]

THERAPIST: What do you feel?

CLIENT: I'm feeling more flexibility in my neck. My head feels like kind of moved around.

[The flexibility indicates a somatic shift, a release of state-dependent sensations that apparently accompanied the original event, during which her head was pinned down.]

THERAPIST: Just notice it. (*leads client in a set of eye movements*)

CLIENT: I hate my uncle. It felt like a little older version of "I hate my uncle." A little older than five.

[The client's words indicate that an adult perspective is emerging.]

THERAPIST: Good. (*leads client in a set of eye movements*) What did you get now?

CLIENT: Starting to feel more adult-like. That I can hate them and I can move on. I'm just angry that it happened at all.

[Notice that the client uses the word "adult" to describe her present feelings. These kinds of client statements serve as an ecology check. Even though the goal of reprocessing is to incorporate this adaptive perspective, the therapist does not use the word "adult" to the client. It emerges spontaneously during processing.]

THERAPIST: Just notice. (*leads client in a set of eye movements*) What did you get now?

CLIENT: Angry that I had to take care of people to get any semblance of nurturing. That I couldn't just get it because I deserved it.

THERAPIST: (*leads client in a set of eye movements*) What do you get now?

CLIENT: A sensation around my neck again.

THERAPIST: How's it feel?

CLIENT: It feels better.

THERAPIST: Good, stay with that. (*leads client in a set of eye movements*)

CLIENT: Now what came up was of keeping men away who are like the men I am attracted to and being able to say no to them.

[The client spontaneously imagines asserting herself to make choices in the future.]

THERAPIST: Good. Stay with it. (*leads client in a set of eye movements*) What do you get?

CLIENT: What came in was the fear that I can't say no and that that connects with my nightmares.

THERAPIST: What happens when you think the words "As an adult I now have choices"?

[The therapist uses cognitive interweave to reinforce further the third plateau of the client now having the ability to choose.]

CLIENT: It feels great.

THERAPIST: Okay, just think of that.

CLIENT: I'm an adult, I now have choices. Okay.

THERAPIST: (*leads client in a set of eye movements*) What do you get now?

CLIENT: What came up is an image of my uncle holding me down and telling me that I didn't have choices and then this image of me kicking him in the face.

[Client's comment indicates a spontaneous change of imagery.]

THERAPIST: Great. Just think of the words "As an adult I now have choices." (*leads client in a set of eye movements*) What do you get now?

CLIENT: Me saying to my uncle, "You have no power over me."

THERAPIST: Good.

CLIENT: And my head just eased up a little bit, too.

THERAPIST: (*leads client in a set of eye movements*) Okay. What do you get now?

CLIENT: Kicking my uncle in the face again and screaming at my father.

THERAPIST: How does it feel?

CLIENT: Still scary.

THERAPIST: Just notice it. (*leads client in a set of eye movements*)

THERAPIST: What do you get now?

CLIENT: Men merging with my father and my uncle again. Me saying to my father, "You broke my heart," and then my ex-boyfriend sort of coming into that. It's all sort of merging together.

THERAPIST: What happens when you go back to the image with your uncle and you think the words "I am an adult and now I have choices"? How does that feel?

[The therapist directs the client back to the pivotal image in order to reinforce the positive cognition.]

CLIENT: It feels empowering, and I still want to kick him in the face.

THERAPIST: Good. If you bring up the statement "As an adult I now have choices," and 1 means completely false and 7 is completely true, how true does it feel?

CLIENT: 6 to 7.

THERAPIST: Okay. Again just hold the image. Hold the statement "As an adult I now have choices." And notice. (*leads client in a set of eye movements*) What did you get?

CLIENT: I kicked my uncle in the face and he got off of me.

THERAPIST: (*leads client in a set of eye movements*) What did you get?

CLIENT: I was telling my uncle that he can't do that to me and telling my father he has to stay in his own room.

THERAPIST: (*leads client in a set of eye movements*) What do you get?

CLIENT: I deserve love.

It is clear from countless EMDR sessions with trauma survivors that the shift to appropriate attributions of responsibility by the client is a necessary condition for positive treatment effects. Theoretically, this shift may reflect the client's need to achieve appropriate developmental stages of maturation, the first of which is personal differentiation, which involves distinguishing appropriate boundaries. Abuse victims often seem buffeted by feelings of guilt and self-denigration because of their participation in the event. Frequently, they identify with the actions of the perpetrator—or hold the almost magical belief that they have caused the abuse—a fact that is manifested by their inability to establish and distinguish appropriate boundaries between self and others.

As long as clients remain at this undifferentiated state, they cannot escape the perceived danger; it is fully internalized. By allowing responsibility for the abuse to rest squarely on the shoulders of the perpetrator, however, the client is able to move from primary identification with the trauma (with the concomitant fear and self-condemnation) to an externalized vantage point of appropriate judgment. This first plateau appears consistently in the processing of childhood traumas. The clinician should initiate the plateau if the client is looping at a high level of disturbance and should test it with a probe question if it has not emerged spontaneously. Clearly, the two subsequent plateaus—reaching an awareness of one's present condition of safety and gaining confidence in one's ability to choose alternatives—are more difficult to achieve if one is unable to differentiate self from the sources of danger.

Once the first plateau is achieved and the danger is externalized, the typical trauma victim generally moves from a state of terror to one of fear. The second plateau, which entails a sense of present safety following recognition that the assault occurred long ago, should then be inaugurated. This usually defuses the fear and allows the client to express anger or disgust with the perpetrator. These emotions should be ventilated in the clinician's office before moving to the final stage, which evokes the client's sense of confidence in being able to make effective choices in the future and which should incorporate an internal locus of control. This stage generally emerges with an accompanying sense of calm and well-being. Each achieved plateau sets the stage for the possibility of the next one, and each may be accessed in turn by using a probe question to elicit the appropriate response or by offering appropriate information in order to educate the client, if necessary.

FITTING THE INTERVENTION TO THE CLIENT

If a probe question—such as "Whose responsibility is it?" or "Whose fault is it?"—does not elicit the desired response, namely, that it is the perpetrator who was at fault, the clinician should engage in a discussion (see next section) that will stimulate it. As soon as the client indicates a cognitive understanding of the issues (although perhaps with some hesitancy), the clinician should add a set with the instruction to "just think of it." If EMDR is properly applied (without major demand characteristics) and if the information offered by the clinician is accurate, a new perspective will be assimilated. If the information is not accurate, it will be rejected. In the latter case, after the set is over, the client will generally remain disturbed; he may also come up with a variety of reasons why the assertion is not true. These counterstatements are generally very productive and worth exploring. If they involve blocking beliefs, they should be processed, and if they involve a lack of understanding, the clinician should offer the proper explanations. If the clinician is wrong, she must acknowledge it.

It is mandatory for this intervention, and for all subsequent variations, that the clinician make the statement "Just think of it" in a suggestive, not directive, tone of voice. The object of this intervention is to assist the client in holding the information in consciousness (stimulating the appropriate neuro network) while the processing system is activated, so that the material can be appropriately assimilated. Any counterexamples or fears initially voiced by the client should be explored cognitively before the clinician repeats the request to "think of it" and initiates another set.

Only when the clinician maintains an open and exploratory manner will the client feel free to report any hesitancies he has regarding the positive resolution and to discuss material that may initially make him feel "disloyal" to his family or to the perpetrator. Unless misdirected feelings of submission and attachment, which are often part of the pathology of the childhood abuse victim, are handled delicately, clients can feel bullied and mistreated. The clinician should take care to assure the client that whatever appropriate connections he has with his parents will remain. Because trauma victims often have great difficulty in asserting themselves, it is vital that the clinician not allow her demand characteristics or position of authority to inhibit the client from revealing his feelings or responding to the interpretations the clinician offers. Attempting to exert undue clinical influence can disrupt processing.

The goal of EMDR treatment is a full integration of the more adaptive material. This means that any feeling of disturbance on the part of the client should be evaluated to determine if the proposed intervention is inappropriate (i.e., not ecologically valid) or if the client needs new or additional information to enhance cognitive understanding. Because EMDR does not appear to allow anything to be assimilated that is not appropriate for the client, the clinician must be willing to accept the possibility of being wrong. If the client does not feel free to disagree or if the clinician is unwilling to admit that she has offered an inaccurate interpretation, the EMDR session may increase, rather than decrease, the client's disturbance.

When an accurate intervention is offered in an appropriate manner and is followed by a set, the client will either accept the clinician's interpretation or become conscious of an important corollary or a significant variant of it. Either response should be viewed as a sign that processing is occurring and should become the focus of a new set. It is important that cognitive progressions be paired with a focus on the corresponding body sensations in a way that is not disruptive to clients. Often, as new material is offered, clients will report a feeling of disturbance such as fear, anxiety, or tension. If so, the body sensations should be targeted to facilitate processing. No new information can be considered fully integrated if the client has any residual feelings of fear or physical tension when it is held in consciousness.

INTERWEAVE CHOICES

According to the Accelerated Information Processing model, the clinician attempts to link the neuro network containing the dysfunctional information with a neuro network containing appropriate, or adaptive, perspectives. Some clients will already have learned and stored the appropriate information and will be able to express it. But this will not be the case for others, owing to deficits in education, parenting, or modeling, and the clinician must offer this information to them. The alternatives discussed in the following paragraphs may be used to introduce or elicit the information necessary for therapeutic resolution with the cognitive interweave.

New Information

The clinician may need to supplement the client's understanding of personality and interpersonal systems dynamics with education about the effects of modeling or physiological imperatives. For instance, if the client's response to the question "Whose responsibility is it?" is self-denigrating because he actually enjoyed the physical stimulation of the abuse, the clinician should explain the automatic nature of physical responses and the occasional unavoidability of sexual arousal in a variety of otherwise unpleasant situations. Likewise, clients may have to be instructed in the dynamics of modeling and in how the need for even negative or forced attention may be the heritage of certain kinds of family dynamics. Once the client accepts the information cognitively, if only with pronounced hesitation, a set should be administered. The following is an example of how a therapist might provide a client with new information:

CLIENT: It was my fault that it happened.

THERAPIST: Children have to be taught how to fight effectively, just as adults have to model social skills and learning skills. It's not something they are born with. Did anyone ever teach you?

CLIENT: No.

THERAPIST: Think of that. (*leads client in a set of eye movements*)

One may view appropriate processing as the transmutation of dysfunctionally stored material as it links up with more adaptive information. When the client lacks sufficient information to modify maladaptive cognitions, knowledge should be gently supplied by the clinician, who then initiates another set, which accelerates the adaptive linkage.

"I'm Confused"

When the clinician believes that the appropriate information already exists within the client, he uses a different alternative to elicit it. This strategic intervention is used to elicit the more adult or adaptive perspective on a cognitive level. Since self-denigrating affect may block progression to more appropriate cognitions, it may be useful to repeat aloud the client's statements of self-blame in order to reveal the cognitive fallacy to her in a nonthreatening way. Once the cognitive link is established, processing may resume. Say, for instance, that a client insists that she is to blame for the sexual abuse she suffered as a child. When the clinician asks why, her response might simply be, "I caused it." The clinician should then introduce a cognitive interweave, perhaps by responding in an apparently bemused fashion: "I'm confused. Are you saying that a 5-year-old girl can cause an adult to rape her?" When the client responds with doubt ("Well, no . . ."), the clinician should gently respond with "Just think of it" and then initiate a set.

"What If It Were Your Child?"

A variation on the previous strategy can be used to great advantage with clients who have children in the family toward whom they are lovingly protective. If the client responds to the probe question with a negative self-judgment, the clinician should respond with the following: "I'm confused. Do you mean that if your child were molested, it would be her fault?" This statement usually elicits a vehement "Of course not!" to which the clinician should gently respond, "Just think of it," and then initiate a set.

Combat veterans as well as molestation victims have been successfully treated with this variation. For instance, one veteran continued a line of self-denigration for having followed a direct order by a commanding officer to keep his head down when his best friend was shot. It was clear that the client would have been killed if he had done otherwise, but he nonetheless blamed himself for not doing something to prevent his friend's death. The clinician gently asked, "If it had been your 19-year-old daughter, what would you have told her to do?" The client responded, "To keep her head down." The clinician asked him to "just think of that" and then began a set. The client's response to the set revealed grief and a lessening of his guilt, and processing then resumed. For another veteran, the ability to forgive himself for his participation in the war (and the deaths that resulted) was evoked by the therapist's asking, "Would you forgive your son if he had been in Vietnam?"

This variation not only appears to link the dysfunctional material with preexisting nodes of appropriate information, but often opens pathways of self-nurturing and acceptance at extremely profound levels. During these sessions there are often tears and other displays of grief for the pain and isolation of the traumatized child or youth the client once was. Quite often, the perception shifts for the client from having been a bad child to having been a scared child, and there emerges a feeling of almost parental care for the wounded self. At this point in treatment an image of the client as a child may spontaneously emerge into consciousness. The client may now offer—or be encouraged to offer (as in other forms of psychotherapy)—to the scared child the appropriate assurances and nurturing so that he feels safe, understood, and protected. While the client imagines this, the clinician initiates additional sets.

Metaphor/Analogy

The use of stories to impart therapeutic lessons is completely compatible with EMDR and may forge the connective links to more adaptive material. By means of fables, fantasies, history, or the therapist's own life story, parallels can be drawn to the client's situation; by following this intervention with a set, information processing may resume. Remember, however, that the session is not complete until the client can reaccess the original traumatic material without disturbance. These strategic interventions are used to jump-start the blocked information-processing system. *Once processing is resumed, by means of any interweave strategy, the standard 11-part EMDR procedure should be fully implemented.*

"Let's Pretend"

Asking the client to visualize a possible positive alternative to the problem can often break through feelings of fear or concerns fed by secondary gains issues. Since the goal of the cognitive interweave is to allow clients to accept the possibility of change, a noncommittal approach can give the client sufficient security to make the useful connections. For instance, to enable the client to express feelings of violation to an authority figure, the clinician might say, "Let's pretend. If you could say something to him, what would it be?" If the client answers in a way that reveals the appropriate attribution of responsibility, the clinician responds, "Good. Now just imagine it and pretend you are saying it," and then initiates another set.

This strategy can also be used to assist a client who is locked in a disturbing scene from the past. In the transcript given earlier, the client spontaneously saw herself kicking the perpetrator. If processing had been blocked, the clinician might have guided the client through a set after asking her to imagine doing exactly that. The clinician can either suggest a particular action or, preferably, invite the client to imagine a new (unspecified) action by asking, "If the perpetrator tried it now, what would you do?" While the client is imagining the new scene, the clinician leads her through a set.

Socratic Method

The clinician can also use the Socratic method to shape the client's thinking processes. In this time-honored tradition a series of easily answered questions is used to lead a person to a logical conclusion. This method is a very useful adjunct to EMDR. It can help educate the client about deficits in his development or in his parents' modeling, allowing him to see that no blame can be attached to his past actions. The following dialogue illustrates the clinical use of the Socratic method. In this part of the client–therapist exchange, the client has just declared that as a young child she was primarily to blame for a dysfunctional relationship with her father.

CLIENT: I feel guilty that it wasn't different.

THERAPIST: Whose responsibility was it that it wasn't different?

CLIENT: Both.

THERAPIST: Both in what way?

CLIENT: Feels like I could have spoke my piece of mind. If I had angry feelings, I could have said something to him.

THERAPIST: How did he usually react to anger?

CLIENT: I don't know. I never got angry at him.

THERAPIST: Did you observe other people getting angry at him?

CLIENT: No.

THERAPIST: Nobody ever got angry towards him?

CLIENT: No.

THERAPIST: So how could you have known that you could do that?

CLIENT: Well, actually I didn't know. I really didn't think I could.

THERAPIST: Right. How were you supposed to know any different? No one ever taught you any different.

CLIENT: Right.

THERAPIST: Just think of it. (*leads client in a set of eye movements*)

The dialogue between clinician and client must be conducted in an exploratory vein, not as a parrying contest. The idea is to open the connective pathways to the new information in a way that is nonthreatening to the client. Any hint of manipulation or intrusion is likely to be detrimental to the therapeutic goals.

ASSIMILATION

The cognitive interweave is used to break through abreactive looping, or blocked processing, as well as to allow new information to be assimilated for use in appropriate future behaviors. As noted earlier, the primary points of focus for the trauma victim during the initial processing of traumatic material are information plateaus regarding (1) responsibility, (2) present safety, and (3) present and future choices. If the recommended procedural variations are used to help the client reach the first plateau of responsibility, processing may spontaneously progress to adaptive resolution. In other instances, after external responsibility has been established, the clinician will observe the client's emotional disturbance diminish from terror to fear and will then need to ask another probe question to help the client reach the plateau of safety.

When dealing with cases of molestation, the clinician must determine early in treatment whether or not the perpetrator is a present danger to children. If he is not, this information can be used to help the client attain the second plateau. For instance, if the perpetrator is dead or disabled or lives in a distant location, the therapist may ask, "Can he hurt you now?" Either the client says no and a set is added, or the clinician employs strategies to instill in the client the recognition that there is no present danger. The clinician may use the Socratic method to lead the client to that recognition, review the differences between the present situation and the past trauma, or use images showing that the relative heights of the client and the perpetrator are different now than when the client was a child.

VERBALIZATIONS

At this point, once the fear is past, it is not unusual for the client to feel extreme disgust or anger at the perpetrator. It is often useful to urge the client to voice her anger or pain to the abuser (e.g., "It was your fault that it happened. You shouldn't have treated me that way"). Earlier (in Chapter 7), the clinician was instructed to regard tension in a client's jaw and throat as an indication of a need to verbalize feelings. If use of the cognitive interweave is indicated, however, the clinician should initiate the verbalization on the basis of the client's emotional state and may even prompt the client with some appropriate words to use. A new interweave reinforcing the client's sense of safety and ability to vocalize may be needed to help her fully ventilate her emotion. The following transcript illustrates the use of this strategy with the client who was molested by her uncle:

CLIENT: I just had another part of my memory, too. Holding my head down.

THERAPIST: How's it feel now?

CLIENT: Okay. My heart's beating pretty quickly.

THERAPIST: Okay, just notice it. (*leads client in a set of eye movements*)

CLIENT: (*cries*)

THERAPIST: What did you get?

CLIENT: I was just thinking of why aren't my parents taking care of me.

THERAPIST: (*leads client in a set of eye movements*) What did you get?

CLIENT: It's still there, particularly my father. Why didn't he take care of me?

THERAPIST: Just notice. (*leads client in a set of eye movements*) What do you feel?

CLIENT: Disgust and anger at him.

THERAPIST: Just notice. (*leads client in a set of eye movements*) What are you feeling?

CLIENT: More of my anger at my uncle. How could he do that?

[By asking the client about her feelings, the therapist is inviting her to vocalize her emotions.]

THERAPIST: Good. If words come up spontaneously to say in your mind or out loud, just let yourself do that.

CLIENT: To tell him what?

THERAPIST: To tell him how you feel about what he did. If you want to do that in your head, that's fine. Just raise your hand for me when you've completed it. Just say what you need to say.

CLIENT: Okay.

[The following dialogue continued during a prolonged eye movement set. Clinicians should encourage clients through both verbal and non-verbal cues.]

THERAPIST: Just say what you need to say.

CLIENT: Just say, "I hate you, you son of a bitch"?

THERAPIST: Right.

[The clinician is acting as a cheerleader to encourage the client to vent her emotions.]

CLIENT: (*to perpetrator*) How do you do that to a 5-year-old girl?

THERAPIST: Really, really.

CLIENT: It's not fair.

THERAPIST: That's right.

CLIENT: It's cruel.

THERAPIST: Whose fault is it?

[The therapist is using the cognitive interweave to reinforce the client's present perspective.]

CLIENT: It's his fault.

THERAPIST: That's right. Tell him.

CLIENT: (*to perpetrator*) You destroyed my childhood. How could you do that? How could you do that?

THERAPIST: Tell him how you feel.

CLIENT: (*to perpetrator*) I hate you!

THERAPIST: Right.

CLIENT: (*to perpetrator*) I hate you, I hate you. I wish you were dead.

[The client states this forcefully and with finality. Therefore, the clinician stops the prolonged eye movement set to attend to any possible dysfunctional emotions or cognitions accompanying the statement. Such possibilities will be discussed later in this chapter.]

THERAPIST: Good, good. What do you feel now?

CLIENT: I feel okay.

THERAPIST: Okay, just notice the feelings. If there's more to say, say it. (*initiates another prolonged set*)

CLIENT: (*to perpetrator*) I just hate you. How could you do that?

THERAPIST: Let it out.

CLIENT: I could never say it, and I still can't.

THERAPIST: (*stopping set to identify what prevents full venting of feelings*) What is it now?

CLIENT: It feels more opened up. My chest feels more opened up. I still feel some stuff in my head.

THERAPIST: When you say you "can't" and you "still can't," what does that mean?

CLIENT: I've never confronted him with it.

THERAPIST: And if you did?

[The therapist is attempting to clarify the client's beliefs so that the cognitive interweave can be used. This does not mean that the therapist is advocating an actual confrontation with the perpetrator. The client will be debriefed about this after processing is completed.]

CLIENT: He'd probably deny it.

THERAPIST: And so? That's not saying you need to.

CLIENT: Right.

THERAPIST: You have a choice to.

CLIENT: Right.

THERAPIST: And if he denies it?

CLIENT: He denies it.

THERAPIST: It's not his salvation you care about.

CLIENT: Right, right, right.

THERAPIST: Just think about it. (*leads client in a set of eye movements*)

[The cognitive interweave is completed.]

THERAPIST: What do you get?

CLIENT: I still feel a little tension in my head—right up here.

THERAPIST: The tension—just notice it. (*leads client in a set of eye movements*) Okay, what do you get?

CLIENT: It's better. It's better up here. (*points to head*)

THERAPIST: Just notice it. (*leads client in a set of eye movements*)

CLIENT: It's like something popped in my head.

THERAPIST: (*leads client in a set of eye movements*) What do you get?

CLIENT: It's all right. It feels like it's breaking up.

THERAPIST: Good. Just notice it. (*leads client in a set of eye movements*)

CLIENT: Something else came up around my mom. My mom was really screaming and raging at me, and there was really no room to tell anybody.

THERAPIST: (*asking for clarification*) No way for you to tell them about him?

CLIENT: Yeah.

THERAPIST: Think of it. (*leads client in a set of eye movements*) What did you get?

CLIENT: What came up is, it's not my fault.

THERAPIST: (*leads client in a set of eye movements*) Good. What do you get now?

CLIENT: It's more the anger at my mom and the statement "It feels safer."

THERAPIST: Okay. Just notice. (*leads client in a set of eye movements*) What do you get now?

CLIENT: The statement came up that "I feel safer and I can sleep."

[The therapist adds an additional set to reinforce the positive cognition.]

As indicated in this transcript inviting the client to say or do what was previously impossible often helps to resolve further the issues of safety and present control. The client may initially choose merely to think the words during the set, but she should be encouraged eventually to say them out loud so that the clinician can assess the level of emotion in her voice. Alternatively, the clinician may ask the client to imagine what she would say to the perpetrator if he were abusing a friend of hers. Clients will generally be able to vocally defend a friend or beloved relative more easily than themselves. The client is asked to vocalize such a statement until it becomes strong and then to substitute herself in it. The following transcript shows the use of this strategy with an assault victim:

THERAPIST: What do you want to say to him?

CLIENT: I don't know. (*shows confusion and fear*) I can't defend myself.

THERAPIST: What would you say if he was hurting your best friend? What would you say to defend her?

CLIENT: (*to perpetrator*) Stop it, get away from her, you have no right to do that.

THERAPIST: (*leads client in a set of eye movements*) That's right. Good. Again.

CLIENT: (*to perpetrator*) Stop it, get away from her. You have no right to do that.

[The clinician repeats encouragement and adds sets until the client's voice is strong and firm. As the client begins to defend her friend emphatically, the clinician prolongs the set and coaches her with the following words.]

THERAPIST: Now try, "Get away from me."

CLIENT: (*to perpetrator*) Get away from me. You have no right to do that.

[The clinician repeats encouragement and continues the set until the client's voice becomes equally strong and firm in her own defense.]

Clients often begin with a hesitant and tentative verbalization, denoting a high level of fear and intimidation. As sets are repeated during the verbalization, the client's fear begins to dissipate and her tone of voice becomes stronger and steadier. The clinician should ask her to repeat the words until her anger is expressed with a sense of sureness and justification.

Specifically requesting clients to vocalize anger may be useful even when processing is not blocked. Even in cases where parental neglect or humiliation did not approach the level of molestation or bodily harm, the pent-up anger and fear can nevertheless be debilitating to clients. The client's inability to express these emotions becomes the target of the EMDR. If a client reports a feeling of holding back or being blocked, this physical sensation should be targeted directly. As the fear is reduced, the client's ability to speak with undiluted anger increases and then, most often, reverts to a calm sense of empowerment. Often, clients who are urged to express themselves during the set make a declaration of independence to the parent. The sets are continued as the clinician urges the client to elaborate or repeat these words until they are said with a firm, confident, and steady voice. The resultant feeling is often described by clients in terms denoting full emancipation and adulthood. This personal resolution also allows adaptive reconciliations, when appropriate, because the reservoir of dysfunctional emotions is drained.

Naturally, in order to time these verbal promptings correctly a good clinical ear is necessary. The clinician should make sure before proceeding that the client either has a cognitive understanding of her anger or spontaneously comments on its meaning. The clinician should also encourage and reinforce the client, regardless of the visual or auditory depictions of violence that may be presented. Anger untapped for an entire lifetime can be extremely frightening to the client. The clinician should reassure him that this anger is simply the manifestation of the childhood rage that has been locked in his nervous system. The clinician might say, for example, "This too is just the scenery passing by while you are on the train."

Regardless of the cause of the client's anger or the words used to express it, the clinician should indicate agreement by means of nonverbal cues (such as nodding), expressions such as "That's right," and encouraging vocalizations. This holds true whether the client's anger is directed at a perpetrator or at the parent who failed to provide protection. The clinician must be careful to give the client complete permission to vent her anger and pain without attempting to redirect it. At this point, logical discussions of how the parent was not omnipotent are neither called for nor helpful. Nevertheless, as processing progresses, the more tempered and judicious view will spontaneously emerge for most clients. However, as with all other facets of EMDR, the client should be allowed to take the lead in the maturation process, as long as no blocking is evident. Appropriate debriefing and checks for ecological validity should supplement all EMDR sessions.

In some instances, the primary emotion that the client may need to verbalize is grief. Whether he is confronting the death of a loved one or the loss of his childhood innocence, the client should be encouraged to give full expression to this grief. The impact of unspoken words of grief was evidenced strongly in a session with a Vietnam veteran. While the initial target was the scene of his best friend being blown up, the death of his parents came quickly to mind, and he made the wrenching declaration "I wasn't able to say good-bye." Using a cognitive interweave, the clinician encouraged the client to visualize his parents and express his emotions and engaged him in successive sets until he experienced a feeling of peace. This feeling was reinforced with further sets.

While some of these aspects of EMDR may appear similar to Gestalt techniques, it is the addition of the sets that appears to facilitate the profound and lasting change usually observed. I believe that staying fully present—that is, being compassionate, aware, and sensitive—with a client during an EMDR session allows the clinician to rediscover the wisdom of every major current psychological modality. Clearly, these modalities all have something to offer therapeutically or they would not have stood the test of time. The purpose of encouraging specific actions or a particular focus during an EMDR session is to inaugurate activities in a deliberate fashion that evolved spontaneously in other clients during effective processing. Many clients have cried out their love, sorrow, anger, or hatred automatically during successive sets. We invite other clients to do the same, that is, to open blockages by stimulating the appropriate neuro networks.

EDUCATION

The third plateau to be addressed is the ability to make adequate and life-enhancing choices in the present and in anticipation of the future. Clearly, for many clients the experience of childhood is one of relative powerlessness, dependence on a dysfunctional family, and attacks by an adult that one had no means of resisting. In general, a client's childhood emotional experience of lacking safety and alternatives is an accurate one. Part of the EMDR treatment is to resolve the past affect, including feelings of low self-worth, and to allow the client to embrace an appropriate sense of adult power in the present. For instance, female clients who have reprocessed early memories of molestation, experiences that have resulted in a fear of men and an inability to forge lasting romantic relationships, might be asked, "How do these words sound: 'As an adult I can now choose who I want to be with.'" Even a tentative approval from such a client is sufficient to start successive sets focusing on any feelings of fear or tension that may exist. Additional sets may focus on the new behavior to be actualized.

Clearly, in many instances it will be necessary to educate the client about social skills, assertiveness, dating customs, and so forth. These can be addressed by helping the client to understand the information at a cognitive level and to imagine the concomitant behavior (actions that would naturally result from such understanding). After this, successive sets should be initiated. As described in Chapter 8, this procedure assists clients in actualizing the material before attempting it in real life. However, this incorporation of a template for appropriate future action cannot generally be inaugurated until the residual primary fears related to the early childhood events have been metabolized. Little behavioral headway can be made until the client feels himself to be at or near a VOC level of 7 concerning the statement "As an adult, I can choose." The clinician should identify for appropriate targeting any blocking beliefs that prevent the attainment of a VOC of 7. However, if the client reports a VOC of 6 (or less) because deficits in her background are causing her to feel too unskilled or inexperienced to cope successfully with a projected situation, the clinician should recognize this as an ecologically valid response and initiate the appropriate education.

The cognitive interweave may be used extensively in the educational process as the clinician alternates sets with instructional and imaginal material. The clinician can offer specific instructions regarding a particular task, ask the client to imagine it, and then add the sets. However, as in all EMDR treatment, the clinician must be prepared for the possibility that the client will remember an earlier event that is connected with some level of disturbance. If this occurs, the memory should become a primary target and education suspended until the memory has been thoroughly reprocessed.

The cognitive interweave allows the clinician to become more creative by including his usual clinical interventions and skills within the EMDR framework. For example, clinicians versed in creative visualization may guide the client through "inner child" or other metaphor explorations, and those trained in art or movement therapy may offer assistance through their use of these creative strategies. Further, clinicians with particular expertise in a specialty population can cognitively assist the client to greater understanding of his problem before helping him assimilate the emotionally corrective material through the sets. The accelerated processing and assimilation of the information can be accomplished within the standard EMDR procedure. The sets are alternated with the individualized creative work, just as the cognitive interweave choices reviewed earlier in this chapter are used to open abreactive blocks.

In addition, the clinician should complete the full procedure, including reaccessing the initial target, initiating sets to discover if other channels of dysfunction are present, and leading the client in the cognitive installation and body scan. This helps ensure that the dysfunctional information is fully processed and that the client will not be hampered in future actions by inappropriate disturbance. As always, the clinician should use the client's log to help reevaluate the treatment effects.

SUPERVISED PRACTICE

The more proactive form of EMDR described in this chapter should not be used until the clinician is comfortable with the standard EMDR procedure and has become familiar with a baseline of client responsiveness to the interventions described in Chapters 7 and 9. At this point, clinicians may practice the cognitive interweave to help bring more challenging cases to a successful resolution. Information from the next chapter should be used to address more difficult clinical populations.

SUMMARY AND CONCLUSIONS

The clinician should use the cognitive interweave to (1) treat looping and other blocked processing, (2) address the lack of generalization of treatment effects, (3) incorporate needed information, and (4) defuse an abreaction or address a multifaceted target when there is not enough time remaining in the session for resolution. According to the present model, the clinician elicits information that links the appropriate neuro networks, that is, allows adaptive perspectives to modify dysfunctional ones. Three specific processing plateaus that the clinician may need to help the client reach, particularly if he is a victim of early trauma, are those associated with issues of (1) responsibility, (2) safety, and (3) choices.

A variety of strategies allow the clinician to elicit the appropriate material and then weave it back into the client's information-processing system. Regardless of the strategy used, it is important to maintain the client's sense of power and to retarget the critical information subsequent to the cognitive interweave to ensure that the client has appropriately integrated it.

Alternative strategies may be used to educate clients who may be suffering from learning deficits or to elicit information and perspectives that have already been incorporated. According to the Accelerated Information Processing model, this adaptive information is held in a neuro network that must be deliberately linked to the targeted material. For instance, the self-denigrating client may fully understand that another child is not responsible for a molestation by an adult; the cognitive interweave will gently lead the client to apply this adaptive perspective to himself, thus dispelling the guilt and self-loathing generated by his own trauma.

With the exception of the instances covered in this chapter, the clinician should generally refrain from using the more proactive version of EMDR so that clients can progress as far as possible on their own. Answers coming from the client are decidedly more empowering to them than answers provided by the clinician.

Cognitive interweave strategies must be used judiciously by a clinician who is willing to accept the client's rejection of her suggestions and who is willing to admit being wrong. Because EMDR appears to neither invalidate perceptions that are true nor add anything that is inappropriate, the cognitive interweave must be used in a flexible, exploratory way so that clients feel free to voice any concerns or counterexamples they may have. This more proactive version of EMDR is mandatory for successful treatment effects with many highly disturbed clients. Furthermore, it is a prime example of the interactive nature of treatment in that clients must be allowed to verbalize their pain and their needs and participate in the creation of the positive templates to be incorporated for future action. In the next chapter we will look at specific populations that may particularly benefit from the cognitive interweave.

CHAPTER 11

• • •

Selected Populations

> Most of us have lost that sense of unity of biosphere and
> humanity which would bind and reassure us all with an
> affirmation of beauty. Most of us do not today believe
> that whatever the ups and downs of detail within our
> limited experience, the larger whole is primarily beautiful.
>
> *Gregory Bateson*

This chapter opens with a discussion of generic issues of noncompliance, which may apply to the more challenging clients in all clinical populations, and then addresses the issues involved in using EMDR to treat trauma with a variety of standard clinical populations: children, couples, sexual abuse victims, combat veterans, and clients with dissociative disorders. As we will see, the cognitive interweave, discussed in Chapter 10, is necessary with most clients suffering from multiple sexual abuse, combat trauma, and dissociative disorders.

It is important for clinicians to remember that EMDR will not be suitable for every client in a given clinical population. For instance, although EMDR is widely applied in the treatment of PTSD, the selection criteria discussed in Chapter 4 preclude its use for certain trauma victims. Likewise, clinicians should not assume that EMDR will be effective with all clinical populations. The applications of the method are guided by the Accelerated Information Processing model, which emphasizes the role of early psychological experience in both the etiology and treatment of dysfunction. Pathologies with organic or biochemical bases are not assumed to be resolvable by treatment with EMDR procedures. It is extremely unlikely, therefore, that EMDR will be found to be the primary treatment of choice for a client with an active psychosis or a purely endogenous depression. However, once again, diagnoses are not as relevant as the individual evaluation. For any client, the experiential factors that contribute to the dysfunction may be amenable to EMDR treatment, even if other aspects of the pathology are not. Further, while EMDR has proven to be effective with a wide variety of clinical diagnoses, additional special protocols and customized treatment regimens are sometimes necessary and will be presented in a future text.

This chapter offers clinicians guidelines to assist them in conceptualizing the problems presented by specific populations. Appropriate case formulation and management are important aspects of any form of psychotherapy, and many suggestions found in this chapter may be broadly applicable. However, thousands of treatment sessions have indicated certain patterns of response that are particularly relevant to focused EMDR work. These guidelines and patterns should help the clinician choose targets and develop useful cognitive interweaves.

While this chapter gives a basic overview of considerations for working with selected populations, it is by no means comprehensive. Clinicians should never use EMDR with any population with which they do not have experience. Nor should clinicians use EMDR with any client they would refrain from treating by means of the other therapeutic tools at their disposal.

ISSUES OF NONCOMPLIANCE

Regardless of the clinical population to which they belong, some clients will be particularly resistant to change. Of course, resistance to treatment or noncompliance with the clinician's recommendations for targeting or homework may arise with any form of therapy. The following is a set of principles that I believe applies to noncompliance and that may prove useful as a clinician checklist. Remember, EMDR is a client-centered model; treatment must move at the client's pace. It is our job to ease the way for clients, not to force them through a protocol.

1. *The boundaries of the therapist's ability should not be construed as the limitations of the client.* Too often, what the clinician dismisses as the result of client resistance is actually due to the limitations of the clinician's model, repertoire of interventions, or ability to interact with the client. While client resistance and noncompliance may certainly be hurdles that need to be overcome, the interaction between the client and the clinician should not be discounted as a factor contributing to the lack of therapeutic effect.

In EMDR the clinician variables that influence the treatment effect include the ability to target the appropriate part of the pathology, and to order the targets appropriately, and comfort with the multifaceted approach. For full therapeutic effect of EMDR the clinician must be able to (1) establish a level of rapport that allows the client to reexperience comfortably the various aspects of the trauma; (2) identify accurately the appropriate targets; (3) use insight and sensitivity to assist in the completion of processing; (4) provide education about a variety of coping skills and systems information; and (5) offer appropriate mod-eling, when necessary.

Fortunately, the client-centered approach allows most of the thera-peutic work to be done in the office, rather than by means of between-sessions homework assignments. Therefore, in the absence of unproc-essed real-world triggers, continued client resistance or noncompliance is most likely due to inflexibility of the clinical approach and indicates the need for more client preparation and appropriate targeting.

2. *Both clinician and client should participate in determining the goals of therapy.* The positive or negative effects of any therapy are based on an interaction among client, clinician, and method. Part of this interac-tion is the appropriate selection of goals agreed upon by both client and clinician. If the client is being asked to reexperience disturbing aspects of a targeted trauma, the reasons for doing so should be acceptable to him. While there can be no guarantees regarding the outcome, the reasons for choosing to experience the discomfort of reprocessing will clearly include the possibility of liberation from the ongoing debilitating effects of the trauma. The client must recognize these potential effects in order to accept the discomfort generated by the processing. In addition, the negative therapeutic consequences of noncompliance should be frankly discussed with the client.

The client should approve of the clinician's goals, and the clinician should evaluate the client's goals for appropriateness. For instance, the client's aim of never getting angry while driving may be impossible to achieve and may be part of an inappropriate self-assessment, such as "I can't succeed," that underlies the reason for noncompliance. Clients should be helped to understand that noncompliance prevents achieve-ment of specific goals that they themselves have chosen, not goals foisted on them by the therapist.

3. *Noncompliance is viewed as a part of the pathology.* If the goals of therapy have been jointly arrived at, noncompliance can be viewed as part of the pathology that needs treatment. Just as we do not tell our clients to return for help when they are less depressed, so we should not ask them not to return until they are more compliant. With this understanding, consequences of noncompliance become part of the ongoing debriefing of the client.

Issues underlying noncompliance can include fear of failure, fear of success, and fear of terminating therapy. Appropriate assessment can be made by asking the client to respond to the question "What would happen if you were successful?" After the clinician addresses these fears, EMDR can be used to target any feeling of tension or resistance that may remain. Unless secondary gains are appropriately identified and addressed, little therapeutic progress can be made.

4. *Targets must be properly prioritized.* EMDR calls for the sequential targeting of memories that influence the pathology. The order in which these targets are accessed and processed is crucial. For instance, memories having to do with lack of worth should be targeted before memories concerned with fear of failure. If blocking beliefs are not appropriately addressed, therapeutic effects will be minimal.

In addition, EMDR calls for addressing directly the appropriateness of the client's fears. When fears appear to be based on real issues, an action plan should be in place before targeting the dysfunction; for example, if the client fears losing a disability check if PTSD is relieved, it is necessary for the clinician to help the client devise a plan for finding a new source of income. When appropriate fears are addressed through education and action plans, the residual fears or concomitant beliefs (such as "I cannot succeed even if I try") are viewed as suitable targets for reprocessing. After these have been processed, the trauma targets may be approached more effectively.

5. *The fears that underlie the lack of compliance may be based on early life experiences.* The clinician should evaluate noncompliance in terms of several factors: the client's spiritual beliefs (such as "Life is suffering"), parental injunctions (or the need to remain loyal to parents through shared suffering), and the client's need to manipulate others or to have power over them. Memories underlying these factors may be targeted before processing the targets that are the cause of the primary presenting complaint; after the memories underlying the noncompliance factors have been reprocessed, the present stimuli that elicit the negative affect or behavior should be targeted and processed. In addition, a positive template for appropriate future action should be installed. With issues of noncompliance, the client should be asked to imagine doing the task easily and comfortably. Targeting with EMDR opens up possibilities of new positive behaviors and allows any residual feelings of discomfort to be reprocessed.

6. *Treatment must be flexible.* The feedback log is an extremely useful part of treatment. If the client does not accurately report to the clinician any disruptive feelings or experiences that occurred subsequent to reprocessing, further targeting may be ineffective. Ironically, except for the client's refusal to engage in the treatment itself, the log is the major source of noncompliance in EMDR treatment and can be used as an appropriate reprocessing target. Specifically, the client can imagine keeping the log, and his feelings of resistance to the task, along with any negative cognitions and pertinent memories, can be addressed as they arise in the office. The clinician may conduct an EMDR session to help install a positive template regarding future use of the log (or of alternatives such as making audiotape recordings or drawings of the triggers and disturbance). Results

are then reported after the client is again assigned homework to do between sessions. Only behavioral changes that occur outside the office are considered signs of successful treatment.

Another example of noncompliance is failure to use the relaxation tape. In this case, other alternatives for relaxation must be explored during the treatment session. The goal of using a relaxation tape is to give the client ongoing instruction in self-control techniques. However, many alternatives to a tape are available as long as flexibility and creativity remain part of the therapeutic process.

In sum, while attending to issues of noncompliance, the clinician should choose a treatment that is flexible enough to work around most clients' resistances until they are resolved. This can often be accomplished by using EMDR, since most of the work is done during the treatment session. However, in some instances, the client's adamant beliefs may resist change. For instance, my most noncompliant client believed that it was spiritually inappropriate to use self-control techniques on an ongoing basis. In his case, I had to accept this as a limitation of treatment and explain the consequences to him. Because of the nature of this client's complaint, we created a contract about what we could and could not accomplish under these conditions before proceeding with therapy. Had the client been more severely dysfunctional, however, I would have been able to use the EMDR framework only to conceptualize the case, assess and identify problem areas, and provide guidance; I would not have been able to use it to process the information. It is important for clinicians to remember that they have other therapeutic methods available and that EMDR processing should be used only when appropriate.

CHILDREN

Life is all memory, except for the one present moment
that goes by so quick you can hardly catch it going.
                                            Tennessee Williams

Included in the many pleasures of working with children is the satisfaction of seeing the traumatic residue disappear quickly and of knowing that the children will be spared years of suffering and will not be driven to engage in behaviors that repeat the abuse on others. To ensure the successful use of EMDR with children, the clinician must pay special attention to creating a safe psychological environment. Clinicians should evaluate their ability to establish rapport with children and to communicate in language appropriate to their age level. As with any other procedure, EMDR should not be used with children unless the clinician is already comfortable working with them.

During the initial history-taking phase it may be useful for the parent to brief the clinician about the problem with the child present and then to leave the room while the child presents his version of the situation. This two-step process may allow the parents' authority to be tacitly transferred to the clinician and may give children a sense of being special when the clinician's full attention is turned exclusively to them.

During the EMDR treatment session the child should be seen without the parents present, if possible, in order to maximize the child's focus on the target. Obviously, there will be times when it is advantageous for parents to be in the room because of the child's fears about separation. However, every effort should be made to create for the child an optimal level of comfort when alone with the clinician. This goal may be facilitated by giving the child permission to bring along a favorite stuffed animal or toy to the next treatment session.

While the clinician must use the language of the child to explain EMDR, it is preferable to refrain from referring to EMDR as a magical cure—even if the child spontaneously adopts such an expression (e.g., "It's magic") when noticing how much better she feels. Rather, as with all EMDR clients, it is preferable to provide the child with a sense of self-healing and self-efficacy. If the clinician indicates instead that the power to remove the negative affect is vested in the method or in his own expertise (e.g., by saying, "I'm going to make it go away"), the child is likely to remain at a level of dependency and powerlessness that is detrimental to overall therapeutic goals.

Before attempting to target dysfunctional material, the clinician should make sure the child has a usable "safe place." A feeling of safety and assurance is induced in the child through use of eye movement sets in the context of an actual positive experience. For example, the clinician might ask the child to remember a time when he was in control and felt good and might have the child imagine looking, feeling, and acting in a positive way. As the child holds this scene in mind, the sets are repeated until the child feels happy or positive, as in the imagined scene. This positive experience with the eye movements (or hand taps) allows children to trust the process, since pleasant feelings are immediately evoked, and they are left with positive associations to the therapeutic experience.

Because the difficulties that clinicians generally encounter with young children are primarily due to concentration problems and relatively short attention spans, the average EMDR treatment session with children is about 45 minutes, during which eye movements are often interspersed with other activities. Fortunately, despite their comparative brevity, such sessions are likely to be therapeutically effective because children appear to respond favorably to EMDR very rapidly.

In order to enhance the child's concentration, the standard EMDR procedure should be adjusted in a variety of ways. In particular, the clinician will need to engage many external stimuli as focal points. Some primary adjustments in the treatment of children are addressed in the following paragraphs.

Concrete Definitions of Feelings

Children typically cannot conceptualize feelings using the SUD Scale because it is too abstract for them. Clinicians should have children use their hands to indicate the magnitude of a feeling. For example, holding the hands at chest level, with arms parallel to the arms of the chair, can be defined as "very bad/terrible/awful" or some other word that evokes the child's negative experience. Clasping the hands can be defined as feeling wonderful or as feeling "as good as looking at bunny rabbits." Children can also be taught to report accurately any changes in distress by indicating these concretely; for example, holding the hand close to the floor can indicate a little hurt whereas a hand held at shoulder height means a big hurt. Another option is for the clinician to draw on a piece of paper a horizontal line with a smiling face on one end and a crying face at the other and to ask the child to indicate where he is located on the line.

Eye Tracking

In order to assist children in eye tracking, the clinician can draw happy faces on her fingers or use puppets or other toys. Puppets or toys may also be used in the two-handed approach described in Chapter 3. The two-handed technique is often useful with young children because of their inability to cross the midline. For instance, when he is asked to draw a line on a piece of paper from the far left to the far right of his body, a young child will start drawing and then lift the pencil in the middle, putting it down again to complete the line. If the single-hand technique is used with a young child, his head will often move along with his eyes. This is acceptable and can achieve treatment effects, but a full range of eye movement should still be attempted.

For children who have an eye-tracking problem because of dyslexia, using small elliptical movements about 3 inches in diameter at the usual 12- to 14-inch distance from the eyes can be effective. Dyslexic children (even when older) cannot track a wide range of motion.

In children with attention-deficit/hyperactivity disorder (ADHD) there is often a tactile defensiveness that makes them uncomfortable when in close contact with the clinician. These children should be asked to move their eyes back and forth between two spots on the wall. To engage their attention these spots may be in the form of colored circles, cartoon figures, or comic book heroes.

Holding the Child's Attention

In order to increase the child's level of involvement when processing a traumatic memory, the clinician should be prepared to engage the child in a variety of ways. For example, during the eye movement sets the clinician might vocalize a lively tune like the William Tell Overture and should be prepared to make rapid rhythmic movements with his upper body to maintain the child's attention.

Clinicians should attempt to harness the child's imagination. For example, the EMDR treatment session may be initiated by asking the child to "imagine what happened" or to "bring up the picture." After the eye movement set the child can be asked to "blow up the picture" or "explode" it. The clinician can assist by making the sound of an explosion and by using gestures that the child can mimic. The clinician then asks, "How does it feel now?"; after redirecting the child's attention to the picture, the clinician adds a set of eye movements and repeats the request to "blow up the picture."

The Positive Cognition

When reprocessing is complete, the positive cognition is installed. The clinician should offer (without any special fuss) an easy cognition such as "I'm fine" or "Mommy/Daddy will take care of it" or "I'm safe now." It can be useful for young molestation victims to address and replace the negative cognition "Don't tell" or "I can't tell." Having the child concentrate on these negative cognitions during successive sets, without pressing for details, allows the fear engendered by these injunctions to dissipate. Then substituting the words "I'm safe now" or "It's okay to tell" can have excellent effects.

Using the Child's Cognitions

When working with school-age children it is preferable to elicit the negative and positive cognitions, rather than merely suggest them, even though they might not be ideally constructed. The clinician initiates a set of eye movements after asking the child to imagine the scene and respond to a question such as "What thoughts do you have?" or "What do you think about in the picture?" Most often, the child will respond with statements that indicate an external locus of control (e.g., "The teacher hates me" as a negative cognition and "The teacher likes me" as a positive cognition). The clinician may ask the child to hold a picture of the "teacher hating" while one or two sets are induced. The child is then asked "What thoughts do you have?" or "What do you think about yourself now?" The child will generally reveal a spontaneous switch from a cognition like "The teacher hates me" to a negative cognition like "I'm not motivated" or "I'm distracted" and a positive cognition like "I can do well in school."

While clinicians will typically attempt to contribute to an initial internal locus of control when working with an adult client, it is important for them to remember that children are frequently in a threatening environment and that they are indeed powerless. In addition, the child may not have a well- developed cognitive structure. Therefore, the clinician should offer the child the closest approximations to self-efficacy statements (e.g., "I'm okay" or "I feel good") without needing to adhere completely to the guidelines about positive cognitions for adults.

Generalizing Treatment Effects

In addition to treating individual memories that a child might reveal, it is advisable with this population to do additional EMDR work with the child concentrating on the perpetrator alone, that is, without imagining the perpetrator engaging in a specific action. Using such a procedure assists in generalizing the treatment effects throughout the entire associated memory network. For instance, a 5-year-old molestation victim was ritually abused by her father while he was wearing a black gown and mask. In addition to targeting her memories of abuse, which included seeing her dog killed, she was asked to hold in mind the picture of her father in his gown and mask. Using a still picture, instead of one in which the perpetrator is taking a particular action, allows a desensitization effect to generalize to all memories that include the cue of the still picture (in this case, the image of the father in mask and gown).

Children as young as 2 years are quite capable of bringing up an image. Be prepared for especially rapid treatment effects (presumably because young children have had relatively few experiences and therefore have fewer associations to be accessed). The child may start smiling happily after only a few sets, which is quite consistent with high therapeutic effectiveness. The clinician should check for subsequent changes in symptomatology, such as bed-wetting, nightmares, and panic attacks, which may disappear after only one or two sessions. However, while bed-wetting and night terrors may end for one child after a single session devoted to processing a molestation incident, cessation of symptoms may require many more sessions for other children. Once again, do not view EMDR sessions as a race. The rate at which treatment effects occur will vary from one client to another.

Creative Therapy

A number of clinicians have recognized the efficacy of the creative process (e.g., drawing, painting, sand-tray play) in the treatment of children (EMDR Network, 1991; Cohn, 1993). One clinical case example involved the pre- and posttreatment pictures drawn by a young boy. When the child was asked to make a picture of the problem, he drew a big black cloud that covered nearly the entire page. He was then asked to hold this picture in mind during successive sets. After showing signs of relief, he was asked to draw the situation again: It now appeared as a small black speck being chased out of the room. The child was then asked to hold this picture in mind for one or two additional sets, after which it was supplemented with a positive cognition.

Sand-tray play, dolls, and pieces of games can all be used as targets for children if the proper foundation is laid to allow them to link their feelings about the negative incident or perpetrator to the object. The full EMDR procedure may be implemented using these targets. However, the clinician should eventually return to the primary trauma images to check for complete resolution.

COUPLES

In order to be utterly happy, the only thing necessary is to refrain from comparing this moment with other moments in the past, which I often did not fully enjoy because I was comparing them with other moments of the future.

Andre Gide

EMDR must be used within the context of an interactional dynamic. Couples therapy may be an appropriate intervention in order to help the client more easily integrate new perspectives and behaviors within the family context. As the client becomes more self-assured and independent, the interpersonal relationship can be threatened by the partner's apparent attempts to sabotage therapeutic effects. In these cases, a therapy appointment with the couple can help reassure the partner and identify potential problems. It can also teach the couple better communication skills and enable the partner to more easily accept the client's changing self-concept and the consequent shift of identified roles.

Alerting the client to possible systems issues can help to minimize areas of confusion and disturbance. The EMDR clinician should consider whether seeing the client and partner jointly is acceptable or whether a referral should be made for couples counseling. If the latter is necessary, the clinician should be sure that an appropriate counselor is available before beginning EMDR treatment with the client. This will ensure a rapid transition if relationship difficulties arise during the client's EMDR treatment.

Early Sexual Abuse in a Marital Partner

Of particular concern is the treatment of sexual abuse survivors. Partners of trauma victims often feel guilty and powerless in the face of the client's pronounced suffering. When memories of molestation are uncovered, sexual dysfunction, depression, and angry accusations on the part of the client often exacerbate the usual relationship tensions and can contribute to a dysfunctional dynamic (Nelson, 1992).

When a molestation victim is treated with EMDR, the disturbance that may arise from continued processing between sessions may cause unease in the partner. In other cases, the dysfunctional relationship dynamics will have preceded any awareness of earlier trauma and the partner may be upset by the client's attempts to be assertive and to establish appropriate boundaries as treatment proceeds. In addition, it is not unusual for sexual abuse survivors to have formed relationships with partners who have also been abused. The emerging traumatic material and labile moods may trigger the partner's own dysfunctional history and consequent responses. In this case, individual therapy, along with joint counseling, is highly advised to defuse the partner's abuse memories and the present triggers.

Joint versus Individual Sessions

Regardless of the obvious reason for referral, the first joint session when working with couples is used to set agreements about why therapy is being sought. If both partners agree that they love each other and that the purpose of the therapy is to improve or save the marriage, this understanding is made explicit and any future disturbance is designated as a "cry for love." Agreements are made with respect to the standard issues of good family therapy, namely, acting as a team, truth telling, time-outs, and so on. The joint meeting also allows the clinician to assess the couple's communication styles and to arbitrate any major problem areas.

Further joint sessions are used to assess progress in communication and interaction, as well as to continue the arbitration process, if necessary. In addition, however, the partners should be seen individually to reprocess all the psychological baggage that has accumulated over the years (i.e., all the why-did- you, how-could-you, and why-didn't-you grievances). The clinical goal is to allow the partners to react to each other in the present rather than continue to be burdened by the weight of the past. Perceptions of early mistakes they made in childrearing or lack of support can cause present recriminations to be triggered by even minor events. By using EMDR to defuse these earlier memories, the couple can achieve a healthier dynamic and give appropriate weight to present problems or disagreements.

In addition to reprocessing the couple's memories of their past problems, it is useful to target the present triggers that cause disturbance. A husband may find that the sound of his wife's voice is similar to a particularly disturbing tone that his mother habitually used, and a look on her husband's face may remind a woman of the expression her father wore during childhood beatings. In addition, by virtue of second-order conditioning, some present situations that habitually provoke the troublesome tone or look may be in themselves highly disturbing. Taking care to reprocess the memories and the present referents can greatly relieve the couple's current dysfunctional interactions. In addition, the present situations that independently cause difficulty (such as the wife staying out late with her women friends or the husband leaving the cap off the toothpaste tube) should also be targeted, the adverse reactions dissipated, and alternatives explored.

In many ways, it is preferable to carry out these individual reprocessing sessions in the absence of the partner. Obviously, if both members of a couple have presented themselves for therapy, it is likely that there are intimacy problems and safety issues that may inhibit full client disclosure. If a painful issue emerges during processing, it is preferable for the client to be able to proceed without worrying about the partner's reaction. For instance, if the client begins to remember an earlier molestation or humiliation, feelings of shame and guilt might cause her to be reticent about revealing the material in the presence of her partner. Or, she might fear that when her partner hears about what was done to her, he will seek out the perpetrator for revenge. Either contingency can cause the client to attempt to dissociate or minimize the disturbance, which can lead to insufficient processing and retraumatization.

Another negative dynamic can emerge if the husband becomes emotional and the wife minimizes his suffering because she needs him to be a stoic male protector. The clinician should therefore proceed with utmost care when considering whether to attempt processing with a client in the partner's presence.

Clinicians need to use their own best judgment about what will be beneficial to clients. For example, one EMDR-trained clinician reported trying the reprocessing sessions with the partner present because she thought that the procedure would increase the bonding of the couple.

When the wife abreacted while processing a memory, the husband was so touched by her level of pain and his own involvement that it became a very beneficial experience for both of them. However, in the case of another couple, the husband fell asleep when the wife began to abreact, a response that, needless to say, did not bring the two partners closer. Since many treatment outcomes are obviously possible, the clinician needs to evaluate the couple carefully before making a decision about whether single or joint EMDR sessions would be more effective.

Infidelity

When a couple presents themselves for therapy because of the aftereffects of an extramarital affair, the clinician should take care to evaluate both the causes and the consequences of the incident. In addition to the couples work already discussed, the clinician should assess the betrayed partner for PTSD-like symptoms. The betrayal of trust can have a devastating effect on the partner's sense of safety in the world and on the ability to trust his or her own perceptions. Accompanying this can be a variety of sequelae consistent with feelings of violation. In addition, many such clients present symptoms of intrusive thoughts of, for example, the actual scene when they discovered the infidelity or of imagined scenes of the partner in a variety of assignations. In order to allow the couple's psychological injuries to heal, the partner's intrusive imagery should be targeted as soon as possible after the appropriate agreements have been made. The feelings of anger and hurt generated by the betrayal can also be targeted most easily if safety has been established by the wronged partner's acceptance of the unfaithful one's apologetic reassurance that the affair has been permanently terminated.

In one case the wife's affair had ended and the couple requested therapy to get their marriage back on track. During the couple's interview the husband declared himself furious at his wife's infidelity and asked for assistance in returning to a state of emotional equilibrium. When he was seen individually, however, the husband admitted that there was a part of himself that did not want to give up the anger. The clinician asked the client where he felt this sense of resistance in his body, and it was targeted with EMDR. The feeling of resistance dissipated, and the anger itself was accessed and reprocessed, along with a variety of intrusive thoughts and images.

Once the aftereffects of the affair are reprocessed, the underlying causes need to be addressed and resolved. As usual in cases of recent trauma, unlike early-trauma processing, the obvious acute cause of PTSD is treated first. In addition to the applications already discussed, EMDR may be used to attempt to clarify the present concerns that one or the other partner might have about continuing the marriage and to reprocess dysfunctional fears that may be dictating inappropriate choices. In the case where one or both partners decide to end the marriage, the clinician should also use EMDR to assist the transition. She should target the intrusive thoughts and feelings of rage and self-denigration felt by either partner. Not only will this improve the present circumstances, but it will help to prevent dysfunction in future relationships. In addition, if there are children involved, negative feelings about their parents' divorce, including self-blame and fear of abandonment, should be reprocessed as early as possible.

SEXUAL ABUSE VICTIMS

It takes two to tell the truth: One to say it and another to hear it.

Henry David Thoreau

Clinicians should already be familiar with many aspects of the issues and cautions listed in the following paragraphs. However, these are especially important during the EMDR treatment of sexual abuse survivors. While such survivors constitute a large proportion of therapy clients, many clinicians have never treated one. This section aims to clarify certain points, but it is not a substitute for adequate supervision and consultation if the clinician has had no previous experience with multiple-molestation survivors.

Appropriate Goals

The ability to accurately retrieve memories of abuse, or large segments of forgotten childhood events, is questionable even under the best of circumstances. While some clients enter therapy to determine whether or not they were molested, the EMDR clinician should not consider this an appropriate therapeutic goal. EMDR is not designed to bring visual memories to the surface but, rather, to process information that is dysfunctionally stored in the nervous system. Clinical observation indicates that even with otherwise full-blown sexual abuse symptomatology only half of EMDR clients experience the emergence of a visual memory of such abuse. Therefore, the clinician should concentrate on the client's symptoms and on what can be done to alleviate the emotional (and possible physical) pain. The following statement can be helpful in explaining to a client how EMDR can bring about a shift in dysfunctional reactions and triggers even without a visual memory of the original trauma: "Just as a VCR can play a videotape whether or not the TV monitor is on, so too can you process past traumatic events without having to actually see them."

As with any type of therapy, the clinician and the client should agree on the specific goals of EMDR. For example, they should explore whether it would be acceptable to the client to alleviate his problems (such as panic attacks, difficulty with intimacy issues, and sleep disturbances) without being 100% certain of their cause. If the client does not agree, EMDR should not be offered as the only treatment, as it is by no means certain that the actual memory will surface.

Ironically, the same restriction applies to a molestation victim who has clear memories of her abuse but insists that the clinician focus exclusively on her present-day problems, such as difficulty with her boss. Since there is no way to prevent the molestation memories from emerging during EMDR treatment (especially if they are part of the memory network associated with the present-day target), the clinician cannot guarantee the client that they will be able to entirely avoid them. Therefore, if the client is adamant in her refusal to think about the molestations, the clinician should probably not use EMDR.

Client Readiness

While many of these factors have been covered in Chapters 4 and 5, I want to stress that the use of EMDR with sexual abuse victims necessitates special attention to the client's emotional containment and current life situation. When there are a number of real problems in the client's present-day life, such as job or family crises, work on early traumas should be kept to a minimum. Until the client is stable enough to handle current problems, the clinician should not risk adding the emotional load of reprocessing early traumatic experiences. Any between-sessions disturbance caused by processing can increase the client's difficulty in handling the anxiety-laden issues in his current life that are out of his control and cannot be put on hold.

Remember that the cautions about using EMDR with a given client include the need to make an appropriate assessment of all of his real-life constraints. If the exhaustion or distress that sometimes arises with EMDR would be detrimental to the client's present functioning, other therapeutic methods should be used for the time being.

Safety and Stability

Of primary importance in dealing with sexual abuse victims are the aspects of safety and stability. It is crucial that clients be carefully prepared for EMDR processing because of the likely emergence of somatic responses, intense fear, and hitherto dissociated memories. Unless the client is prepared for the potential speed with which these can emerge and the potential intensity of the emotional response, she may break off EMDR in the middle of an abreaction and refuse to resume treatment. Therefore, all of the cautions and criteria for client selection described in Chapters 4 and 5 should be implemented with even greater thoroughness when working with sexual abuse victims. The clinician should always give the client an initially positive experience with EMDR by using the safe-place exercise and teaching him a variety of relaxation techniques to relieve any disturbance that may arise between sessions. Also, when sexual abuse is suspected, it is vital that the clinician adequately screen the client for the possibility of a dissociative disorder.

Evaluating indicators of clinical safety and the client's sense of control is mandatory when working with this population and extends even to the use of the eye movements. Because some molestation clients may find the clinician's moving fingers threatening, it may be necessary to use objects, such as a pen or ruler, or to switch to the use of hand taps. In addition, because of their tendency to feel that their personal space has been violated when people are in close proximity to them, some molestation victims may prefer that the clinician sit at a greater distance from them than is usually recommended with EMDR treatment. In short, the clinician should be flexible enough to adapt the standard format in any way necessary for client safety and comfort.

Structure

While clinicians should be flexible in their choice of the focal points they use with molestation clients, they should nevertheless stick closely to the structure of the standard protocols. Specific old memories, when available, should be targeted first because they have the greatest likelihood of rapid and complete processing, which in turn will give the client a sense of accomplishment. When a specific old memory is available, using the associated image, cognition, and body sensation will generally result in a more controlled and contained session than attempting to target diffuse feelings of despair, hopelessness, or generalized negative statements such as "I wish I were dead."

A specific old memory that incorporates the negative aspects can be more easily processed and put in perspective than a more recent one, since the former is already part of the historical past and is no longer a danger. Targeting only a current emotion or cognition rather than a specific event can start the processing, but it may be much more difficult to complete it, inasmuch as current material is stimulated without the specific goal of laying an old memory to rest.

The controlled use of the EMDR eight-phase approach (explained in Chapters 4, 5, 6, and 8), along with the standard 11-part procedure (summarized in Chapter 9), offers specific baseline and assessment measures, such as the SUD and VOC ratings, that set realistic expectations for the client and help strengthen her sense of structure, safety, and understanding. While flexibility is vital when working with sexual abuse survivors, it should not circumvent the many safeguards that are built into the standard EMDR protocols and procedures. The clinician should try to use the standard approach first, deviating from it only if the client is uncomfortable or unresponsive. The more specific the targets and goals, the greater the likelihood of success.

Integration

The clinician should be especially sensitive to the amount of time the client needs in order to integrate the material that surfaces. Many sessions may be needed to discuss the intrapsychic and interpersonal needs revealed by a new information plateau, to offer modeling of new behavior, to identify interactional pressures, or to target dreams and present reactions that have arisen from the processing of earlier traumatic material.

The clinician should not continue to target new memories until the previously elicited ones and their reverberations have been treated. For instance, the week after reprocessing a major molestation memory a client reported a pronounced sense of sorrow, stating, "I never before grieved for my father's death." The clinician realized that it was necessary for the client to focus on this plateau next, rather than attempt to move on to another memory. The log that clients are asked to keep is vital for identifying any new avenues, emotions, or perspectives that are emanating in a troubling way from a previous target and should be used to explore the ramifications of the memory work. This record-keeping should include nightmares, disturbing or unsettling aspects of the revelations, emerging interpersonal needs in relation to integration, and so on.

Just as clients vary in their need to rest or talk or integrate between sets, so too do they vary in the amount of time they need between EMDR sessions. The clinician must be certain that the client has an adequate repertoire of self-control techniques to deal with any discomfort that arises between sessions. If the client's log reveals a great deal of distress, the clinician should take measures to relieve her from emotional pressure. Prolonged distress is detrimental to therapeutic effectiveness because it can reinforce the client's feelings of low self-esteem and lack of control.

The clinician should also encourage the client to allow sufficient time to pass to assimilate treatment effects before she determines the objective truth of any emerging memories or decides to confront her suspected perpetrator, either personally or legally. Traumatic events are often stored as fragments, a fact that makes their interpretation difficult.

For instance, one client whose sexual dysfunctions and intimacy problems were targeted by EMDR reported experiencing sensations of being violated at the same time that an image of her father's face emerged into consciousness. Given this association, it would have been logical for both clinician and client to conclude that she had been assaulted by her father. However, a subsequent targeting of the memory fragment revealed that her attacker was a high school boy and that the image of her father involved his coming to her rescue.

The aforementioned case underscores two important points: (1) Clinicians should refrain from interpreting clients' memory fragments, and (2) clients should be cautioned to "just let whatever happens, happen without judging it" or launching into confrontations with presumed perpetrators because of it. The need of clients to confront or receive acknowledgment from relevant family members is strongest during the early stages of therapy, when the memories are unmetabolized and a source of great distress. Once the client has processed these memories and much of his disturbance is removed, he is better able to judge the need or advisability of confrontation. Therefore, recommending that the client take sufficient time to integrate the therapy effects is strongly urged, regardless of the clinical modality being used.

Information Plateaus

When reprocessing a sexual trauma, remember to utilize the cognitive interweave, if necessary, to establish the plateaus of (a) appropriate responsibility, (b) safety, and (c) choice. These plateaus seem particularly relevant for the molestation victim who is psychologically frozen in the horror of a childhood assault.

In addition, many clients feel an urge to imbue the tragedy with some meaning. The clinician can often assist this goal by using the cognitive interweave to explore the ways in which the abuse has resulted in the client's having achieved higher levels of sensitivity, compassion, or understanding for other people's suffering. (Indeed, it is not unusual for victims of abuse to become mental health professionals.) This awareness assists many clients by engendering in them a sense of significance (purpose, self-esteem, or success) in that they were able to triumph by abstracting meaning from their pain. The sense of a spoiled or wasted childhood is, of course, deeply distressing for many clients and should be directly targeted by the clinician if it emerges.

Emotional Stages

When processing a sexual trauma, it is not unusual for the client to go through a variety of emotions and stages of healing. The denied or dissociated material can shift to feelings of guilt and shame and then to rage, anger, sadness, and, finally, acceptance—and possibly forgiveness. The stage of sadness can occur before, during, or after the rage or anger. As one client expressed it, "He stole my childhood from me. How can anyone steal something so precious?" While anger might be the client's dominant emotion, the underlying sadness must also be carefully targeted and addressed.

The importance of the client-centered approach is vital when working with sexual abuse victims; other clinical models can actually be detrimental to full therapeutic effect. For instance, many clinicians believe that the client should get in touch with her anger about the molestation and that this is an empowering state of being. While anger is undoubtedly of great consequence for almost all victims, it may be useful to recognize it as indicative of only a single stage of processing. Rather than terminating the EMDR session once the client has started to experience her anger, the clinician may find it more productive to continue by targeting the rage or anger and requesting the client to verbalize it during the set. This invitation often allows the client to engage fully with the emotion and make a declaration of independence that firmly establishes her personal boundaries.

During the stage of rage, the client may also experience images and thoughts of taking revenge on the perpetrator. He should be assured that this is childhood rage surfacing and that the images should simply be noticed and the thoughts safely verbalized during the session. Completing this cycle of processing allows the client to release the accumulated tension of all the suppressed pain. Processing these images and verbalizations may obviate the client's need for direct confrontation, an action that might ultimately be futile or disruptive to the family relationships the client wishes to maintain. For instance, a client may feel at peace after her verbalization to her dead father, who molested her, and may not require further acknowledgment from her psychologically unstable elderly mother. However, the clinician should ensure that the client reprocesses all of the dysfunctional emotions related to the abuse, including the rage and feelings of betrayal toward the parent who, knowingly or not, allowed the abuse to occur.

After the client's rage has been processed, he may experience a nondisruptive level of anger, which may be an appropriate and healthy final stage for him, at least at this point in his life. It is not unusual, however, for clients to move into a stage of calm acceptance. In addition, the client may spontaneously remember certain aspects of the perpetrator's history that contribute to a genuine feeling of forgiveness. For example, the client may recall that "Mother was also molested," or "Father was abused." Such realizations may help the client recognize a repetition compulsion or dissociation that explains why her parent abused her. This in turn may precipitate a feeling of compassion for the perpetrator and a sense of forgiveness that transcends the injury and gives the client a profound sense of peace.

If the stage of anger does not evolve into forgiveness, it is probably because this shift is not yet appropriate for the particular client. However, the clinician should discriminate between dysfunctional rage and appropriate anger. With EMDR the violence and personal turmoil of the rage can transmute into an appropriate level of justified anger that is outwardly directed at the perpetrator and no longer fed by unremitting feelings of pain and fear. Remember, EMDR is a client-centered approach that allows the client to process information appropriate for health and integration. If the client does not process his anger after verbalizing it in alternation with successive sets, the anger should be viewed as ecologically sound and a suitable positive cognition should be installed. The client may need to integrate this plateau by setting firmer boundaries with family members and by having appropriate conversations or even confrontations. It would be unfortunate, however, if the client remained stuck in his anger simply because the clinician felt that forgiveness of the perpetrator was inappropriate and therefore prematurely closed the EMDR session.

Remember that reprocessing does not eliminate anything that is healthful or ecologically valid for the client. If the client does move on to forgiveness, it does not mean that she has forgotten the abuse or condones the perpetrator's behavior. Rather, achieving forgiveness may entail a strong sense of self-renewal and empowerment, a sense that the victimization no longer defines the self. Unfortunately, however, some mental health professionals tell victims that it is necessary to forgive their perpetrators in order to be completely healed. Insisting to the client that she achieve this stage of acceptance can often be traumatizing in its own right, since she is powerless to attain it by force of will. Since forgiveness can neither be mandated nor controlled, the EMDR clinician is advised to allow it to emerge spontaneously, when (and if) it is ready to do so.

False Memory

Currently there is a great deal of controversy regarding the possibility that false allegations of sexual abuse are being made as a result of inappropriate therapy. Although some of these claims may well be coming from perpetrators in denial, it is clear that there is a need for quality control in the mental health profession. There is no question that some therapists are using psychological tools, such as hypnosis, with little or no training and are therefore ignorant of the limitations of these tools and of their potential for contaminating memories or creating false impressions.

Consequently, it is not surprising to learn that some clients have been led to accept images that have surfaced under hypnosis, guided visualization, or dream analysis as definitive evidence of actual memories, even when corroboration is often impossible. Clinicians should be aware of their boundaries of competence and of the limitations of their methods before utilizing them in clinical practice. This is why it is vital that the use of EMDR be restricted to trained, licensed clinicians who have been supervised in its practice. Simply reading the cautions offered in the following pages is not a substitute for adequate training.

Cautions Regarding Memory Work

When treating victims of sexual abuse, the clinician must carefully evaluate the interaction between EMDR and other forms of treatment. For instance, since one of the legacies of the psychodynamic model is the belief that uncovering memories is a necessary prerequisite for working them through, it may be tempting for the clinician to use a combination of EMDR and hypnosis for memory retrieval. While hypnosis has been a highly successful and standard procedure for many years, its potential interaction with EMDR has not been systematically investigated. Therefore, some words of caution seem appropriate, since each clinician is bound to approach issues of possible "repression" and "resistance" in a highly subjective manner. The points made in the following paragraphs are offered in order to highlight factors that might be overlooked by some clinicians in the merging of various therapeutic orientations.

Hypnosis

Hypnosis and EMDR may not be an appropriate combination. Some clinicians using EMDR have been successful in inducing light trances in dissociative disorder clients to assist in stabilization and to close incomplete sessions. In addition, a light trance may be used to assist targeting. However, inducing deep trances during the EMDR treatment session may be contraindicated because the altered physiological state of hypnosis may not permit all the information to be processed adequately. Just as clinicians should retarget any traumas after the client has been taken off medication in order to check for any unprocessed material left in state-specific form, so too should they retarget events if hypnosis has been used with the client.

Clinical observations indicate that delusions may not be susceptible to change with EMDR until the experiential origin has been targeted. For example, in order to treat a husband's delusion that his wife had been kidnapped, it was necessary to target, in one of his more lucid moments, the actual event of her leaving him by choice. Similarly, some hypnotically induced fantasies and memories may not be modifiable with EMDR. It is important for clinicians to realize that, while they may take a judicious approach to the use of hypnosis with clients, they may have inherited clients who were ineptly handled by previous therapists.

When targeted memories do not undergo the expected treatment effect, either during the session or in follow-up, the clinician should implement a more thorough screening for dissociative disorder and for the presence of previously implanted hypnotic suggestions. For instance, some victims are the recipients of hypnotically induced "memories" that were implanted during abuse but are unaware of the fact. When targeted with EMDR, these "memories" may be resistant to processing and are therefore extremely disturbing to clients. There is currently insufficient clinical feedback to definitively address this concern.

More importantly, in many courts the use of hypnosis in any phase of a client's treatment can contaminate his ability to take legal action against the perpetrator. EMDR is clinically very dissimilar to hypnosis, and recent EEG studies indicate that the brain waves produced during EMDR treatment and those produced during hypnosis are quite different from each other (Nicosia, in press). In addition, in a recent court case involving alleged sexual abuse the judge ruled that EMDR was not akin to hypnosis and could not implant false memories (Shapiro, 1994d). Another legal ruling in Australia stated that EMDR does not cause memory distortion. These, however, are the only court cases to date, and EMDR may face more legal challenges in the future. Consequently, the clinician should inform the client of the possible legal issues before EMDR treatment is commenced. However, refraining from using hypnosis along with EMDR may make the case more forensically tenable.

The Fallibility of Memory

There is often no way of knowing whether a memory that emerges is true or not. Indeed, the very attempt at memory retrieval as a therapeutic goal may establish the belief in the client that a memory of abuse exists, that it should be revealed, and that there was indeed a perpetrator. Thus, this scenario could provide the perfect conditions for eliciting "false" or mistaken memories. When a memory is reported during EMDR, there is a possibility that (1) the image is a symbolic representation, (2) the event in question was only vicariously experienced (e.g., through identification with a character in a story), (3) the image is the result of trickery (such as a perpetrator in disguise), or (4) that it is valid.

The fallibility of even a "nondelayed" memory is illustrated by the following case. A client presented the intrusive thoughts and images of having been raped by Satan (Young, 1992). She was quite definite that the event had occurred because she had retained a clear image of it since childhood. When the memory was reprocessed, she noticed that the horns appeared to be made of plastic and recognized the voice of a friend of her father's. She was then able to recognize that she had been tricked, and the real identity of the perpetrator became clear (although without appropriate corroboration it should not be accepted at face value). The important point here, however, is that the incident was so abusive that it might easily have been dissociated at the time it occurred and might only have emerged decades later during EMDR. If the friend had been better at disguise—perhaps using a full face mask, wearing a costume, and changing his voice—the memory would have emerged as an apparent rape by Satan. This obvious fallacy should underscore the point that perpetrators can also convince children that their parents are witnessing and approving of the abuse from a different part of the room. If a memory of an abuse incident that occurred under such a circumstance emerges during processing, there is no way to guarantee that EMDR will adequately disclose the trickery. Clinicians should be cognizant of the limitations and distortions of memory itself before advising clients about the accuracy of any memory that emerges during EMDR.

The issue of vicarious traumatization (Figley, 1995) is also significant here. In one case, a client asked for help with PTSD symptomatology that included flashbacks of having been killed at Auschwitz during the Holocaust. While two specific scenes had repeated themselves in nightmares and flashbacks for many years, the client had no idea of their genesis. In fact, he was not old enough even to have been in the Holocaust. The first scene, of standing in line to enter the concentration camp, was targeted for reprocessing, and the client reported a rapid reduction in SUD level after completing the sets. It was not until the second memory, of being gassed in a chamber, was treated that the client suddenly exclaimed after two sets, "It's not me, it's my uncle!" He then remembered all the stories he had been told as a child about his uncle dying in Auschwitz during the war. The impact of the vicarious traumatization was sufficient to cause the client's pronounced symptomatology, although the actual trauma happened to someone else. It is vital for clinicians to remember that the genesis of a symptom may be masked by a representation or screen image that may never be penetrated. For instance, in this case the first "memory" was reprocessed without revealing the true cause.

Likewise, symptoms of sexual dysfunction or of difficulty with intimacy issues may be caused by vicarious traumatization or by traumatic events that have no relation to sexual abuse. For instance, sexual abuse was suspected in another client because she manifested many of the attendant symptomatology: panic reactions; problems with men; and fears of intimacy, betrayal, and abandonment. However, during

EMDR she discovered that she had dissociated a memory of her father being killed while he was driving her to her birthday party. Her symptoms had nothing to do with sexual assault.

Remember that the use of EMDR involves a client-centered approach that attempts to follow rather than lead clients. The clinician should specifically refrain from asking for details or interpreting events. This will decrease the possibility of contaminating memories or creating false impressions. All clients should be instructed regarding the fallibility of memory in a way that does not denigrate their experience. Many true memories will surface for the first time, and clients should be supported in any appropriate action they choose to take as a result. Nevertheless, it is important that clients draw their own conclusions about these memories, using all possible sources of corroboration, and not be led by the clinician.

Clinicians must keep in mind that the emergence of a scene during an EMDR session does not mean that it is true in a literal sense—even though it may have been truly experienced by the person. For instance, a client may have been tricked by the perpetrator into thinking that a cult or large group was involved. This might have been done in order to increase the client's fear and the likelihood of her future silence or to make any later revelations about such ritual abuse appear too fantastic to be true. As previously stated, perpetrators can also fool children into believing that their parents are present and approve of the abuse. Because of this ambiguity it is necessary to exercise clinical caution and to encourage the client who is determined to discover the truth to attempt to find corroborating evidence, including physical signs, witnesses, or hospital records. Whether there are corroborating data or not, the primary emphasis must be on client safety and appropriate support during the therapeutic process.

Remember that revelations of horrible abuse (whether true or not) can be extremely disturbing to the client; for the clinician to insist that the memories are true (or false) may only add to the client's distress. A more appropriate stance for the clinician to take is that it may be impossible to know for certain that a specific memory is true and that the focus of therapy should be on the present symptomatology or distress. Clearly, focusing on the client's internal reaction to the event or possible perpetrator is necessary whether or not the memory is accurate. Supporting clients through the experience and reprocessing of their targeted images remains crucial, whether the event is true, symbolic, or due to vicarious traumatization.

On the other hand, if extensive or ritual abuse is suspected, it is also vital that a thorough check for dissociative disorder be done. Chronic abuse is a leading cause of dissociative disorder, and it may remain hidden unless a thorough screening is performed. No client with dissociative disorder should be treated with EMDR unless the clinician is skilled in that specialty area (see the Dissociative Disorders section later in this chapter).

COMBAT VETERANS

> Blessed is the warrior who hears the whisper of peace in his heart.
>
> *Anonymous*

Dealing with Self-Denigration

Eric, one of the first veterans ever treated with EMDR, showed me—in a way I will never forget—that his 20 years of postcombat suffering were based on his nobility. Put simply, Eric's most painful memories were not those in which bombs fell around him or machine gun fire rattled past his helmet. They were memories in which he had tried to save someone's life and failed or in which he believed he was responsible for someone's death. The tragedy is that a great many young men and women who go off to war believe deeply in the fundamental principle, taught by their religion, that life is sacred. They go to do their duty but discover that they have to take the lives of others or are unable to save or protect lives or must witness the kinds of horror only war can generate. One of Eric's most painful memories was of learning that the artillery fire he had to call in to protect the position of his platoon caused shells to land near a village, probably causing the death of many children. Although he had no choice but to follow his sense of duty and save the lives of his men, the shelling of the village haunted him for two decades.

There are two basic concepts that a veteran with PTSD needs to understand. First, if he is as bad as he thinks he is, he would not still be suffering; bad people do not suffer over something they did 20 years ago. Second, his suffering now does not help those who were harmed, but it does keep him from doing something worthwhile.

In order to help defuse the feelings of self-denigration that have accumulated over the years of pain and irrational behaviors, the veteran must be led to understand that his continued symptomatology, including the bouts of intense anger, are caused by the experiences in combat that are locked in his nervous system. Continued substance abuse, if present, is often caused by a need to medicate the pain. In some cases it is triggered by old habit patterns from combat: Since alcohol or drugs were sometimes used to decompress after battles, the desire to use them now may be integrally linked with combat-related thoughts or feelings that currently arise.

Dealing with Feelings of Lack of Control

The appropriate clinical framework for treatment of combat veterans is crucial for positive therapeutic results. Because EMDR is being offered to the client as a new treatment, it can arouse fears about experimentation or depressing reminders of repeated treatment failures. Since veterans are typically survivors of multiple traumatic events and decades of often unremitting pathology, the clinician must take care to prepare the client well for the intensity of the emotional processing that occurs both during and between sessions. These precautions are important because of the generally high attrition rate of veterans in treatment programs.

It can greatly help veterans if they understand that their symptomatology is actually governed by cause-and-effect principles. Since the combat experience was often one of chaos and lack of control, veterans may experience the same feelings during therapeutic exploration of the material and the triggered symptomatology. For greater clinical effectiveness, the clinician should provide the client with a sense of order and explain the guiding principles of treatment. This can help set the parameters for a systematic approach to overcoming the pathology.

It is important for the clinician to convey to the veteran the idea that memories of childhood may emerge during EMDR and that these should be reported to her. Because the emphasis on treating veterans has been so heavily focused on the impact of combat, the premorbid history of the client has often been ignored. It can safely be said that many veterans did not enter the war with ideal childhoods behind them. If the veteran was abused as a child or victimized by situations out of his control (such as having an alcoholic parent), the war experiences may be associated to these already-established nodes. During EMDR the client will often recall childhood experiences that must be reprocessed. If the veteran purposely ignores these images because he considers them to be unimportant, beneficial therapeutic effects will be hampered. Therefore, the clinician should help the veteran to understand the importance of his childhood experiences and should encourage him to disclose the memories if they arise.

Secondary Gain Issues

It is also important to consider carefully the secondary gain aspects of the clinical presentation. As discussed in Chapter 4, secondary gain is considered part of the pathology and needs to be addressed and targeted directly if positive therapeutic effects are to be obtained. Secondary gains particularly applicable to veterans include their identification as warriors, their reliance on wartime trauma as justification for years of failure, the postservice vigilance that provides safety, and the need for financial security in the form of VA benefits.

The clinician should keep in mind that offering to use EMDR to take away the veteran's nightmares, intrusive thoughts, and flashbacks, may also threaten his and his family's livelihood, which comes from a disability check. Obviously, for the veteran who has not successfully held gainful employment and has few marketable skills, this prospect can be terrifying. Therefore, if the clinician fails to make a realistic assessment of the potential secondary gains, give appropriate reassurance, and take steps to allay the veteran's fears through realistic and reasonable action plans, there is a risk of inhibiting the therapeutic effect.

Affiliation and the Fear of Forgetting

Another fear that EMDR can stimulate, one that is of particular importance to veterans, is the fear of forgetting. The clinician should make clear to the veteran that losing his pain or a particular image does not represent amnesia and that he will not forget about the combat experience or forget to honor the dead. Further, he should be assured that by gaining the ability to live a healthier and more productive life, he will have more choices and a greater capacity for honoring his comrades' sacrifices. For instance, after successful treatment, the client can offer more useful help to other veterans and to the widows and children of fallen comrades, which will continue a sense of connection to those who served and died. Also worth addressing with some veterans is their fear of losing their "edge"; the clinician should make clear that the client's ability to react appropriately to any real danger will not be diminished by EMDR. After the appropriate debriefing of any secondary gain issues, the clinician should directly target any residual client fears.

The question of affiliation is extremely important to the veteran population. For many, war constitutes the deepest bonding experience of their life. Through shared horror and heroism, a sense of deep connection emerges, a connection that can appear threatened if the veteran feels the pain of wartime memories dissipating. Therefore, it is important that veterans be reassured of their continued connection, especially during the periods when they may be making more therapeutic progress than members of their peer group. This precaution is particularly important when working with veterans who are in inpatient units or in groups within a VA hospital. A sense of alienation may arise when the client is no longer fixated on wartime memories but hears the same stories being rehashed by other veterans. The clinician should take care to defuse any attendant frustration or sense of impending loss of companionship. Using these emotions as targets for EMDR may assist the client during this transitional state.

Dealing with Denial and Transition States

Other issues that must be carefully addressed concern veterans who have been in denial about harmful actions they took in the past. Because of the ability of EMDR to engender appropriate client insight, this may represent the first time the veteran's actual level of responsibility for certain incidents is brought to light. In one instance, a veteran continued to feel a great deal of rage for the enemy. Having gone to war with his best friend and watched him die, he had vowed to avenge his friend's death and had returned for five tours of duty in order to kill as many of the enemy as he could. He became a "cowboy," recklessly leading his platoons into dangerous situations because of his need to kill. During EMDR treatment this veteran's anger began to dissipate, and he remarked suddenly, "Maybe I was just as bad as the people I was trying to kill. I didn't care at all about my own men dying around me."

This transitional stage, in which past actions are acknowledged, is one in which veterans are very vulnerable. They are in great danger of terminating the therapy because of the pain that accompanies their insights. They need to be thoroughly supported in order to make the transition to the next plateau. The clinician should take great pains to help clients address the issue of responsibility, pointing out, with a cognitive interweave, how young they were when they went to war and how the pressures, chaos, drugs, pain, and anger contributed to their actions. The memory of forgotten events can emerge suddenly during processing for some veterans who have denied culpability for harmful actions. Whether the denial of such actions is caused by lack of insight or by dissociation, EMDR can cause an emotional breakthrough—but only with the appropriate therapeutic alliance and clinician availability. If these psychological supports are not in place, the client may respond to the emotional pain with self-medication or self-sabotage and all therapeutic benefits may be lost.

When working with disturbing transitional states in veterans, it is vital not only to schedule 90-minute sessions, but to offer increased clinical availability in order to rapidly target the distressing material and complete the processing. It is unnecessary for the veteran to remain in a state of prolonged guilt or sorrow just because these emotions have only recently arisen. Remember, it is not useful to mandate a set amount of time for client grief and suffering, because the appropriate levels of insight and meaning will be gained by the client as the reprocessing of the information occurs.

Emotions are considered dysfunctional when they are not empowering and enhancing for the client. Immediately targeting the veteran's feelings of intense guilt as they emerge can assist him in the transition to an appropriate level of responsibility for his actions. For many clients, this entails a desire to expiate past acts. In these cases it may be useful for the clinician to suggest to such clients that they offer their assistance to war widows and children and to other veterans. Such acts are likely to provide the veteran with a sense of fulfillment and purpose. Giving talks to high school students on their war experience or offering their services as a Big Brother or Big Sister are other ways in which clients can seek a sense of redemption for the horrors they may have perpetrated during wartime. All of these explorations and suggestions can be accomplished, when necessary, with the help of the cognitive interweave.

Dealing with Anger

Issues of anger can be extremely difficult for the combat veteran. Many veterans suffer from uncontrollable bouts of anger in response to minor disturbances, a symptom of special consequence because of the spouse or child abuse that may occur as a result. Not surprisingly, many marriages have suffered or been destroyed by the veteran's overpowering attacks of rage. It may be useful to explain to the veteran that much of this anger may also be directly linked to the war experience. The client should be assured that reprocessing the memories and targeting the appropriate present-day triggers will allow him to be in greater control because, among other things, his rage will be reduced. Metaphorically, the information processing will drain the pool of anger so that it will be less likely to overflow. In addition, it is important to offer clients a variety of self-control techniques (described in Chapter 9) to use in the meanwhile if the anger wells up. The safe-place exercise is particularly useful for this population, because part of the client's pathology may involve the need to remain vigilant under almost all conditions.

A variety of creative interventions may have to be employed to assist clients in dealing with their rage. For inpatient treatment of veterans in VA hospitals (Lipke, 1992a), a set of agreements is offered before EMDR treatment is commenced. One agreement is that the veteran will not leave his chair during an EMDR session without first discussing it with the clinician. The clinician can assist the veteran in keeping this agreement by suggesting that he strenuously grip the arms of his chair during fits of anger or other emotional outbursts. This activity also reminds the veteran that he is in the United States, not back in wartime Vietnam or Iraq. The dual-processing aspect of EMDR is extremely important for these clients. In addition, whenever possible, they should be encouraged to voice any feelings of anger, betrayal, or fear they may have.

An example of the need for innovation during treatment came to light during a session targeting a client's reaction of extreme anger about a variety of seemingly innocuous business situations. Since most of this client's Vietnam experiences had already been reprocessed, these incidents were noted as part of his log report. As per the standard EMDR protocol, these stimuli were discussed and targeted. However, in the middle of the first set, the client held up his hand to stop and declared his unwillingness to continue. When asked for a reason, he said, "I just realized that this is the same anger that kept me alive in Vietnam and let me do what I had to do. I'm afraid if we continue that I will hurt you." The client was thanked for his concern, and the parameters of his fear were examined. He said he was afraid that if he allowed himself to access the full force of his emotion, he would automatically act out against anyone around him. The clinician felt sure of the client's actual level of stability, but honoring the client's need for safety was vital. The clinician therefore instructed the client to go to a nearby area that contained no people and to allow himself to feel the emotion and pound the ground while verbally expressing any thoughts that arose. The clinician instructed him to return when he felt ready. Approximately 1/2 hour later the client emerged with a face of happy wonder. He had found that he had not been overwhelmed by the emotion; instead, as he allowed himself to express it, it had subsided. The client said that he felt he would no longer be the victim of his emotion but, rather, its master. These thoughts were used as the positive cognitions in successive sets. The present stimuli were then reprocessed without further incident. Follow-up sessions revealed that the client's anger was now rarely triggered at work, was at a much reduced level when it did occur, and was easily handled with self-control techniques.

Using the Cognitive Interweave

The plateaus of processing discussed in relation to the sexual abuse victim also apply to the treatment of the combat veteran. Using the cognitive interweave to help clients recognize the appropriate level of responsibility, present safety, and future ability to choose can be extremely helpful. For instance, a veteran was abreacting with respect to an incident in which a new recruit was killed because the two men exchanged positions on patrol. The exchange had been unavoidable because it followed a direct order, but the client's guilt was nevertheless overwhelming. The clinician used the cognitive interweave by asking, "If your nephew had been in your situation, what would you have wanted him to do?" The veteran freely admitted that he would have wanted his nephew to obey the order, since it was the right thing to do. The addition of a set shifted the plateau, and the memory was successfully processed.

Another veteran was similarly relieved of his guilt about participating in the war by being asked if he would blame his own son for participating. The veteran reacted with tears, and the remnants of 20 years of guilt were effectively drained. While this cognitive interweave will not work with every veteran, it frequently proves useful, particularly when posed as a question. Even if an answer is not immediately forthcoming, all the veteran need do is think about the question during successive sets. Veterans suffering primarily from the locked-in fear of the life-threatening combat itself can often be assisted by a cognitive interweave that elicits the statement, "It's over; I'm safe now."

Therapy with Older Veterans

Special care must be taken with World War II and Korean War veterans, who are beginning to present themselves for the treatment of greatly delayed PTSD symptomatology, seemingly as a consequence of reaching retirement age. Clinicians should carefully assess older veterans for physical conditions, including cardiac or respiratory problems, that might exclude them from treatment because of potential health risks from abreactive responses. As a precaution, some veterans' programs are inaugurating inpatient care for older veterans during EMDR treatment.

Therapy with Female Veterans

Special attention should be paid to female veterans, both those who were involved in direct combat and those who served as nurses and were confronted daily with the pain and futility of being unable to save the soldiers in their charge. Many of these women have not yet directly addressed the PTSD symptomatology associated with the chaotic conditions under which they were forced to serve; nor have they confronted the misplaced guilt they feel over the soldiers' deaths. In addition, many of the nurses have been haunted for years by intrusive thoughts of the faces of the dying soldiers and of the scenes of suffering and disfigurement. The clinician should carefully nurture these women through the abreactions that may be precipitated by EMDR and should use the cognitive interweave, when necessary, to remind them of the comfort they brought to those men who would otherwise have died alone. The clinician should be mindful of the level of suffering engendered by the grief and should recognize that this suffering is no less severe than that born of the combat experience itself.

DISSOCIATIVE DISORDERS

Let us be kinder to one another.
Aldous Huxley (on his deathbed)

To date, I have received 5 years of feedback from clinicians regarding the use of EMDR, and these responses have shaped the format of training and the cautions covered in this book. By far, the greatest number of reported difficulties and stories of clinical problems and potential harm through the improper use of EMDR have involved clients with dissociative disorders. On the other hand, trained clinicians report that the proper application of EMDR greatly accelerates and eases treatment of this population. Therefore, I will review particular issues regarding these clients to emphasize their importance.

No clinician should use EMDR with a client suffering from dissociative disorder unless he is educated and experienced in working with this population and has been trained in the use of the cognitive interweave. The potential for harm with this type of client is great if EMDR is used inappropriately or injudiciously (as discussed in Appendix B). It is mandatory that clinicians feel extremely comfortable in their use of EMDR, since the cognitive interweave and the alternative abreactive strategies (see Chapter 10) are often necessary for treatment success.

This section provides an overview that should be used in conjunction with supervision and consultation. It is offered in order to provide a general description and to act as a reminder for clinicians who have received the proper instruction from experienced, trained EMDR clinicians qualified to act as consultants with this population. (Because of their assumed background, the texts cited and the terms used in this discussion should already be familiar to these clinicians.)

Since multiple personality disorder (MPD) is now designated as dissociative identity disorder (DID) in the DSM-IV, the new abbreviation will be employed here.

The lack of adequate screening, preparation, or implementation of EMDR can have literally fatal consequences for this population. For instance, an apparently successful EMDR treatment session can exacerbate the dysfunction for a number of DID "alters" and result in suicide attempts, other self-injury, or the need for emergency medical services. Regardless of the modality used, the treatment of DID by clinicians uneducated in the nuances and special needs of this population is a matter of grave concern and should be addressed throughout the mental health field. The "false memory" controversy has dramatically drawn attention to the lack of quality control in psychotherapy.

While clearly a separate category in the DSM, dissociative disorders are viewed by the Accelerated Information Processing model as a neurological configuration created by pronounced and sustained abuse. The result of this abuse is a variety of compartmentalizations of experiences held in state-specific form (Braun, 1988). According to the model, the DID alters represent network configurations that perceive themselves to have lives of their own. The personality components represent information stored in alter states within the separated neurological networks.

The amnestic barriers that characterize DID are symptomatic of state-specific compartmentalizations around pivotal incidents or affects associated with the abuse. Once EMDR has reprocessed the traumatic memories and thus metabolized them, the networks are able to link with each other and the amnestic barriers dissolve. After appropriate exploration and stabilization, fears of integration or fusion and of loss of identity or "death" may be addressed as negative cognitions and reprocessed accordingly. However, many EMDR clinicians are reporting that spontaneous integration and fusion also occur. For instance, after traumas are reprocessed, clients report that some alters spontaneously say, "I feel it's time to say good-bye."

As with other methods (such as hypnosis) that may precipitate abreactions, appropriate client preparation, including understanding the system and how it is organized, is paramount (Kluft & Fine, 1993; Putnam, 1989). When possible, clients should be educated about the necessity for all parts of themselves to participate. Many clinicians educate DID clients about ways to focus the attention of all the participating alters through the eyes of the host or of the particular alter being treated. Other clinicians implement EMDR with the individual alters, but only after making sure that there is no opposition from the internal states that represent the rest of the system. If appropriate diagnosis and preparation are not carried out (unless the system as a whole consents to the work), a seemingly successful session may prove only temporary and may result in the activation of uncontrolled switching and the emergence between sessions of distraught or harmful alters.

While standard abreactive protocols for using hypnosis with this population often include time distortions, this intervention should not generally be attempted with EMDR. Although light hypnosis may be used for relaxation or to enhance a sense of safety, the clinician should evaluate the client's needs in relation to time-distortion suggestions, bearing in mind that EMDR causes the material to move very rapidly on its own. Additional time distortion can cause the client to feel overwhelmed and is therefore not recommended. In addition, since many clinicians report that clients do not generally submerge into the material (as they generally do during hypnosis), physical or hypnotic restraints may not be necessary when using EMDR. Further, needing restraints is an important cue and may mean that EMDR is not yet appropriate; for instance, the patient may be on the verge of dyscontrol and may need inpatient therapy.

The fractionated abreaction protocol (Fine, 1991) dovetails quite well with EMDR. This protocol often enables the creation of a more stable environment for the DID client and is currently being used by a number of EMDR clinicians on an outpatient basis. Regardless of the protocol used, all usual clinical cross-checks employed by the clinician experienced in treating dissociative disorders should be administered to determine whether the material has actually been integrated or merely further dissociated. This precaution also includes checking the continuity of memory by obtaining detailed narratives of the targeted event.

The standard EMDR protocol may be used as long as special attention is paid to the negative and positive cognitions and body scan. The negative cognitions may be difficult to ascertain because different alters hold different beliefs. In certain instances, utilizing phrases with such themes as danger or loss may be appropriate to activate the target event. Positive cognitions must be carefully defined to include all the pertinent alters. Using a standard positive cognition such as "I am in control" or "I am powerful" can be problematic in view of the systems configuration and the interpretation of suicidal or homicidal alters.

After some reprocessing has occurred, memories should be retargeted to determine if all of the dysfunctional emotions have been appropriately resolved. Visual, cognitive, and somatic checks are necessary for this purpose. The body scan should be utilized and, according to many clinicians in the field, carefully addressed to each alter separately. This procedure may be time-consuming, but unless a somatic check has been carried out and no disturbance has been observed in any alter after memory material is retargeted, the clinician should not assume that the dysfunctional material has been metabolized.

Once again, the treatment of dissociative disorders with EMDR should be undertaken only after the clinician has received appropriate education, training, and supervision for DID and other dissociative disorders. The EMDR protocols for these diagnoses are changing rapidly as more expertise in these areas is tapped, and clinicians should make efforts to acquaint themselves with the latest suggestions. In Appendix B are the guidelines for assessment and treatment drafted by the Dissociative Disorder Task Force. In addition, all the selection criteria and cautions outlined in previous chapters should be followed with extra diligence when dealing with this population. This holds true along the whole spectrum from ego-state disorders to full-blown DID.

OVERALL EVALUATIONS

EMDR is neither a panacea nor a magic bullet. Appropriate clinical cross-checks should be used to determine if a memory has been fully processed, a dissociation adequately resolved, or a complaint satisfactorily handled. No method should be assumed to have been successful without applying appropriate clinical and behavioral measures over an adequate period of time. This caveat underscores the importance of a log and an ongoing feedback system. The clinician should maintain an open line of communication with clients after treatment so that they can report subsequent problems, if any. Additionally, other memories may surface because of client readiness or the convergence of particular triggers. Clearly, not all dysfunctional material will (or needs to) surface at any given time. The clinician should always leave the door open for the emergence of new memories.

While flexibility and creativity on the part of the clinician are often central to clinical success, it is important to remember that EMDR is new and that its suitability for every new client should be rigorously evaluated. The efficacy of combining methods, such as EMDR and hypnosis, should be carefully assessed, rather than assumed, by the clinician.

Evidence of prolonged distress and inadequate resolution of memories after the use of EMDR is a sign that other methods should be used in addition to or in place of it. Some clients will be unable to process memories without the clinician's use of the cognitive interweave and additional abreactive strategies (see Chapter 10). These are offered for use with clients who remain blocked on a plateau of information, with no more processing taking place.

If the clinician is uncomfortable using the cognitive interweave and finds that a client continues to evidence distress with regard to targeted memories, he should discontinue EMDR treatment until appropriate supervision and additional practice are obtained. If the clinician has been adequately supervised in the use of the cognitive interweave, yet finds that a client continues to "loop," she should discontinue the use of EMDR and contact a more experienced consultant or send a written report of the case to the EMDR Network Newsletter (see Appendix C).

Obviously, EMDR will not work for every client. It requires only a few sessions to determine its suitability in a particular case; one simply observes the level of processing that has (or has not) occurred. Clearly, the clinician should not let months go by while the client experiences pronounced distress before deciding to change methods. If adequate processing does not occur during the first few sessions, and especially if exacerbated disturbance appears, then either the method is being inadequately applied or it is inappropriate for the client at that time. Indeed, for some clients it may never be appropriate.

It is important to remember that the evidence for the efficacy of various EMDR protocols is still largely based on clinical observation rather then controlled research. Therefore, it is the responsibility of the clinician to use all of his clinical skills to assess its effectiveness with a given client or population. At this point the only adequate measure of success is the individual client's response. As I have said repeatedly, EMDR is client-centered in terms of servicing the needs of the client. Using demand characteristics to pressure clients into continuing EMDR or intimating that the treatment they are receiving is the only way they can be healed can easily backfire. Remember, respect for client defenses is paramount. Clinical work with EMDR is a dance—and the client is the one who leads.

SUMMARY AND CONCLUSIONS

For work with clients in the populations covered in this chapter, the issues of resistance and noncompliance may be of concern. The clinician should make sure that the appropriate therapeutic relationship, goals, and prioritization of targets have been established. Flexibility and creativity are also critical.

Clinicians working with clients who have suffered sexual abuse, war trauma, or dissociative disorders will find the cognitive interweave indispensable for achieving consistent therapeutic success. In addition to being comfortable with EMDR, the clinician should also be well versed in working with the clinical population with whom she proposes to use EMDR. Put simply, clinicians should never use EMDR with a client they would not treat without it. Education, consultation, and supervised experience are highly recommended for any specialized clinical population.

Children as young as 2 years old can be treated successfully if appropriate alterations of the standard EMDR procedures are made. A safe environment must be provided in which the child sees that the parents' authority has been tacitly given to the therapist. The creation of a positive initial experience with EMDR, plus the use of techniques for assisting concentration, produces rapid positive effects for children. As always, the creativity of the clinician is vital for success.

Couples should be treated only by clinicians with a background in family or couples therapy. However, in general, individual partners should be treated singly with respect to disturbing memories of past interactions, childhood experiences that contribute to present problems, and present circumstances that exacerbate the disturbance. Special attention must be given to partners of sexual abuse survivors, as well as to partners suffering the aftermath of an extramarital affair.

It is important that sexual abuse survivors be given an initial positive experience with EMDR through the safe-place exercise and that they learn a variety of relaxation techniques to enhance their sense of safety and control. Because of the special vulnerability of these clients all clinical cautions should be intensified. It is vital that appropriate goals be established before treatment begins and that informed consent regarding possible forensic issues be obtained. While a variety of previously dissociated and unresolved memories may surface during treatment, it is important to recognize that they may be based on vicarious traumatization or trickery. Clients should be given sufficient time to integrate the new information plateaus and emotional stages they attain before proceeding with the processing of new issues.

The treatment of combat veterans is often hampered by secondary gain issues, not the least of which is the fear of losing disability compensation. A treatment plan is necessary that takes into account such factors, as well as the client's premorbid history, possible perpetrator guilt, and excessive anger. There are also special concerns related to the treatment of older veterans and female veterans.

The category of dissociative disorder includes some of the highest-risk clients to be treated with EMDR. While success rates have been high, clinicians must be not only knowledgeable in this specialty area but comfortable with the cognitive interweave and familiar with the necessary adjustments to the standard EMDR procedure. All clients should be screened for dissociative disorder before EMDR is initiated. Additional guidelines and suggestions for training in the area of dissociative disorders appear in Appendix B.

It is vital that the clinician use all pertinent cross-checks and cautions to evaluate apparent treatment effects. Open lines of communication with clients are necessary to continue work, if needed. It should be remembered, however, that some clients will not be amenable to EMDR treatment. Continued distress in any client is a red flag indicating that other methods should be initiated. Although consultants are available through the EMDR Network, the ultimate arbiter of a client's suitability for EMDR treatment is the clinician's own observation.

CHAPTER 12

Theory, Research,
and Clinical Implications

> Five senses; an incurably abstract intellect; a haphazardly
> selective memory; a set of preconceptions and
> assumptions so numerous that I can never examine
> more than a minority of them—never become even
> conscious of them all. How much of total reality can
> such an apparatus let through?
>
> *C. S. Lewis*

In the first section of this chapter we will examine some theories
regarding the underlying basis for EMDR treatment effects. Unfortunately, there is not yet enough known in the area of brain physiology to
confirm these theories, and this situation is unlikely to change in the
foreseeable future. However, because of EMDR's dramatic treatment
effects, theories about why it works abound. In the second section we
will delineate some basic research criteria, review the research that has
been done on EMDR for PTSD, examine the shortcomings of this
research, and make suggestions for further studies. The final section of
this chapter deals with the clinical implications of current research and
the use of EMDR.

THEORETICAL EXPLANATIONS

EMDR was launched because of my chance observation in the park, and
its development and continued refinement are the result of clinical
observation. Theories that explain why EMDR works have arisen after
the fact and have not yet been confirmed. However, the lack of definitive
explanation of the underlying mechanisms of EMDR in no way detracts
from the demonstrated effectiveness of the method. At the very least,
some of these theories are clinically useful because they have helped us
to improve the methodology.

The Accelerated Information Processing model uses the language of neurobiology. Its physiological foundations, while undeniable, are currently unknown, as are those of any other information-processing model. However, I believe that the identification of the underlying physiological mechanisms is not as relevant as the development of the clinical procedures derived from the conceptual paradigms, the efficacy of which are testable. It was the observations of EMDR treatment effects that led to the Accelerated Information Processing model. The principles that evolved as the model was developed were successful in predicting new treatment applications, procedural variations, and protocols for clinical practice. The neurobiological model has proved useful as a therapeutic road map and as a unifying concept that integrates the salient aspects of most of the major psychological modalities.

In its simplest form, the model incorporates the physiological notions of network activation, counterconditioning, and assimilation of emotionally corrective, adaptive information. During EMDR treatment, the neuro network containing the target information is activated, the negative effects are mitigated, and the resultant information is weighted positively and then functionally stored in memory. By whatever means, EMDR causes this delayed learning to take place and to do so at an accelerated rate.

Theories as to why EMDR works are currently only speculations—and will probably remain so for many years. Fortunately, we do not have to know why a demonstrably effective treatment works before using it. By analogy, although it took decades to discover why penicillin works, it was used in the meantime because its positive effects were dramatic and reliable.

In order to explore the theories of how EMDR works, I will first review explanations that were advanced in an earlier article (Shapiro, 1991a) and then move on to more recent suggestions regarding the cortical functions that may be involved. One thing is certain: Whatever explanation is finally confirmed will have to encompass the complex interaction of a number of factors, including both procedural elements operating during EMDR clinical practice and neurophysiological mechanisms.

Procedural Elements

Any assessment of the therapeutic effectiveness of EMDR must take account of all of its procedural elements. Many of these elements are designed to provide an emotionally corrective experience, traditionally considered to be important for effective psychotherapy (Alexander, 1956; Alexander & French, 1946; Foa & Kozak, 1986; Lang, 1979; Watzlawick, 1987). The following are some aspects of EMDR that may foster such an experience:

1. Dosed exposure with clients who have been thoroughly pre-pared for the experience is considered to be an important procedural element of EMDR. As reviewed in Chapter 1, exposure is generally thought to be the primary active ingredient in behavioral treatments of PTSD, and a number of studies have focused on the efficacy of techniques such as desensitization (Brom, Kleber, & Defares, 1989; Peniston, 1986) and direct therapeutic exposure (Boudewyns & Hyer, 1990; Cooper & Clum, 1989; Foa et al., 1991; Keane et al., 1989) in which this element is paramount. The therapeutic effects in these studies were achieved by means of 6–16 treatment sessions of 60–90 minutes each. The most significant clinical effects (approximately 60% success) were reported by two studies by Brom et al. (1989), who used 15 desensitization sessions, and by Foa et al. (1991), who examined the effects of seven sessions of prolonged exposure, plus approximately 20 hours of assigned exposure homework. In contrast, a recently published pilot study of EMDR with diagnosed PTSD subjects (Forbes et al., 1994) obtained treatment efficacy, comparable to the preceding studies as assessed by equivalent measures, after only four treatment sessions and no assigned homework. To date, the most consistent treatment effects using exposure techniques with a PTSD population have been reported by Richards, Lovell, and Marks (1994), who used a combination of eight sessions of imaginal and live exposure and 1 hour of daily exposure homework over a 2-month period. A symptom improvement of 65–80% was reported in this study, compared to the 30–60% improvement found in the previously mentioned studies. However, a total of approximately 50 exposure hours (therapist sessions plus homework) was necessary to achieve these results. In contrast, a recent study of 80 trauma victims (Wilson et al., in press) reported that a total of three EMDR sessions yielded therapeutic effects that were equivalent to those found in the Richards et al. (1994) study. A recent study comparing four sessions of EMDR and approximately 20 hours of exposure (Vaughan, Wiese, et al., 1994) found that the two procedures yielded comparable results.

Although exposure is most certainly a necessary element of EMDR treatment, it appears insufficient as the sole explanation for the rapidity of the treatment effects obtained. Nevertheless, the clinician's prepara-tion of the client, which increases the client's ability to remain in contact with the disturbing imaginal experience, and the alternation of short doses of exposure with cognitive debriefing are probably very impor-tant aspects of EMDR treatment. It may be that it is this alternating exposure to high levels of disturbance that is the unique contribution of EMDR methodology to standard exposure procedures. The exact physiological reasons for the success of this type of exposure regimen are, however, beyond the scope of this text (except for the clinically based conjectures described below). However, evaluating the effects of interrupted exposure alone should be considered in light of the apparently contradictory observation that a similar interruption of exposure in the context of systematic desensitization does not cause the remission of disturbance at the high end of the anxiety continuum (Wolpe, 1958). In addition, it will be necessary to address the report that, with flooding, a minimum of 25 minutes of continuous exposure seems necessary for a significant decrease in distress (Chaplin & Levine, 1981; Foa & Kozak, 1986), as well as the fact that prolonged rather than brief exposure has been proposed as the most effective form of the treatment (Chaplin & Levine, 1980; Foa, Steketee, & Rothbaum, 1989; Marks, 1972). However, the clinical observation of decreased disturbance (by one-to-five SUD units within the first 15 minutes of EMDR reprocessing), the results of the aforementioned EMDR studies, and the consistent reports of complete and long-lasting desensitization of target memories after only one-to-three EMDR sessions strongly suggest either that thorough preparation of clients undergoing interrupted exposure yields the most pronounced treatment results or that aspects of EMDR in addition to exposure are responsible for its success. Some of the factors that may contribute to the effectiveness of dosed exposure, as well as other potentially important aspects of EMDR, are explored in the following sections.

2. Clients are assisted in the repeated creation and dismissal of their traumatic imagery, processes that may give them a sense of mastery in their ability to mentally circumscribe and manipulate the disturbing internal stimuli. In addition, focusing attention on the disturbing material for short periods of time while hearing reassuring therapeutic statements from the clinician and becoming aware of the safety of the clinical context may foster counterconditioning. At the very least, the client's short bursts of attention to the traumatic memories, along with the therapist's reassurance, provide a therapeutic context offering the benefits of repeated exposure, a condition antithetical to the avoidance reaction that is part of the pathology and that maintains it.

3. Clients are encouraged to attend for a prescribed amount of time to the physical sensations created by the traumatic imagery. This contact may allow them to identify and separate the sensory effects of the trauma from the cognitively laden affective interpretations of these sensations (which can result in identification with a labeled emotion such as "I am afraid" or "I am angry"). Clients can come to perceive themselves as larger than the pathological cognition by observing their reaction to the target. They do this by shifting focus from an undifferentiated, overwhelming feeling of fear to a cognitive awareness such as: "I am feeling sensations in my stomach that are associated with a feeling of fear. Now I am feeling sensations in my chest that are associated with feelings of fear. . . ." This cognitive separation allows clients to recognize

nize the changeability of the sensations, a recognition that can increase their sense of self-awareness and self-efficacy. These short periods of attention to sensations may afford the same benefits of counterconditioning and exposure as does the repetition of alternating periods of creation and dismissal of traumatic imagery.

4. Assisting clients to identify the negative self-assessment stemming from the trauma may allow them to perceive its irrationality. The restructuring and reframing inherent in formulating positive cognitions can also facilitate the therapeutic process.

5. The alignment of the primary aspects of the trauma by focusing on the image, the negative cognition, and physical sensations assists clients in accessing the dysfunctional information. This state-specific information is then linked to emotionally corrective information through the positive cognition. The therapeutic alignment of target components in EMDR appears consistent with the BASK (behavioral, affect, sensation, and knowledge) model of dissociation posited by Braun (1988). The procedural reconnection of the traumatic material, which helps the client make sense of the experience, then facilitates its storage in narrative memory.

6. The clients are asked, "What do you get now?" at the end of every set of eye movements, which automatically brings new pieces of information to mind. These are targeted in the order of their appearance. This sequential targeting may be a much more effective way to access the most relevant distressing material than is the procedure (used in systematic desensitization or direct therapeutic exposure) of returning repeatedly to the initial traumatic image.

7. The instructions to "just notice" the trauma and the attendant disturbance increase the counterconditioning and exposure benefits by interfering with the client's tendency to be afraid of the fear, an inclination that has contributed to the client's ongoing distress and that can continue to interfere with treatment effects. This interference may be facilitated by the eye movements (or other stimuli used in EMDR) themselves.

Eye Movements (and Alternative Stimuli)

A variety of physiological mechanisms may be activated by the eye movements (and alternative stimuli) used in EMDR. These may contribute to EMDR's therapeutic effect by maintaining the client's simultaneous external awareness during a period of internal distress or by activating brain functions inherent in the movements or in the attention paid to two simultaneously present stimuli. These possibilities are explored in the following sections.

Distortion of Response Stereotype

One of my early conjectures about EMDR (Shapiro, 1991a) was that the client's response to accessing the traumatic memory involves automatic physiological states (fused in state-specific configuration). The addition of the eye movements may cause another configuration of physiological states and responses to intrude on the earlier associations. This may in turn cause a disruption of the complex of habitual physiological responses elicited by the traumatic memory. The disruption engendered by the simultaneous dual configurations may allow further processing to occur. Lipke (1992a) has suggested that the latter is accomplished by the simple inauguration of an orienting response, in which the external focus elicited by the eye movements disrupts the traumatic associative network so that learning can occur. Armstrong and Vaughan (1994) believe that the learning occurs because of the triggered orienting response, which interrupts escape/avoidance behavior.

Marquis (1991) has suggested further that "the field currents generated by the eye movements (the same used to detect REM sleep) interfere with the tracts connecting the frontal lobes with the hypothalamus and hippocampus in such a way as to weaken the connection between stimulus and emotional response" (p. 192). Such a process would aid in a deconditioning effect. However, this suggestion alone is insufficient to explain the increase in positive emotions that are observed during the treatment session.

Distraction

One obvious interpretation of the role of the eye movements is that they distract the client from the trauma (Shapiro, 1991a). According to Dyck (1993), this presumed distraction causes deconditioning because of the client's inability to concentrate on the traumatic image; that is, the distraction prevents the traumatic material from being reinforced by the previously anticipated anxiety. This, according to Dyck, constitutes an extinction trial.

While investigations of this interpretation may be fruitful, a number of problems with it are worth noting. First, Dyck suggests that the kind of distractor that should be used is related to the dominant modality of the trauma. For instance, auditory distractors would be most effective on auditory components of the traumatic memory and visual distractors most effective on visual images. However, this conjecture has not been supported clinically, because thoughts and cognitions have also undergone immediate therapeutic modification as the result of eye movements alone. Second, Dyck posits that a series of traumas or traumas that occurred over extended periods of time would be less amenable to treatment by EMDR than would single events. Once again, however, this possibility has not been observed in clinical settings. Further, a number of experiments have indicated that distraction lessens, rather than increases, therapeutic effectiveness (Grayson, Foa, & Steketee, 1982, 1986; Satory, Rachman, & Grey, 1982). It would appear, therefore, that the present conception of distraction does not make a significant contribution to understanding EMDR effects. It is possible, however, that the eye movements serve to titrate the client's response to the memory in other ways which, as Dyck suggests, make the dosed exposure a deconditioning experience.

Hypnosis

It is reasonable to suspect that any rapid psychotherapeutic effect is due to hypnotic suggestion. However, EMDR and hypnosis are very dissimilar in their clinical effects. For instance, hypnotic abreactions seem to involve a moment-by-moment ("frame-by-frame") sequence of events, whereas clients treated with EMDR tend to jump from one key element of the memory to another. EMDR clients appear more alert and conscious and less susceptible to inappropriate suggestion than are hypnosis clients. For instance, clinical reports consistently indicate that EMDR alone cannot instill anything that is false. Thus, the client will reject a suggestion that is not ecologically valid and may even become agitated as a result. Likewise, EMDR has not been reported to take away any belief that is true. Beliefs, as well as anxiety, that are appropriate and currently useful remain intact.

The lack of suggestibility of clients during the EMDR process compared to those in a hypnotic state may be a result (or correlate) of differences in the dominant brain waves elicited by the two procedures. EEG readings taken during EMDR show a brain wave pattern within normal waking parameters (Nicosia, in press), whereas pronounced theta (Sabourin, Cutcomb, Crawford, & Pribram, 1990), beta (DePascalis & Penna, 1990), or alpha (Meares, 1960) waves are characteristic of hypnotized subjects. Thus, EEG readings indicate that EMDR clients are not in a state of hypnosis.

Synaptic Changes

Animal studies have indicated that repetitive low-voltage currents change the synaptic potentials that are directly related to memory processing (Arai & Lynch, 1992; Barrionuevo et al., 1980; Larson & Lynch, 1989). In earlier articles (Shapiro, 1989a, 1991a) I suggested that the neuronal bursts caused by the eye movements may be essentially equivalent to a low-voltage current and therefore responsible for the same synaptic changes. It may be that the repetitive action of any of the alternative stimuli—or even repetitive bursts of attention—generates such a current. The shifting of the synaptic potential of the neural networks that include the dysfunctional material may cause the information to undergo progressively more processing with each set, until it arrives at an adaptive resolution.

While this hypothesis is ethically impossible to test on humans, given the present state of neurobiological science and its invasive measurement devices, it affords some interesting speculations, as detailed in the following paragraphs. It is important to understand that these speculations are offered primarily as intellectual stimulation, not as a necessary precursor to establishing or obtaining EMDR treatment efficacy.

As discussed earlier, the resolution of many traumatic memories appears to entail a transmutation from the dysfunctional to the adaptive perspective. Because it appears that the adaptive perspective can emerge progressively and rapidly during EMDR treatment, it may be useful to imagine a sequential linkage of information that is brought about by a shift in the synaptic potential (receptor valence or level of resistance) of the targeted network. Although these constructs are *hypothetical,* they may nevertheless prove to be useful to information processing theorists (and perhaps clinicians) as a way of conceptualizing the transmutation process.

The present formulation (Shapiro, 1992) is based on the pivotal relationship observed in EMDR between affect and the transition from dysfunction to resolution. The initial dysfunctional state, the intervening stages of processing, and the final functional perspective revealed by the client may be conceptualized as verbalizations of the sequential stages of affect during the adaptive integration of the past and present experiences. The observation in EMDR treatment sessions that information is at least partially organized through affect is not unique to this method (Bower, 1981; Reiser, 1990). Extrapolating from the concepts elucidated earlier in this text, Figure 14 depicts my additional speculations that neuro networks (and associated cognitive content) are organized, in part, by affect, which is linked to a particular bioelectric valence (level of charge). The greater the dysfunctional affect, the stronger the network's synaptic potential. Therefore, the target trauma is prevented from linking with any more adaptive information by the high resistance of its neural receptors.

Let us say that the target memory (Z) in Figure 14 has been observed clinically to contain the affect of guilt and shame and the accompanying cognition "I am detestable and worthless." The information stored regarding this memory is encapsulated in a neuro network with a high bioelectric valence associated with the high level of dysfunctional affect. It is hypothesized that the networks with the

Z valence contain information with the most self-destructive affect and self-assessment, whereas the networks with the A valence are associated with the most adaptive and appropriate affect and assessment, such as "I am a lovable/worthy/healthy." That is, the valences of the neural receptors (synaptic potential) of the respective neuro networks, which separately store various information plateaus and levels of adaptive information, are represented by the letters Z through A. It is hypothesized that the high-valence target network (Z) cannot link up with the more adaptive information, which is stored in other networks with a lower valence. That is, the synaptic potential is different for each level of affect held in the various neuro networks. Lower-valence networks would contain memories of positive material (e.g., mastery experiences, compliments, information from self-help books). The theory is that when the processing system is catalyzed by EMDR, the valence of the receptors is shifted downward so that they are capable of linking with the receptors of neuro networks with progressively

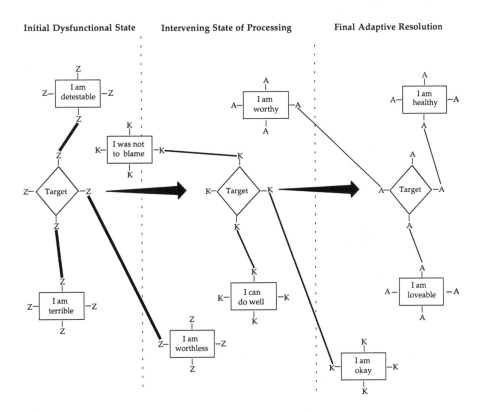

FIGURE 14. The relationship between bioelectrical valence, affect, and cognition in information processing.

lower valences and will thus incorporate the more adaptive information that is stored there. An example of such a linkage would be the movement from a high level of dysfunction, say, from the T valence associated with a cognition like "I'm always to blame" to the lower valence of K, which is associated with a cognition like "I can do well." This shift is made evident by the progressive discharge of the negative affect, the evolution of more adaptive cognitions, and the emergence of positive memories into conscious awareness.

There are various clinical implications of the affect/valence hypothesis. For example, molestation victims often report horrific nightmares in which they are being dismembered by monsters. If we suppose that an attempt is being made by the REM sleep mechanism to process early traumatic events, then a nightmare of being dismembered by monsters is the cognitive counterpart to the high level of affect locked in the network containing the early memories. Let us say, for example, that at the time of the original trauma, a molested child experienced great terror when an adult entered the room and pulled her legs apart. The affect associated with this memory is now locked in her nervous system and is generated by the attempted reprocessing during REM sleep. Such a level of terror would not be generated in the adult client by another adult in the present but could be associated with a confrontation with an uncontrollable monster. The symbolism of the monster is the cognitive construction of the affect state during the period of processing in REM sleep.

When EMDR is used to target the dream image, a high level (Z valence) of terror is evoked. As a sufficient amount of information is processed, the affect shifts downward. The lowered valence allows the appropriate cognitive connections to be made by the linking of different neuro networks. With the shift in affect, the symbolic representation, or cognitive construction, can be removed and the client perceives the present without distortion. For instance, a molestation victim who dreamed of being chased by a monster through a cave exclaimed, after a number of eye movement sets, "That's my stepfather chasing me through my childhood home."

Other symbolic representations are often found to be the cognitive counterpart of an affective state or physical sensation. One example, described in Chapter 11, is from the case of the client whose intrusive images of being raped by Satan resolved during EMDR treatment into a memory of being raped by her father's friend, who assaulted her while he wore a set of plastic horns. The two different interpretations may be due to the activation of a cognitive network of parallel valence that contains different information. Thus, the level of affect stimulates cognitive content of equivalent valence.

Another possible extrapolation from the affect/valence hypothesis is the escalation of self-destructive behavior such as increasingly severe self-mutilation (cutting) or increasingly dangerous sexual encounters observed in many clients. Clients may be driven to maintain a high level of pain because of the restimulation of early abuse memories that incorporate states of self-loathing or other aspects of disturbance (Calof, 1992). It is possible that the affect of the core memories and the corresponding valence become associated with certain behaviors that are consistent with that client's subjective level of pain. As the behaviors become desensitized through repeated exposure, the valence of the core memories stimulates other behaviors that had been higher on the disturbance hierarchy but are now merely parallel to that level of affect. For example, relationships appear to get more abusive, but the client experiences them with the same level of affect. This progressive desensitization process can be seen clinically in the way that SUD levels drop throughout the hierarchy during systematic desensitization (Wolpe, 1991). Therefore, what appears to be a level of escalation when viewed by an observer is actually behavior generated internally from the client's unchanged level of affect.

The processing of information due to a change in receptor valence, which in turn influences affect, may also work in reverse. In other words, some aspect of the alternative stimuli may cause a deconditioning on an affective level, which then stimulates certain receptors and causes associative processing.

Once again, while these mechanisms are pure conjecture, such attempts to understand what is observed clinically in EMDR treatment may prove to be useful in furthering our understanding of dream imagery, self-destructive behaviors, and other clinical phenomena. Theorizing about observed clinical behaviors can also contribute to the development of therapeutic methodology. For example, conceptualizing the eye movements in EMDR as causing the equivalent of a low-voltage current affecting receptors (i.e., their synaptic potential) resulted in the successful innovation in EMDR practice of using different directions and speeds for the eye movements. Presumably, each kind of movement has a unique effect on the target network.

Dream Sleep

One of my earliest suggestions (Shapiro, 1989a) was that the directed eye movements may be stimulating the same processes that occur in REM sleep. I posited that the relationship of eye movements and stress may be one of reciprocal inhibition; that is, the eye movements help inhibit the stress, but sufficiently high stress inhibits the eye movement. As reviewed in Chapter 1, independent sleep studies have offered some support for these ideas inasmuch as the most traumatized individuals appear to suffer from dysfunctional REM sleep states. For instance, the combat veteran awakens in the middle rather than at the end of the nightmare (Ross et al., 1990). Additionally, a recent study has shown a direct correlation between the intensity of negative affect in the dream and the amount of REM observed (Hong et al., 1992); this study disputes an earlier theory that eye movements during dreaming are simply evidence that the dreamer is scanning the dream environment. Furthermore, the conjecture that cognitive or memory processing is linked to eye movements seems to be supported by a recent study showing that newly taught skills will be lost if REM is subsequently disrupted (Karni et al., 1992).

While this hypothesis about the role of the eye movements in EMDR is interesting, particularly in view of the work in neuroscience suggesting that the function of the REM state is the processing and storage in memory of information (Fishbein & Gutwein, 1977; Gabel, 1987; Sutton, Mamelak, & Hobson, 1992; Winson, 1993), there is currently no direct support for it. It would be interesting to compare sleep and REM patterns in clients before and after successful EMDR treatment. Brain wave studies comparing EMDR and REM patterns might also provide useful information.

Relaxation Response

I have posited (Shapiro, 1989a, 1991a) that the eye movements may induce a conditioned relaxation response. This response might be induced by way of the reticular formation (which causes muscular inhibition in REM state) or other mechanisms that activate the parasympathetic nervous system. The parasympathetic system would inhibit the sympathetic nervous system, which is associated with the "fight or flight" fear responses engendered by trauma. One study involving biofeedback equipment has supported this hypothesis by finding that eye movements appear to cause a compelled relaxation response (Wilson et al., 1995). However, this observation does not explain the clinical effectiveness of the alternative stimuli that have been used with EMDR; the same relaxation response (as determined by physiological measures) was not found in a control group stimulated by finger tapping. There may be some essential difference between clinician-initiated hand taps and the client-controlled finger taps used in the study, or a different mechanism may be responsible for their effects. However, the finding that the parasympathetic nervous system is activated during tasks that demand visual convergence (Monnier, 1968) may explain the positive treatment effects also noted in studies using eye fixation control (Pitman et al., 1993; Renfrey & Spates, 1994).

Much more physiological research is needed on populations other than chronically impaired veterans, who may not show positive effects because of ancillary trauma, and normal subjects, who may not show effects because the target material is insufficiently disturbing. Single-trauma PTSD-level subjects should be used to test these hypotheses further.

Cortical Functions

The hypotheses I raised in 1989 included reference to Pavlov's (1927) theory of psychotherapeutic effect and the basis of neurosis. Setting aside any notion of "excitatory-inhibitory" balance and of specific neural blockages inherent in Pavlov's conception, there is little doubt that something about the trauma causes information processing to be blocked. This blockage keeps the original incident in its anxiety-producing form.

According to Pavlov (1927), the essence of any psychotherapeutic treatment is the restoration of a neurological balance. This view is consistent with the positions of major historical figures such as Freud (1919/1955) and Janet (1989/1973) and of neurological and biochemical experts today (Krystal et al., 1989; van der Kolk, 1994; van der Kolk & van der Hart, 1991; Watson et al., 1988). If this assumption is valid, it is logical to conclude that EMDR facilitates a rebalancing or stimulation of the information-processing system. In this regard, I proposed that eye movements might have a direct effect on cortical functions. Two independent theories regarding this possibility have been offered, based on neurobiological research, and both posit bihemispheric involvement as a cause.

Examination of EMDR clients by means of quantitative analysis of electroencephalography (QEEG) has shown a normalization in the synchronization of slower brain wave activity in the two cortical hemispheres (Nicosia, 1994). The normalization of depressed function shown after EMDR treatment corresponds to clinically observed improvement in memory retrieval and information processing. Nicosia posits that the phase relationship of the two cortical hemispheres is disrupted by the suppression of REM caused by the norepinephrine released during trauma. This interhemispheric asynchrony prevents integrative memory processing. He suggests that the eye movements in EMDR resynchronize the activity of the two hemispheres because their rhythmic and repetitive alternation mimics the activity of pacemaker mechanisms within the cortex, which exist for this purpose but which were suppressed by the trauma.

The notion that synchronized hemispheric activation produces beneficial information-processing effects is supported by independent research on the differential effects of gaze manipulation on the positive and negative assessments of initially neutral stimuli (Drake, 1987). The results of a number of controlled studies have shown that directing the gaze of right-handed subjects to objects located to the right results in more positive evaluative responses than directing their gaze to objects on the left. This research was based on hypotheses involving hemisphere asymmetry in emotional processing, one of which states that the left hemisphere processes information related to positive affect, whereas the right hemisphere processes negative affect (Drake, 1984; Drake, 1993; Drake & Seligman, 1989; Merckelback & van Oppen, 1989). These studies provide some support for Nicosia's suggestion that alternately activating the two hemispheres induces integrative information processing.

Just as EMDR treatments have shown positive clinical effects through the use of alternating hand taps and tones, so too have recent studies regarding lateral activation of positive and negative reactions to the same stimulus (e.g., scripted "persuasive" arguments) found predicted differential reactions through the use of auditory and physical manipulation; that is, subjects responded positively to (e.g., thought well of) a script heard through the right headphone and negatively to one heard through the left headphone (Drake, 1991; Drake, 1993; Drake & Bingham, 1985; Drake & Sobrero, 1987). Even more interesting is the fact that investigators in this independent line of research recognized the possibility of clinical effects that are, in fact, currently being realized with EMDR in their suggestion that "future investigations should examine whether experimentally induced gaze shifts affect fundamental processes such as conditioning" (Merckelback & van Oppen, 1989, p. 150).

One conclusion that might be drawn from this research is that the type of stimulation used is not as important as the focused attention itself. Hemispheric activation is clearly induced by simply laterally shifting foci of attention, whether or not any lateral motoric activity takes place. For instance, several studies in perceptual psychology have demonstrated that the initiation of a saccadic eye movement causes the subject to feel that the movement has been completed even when it has actually been prevented from occurring. If, for example, the eye muscles are immobilized and subjects try to turn their eyes to one side, they feel as if the eyes have moved although they have not (Brindley & Merton, 1960). In short, when it comes to saccadic eye movements, the brain registers the intention, not the completed act. This finding is consistent with the hypothesis that the orienting response alone, and not any specific movement, is necessary for the activation of information-processing mechanisms (Lipke, 1992a). Self-focused attention to an internal state in conjunction with bilateral activation has also been posited as necessary for therapeutic EMDR effect (Russell, 1992).

If alternating hemispheric activity is one of the factors in EMDR effects, it can be expected that many more stimuli besides eye movements, hand taps, and tones will be found to be useful. In fact, because the optic nerve from each eye is linked to both hemispheres, it may turn out that a forced focus on a single spot induces processing shifts. Alternatively, it may be that rhythmic stimulation alone is conducive to the more rapid therapeutic effects.

In either instance, the clinical objective would be to maintain the client's awareness of the traumatic memory while continually activating the processing mechanism through bursts of concentrated attention on a currently presented stimulus. Presumably, then, the best alternative stimuli would be those that allow the processing effect to occur, but that also allow the clinician to monitor the client's compliance with the instruction to attend simultaneously to the traumatic memory and the present stimulus (and additional reinforcers that assist the therapeutic effect).

Integrative Effect

One of the simplest ways of describing EMDR effects is to say that the target event has remained unprocessed because the immediate bio-chemical responses to the trauma have left it isolated in neurobiological stasis. When the client tracks a moving finger or attends to a hand tap, tone, or even a fixed point on a wall, active information processing is initiated to attend to the present stimulus. If the client is asked to attend simultaneously both to this stimulus and to the traumatic memory, the active information-processing mechanism is linked to and processes the target event as well as the current stimulus. This processing mechanism is physiologically configured to take the information to an adaptive resolution.

Perhaps the accelerated processing occurs because the clinician continually guides the client to the appropriate targets (and to the proper alignment of the components of the targeted experience) and because other procedural elements prevent client avoidance. Since it is well documented that the amount of time necessary for positive treat-ment effects with EMDR is substantially less than that required with simple exposure (Fine, 1994; Forbes et al., 1994; Goldstein & Feske, 1994; Kleinknecht, 1992; McCann, 1992; Paulsen et al., 1993; Steketee & Goldstein, 1994; Vaughan, Wiese, et al., 1994; Wilson et al., 1995; Wilson et al., in press), some other mechanism besides exposure must be at work. However, the actual neurological concomitants may not be discovered for decades. In the meanwhile, clinical observations of EMDR effects may provide investigators in the areas of neurobiology and memory research with a better understanding of physiological processes. The rapid treatment effects of EMDR provide an opportunity to observe the standard patterns of memory association and emotional or cognitive processing, as well as the differential effects of processing long-standing and more recent memories. Thus, in many ways, EMDR may offer a window into the brain.

CONTROLLED RESEARCH

The investigation of any new method should include both clinical observations and experimental findings. EMDR studies will now be evaluated within the context of research on PTSD.

General Scarcity of PTSD Treatment Studies

Controlled clinical outcome research in many areas of mental health is unfortunately scarce and traditionally lags far behind clinical practice. For instance, although systematic desensitization was introduced by Joseph Wolpe in 1952 and numerous case histories were reported 6 years later (Wolpe, 1958), the first controlled study establishing its effectiveness did not appear for another 8 years (Paul, 1966). Similarly, while flooding is now a standard treatment for PTSD, the first clinical reports on it were presented in 1982 (Fairbank & Keane, 1982; Keane & Kaloupek, 1982) and the first independent controlled study validating its effectiveness did not appear until 7 years later (Cooper & Clum, 1989).

In general, there appears to be very little clinical outcome research in the field of psychological trauma. By the end of 1993, 13 years after PTSD was officially recognized and classified in the 1980 DSM-III, only six randomized controlled clinical outcome studies (excluding studies of drug effects) were to be found in the published literature (Solomon et al., 1992), and four of these were limited to male Vietnam combat veterans. Clearly, there is a strong need for more clinical outcome research on trauma populations.

Suggested EMDR Research Criteria

This section will delineate some basic research criteria which appear both reasonable and necessary for a valid test of the method. The principles will then be used to evaluate the results of extensive research already completed.

Method Validity

Researchers should be trained in the entire EMDR methodology and should implement the protocols actually used in clinical practice. Fidelity checks should be performed by competent EMDR instructors or clinicians to assess the validity of the researcher's use of the method.

Clearly, methods used incorrectly or incompetently by researchers contribute little or nothing to the knowledge base about these methods and, indeed, can lead to false conclusions.

Because EMDR entails a complex methodology, adequately supervised practice sessions should take place before it is used. However, training alone does not ensure competency, and this is especially true for students or researchers who have not perfected their general clinical skills through extensive practice and clinical experience.

Ideally, researchers should observe the use of EMDR as practiced by fully trained, thoroughly experienced clinicians who are comfortable with and have been assessed as competent in the use of the method. When this is not possible, researchers should receive formal training in the method, practice it sufficiently on subjects in a pilot study to obtain consistently positive fidelity checks (assisted by appropriate consultation and supervision, if necessary), and feel comfortable in using it before systematically examining it in controlled research. Of course, these precautions should be taken with any therapeutic procedure. Indeed, it is the format used by researchers in the hard sciences when conducting formal studies, and it should be an established part of general research practice in clinical psychology, as should continued supervision and checks of procedure fidelity and protocol maintenance.

Selection of Psychometrics

EMDR researchers should use measurement tools that are capable of assessing change when a single memory has been successfully processed. Unfortunately, practically no psychometrics have been developed for this purpose. The limited number of sessions used in clinical research make the creation of such tools mandatory. For instance, if only one disturbing memory (or a small number of memories) is being treated in subjects who are suffering from multiple-event trauma (such as molestation or military combat), global psychometrics such as Goal Attainment Scaling (GAS), the Standard Interview of PTSD, the Minnesota Multiphasic Inventory (MMPI), and the Symptom Checklist 90 (SCL-90) are not likely to detect changes. Further, clinical observation indicates that if global measurements are used with multiple-event trauma, subjects should receive no less than 12 weeks of EMDR treatment on enough memories to represent all their major clusters. (Even more sessions may be needed to address secondary gains.)

The only standardized measure generally used to assess the effects of single-memory reprocessing is the Impact of Event Scale. However, while this device may be used to measure change after the treatment of one memory, subjects must be specifically instructed to rate the number of intrusions that are related only to the memory already targeted and to ignore any other intrusions. This discrimination may be very difficult for subjects. Additionally, if a single traumatic event out of many is successfully treated, intrusions of that specific memory will not be detected by the Impact of Event Scale, while other memories can continue to be troublesome and can influence the Avoidance subscale. If the number of memories treated is sufficient, the Intrusion subscale of the Impact of Event Scale may show an immediate effect, although the present stimuli and a future template (see Chapter 8) generally will need to be targeted with EMDR (with adequate time for real-life exposure) in order to reveal a treatment effect on the Avoidance subscale. This procedural sequence applies to all similar measures and is relevant to any PTSD treatment method being evaluated.

Also valuable, and one of the few self-report measures that can detect changes in a single target memory (out of many), is the SUD Scale. It has been found to correlate with objective physiological indicators of stress (Thyer, Papsdorf, Davis, & Vallecorsa, 1984) and has shown a high concordance with other measures of treatment outcomes (Hyer, 1994a). The SUD Scale was recently cited as the best indicator of PTSD as assessed by the Structured Clinical Interview for DSM (SCID; Keane, Thomas, Kaloupek, Lavori, & Orr, 1994).

Subject Selection

Research subjects should meet reasonable criteria for the possibility of clinical change. For example, adequate clinical work cannot be done with clients without first addressing potential secondary gains. Clearly, subjects who are in danger of losing their disability check if their PTSD is cured are likely to be resistant to any therapeutic procedure. Just as dual diagnoses and active drug abuse are generally used as exclusion criteria, so too should such secondary gains issues as financial compensation disqualify prospective subjects. The exception would be any long-term experiment that targets these factors first. However, the establishment of new clinical methodologies, whether EMDR or others, should not depend on obtaining large treatment effects with chronically impaired combat veterans presently receiving disability compensation.

Comparative Research

Controlled comparative clinical outcome research should be done using PTSD populations. EMDR should be tested against other standard treatments, such as direct therapeutic exposure (including systematic desensitization and prolonged exposure), stress inoculation therapy, and other cognitive behavioral therapies. The treatments should be compared to a nontreatment control. Evaluations should be done on comparative efficacy, length of treatment, and generalization of effects, issues that are of vital concern to clinicians in standard clinical practice.

Diverse Protocols

In addition to adequate replication of results from studies of trauma victims, controlled comparative research should be done on the many EMDR protocols that have been developed for specific clinical populations. Initial reports have shown very favorable results in studies of EMDR with panic disorder and agoraphobia (Goldstein & Feske, 1994) and with somatic disorders (Weston, 1994). Additional research is needed on protocols for other anxiety disorders, dissociative disorders, substance abuse, and depression. These populations will be explored in a future book on the advanced clinical applications of EMDR.

Component Analyses

Component analyses can be useful to determine whether alterations to the standard protocols enhance or detract from treatment efficacy. For these purposes, victims of single-event trauma would be the most appropriate subjects. Fine discriminations can also be made regarding what aspects of the eye movement and alternative stimulation are responsible for the therapeutic effect. Furthermore, although the eye movement is the most unique aspect of EMDR as it is typically practiced, there are many other components in the procedure that require separate evaluation. In addition to the standard EMDR procedure, a number of protocols are used to treat a variety of complaints. These protocols are an integral part of EMDR treatment and should be used with the appropriate populations. The clinical outcomes derived from the entire methodology, procedures, and protocols should be tested and suitably employed while attempting to examine the various components of EMDR.

It will be useful to perform a series of component analysis studies in which eye movement, closed eye, forced eye focus, unilateral and bilateral rhythmic stimulation (e.g., sounds and hand taps), and other tasks are examined separately in comparison to more standard placebo treatment controls. These studies should, of course, include a sufficient number of subjects to ensure statistical power. Measures should include standard objective tests of therapeutic results (including behavioral measures) and should use treatment time as one of the independent variables. Furthermore, component analyses should be done in the context of the complete EMDR methodology and should include checks of treatment fidelity. A possible outcome of such a research program is that the complete EMDR methodology can afford powerful treatment effects without the use of eye movements or other external stimuli (particularly with selected clinical populations), but that the addition of such dual attention stimuli increases the overall speed and efficacy of treatment to a measurable degree, with the various stimuli being differentially effective.

It is clear that the eye movements are not unique in producing positive therapeutic effects and that the existence of successful alternative stimuli adds to the versatility of the method. However, whatever the alternative mode of stimulation used, it is important that the clinician or researcher be able to monitor the client's focus of attention so that severely disturbed clients do not dissociate into the target material. The use of directed eye movements makes such monitoring relatively easy since a client who becomes too engrossed in the dysfunctional material will generally cease tracking the clinician's fingers. If eye movements are not used, extra care should be taken to offer continuous verbal prompts to the client/subject to remain aware of the alternate stimulation, since concentrating solely on the disturbing information interferes with the orienting response or dual-attention mechanism that may be responsible for the therapy's effectiveness.

The Initial Study of EMDR

I introduced EMDR in 1989 with a controlled study (Shapiro, 1989a, 1989b), which was discussed in detail in Chapter 1. This study, which has attracted much attention, served the important purpose of stimulating further investigation. It is noteworthy that the initial study of EMDR provided one of the first controlled treatment outcome assessments in the area of PTSD. Because of the small number of subjects used, the 1989 study is best viewed as preliminary and in need of confirmation by independent replications and careful clinical observation. Subsequent EMDR studies (reviewed below) have been strengthened by the incorporation of more standardized diagnostic criteria and measures of symptomatology, as well as by a separation between the therapist and the measurement of effects.

Review of EMDR Research

In the 5 years since the initial study, there have been more published reports in support of EMDR than of either systematic desensitization or flooding in the treatment of PTSD during a comparable time period (see Chapter 1). In fact, to date, more controlled studies on EMDR have been done than on any other method used in the treatment of PTSD.

Table 1 lists the controlled studies investigating PTSD symptomatology that involve more than 10 subjects, and examines them along the dimensions delineated in the previous section. I will first briefly review the studies and then delineate some of the flaws that should be avoided in future research.

The studies represented in Table 1 are as follows:

TABLE 1. EMDR Controlled Studies Investigating PTSD Symptomatology

	(1) Boudewyns	(2) Jensen	(3) Levin	(4) Pitman	(5) Renfrey	(6) Shapiro	(7) Vaughan	(8) D. Wilson	(9) S. Wilson
Principal investigator									
Method validity and fidelity checks	None	Low	High	Variable	None	High	None	High	High
No. of sessions	2	2	1	12	2–6	1	3–5	1	3
Psychometrics									
SUDs	Decreased	Decreased	Decreased	Decreased	Decreased	Decreased		Decreased	Decreased
IES	Unchanged	Decreased	Decreased	Decreased	Decreased		Decreased		Decreased
Global	Unchanged	Unchanged		Mixed	Decreased		Decreased		Decreased
Physiological	Unchanged				Decreased	Decreased	Decreased	Decreased	
Behavioral	Unchanged							Decreased	
Subjects (primary)									
Single trauma			X		X	X	X	X	X
Multitrauma	X	X		X					
Compensation	X	X		X					
Design									
Comparative	X		X			X	X		
Component	X							X	
Delayed treatment				X	X	X			X
Wait list only (no treatment control)		X							

1. *Boudewyns, Stwertka, Hyer, Albrecht, and Sperr (1993).* A pilot study randomly assigned 20 chronic inpatient veterans to EMDR, exposure, and group therapy conditions and found significant positive results from EMDR for self-reported distress levels and therapist assessment. No changes were found in standardized and physiological measures, a result attributed by the authors to insufficient treatment time considering the secondary gains of the subjects who were receiving compensation. Results were considered positive enough to warrant further extensive study, which has been funded by the VA. Preliminary reports of the data (Boudewyns, Hyer, Peralme, Touze, & Kiel, 1994) indicate that EMDR is superior to a group therapy control.

2. *Jensen (1994).* A controlled study of the EMDR treatment of 25 Vietnam combat veterans suffering from PTSD, as compared to a nontreatment control group, found small but statistically significant differences after two sessions for in-session distress levels, as measured on the SUD Scale, but no differences on the Structured Interview for Posttraumatic Stress Disorder (SI-PTSD), VOC, GAS, and Mississippi Scale for Combat-Related PTSD (M-PTSD; Jensen, 1994). This study was done by two psychology interns who had not completed formal EMDR training. Furthermore, the interns reported low fidelity checks of adherence to the EMDR protocol and skill of application, which indicated their inability to make effective use of the method to resolve the therapeutic issues of their subjects.

3. *Levin, Grainger, Allen-Byrd, and Fulcher (1994).* A controlled study of 45 Hurricane Andrew (Florida) survivors found significant differences in scores on the SUD and Impact of Event scales, indicating a superiority of EMDR treatment to supportive crisis counseling and nontreatment controls at 1-month and 3-month follow-ups.

4. *Pitman et al. (1993).* In a controlled component analysis study of 17 chronic outpatient veterans, using a crossover design, subjects were randomly divided into two EMDR groups, one using eye movement and a control group that used a combination of forced eye fixation, hand taps, and hand waving. Six sessions were administered for a single memory in each condition. Both groups showed significant decreases in self-reported distress, intrusion, and avoidance symptoms. SCL-90-R changed in the eye movement condition only, while the Clinician-Administered PTSD Scale (CAPS), Mississippi Scale for Combat-Related PTSD, and State Anxiety remained unchanged in both.

5. *Renfrey and Spates (1994).* A controlled component study of 23 PTSD subjects compared EMDR with eye movements initiated by tracking a clinician's finger, EMDR with eye movements engendered by tracking a light bar, and EMDR using fixed visual attention. All three conditions produced positive changes on the CAPS, SCL-90-R, Impact of Event Scale, and SUD and VOC scales.

6. *Shapiro (1989a).* The initial controlled study of 22 rape, molestation, and combat victims compared EMDR and a modified flooding procedure that was used as a placebo to control for exposure to the memory and to the attention of the researcher. Positive treatment effects were obtained for the treatment and delayed treatment conditions on SUDs and behavioral measures, which were independently corroborated at 1- and 3-month follow-up sessions.

7. *Vaughan, Armstrong, et al. (1994).* In a controlled comparative study, 36 subjects with PTSD were randomly assigned to treatments of (1) imaginal exposure, (2) applied muscle relaxation, and (3) EMDR. Treatment consisted of four sessions, with 60 and 40 minutes of additional daily homework over a 2- to 3-week period for the image exposure and muscle relaxation groups, respectively, and no additional homework for the EMDR group. All treatments led to significant decreases in PTSD symptoms for subjects in the treatment groups as compared to those on a waiting list, with a greater reduction in the EMDR group, particularly with respect to intrusive symptoms.

8. *D. Wilson, Covi, Foster, and Silver (1995).* In a controlled study, 18 subjects suffering from PTSD were randomly assigned to eye movement, hand tap, and exposure-only groups. Significant differences were found using physiological measures (including galvanic skin response, skin temperature, and heart rate) and the SUD Scale. The results revealed, with the eye movement condition only, a one-session desensitization of subject distress and an automatically elicited and seemingly compelled relaxation response, which arose during the eye movement sets and which appears to support a conditioning model.

9. *S. Wilson, Becker, and Tinker (in press).* A controlled study randomly assigned 80 trauma subjects (37 diagnosed with PTSD) to treatment or delayed-treatment EMDR conditions and to one of five trained clinicians. Substantial results were found at 30 and 90 days and 12 months posttreatment on the State–Trait Anxiety Inventory, PTSD-Interview, Impact of Event Scale, SCL-90-R, and the SUD and VOC scales. Effects were equally large whether or not the subject was diagnosed with PTSD.

Nonrandomized studies involving PTSD symptomatology (not noted in Table 1) include:

1. An analysis of an inpatient veterans' PTSD program ($n = 100$) compared EMDR, biofeedback, and relaxation training and found EMDR to be vastly superior to the other methods on seven of eight measures (Silver, Brooks, & Obenchain, 1995).

2. A study of 100 Hurricane Andrews survivors found significant differences on the Impact of Event Scale and SUD scales in a compari-

son of EMDR and nontreatment conditions (Grainger, Levin, Allen-Byrd & Fulcher, 1994).

3. A study of 60 railroad personnel, suffering from high-impact critical incidents, compared a peer counseling debriefing session alone to a debriefing session that included approximately 20 minutes of EMDR (Solomon & Kaufman, 1994). The addition of EMDR produced substantially better scores on the Impact of Event Scale at 2- and 10-month follow-ups.

4. Of 445 respondents to a survey of trained clinicians who had treated over 10,000 clients, 76% reported greater positive effects with EMDR than with other methods they had used. Only 4% found fewer positive effects with EMDR (Lipke, 1992b, 1994; see Appendix D).

While most of these studies obtained clinically positive results, in the following paragraphs I indicate some of the replication problems I hope will be addressed in future studies of EMDR. These problems include the lack of treatment fidelity (i.e., how well the procedure is administered), lack of appropriate clinical assessment measures, inappropriate component analyses, and use of subjects with secondary gain issues.

1. *Some published research on EMDR has not conformed to the way the method is used in clinical practice.* For instance, in two non-PTSD studies (not shown in Table 1), researchers untrained in the method and using only a restricted number of directed eye movements nevertheless drew conclusions about the entire method (Sanderson & Carpenter, 1992; Tallis & Smith, 1994). Both of these studies reported effects that were essentially equivalent to simple exposure.

While these studies may allow for conjectures about the efficacy of isolated and restricted eye movements, the results shed no light on the use of the overall EMDR method. As this book makes clear, EMDR is a complex methodology that entails much more than directed eye movements. Furthermore, to maximize effects in clinical practice, the eye movements must be tailored to the client. As we have seen, some clients do not respond to certain eye directions or speeds and others require that the eye movements be systematically altered during the course of therapy if treatment effects are to continue.

It is not surprising, therefore, that studies by researchers who are untrained in EMDR and who use four to seven sets of eye movements that are restricted to the same direction, rate, and number report only marginal improvement in their subjects. The Sanderson and Carpenter (1992) study of phobic clients, for example, reported a decrease of distress equivalent to only two SUD Scale units after seven sets of restricted eye movements, a finding that led readers to conclude that

phobics could not receive substantial relief with EMDR. This erroneous conclusion was compounded by an additional case report (Acierno, Tremont, Last, & Montgomery, 1994) of a multiphobic subject who was also treated unsuccessfully with restricted eye movements. In addition, these researchers inaccurately implemented the procedure described in my early articles (Shapiro, 1989a, 1989b) in that the subject was instructed to relax after each set and treatment was not commenced until physiological measures returned to baseline (thereby repeatedly interrupting processing). Predictably, no significant positive results were obtained. On the other hand, an EMDR-trained researcher (Kleinknecht, 1993) reported the complete desensitization of a blood phobia (a decrease of 10 SUD Scale units) after a period of treatment equivalent to one session. Self-report, physiological, and behavioral measures validated Kleinknecht's reported clinical effects, thus supporting the claim of numerous clinicians over the past 5 years that EMDR is a powerful treatment for phobias.

As indicated earlier, the effects of the eye movements, or alternative stimulation, while considered a central factor in EMDR, are clearly augmented and facilitated by other aspects of the standardized procedure and protocols. Thus, the results of studies by researchers who have never been trained in the use of EMDR cannot provide definitive conclusions about the efficacy of the method as it is actually used in clinical practice.

Even with EMDR-trained researchers, validity checks should be performed on their use of the method, since training alone does not guarantee competence and treatment integrity. For instance, validity checks reported in a recent study (Pitman et al., 1993), noted in Table 1, revealed variable treatment fidelity and a positive correlation between how well the method was used and the magnitude of the treatment effect. In addition, the study by two inexperienced interns who had not completed formal EMDR training (Jensen, 1994) also reported a low fidelity evaluation, which explicitly warned them before the study was completed that they were exploring difficult and complex areas without the necessary skills.

2. *Standard psychometrics have been used that are incapable of reflecting successful treatment results.* Unfortunately, there is a general lack of standard psychometrics capable of revealing therapeutic change when a single memory out of many is reprocessed. For example, although the Boudewyns et al. (1993) and Jensen (1994) studies found a reduction in subjects' SUD level, their other measures were global (e.g., the M-PTSD), which are insensitive to therapeutic improvement when only one of a dozen traumatic combat memories has actually been treated (Fairbank & Keane, 1992). Further, the physiological measures used in the Boudewyns et al. study have not been found to shift in *any* clinical

studies using chronic multi-traumatized combat veterans (Boudewyns & Hyer, 1990).

3. *Component analyses (Pitman et al., 1993; Renfrey & Spates, 1994; Wilson et al., 1995) have compared eye movements to other forms of stimulation or to forced eye fixation without using a conventional treatment or a true placebo condition for comparison.* Except for the signature physiological response revealed by Wilson et al.'s use of biofeedback equipment, this design sheds little light on treatment efficacy because alternate stimulation has been used with success by EMDR clinicians for years. Furthermore, the other procedural elements of EMDR produce positive treatment effects and therefore should not be used as a placebo condition. That is, while EMDR was named for its use of directed eye movements, these represent only one component of the methodology; furthermore, the eye movements are not the only form of external stimulation to have therapeutic impact. Perhaps it would be helpful for researchers who attempt a component analysis to view EMDR in terms of its overarching principles and to consider EMDR as an abbreviation for Exposure-Mediated Dual Reprocessing. In other words, the observed reprocessing effects of EMDR may be initiated by a combination of exposure to the memory and other procedural elements and facilitated by the awareness of the trauma and the simultaneous focus of attention on an external stimulus. For now, we can assume that many alternative stimuli will activate processing when the researcher helps subjects to concentrate on the dysfunctional target in the properly aligned components, (e.g., image, cognition, physical sensation) and guides them according to EMDR procedures.

Four investigators have attempted to study the efficacy of EMDR in the treatment of PTSD by singling out its most salient component, the repeated eye movements. Unfortunately, definitive findings have been hampered by inappropriate controls, a number of subjects insufficient to ensure statistical power, and the use of subjects with secondary gain issues who reveal only marginal treatment effects. At this time, the four studies of this component have produced contradictory reports. Two of these studies (Boudewyns et al., 1993; Wilson et al., 1995) found an eye movement condition to be superior to a no-eye-movement control, while two studies (Pitman et al., 1993; Renfrey and Spates, 1994) found equivalent effects for the two conditions.

All four studies used a small number of subjects. However, there were major differences in the size of the treatment effects between those studies that used single-trauma subjects (Renfrey & Spates, 1994; Wilson et al., 1995) and those that used chronic combat veterans (Boudewyns et al., 1993; Pitman et al., 1993). This suggests that studies using single-trauma subjects without secondary gains are the appropriate means of making fine discriminations among component effects. The other implementation problems are reviewed below.

Pitman et al. compared a condition of the EMDR procedure using eye movements to a condition of the EMDR procedure entailing a combination of (1) visual fixation of a dot on the wall, (2) hand tapping, and (3) rhythmic visual stimulation caused by the therapist repetitively moving his hand in front of the subject. The second complex condition was considered to be a placebo (or equivalent to exposure-only). However, this is essentially comparing EMDR to itself, for, as should be abundantly clear from the preceding chapters, EMDR entails many different elements, any and all of which may be crucial for maximal therapeutic effectiveness. Furthermore, other attention-focusing tasks such as hand tapping have been used clinically in the place of the eye movements with comparable results. It is not surprising, therefore, that Pitman et al. found little difference in the effectiveness of their two conditions. A true placebo (or exposure-only) condition would be one that does not include any of the major components of EMDR or factors inherent in the eye movements themselves. In addition, the complexity of the combined control condition used by Pitman et al. precludes any determination of what aspect of the eye movements might be responsible for their therapeutic effect.

The Renfrey and Spates (1994) study, which was conceptualized more rigorously than the Pitman et al. study, raises some interesting questions. In a comparison of different lengths of treatment, the subjects in a standard eye movement group received a mean of 3.9 sessions, with 43.5 cumulative sets of eye movements, whereas the subjects in a focused eye control group received a mean of 5.4 sessions, with a total of 57.6 sets of visual attention. In a comparison of efficacy, 21 of the 23 subjects initially met the criteria for PTSD, while at a posttest only one in the standard eye movement group, compared to three in the fixation group, met criteria. Therefore, the reported lack of statistical significance between the two conditions with respect to treatment length, number of sets, and treatment efficacy may be due to the small number of subjects used (i.e., 8 in the EMDR group and 7 in the visual attention group), which unfortunately limits the usefulness of the conclusions.

The existence of clinically effective alternatives to the eye movements should not be used to discount the treatment's efficacy, because there is no reason to suppose that the eye movements are unique. The eye movements may be effective because of an interaction of such factors as focused attention, stimulation of an orienting response or of dual-processing mechanisms, rhythmic activity, or bilateral activation, to name a few. However, many of these elements are also present in the alternative stimuli that have been used (including focusing on a dot on the wall) and each may have some degree of therapeutic effect. It is important that when designing placebo conditions to evaluate possible treatment effects researchers not discount the complex brain activity involved in even the smallest act of attention.

4. *The subjects used in some of the EMDR research have too many secondary gain issues to allow an accurate assessment of psychological methods in only a few sessions.* The size of the effects in these studies (Boudewyns et al., 1993; Jensen, 1994; Pitman et al., 1993) must be evaluated with this condition in mind. Unlike the clients treated by most clinicians, chronic populations receiving compensation for their psychological disability are the primary subjects used in PTSD research. Unfortunately, as most clinicians would attest, the secondary gains (e.g., VA benefits) that are frequently a part of life for these individuals (as noted in Chapters 4 and 11) must be addressed before anything more than small or uneven treatment effects can be expected.

BROADER CLINICAL AND PROFESSIONAL IMPLICATIONS

The aforementioned replication problems are not unique to EMDR. I hope that the present discussion will serve as a wake-up call to clinical researchers in general. Although millions of people suffer from the effects of trauma and millions of dollars are spent yearly on mental health research in general, there are too few controlled clinical outcome studies of PTSD. Furthermore, the quality of the few published studies on this pathology leaves much to be desired (Blake et al., 1993; Hyer, 1994b; Solomon et al., 1992). Unfortunately, there is no generally accepted standard of quality for clinical outcome research, nor any universally accepted definitive editorial guidelines for the publication of research on therapeutic procedures. These drawbacks vastly decrease the value of published research for clinicians, because the findings of any individual study may not accurately represent the effects of the methodologies as they are actually practiced by the experienced therapist. It would greatly advance the field of psychotherapeutic practice if representatives of professional research organizations and the most respected journals jointly issued a position paper aimed at upgrading and standardizing the caliber of clinical research articles. In addition, yearly updates of suggested psychometrics for the major DSM categories would help to standardize the efforts of new researchers in the field.

The need to upgrade the level of clinical research is becoming extremely important for the practicing clinician. No single study causes a method to be accepted or discarded, but the principles underlying the selection and publication of acceptable research studies have far-reaching ramifications for clinicians. While psychologists have long voiced the desire to be guided by the scientific principles of research, the question remains whether scientific principles are actually guiding the researchers themselves. For instance, if the purpose of research is to objectify subjective experience, then clearly there must be some external validation of the researcher's subjective utilization of the clinical method.

The issue of treatment fidelity in clinical research is of great concern. Is the method being tested actually the method being used in clinical practice? An examination of the EMDR research, and clinical research in general, indicates that checks of treatment fidelity have been minimized or ignored. Therefore, the ability of research to guide therapists in their clinical practice is unfortunately limited. This is underscored by the comparatively small treatment effects found in the three EMDR studies on combat veterans (Boudewyns et al., 1993; Jensen, 1994; Pitman et al., 1993), where the fidelity checks were nonexistent, poor, and variable, respectively. The treatment outcomes of these studies can be compared to the reports of experienced licensed clinicians and directors of PTSD programs within the VA system who have consistently reported substantial positive treatment effects using EMDR with veterans from World War II through Desert Storm (Carlson et al., in press; Daniels et al., 1992; Lipke & Botkin, 1992; Silver et al., 1995; Taber, in press; Thomas & Gafner, 1993; Viola & McCarthy, 1994). Although controlled studies may indeed be invaluable in helping to weed out the effects of expectancy and experimenter bias, these effects are typically small and short-lived (Rosenthal, 1976). In addition, an extensive meta-analysis of studies using placebo controls (Lipsey & Wilson, 1993) indicates that placebo effects are extremely small. Therefore, the achievement of substantial and persistent treatment effects with subjects suffering from PTSD would seem to minimize the significance of any of these confounds in interpreting these findings, particularly as a review of the trauma literature indicates that PTSD is highly resistant to placebo effects (Solomon et al. 1992).

The dearth of acceptable clinical norms evinced in many published studies points up the lack of reliability and validity to which therapists have grown accustomed in clinical research. On the other hand, the publication of such studies suggests a presumption by some journal editors and researchers of a prevalent and seemingly acceptable laxness of clinical standards on the part of therapists. This juxtaposition serves neither clients nor science. Now is not the first time that such questions have been raised, and it is vital that we continue to address them throughout the mental health community (Fensterheim, 1994a; Goldfried, 1993; Hill, 1994; Orlinsky & Russell, 1994; Persons, 1994; Raw, 1993, in press; D. A. Shapiro et al., 1994; Wolfe, 1994).

The question of how well clinical treatment outcome studies are conducted is no longer primarily an academic issue, but one that directly relates to the practicing clinician, now that managed care companies are being guided by research results. If clinicians are to be directed toward or away from using any specific treatment methods for clients in their care, such guidance should result only from the testing of methods that are utilized in a way consistent with clinical practice, using adequately prepared subjects and the appropriate psychometrics.

Clinical Responsibility

In addition to questions of research validity, there are also issues of personal responsibility and treatment fidelity. Any positive treatment effect is the result of an interaction among clinician, method, and client. Clearly, the clinician must evaluate a prospective client to assess readiness and appropriateness for a given intervention. A treatment may fail if the client is inappropriately assessed, and the clinician must make consideration of this possibility a part of any treatment evaluation process.

Of course, a particular therapeutic method may simply be ineffective. In the case of EMDR, however, not only has the preponderance of controlled research revealed positive treatment effects, but reports of the successful application of EMDR in single and group case studies with standardized evaluations abound (see Chapter 1), along with an overwhelmingly positive response from a survey of trained clinicians who as a group had treated over 10,000 clients with EMDR. Therefore, if the clinician using EMDR is failing to achieve positive effects with a high percentage of clients, he should not automatically assume that it is the method that is at fault but should at least consider the possibility that the problem is the way it is being used.

Clinicians who fail to get positive treatment effects with EMDR may simply be those who cannot incorporate it into their therapeutic style. EMDR entails highly focused, interactive clinical work that can bring up a great deal of disturbing affect. Any of its procedural factors may be disturbing to some clinicians. For example, some therapists may find it difficult to follow the injunction "Stay out of the way of the client during successful processing," whereas others may find the cognitive interweave too directive. Thus, some otherwise excellent clinicians may never become skilled in EMDR simply because they are uncomfortable with it. This is one of the hazards of attempting to learn any new method midway or late in one's clinical career. We can hope this problem will be alleviated when EMDR courses become part of the standard graduate school curriculum.

Clinicians who find EMDR principles and practices appealing will still find EMDR a challenging modality and will need to work to upgrade their skill levels. In our formal EMDR training sessions we continually stress that EMDR is not a "cookie cutter" approach but must be tailored to each client. It is also emphasized that EMDR training does not ensure EMDR competency; it is merely the beginning of an ongoing learning experience. This book will assist the learning and retention process by serving as a training guide and clinical handbook. However, each clinician (and researcher) will have specific weaknesses that can only be addressed with supervision and consultation with other trained clinicians. This makes it mandatory that research be accompanied by appropriate fidelity checks to make sure that the method that is being tested is the one actually used in clinical practice.

Clinical observation suggests that therapists trained formally or through supervision by experienced EMDR clinicians can expect a high success rate (perhaps as much as 80–90%) for appropriately selected clients. If this level of success is not being achieved, the clinician should take responsibility for becoming more skilled in the method. Assessment and application are equally important: Education in the appropriate use of a method includes not only how but when (and on whom) to use it. A valid opportunity for informed consent cannot be given to clients contemplating therapy unless the clinician is sufficiently educated and practiced in the method.

At the time of this writing, there are over 10,000 clinicians worldwide who have been trained in EMDR. Some are more skilled and experienced than others. Among the most highly skilled group are the approximately 200 facilitators who have assisted in the formal EMDR training sessions. They are accessible through the EMDR Network, a nonprofit professional organization dedicated to ongoing education and development of therapist resources. Membership in the EMDR Network is open to clinicians, researchers, and students who have been formally trained. Because this book will make instruction more widely available through graduate school courses and supervision by previously trained clinicians, equivalency standards for membership will be made available. Interested readers should review the information in Appendix C.

An independent EMDR Professional Issues Committee (EPIC) has also been established that oversees training policies and professional activities. Their recommended guidelines regarding formal training are found in Appendix B.

The skill level of each clinician has a profound effect on individual clients and on those with whom these clients come in contact. The successful treatment of one client can inspire others to seek assistance, while a failure can discourage many others. The joy of good clinical work is the ability to participate in a client's personal healing. Successful therapy causes a ripple effect through the population and through succeeding generations. But along with the potential for great impact comes a tremendous responsibility. If we do not take sufficient care to learn our methods well, we fail in our responsibility as therapists. The first rule is "Do no harm," yet we harm when we do not prepare enough to do our best. Our clients place their lives and their psyches (the Greek word for "soul") in our care. Only our highest integrity, our most educated level of skill, and our most profound compassion should answer their need.

SUMMARY AND CONCLUSIONS

The clinical effects of EMDR have been demonstrated in numerous case reports and several studies. However, the mechanisms that underlie this information processing are unknown and will probably remain so for years to come, owing to lack of neuropsychological knowledge and appropriate measuring devices. Even descriptions such as interhemispheric synchrony speak to observed effects rather than causes.

However, a number of theories have been proposed to explain EMDR's therapeutic effects. The theories involve the method's procedural elements, and specific hypotheses address the eye movement component. The latter attribute the therapeutic effect of the eye movements to the disruption of stereotypic responses, distraction, hypnosis, synaptic alterations, REM sleep concomitants, a compelled relaxation response, or activation of cortical functions, including the rhythmical stimulation of an external pacemaker and a bihemispheric activation that induces integrative processing.

The meteoric rise in popularity of EMDR, due largely to the clinical observations of many trained clinicians, has far outstripped the amount of controlled research on this method. In part, this is symptomatic of the scarcity of clinical outcome research in the area of posttraumatic stress in general. Much more scientific investigation needs to be done, and issues such as treatment fidelity, the use of appropriate standardized psychometrics and treatment comparisons, and the identification of suitable populations must be directly addressed in order to test methods adequately.

This book has been written to supplement supervised practice conducted by trained, experienced EMDR instructors. Whether EMDR education takes place in formal, dedicated training sessions, within mental health agencies, or as part of a graduate school curriculum, it is only the beginning of the learning process. Once formal training is complete, it becomes the responsibility of all therapists and researchers using EMDR to continue to upgrade their skills through ongoing practice, supervision, and consultation with more experienced practitioners.

EMDR has already helped to relieve suffering for thousands of clients and has affected many thousands more through clients' associations with friends and family. However, the method is only as good as the clinicians who are trained to use it. EMDR's therapeutic potential is enormous—and so is each clinician's personal responsibility to use it judiciously and well.

> We cannot live only for ourselves. A thousand fibers
> connect us with our fellow men; and among those
> fibers, as sympathetic threads, our actions run as
> causes, and they come back to us as effects.
> *Herman Melville*

References

Abruzzese, M. (1994, September). *Behavioral play therapy with very young children.* Paper presented at the 24th Congress of the European Association for Behavioral and Cognitive Therapies, Korfu, Greece.

Acierno, R., Tremont, G., Last, C., & Montgomery, D. (1994). Tripartite assessment of the efficacy of eye-movement desensitization in a multi-phobic patient. *Journal of Anxiety Disorders, 8,* 259–276.

Alexander, F. (1956). *Psychoanalysis and psychotherapy.* New York: Norton.

Alexander, F., & French, T. (1946). *Psychoanalytic therapy.* New York: Ronald Press.

Amadeo, M., & Shagass, C. M. (1963). Eye movements, attention and hypnosis. *Journal of Nervous and Mental Disease, 136,* 139–145.

American Psychiatric Association. (1980). *Diagnostic and statistical manual of mental disorders* (3rd ed.). Washington, DC: Author.

Anisman, H. (1978). Neurochemical changes elicited by stress. In H. Anisman & G. Bignami (Eds.), *Psychopharmacology of aversively motivated behavior.* New York: Plenum.

Antrobus, J. S., & Singer, J. (1964). Eye movements, accompanying daydreams, visual imagery, and thought suppression. *Journal of Abnormal and Social Psychology, 69,* 244–252.

Arai, A., & Lynch, G. (1992). Factors regulating the magnitude of long-term potentiation induced by theta pattern stimulation. *Brain Research, 598,* 173–184.

Armstrong, N., & Vaughan, K. (1994, June). *An orienting response model for EMDR.* Paper presented at the meeting of the New South Wales Behaviour Therapy Interest Group, Sydney, Australia.

Aserinsky, E., & Kleitman, N. (1953). Regularly occurring periods of eye motility and concomitant phenomena during sleep. *Science, 118,* 273.

Baker, N., & McBride, B. (August, 1991). *Clinical applications of EMDR in a law enforcement environment: Observations of the psychological service unit of the L.A. County Sheriff's Department.* Paper presented at the Police Psychology (Division 18, Police & Public Safety Sub-section) Mini-Convention at the 99th annual meeting of the American Psychological Association, San Francisco.

Barrionuevo, G., Schottler, F., & Lynch, G. (1980). The effects of repetitive low-frequency stimulation on control and "potentiated" synaptic responses in the hippocampus. *Life Sciences, 27*, 2385-2391.

Bart, P. B., & Scheppele, K. L. (1980, August). *There ought to be a law: Women's definitions and legal definitions of sexual assault.* Paper presented at the meeting of the American Sociological Association, New York.

Bauman, W., & Melnyk, W. T. (1994). A controlled comparison of eye movement and finger tapping in the treatment of test anxiety. *Journal of Behavior Therapy and Experimental Psychiatry, 25*, 29-33.

Beck, A. T. (1967). *Depression.* New York: Hoeber-Harper.

Beere, D. B. (1992). More on EMDR. *the Behavior Therapist, 15*, 110-111.

Bernstein, C., & Putnam, F. W. (1986). Development, reliability, and validity of a dissociation scale. *Journal of Nervous and Mental Diseases, 174*, 727-735.

Black, J. L., & Keane, T. M. (1982). Implosive therapy in the treatment of combat-related fears in a World War II veteran. *Journal of Behavior Therapy and Experimental Psychiatry, 13*, 163-165.

Blackburn, A. B., O'Connell, W. E., & Richman, V. W. (1984). PTSD, the Vietnam veteran, and Adlerian natural high therapy: Individual psychology. *Journal of Adlerian Theory, Research and Practice, 40*, 317-332.

Blake, D. D., Abueg, F. R., Woodward, S. H., & Keane, T. M. (1993). Treatment efficacy in posttraumatic stress disorder. In T. R. Giles (Ed.), *Handbook of effective psychotherapy.* New York: Plenum.

Blanchard, E. B., & Abel, G. G.(1976). An experimental case study of the biofeedback treatment of a rape-induced psychophysiological cardiovascular disorder. *Behavior Therapy, 7*, 113-119.

Blanchard, E. B., Kolb, L. C., Pallmayer, T. P., & Gerardi, R. J. (1982). The development of a psychophysiological assessment procedure for posttraumatic stress disorder in Vietnam veterans. *Psychiatric Quarterly, 54*, 220-228.

Boudewyns, P. A. (1976). A comparison of the effects of stress vs. relaxation instrumentation on the finger temperature response. *Behavior Therapy, 7*, 54-67.

Boudewyns, P. A., & Hyer, L. (1990). Physiological response to combat memories and preliminary treatment outcome in Vietnam veteran PTSD patients treated with direct therapeutic exposure. *Behavior Therapy, 21*, 63-87.

Boudewyns, P. A., Hyer, L. A., Peralme, L., Touze, J., & Kiel, A. (1994, August). *Eye movement desensitization and reprocessing for combat-related PTSD: An early look.* Paper presented at the 102nd annual meeting of the American Psychological Association, Los Angeles.

Boudewyns, P. A., Hyer, L., Woods, M. G., Harrison, W. R., & McCranie, E. (1990). PTSD among Vietnam veterans: An early look at treatment outcome with direct therapeutic exposure. *Journal of Traumatic Stress, 3*, 359-368.

Boudewyns, P. A., & Shipley, R. H. (1983). *Flooding and implosive therapy: Direct therapeutic exposure in clinical practice.* New York: Plenum.

Boudewyns, P. A., Stwertka, S. A., Hyer, L. A., Albrecht, J. W., & Sperr, E. V. (1993). Eye movement desensitization and reprocessing: A pilot study. *Behavior Therapy, 16*, 30-33

Bower, G. H. (1981). Mood and memory. *American Psychologist, 36,* 129–148.

Braun, B. G. (1988). The BASK model of dissociation. *Dissociation, 1,* 4–23.

Brende, J. O. (1981). Combined individual and group therapy for Vietnam veterans. *International Journal of Group Psychotherapy, 31,* 367–378.

Brende, J. O., & McCann, I. L. (1984). Regressive experiences in Vietnam veterans: Their relationship to war, posttraumatic symptoms and recovery. *Journal of Contemporary Psychotherapy, 14,* 57–75.

Brindley, G. S., & Merton, P. A. (1960). Absence of position sense in the human eye. *Journal of Physiology, 153,* 127–130.

Brom, D., Kleber, R. J., & Defares, P. B. (1989). Brief psychotherapy for posttraumatic stress disorders. *Journal of Consulting and Clinical Psychology, 57,* 607–612.

Burgess, A. W., & Holmstrom, L. L. (1974). *Rape: Victims of crisis.* Bowie, MD: Robert J. Brady.

Calof, D. (1992, June). *Self-injurious behavior: Treatment strategies.* Paper presented at the 4th annual Eastern Regional Conference on Abuse and Multiple Personality, Alexandria, VA.

Carlson, E. B., & Putnam, F. W. (1993). An update on the dissociative experience scale. *Dissociation, 6,* 16–27.

Carlson, J. G., Chemtob, C. M., Rusnak, K., & Hedlund, N. L. (in press). Eye movement desensitization and reprocessing as an exposure intervention in combat-related PTSD. *Journal of the Vietnam Veterans Institute.*

Chaplin, E. W., & Levine, B. A. (1981). The effects of total exposure duration and interrupted versus continuous exposure in flooding therapy. *Behavior Therapist, 12,* 360–368.

Chemtob, C., Roitblat, H., Hamada, R., Carlson, J., & Twentyman, C. (1988). A cognitive action theory of posttraumatic stress disorder. *Journal of Anxiety Disorders, 2,* 253–275.

Christi, M. J., & Chesher, G. B. (1982). Physical dependence on physiologically released endogenous opiates. *Life Science, 30,* 1173–1177.

Cocco, N., & Sharpe, L. (1993). An auditory variant of eye movement desensitization in a case of childhood posttraumatic stress disorder. *Journal of Behavior Therapy and Experimental Psychiatry, 24,* 373–377.

Cohn, L. (1993). Art psychotherapy and the new eye treatment desensitization and reprocessing (EMD/R) method, an integrated approach. In E. Dishup (Ed.), *California art therapy trends.* Chicago: Magnolia Street.

Cooper, N. A., & Clum, G. A. (1989). Imaginal flooding as a supplementary treatment for PTSD in combat veterans: A controlled study. *Behavior Therapy, 20,* 381–391.

Cousins, N. (1979). *Anatomy of an illness.* New York: Norton.

Cousins, N. (1989). *Head first: The biology of hope.* New York: Dutton.

Crump, L. E. (1984). Gestalt therapy in the treatment of Vietnam veterans experiencing PTSD symptomatology. *Journal of Contemporary Psychotherapy, 14,* 90–98.

Daniels, N., Lipke, H., Richardson, R., & Silver, S. (1992, October). *Vietnam veterans' treatment programs using eye movement desensitization and reprocessing.* Symposium presented at the annual meeting of the International Society for Traumatic Stress Studies, Los Angeles.

Day, M. E. (1964). An eye movement phenomenon relating to attention, thought and anxiety. *Perceptual and Motor Skills, 19,* 443–446.

DePascalis, V., & Penna, P. M. (1990). 40 hz EEG activity during hypnotic induction and hypnotic testing. *International Journal of Clinical and Experimental Hypnosis, 38,* 125–138.

Doctor, R. (1994, March). *Eye movement desensitization and reprocessing: A clinical and research examination with anxiety disorders.* Paper presented at the 14th annual meeting of the Anxiety Disorders Association of America, Santa Monica, CA.

Drake, R. A. (1984). Lateral asymmetry of personal optimism. *Journal of Research in Personality, 18,* 497–507.

Drake, R. A. (1987). Effects of gaze manipulation on aesthetic judgments: Hemisphere priming of affect. *Acta Psychologica, 65,* 91–99.

Drake, R. A. (1991). Processing persuasive arguments: Recall and recognition as a function of agreement and manipulated activation asymmetry. *Brain and Cognition, 15,* 83–94.

Drake, R. A. (1993). Processing persuasive arguments: Discounting of truth and relevance as a function of agreement and manipulated activation asymmetry. *Journal of Research in Personality, 27,* 184–196.

Drake, R. A., and Bingham, B. R. (1985). Induced lateral orientation and persuasibility. *Brain and Cognition, 4,* 156–164.

Drake, R. A., & Seligman, M. E. P. (1989). Self-serving biases in causal attributions as a function of altered activation asymmetry. *International Journal of Neuroscience, 45,* 199–204.

Drake, R. A., and Sobrero, A. P. (1987). Lateral orientation effects upon trait-behavior and attitude-behavior consistency. *Journal of Social Psychology, 127,* 639–651.

Dyck, M. J. (1993). A proposal for a conditioning model of eye movement desensitization treatment for posttraumatic stress disorder. *Journal of Behavior Therapy and Experimental Psychiatry, 24,* 201–210.

Ellis, A. (1962). *Reason and emotion in psychotherapy.* Secaucus, NJ: Citadel.

EMDR Network. (1991, September). *Treating children with EMDR and artwork.* Special report of the Children/Adolescents Special Interest Group, Sunnyvale, CA.

Fairbank, J. A., & Brown, T. (1987a). Current behavioral approaches to the treatment of posttraumatic stress disorder. *Behavior Therapist, 3,* 57–64.

Fairbank, J. A., & Brown, T. (1987b). Heterogeneity of posttraumatic stress reactions. *Behavior Therapist, 10,* 242.

Fairbank, J. A., Gross, R. T., & Keane, T. M. (1983). Treatment of posttraumatic stress disorder: Evaluating outcome with a behavioral code. *Behavior Modification, 7,* 557–568.

Fairbank, J. A., & Keane, T. M. (1982). Flooding for combat-related stress disorders: Assessment of anxiety reduction across traumatic memories. *Behavior Therapy, 13,* 499–510.

Fairbank, J. A., & Nicholson, R. A. (1987). Theoretical and empirical issues in the treatment of posttraumatic stress disorder in Vietnam veterans. *Journal of Clinical Psychology, 43,* 44–45.

Fensterheim, H. (1994a, July). *Eye movement desensitization and reprocessing with personality disorders*. Paper presented at the 10th annual meeting of the Society for the Exploration of Psychotherapy Integration, Buenos Aires, Argentina.

Fensterheim, H. (1994b). Outcome research and clinical practice. *Behavior Therapist, 17*, 140.

Figley, C. R. (1978a). Symptoms of delayed combat stress among a college sample of Vietnam veterans. *Military Medicine, 143*, 107–110.

Figley, C. R. (1978b). Psychosocial adjustment among Vietnam veterans. In C. R. Figley (Ed.), *Stress disorders among Vietnam veterans: Theory, research, and treatment*. New York: Brunner/Mazel.

Figley, C. R. (1995). *Compassion fatigue: Secondary traumatic stress disorder from helping the traumatized*. New York: Brunner/Mazel.

Figley, C. R., & Carbonell, J. L. (1995, May). *Memory based treatments of traumatic stress: A systematic clinical demonstration program of research*. Paper to be presented at the Fourth European Conference on Traumatic Stress, Paris, France.

Fine, C. G. (1991). Treatment stabilization and crisis prevention: Pacing the therapy of the multiple personality disorder patient. *Psychiatric Clinics of North America, 14*, 661–675.

Fine, C. G. (1994, June). *Eye movement desensitization and reprocessing (EMDR) for dissociative disorders*. Paper presented at the Eastern Regional Conference on Abuse and Multiple Personality, Alexandria, VA.

Fisch, R., Weakland, J. H., & Segal, L. (1982). *The tactics of change: Doing therapy briefly*. San Francisco: Jossey-Bass.

Fishbein, W., & Gutwein, B. M. (1977). Paradoxical sleep and memory storage processes. *Behavioral Biology, 19*, 425–464.

Foa, E. B., & Kozak, M. J. (1986). Emotional processing of fear: Exposure to corrective information. *Psychological Bulletin, 99*, 20–35.

Foa, E. B., Rothbaum, B. O., Riggs, D., & Murdock, T. (1991). Treatment of posttraumatic stress disorder in rape victims: A comparison between cognitive-behavioral procedures and counseling. *Journal of Consulting and Clinical Psychology, 59*, 715–723.

Foa, E. B., Steketee, G., & Rothbaum, B. O. (1989). Behavioral/cognitive conceptualizations of post-traumatic stress disorder. *Behavior Therapy, 20*, 155–176.

Forbes, D., Creamer, M., & Rycroft, P. (1994). Eye movement desensitization and reprocessing in posttraumatic stress disorder: A pilot study using assessment measures. *Journal of Behavior Therapy and Experimental Psychiatry, 25*, 113–120.

Forman, B. D. (1980). Psychotherapy with rape victims. *Psychotherapy: Theory, Research and Practice, 17*, 304–311.

Frank, E., Anderson, B., Stewart, B. D., Dancu, C., Hughes, C., & West, D. (1988). Efficacy of cognitive behavior therapy and systematic desensitization in the treatment of rape trauma. *Behavior Therapy, 19*, 403–420.

Frank, E., & Stewart, B. D. (1983a). Physical aggression: Treating the victims. In E. A. Bleckman (Ed.), *Behavior modification with women*. New York: Guilford Press.

Frank, E., & Stewart, B. D. (1983b). Treatment of depressed rape victims: An approach to stress-induced symptomatology. In P. J. Clayton & J. E. Barrett (Eds.), *Treatment of depression: Old controversies and new approaches*. New York: Raven Press.

Frank, E., Turner, S. M., & Duffy, B. (1979). Depressive symptoms in rape victims. *Journal of Affective Disorders, 1,* 269–277.

Freud, S. (1953). Interpretation of dreams. In J. Strachey (Ed. & Trans.), *The standard edition of the complete psychological works of Sigmund Freud* (Vols. 4 & 5). London: Hogart Press. (Original work published in 1900)

Freud, S. (1955). Introduction to psychoanalysis and the war neuroses. In J. Strachey (Ed. & Trans.), *The standard edition of the complete psychological works of Sigmund Freud* (Vol. 17). London: Hogarth Press. (Original work published in 1919)

Freud, S. (1964) Moses and monotheism. In J. Strachey (Ed. & Trans.), *The standard edition of the complete psychological works of Sigmund Freud* (Vol. 23). London: Hogarth Press. (Original work published in 1939)

Freud, S., Ferenczi, S., Abraham, K., Simmel, E., & Jones, E. (1921). *Psychoanalysis and the war neurosis*. New York: International Psychoanalytic Press.

Friedman, M. J. (1988). Toward rational pharmacotherapy for posttraumatic stress disorder: An interim report. *American Journal of Psychiatry, 145,* 281–285.

Gabel, S. (1987). Information processing in rapid eye movement sleep: Possible neurophysiological, neuropsychological, and clinical correlates. *Journal of Nervous and Mental Disease, 175,* 193–200.

Gale, A., & Johnson, F. (Eds.). (1984). *Theoretical and applied aspects of eye movement research*. New York: Elsevier.

Goldfried, M. R. (1980). Toward the delineation of therapeutic change principles. *American Psychologist, 35,* 991–999.

Goldfried, M. R. (1993, November). Implictions of research for the practicing therapist: An unfulfilled promise? *Clinician's Research Digest* (Suppl. 10).

Goldstein, A., & Feske, U. (1993). Eye movement desensitization and reprocessing an emerging treatment for anxiety disorders. *ADAA Reporter, 4,* 1, 12.

Goldstein, A., & Feske, U. (1994). Eye movement desensitization and reprocessing for panic disorder: A case series. *Journal of Anxiety Disorders, 8,* 351–362.

Gould, E. (1994, March). *EMDR treatment of adult survivors of sexual abuse*. Paper presented at the 14th annual meeting of the Anxiety Disorders Association of America, Santa Monica, CA.

Grainger, R. K., Levin, C., Allen-Byrd, L., & Fulcher, G. (1994, August). *Treatment project to evaluate the efficacy of eye movement desensitization and reprocessing (EMDR) for survivors of a recent disaster*. Paper presented at the 102nd annual meeting of the American Psychological Association, Los Angeles.

Grayson, J. B., Foa, E. B., & Steketee, G. (1982). Habituation during exposure treatment: Distraction versus attention-focusing. *Behaviour Research and Therapy, 20,* 323–328.

Grayson, J. B., Foa, E. B., & Steketee, G. (1986). Exposure *in vivo* of obsessive-compulsives under distracting and attention-focusing conditions: Replication and extension. *Behaviour Research and Therapy, 24,* 475–479.

Greenberg, R., Katz, H., Schwartz, W., & Pearlman, C. (1992). A research-based reconsideration of the psychoanalytic theory of dreaming. *Journal of the American Psychoanalytic Association, 40,* 531–550.

Greenwald, R. (1994). Applying eye movement desensitization and reprocessing (EMDR) to the treatment of traumatized children: Five case studies. *Anxiety Disorders Practice Journal, 1,* 83–97.

Haynes, S. N., & Mooney, D. K. (1975). Nightmares: Etiological, theoretical and behavioral treatment considerations. *Psychological Record, 25,* 225–236.

Hedstrom, J. (1991). A note on eye movements and relaxation. *Journal of Behavior Therapy and Experimental Psychiatry, 22,* 37–38.

Hekmat, H., Groth, S., & Rogers, D. (1994). Pain ameliorating effect of eye movement desensitization. *Journal of Behavior Therapy and Experimental Psychiatry, 25,* 121–130.

Hepper, P. P., & Hepper, M. (1977). Rape: Counseling the traumatized victim. *Personnel and Guidance Journal, 56,* 77–80.

Hill, C. E. (1994). From an experimental to an exploratory naturalistic approach to studying psychotherapy process. In R. L. Russell (Ed.), *Reassessing psychotherapy research.* New York: Guilford Press.

Hong, C., Gillin, C., Callaghan, G. A., & Potkin, S. (1992). Correlation of rapid eye movement density with dream report length and not with movements in the dream: Evidence against the scanning hypothesis. *Annual Meeting Abstracts, Association of Professional Sleep Societies,* Poster #12.

Horowitz, M. J. (1973). Phase-oriented treatment of stress response syndromes. *American Journal of Psychotherapy, 27,* 506–515.

Horowitz, M. J. (1974). Stress response syndromes, character style, and dynamic psychotherapy. *Archives of General Psychiatry, 31,* 768–781.

Horowitz, M. J. (1976). *Stress response syndromes.* New York: Aronson.

Horowitz, M. J. (1979). Psychological response to serious life events. In V. Hamilton & D. M. Warburton (Eds.), *Human stress and cognition.* New York: Wiley.

Horowitz, M. J. (1983). Post-traumatic stress disorders. *Behavioral Sciences and the Law, 1,* 9–23.

Horowitz, M. J., & Becker, S. S. (1972). Cognitive response to stress: Experimental studies of a "compulsion to repeat trauma." In R. Holt & E. Peterfreund (Eds.), *Psychoanalysis and contemporary science* (Vol. 1). New York: Macmillan.

Horowitz, M. J., & Kaltreider, N. B. (1980). Brief psychotherapy of stress response syndromes. In T. B. Karasu & L. Ballak (Eds.), *Specialized techniques in individual psychotherapy.* New York: Brunner/Mazel.

Horowitz, M. J., Marmar, C., Weiss, D. S., Dewitt, K. N., & Rosenbaum, R. (1984). Brief psychotherapy of bereavement reactions: The relationship of process to outcome. *Archives of General Psychiatry, 41,* 438–448.

Horowitz, M. J., Wilmer, N., & Alvarez, W. (1979). Impact of event scale: A measure of subjective stress. *Psychosomatic Medicine, 41,* 209–218.

Hyer, L. (1994a). *A treatment outcome study of PTSD in rape victims.* Research proposal submitted to NIMH.

Hyer, L. (1994b). The trauma response: Its complexity and dimensions. In L. Hyer (Ed.), *Trauma victim: Theoretical issues and practical suggestions*. Muncie, IN: Accelerated Development.

Hyer, L., Fallon, J. H., Harrison, W. R., & Boudewyns, P. (1987). MMPI overreporting by Vietnam combat veterans. *Journal of Clinical Psychology*, *43*, 79–83.

Jacobson, E. (1938). *Progressive relaxation*. Chicago: University of Chicago Press.

Janet, P. (1973). *L'Automatisme psychologique*. Paris: Societe Pierre Janet. (Original work published in 1889)

Janoff-Bulman, R. (1985). The aftermath of victimization: Rebuilding shattered assumptions. In C. R. Figley (Ed.), *Trauma and its wake*. New York: Brunner/Mazel.

Jensen, J. A. (1994). An investigation of eye movement desensitization and reprocessing (EMD/R) as a treatment for posttraumatic stress disorder (PTSD) symptoms of Vietnam combat veterans. *Behavior Therapy*, *25*, 311–326.

Johnson, C. H., Gilmore, J. D., & Shenoy, R. S. (1982). Use of a feeding procedure in the treatment of a stress-related anxiety disorder. *Journal of Behavior Therapy and Experimental Psychiatry*, *13*, 235–237.

Jung, C. G. (1916). *Analytic psychology*. New York: Moffat.

Kadushin, C., Boulanger, G., & Martin, J. (1981). Long-term stress reactions: Some causes, consequences, and naturally occurring support systems. In A. Egendorf, C. Kadushin, P. S. Laufer, G. Rothbart, & L. Sloan (Eds.), *Legacies of Vietnam: Comparative adjustment of veterans and their peers* (Vol. 4). Washington, DC: Government Printing Office.

Karni, A., Tanne, D., Rubenstein, B. S., Askenasi, J. J., & Sagi, D. (1992). No dreams, no memory: The effect of REM sleep deprivation on learning a new perceptual skill. *Society for Neuroscience Abstracts*, *18*, 387.

Keane, T. M., Caddell, J. M., Martin, B., Zimering, R. T., & Bender, M. E. (1985). A behavioral approach to assessing and treating posttraumatic stress disorder in Vietnam veterans. In C. R. Figley (Ed.), *Trauma and its wake*. New York: Brunner/Mazel.

Keane, T. M., Fairbank, J. A., Caddell, J. M., & Zimmering, R. T., (1989). Implosive (flooding) therapy reduces symptoms of PTSD in Vietnam combat veterans. *Behavior Therapy*, *20*, 245–260.

Keane, T. M., Fairbank, J. A., Caddell, J. M., Zimering, R. T., & Bender, M. E. (1985). A behavioral approach to assessing and treating posttraumatic stress disorder in Vietnam veterans. In C. R. Figley (Ed.), *Trauma and its wake*. New York: Brunner/Mazel.

Keane, T. M., & Kaloupek, D. G. (1982). Imaginal flooding in the treatment of a posttraumatic stress disorder. *Journal of Consulting and Clinical Psychology*, *50*, 138–140.

Keane, T. M., Scott, W. O., Chavoya, G. A., Lamparski, D. M. J., & Fairbank, J. A. (1985). Social support in Vietnam veterans with posttraumatic stress disorder: A comparative analysis. *Journal of Consulting and Clinical Psychology*, *53*, 95–102.

Keane, T. M., Thomas, R. S., Kaloupek, D. G., Lavori, P., & Orr, S. (1994, August). *Psychophysiology of posttraumatic stress disorder: Results of a multisite clinical trial.* Symposium conducted at the 102nd annual meeting of the American Psychological Association, Los Angeles.

Keane, T. M., Zimering, R., & Caddell, J. M. (1985). A behavioral formulation of posttraumatic stress disorder in Vietnam veterans. *Behavior Therapist, 8,* 9-12.

Kilpatrick, D. G., & Best, C. L. (1984). Some cautionary remarks on treating sexual assault victims with implosion. *Behavior Therapy, 15,* 421-423.

Kilpatrick, D. G., & Calhoun, K. S. (1988). Early behavioral treatment for rape trauma: Efficacy or artifact? *Behavior Therapy, 19,* 421-427.

Kilpatrick, D. G., & Veronen, L. J. (1983). Treatment for rape-related problems: Crisis intervention is not enough. In L. H. Cohen, W. L. Claiborn, & G. A. Specter (Eds.), *Crisis intervention.* New York: Human Sciences Press.

Kilpatrick, D. G., Veronen, L. J., & Resick, P. A. (1982). Psychological sequelae to rape: Assessment and treatment strategies. In D. M. Doleys & R. L. Meredith (Eds.), *Behavioral medicine: Assessment and treatment strategies.* New York: Plenum.

Kitchen, R. H. (1991). Relapse therapy. *EMDR Network Newsletter, 1,* 4-6.

Kleinknecht, R. A. (1992). Treatment of post-traumatic stress disorder with eye movement desensitization and reprocessing. *Journal of Behavior Therapy and Experimental Psychiatry, 23,* 43-50.

Kleinknecht, R. A. (1993). Rapid treatment of blood and injection phobias with eye movement desensitization. *Journal of Behavior Therapy and Experimental Psychiatry, 24,* 211-217.

Kluft, R. P. (1985). The natural history of multiple personality disorder. In R. P. Kluft (Ed.), *Childhood antecedents of multiple personality.* Washington, DC: American Psychiatric Press.

Kluft, R. P. (1987a). First rank symptoms as a diagnostic clue to multiple personality disorder. *American Journal of Psychiatry, 144,* 293-298.

Kluft, R. P. (1987b). Making the diagnosis of multiple personality disorder. In P. Flach (Ed.), *Diagnostics and psychopathology.* New York: Norton.

Kluft, R. P., & Fine, C. G. (1993). *Clinical perspectives on multiple personality disorder.* Washington, DC: American Psychiatric Press.

Kolb, L. C. (1984). The posttraumatic stress disorders of combat: A subgroup with a conditioned emotional response. *Military Medicine, 149,* 237-243.

Kolb, L. C. (1987). Neurophysiological hypothesis explaining posttraumatic stress disorder. *American Journal of Psychiatry, 144,* 989-995.

Krupnick, J. L., & Horowitz, M. J. (1981). Stress response syndromes: Recurrent themes. *Archives of General Psychiatry, 38,* 428-435.

Krystal, J. H., Kosten, T. R., Southwick, S., Mason, J. W., Perry, B. D., & Giller, E. L. (1989). Neurobiological aspects of PTSD: Review of clinical and preclinical studies. *Behavior Therapy, 20,* 177-198.

Kuch, K. (1987). Treatment of PTSD following automobile accidents. *Behavior Therapist, 10,* 224, 242.

Lang, P. J. (1977). Imagery in therapy: An information processing analysis of fear. *Behavior Therapy, 8,* 862-886.

Lang, P. J. (1979). A bioinformational theory of emotional imagery. *Psychophysiology, 16,* 495-512.

Larson, J., & Lynch, G. (1989). Theta pattern stimulation and the induction of

LTP: The sequence in which synapses are stimulated determines the degree to which they potentiate. *Brain Research, 489,* 49–58.

Laufer, R. S., Yager, T., Frey-Wouters, E., & Donnellan, J. (1981). Post-war trauma: Social and psychological problems of Vietnam veterans in the aftermath of the Vietnam War. In A. Egendorf, C. Kadushin, P. S. Laufer, G. Rothbart, & L. Sloan (Eds.), *Legacies of Vietnam: Comparative adjustment of veterans and their peers.* New York: Center for Policy Research.

Lazrove, S. (1994, November). *Integration of fragmented dissociated traumatic memories using EMDR.* Paper presented at the 10th annual meeting of the International Society for Traumatic Stress Studies, Chicago.

Leigh, J., & Zee, D. (1983). *The neurology of eye movements.* Philadelphia: F. A. Davis.

Levin, C. (1993, July/August). The enigma of EMDR. *Family Therapy Networker,* pp. 75–83.

Levin, C., Grainger, R. K., Allen-Byrd, L., & Fulcher, G. (1994, August). *Efficacy of eye movement desensitization and reprocessing for survivors of Hurricane Andrew: A comparative study.* Paper presented at the 102nd annual meeting of the American Psychological Association, Los Angeles. (Article being prepared for journal submission.)

Levine, S. (1991). Additional visualizations for emotional and physical pain contained. In *Guided meditations, explorations, and healings.* New York: Doubleday.

Levis, D. J. (1980). Implementing the technique of implosive therapy. In A. Goldstein & E. B. Foa (Eds.), *Handbook of behavioral interventions: A clinical guide.* New York: Wiley.

Lindy, J. D., Green, B. L., Grace, M., & Titchener, J. (1983). Psychotherapy with survivors of the Beverly Hills Supper Club fire. *American Journal of Psychotherapy, 37,* 593–610.

Lipke, H. (1992a). *Manual for the teaching of Shapiro's EMDR in the treatment of combat-related PTSD.* Unpublished manuscript available from author.

Lipke, H. (1992b, October). *Preliminary survey results of 1200 EMDR-trained clinicians.* Paper presented at the annual meeting of the International Society for Traumatic Stress, Los Angeles.

Lipke, H. (1994, August). *Survey of practictioners trained in eye movement desensitization and reprocessing.* Paper presented at the 102nd annual meeting of the American Psychological Association, Los Angeles.

Lipke, H., & Botkin, A. (1992). Brief case studies of eye movement desensitization and reprocessing with chronic post–traumatic stress disorder. *Psychotherapy, 29,* 591–595.

Lipsey, M. W., & Wilson, D. B. (1993). The efficacy of psychological, educational, and behavioral treatment: Confirmation from meta-analysis. *American Psychologist, 48,* 1181–1209.

Litz, B. T., & Keane, T. (1989). Information processing in anxiety disorders: Application to the understanding of post-traumatic stress disorder. *Clinical Psychology Review, 9,* 243–257.

Lohr, J., Tolin, D., & Kleinknecht, R. A. (in press-a). An intensive investigation of eye movement desensitization and reprocessing of claustrophobia. *Journal of Anxiety Disorders.*

Lohr, J., Tolin, D., & Kleinknecht, R. A. (in press-b). An intensive investigation of eye movement desensitization of medical phobias. *Journal of Behavior Therapy and Experimental Psychiatry.*

London, P. (1964) *The modes and morals of psychotherapy.* New York: Holt, Rinehart & Winston.

Malleson, N. (1959). Panic and phobia. *Lancet, 1,* 225.

Malloy, P. F., Fairbank, J. A., & Keane, T. M. (1983). Validation of a multimethod assessment of PTSD in Vietnam veterans. *Journal of Consulting and Clinical Psychology, 51,* 488–494.

Mandai, O., Guerrien, A., Sockeel, P., Dujardin, K., & Leconte, P. (1989). REM sleep modifications following Morse code learning session in humans. *Physiology and Behavior, 46,* 639–646.

Marks, I. M. (1972). Flooding (implosion) and allied treatments. In W. S. Agras (Ed.), *Behavior modification: Principles and clinical applications.* Boston: Little, Brown.

Marquis, J. N. (1991). A report on seventy-eight cases treated by eye movement desensitization. *Journal of Behavior Therapy and Experimental Psychiatry, 22,* 187–192.

Marquis, J. N., & Puk, G. (1994, November). *Dissociative identity disorder: A common sense and cognitive-behavioral view.* Paper presented at the annual meeting of the Association for Advancement of Behavior Therapy, San Diego, CA.

Martinez, R. A. (1991). Innovative uses. *EMDR Network Newsletter, 1,* 5–6.

Martinez, R. A. (1992, March). *The alchemy of success: Turning losses into wins.* Keynote speech presented at the International EMDR Annual Conference, Sunnyvale, CA.

Maslow, A. H. (1970). *Motivation and personality.* New York: Harper & Row.

McCann, D. L. (1992). Post-traumatic stress disorder due to devastating burns overcome by a single session of eye movement desensitization. *Journal of Behavior Therapy and Experimental Psychiatry, 23,* 319–323.

McCann, L., & Pearlman, L. A. (1990). Vicarious traumatization: A framework for understanding the psychological effects of working with victims. *Journal of Traumatic Stress, 3,* 131–150.

McDermott, W. F. (1981). *The influence of Vietnam combat on subsequent psychopathology.* Paper presented at the 89th annual meeting of the American Psychological Association, Los Angeles.

Meares, A. (1960). *A system of medical hypnosis.* New York: Julian Press.

Meichenbaum, D. (1977). *Cognitive-behavior modification.* New York: Plenum.

Merckelback, H., & van Oppen, P. (1989). Effects of gaze manipulation on subjective evaluation of neutral and phobia-relevant stimuli. *Acta Psychologica, 70,* 147–151.

Miller, E. (1994). *Letting go of stress.* Menlo Park, CA: Source Cassette Tapes.

Miller, T. W., & Buchbinder, J. T. (1979, December). *Clinical effects of cognitive-behavior therapy with a posttraumatic war neurosis Vietnam veteran.* Paper presented at the meeting of the Association for Advancement of Behavior Therapy, San Francisco.

Mineka, S., & Kihlstrom, J. F. (1978). Unpredictable and uncontrollable events:

A new perspective on experimental neurosis. *Journal of Abnormal Psychology, 87,* 256.

Monnier, M. (1968). *Functions of the nervous system.* London: Elsevier.

Monty, R. A., Fisher, D. F., & Senders, J. W. (1978). *Eye movements and the higher psychological functions.* Hillsdale, NJ: Erlbaum.

Monty, R. A., & Senders, J. W. (1976). *Eye movements and psychological processes.* Hillsdale, NJ: Erlbaum.

Mowrer, O. H. (1960). *Learning theory and behavior.* New York: Wiley.

Neilsen, T. (1991). Affect desensitization: A possible function of REMs in both waking and sleeping states. *Sleep Research, 20,* 10.

Nelson, S. (1992, March). *Partners of sexual abuse victims.* Paper presented at the annual EMDR International Conference, Sunnyvale, CA.

Neurotek. (1994). Eye tracking device to assist the EMDR clinician. Pacific Grove, CA: EMDR Institute.

Nicosia, G. (1994, March). *A mechanism for dissociation suggested by the quantitative analysis of electroencephalography.* Paper presented at the International EMDR Annual Conference, Sunnyvale, CA.

Nicosia, G. (in press). Brief note: EMDR is not hypnosis: EEG evidence. *Dissociation.*

Norcross, J. C. (Ed.). (1986). *Handbook of eclectic psychotherapy.* New York: Brunner/Mazel.

O'Brien, E. (1993, November/December). Pushing the panic button. *Family Therapy Networker,* pp. 75–83.

Ochs, L. (1993). *EEF [Electroencephalographic entrainment feedback]: Preliminary head injury data.* Paper presented at the Association of Applied Psychophysiology and Biofeedback Convention, Los Angeles.

Orlinsky, D. E., & Russell, R. L. (1994). Tradition and change in psychotherapy research: Notes on the fourth generation. In R. L. Russell (Ed.), *Reassessing psychotherpay research.* New York: Guilford Press.

Page, A. C., & Crino, R. D. (1993). Eye-movement desensitisation: A simple treatment for post-traumatic stress disorder? *Australian and New Zealand Journal of Psychiatry, 27,* 288–293.

Parnell, L. (1994, August). *Treatment of sexual abuse survivors with EMDR: Two case reports.* Paper presented at the 102nd annual meeting of the American Psychological Association, Los Angeles.

Paul, G. L. (1966). *Insight versus desensitization in psychotherapy: An experiment in anxiety reduction.* Stanford, CA: Stanford University Press.

Paulsen, S. (in press). Eye movement desensitization and reprocessing: Its cautious use in the dissociative disorders. *Dissociation.*

Paulsen, S., Vogelmann-Sine, S., Lazrove, S., & Young, W. (1993, October). *Eye movement desensitization and reprocessing: Its role in the treatment of dissociative disorders.* Symposium presented at the 10th annual meeting of the International Society for the Study of Multiple Personality Disorders, Chicago.

Pavlov, I. P. (1927). *Conditioned reflexes.* New York: Liveright.

Pearson, M. A., Poquette, B. M., & Wasden, R. E. (1983). Stress-inoculation: The treatment of post-rape trauma: A case report. *Behavior Therapist, 6,* 58–59.

Pelletier, K. R. (1977). *Mind as healer, mind as slayer.* New York: Delacorte.

Pellicer, X. (1993). Eye movement desensitization treatment of a child's nightmares: A case report. *Journal of Behavior Therapy and Experimental Psychiatry, 24*, 73–75.

Peniston, G. E. (1986). EMG biofeedback-assisted desensitization treatment for Vietnam combat veterans post-traumatic stress disorder, *Clinical Biofeedback Health, 9*, 35–41.

Perry, G. L. (in press). EMDR versus PTSD: A case study. *Journal of the Vietnam Veterans Institute.*

Persons, J. (1994). Why don't my patients do as well as the ones in outcome studies?. *Behavior Therapist, 17*, 60.

Pitman, R. K., Altman, B., Greenwald, E., Longpre, R. E., Macklin, M. L., Poire, R. E., & Steketee, G. S. (1991). Psychiatric complications during flooding therapy for posttraumatic stress disorder. *Journal of Clinical Psychiatry, 52*, 17–20.

Pitman, R. K., Orr, S. P., Altman, B., Longpre, R. E., Poire, R. E., & Lasko, N. B. (1993, May). *A controlled study of EMDR treatment for post-traumatic stress disorder.* Paper presented at the 146th annual meeting of the American Psychiatric Association, Washington, DC

Puk, G. (1991a). Treating traumatic memories: A case report on the eye movement desensitization procedure. *Journal of Behavior Therapy and Experimental Psychiatry, 22*, 149–151.

Puk, G. (1991b, November). *Eye movement desensitization and reprocessing: Treatment of a more complex case, borderline personality disorder.* Paper presented at the annual meeting of the Association for Advancement of Behavior Therapy, New York.

Puk, G. (1992, May). *The use of eye movement desensitization and reprocessing in motor vehicle accident trauma.* Paper presented at the 8th annual meeting of the American College of Forensic Psychology, San Francisco.

Puk, G. (1994, July). *Eye movement desensitization and reprocessing in the treatment of multiple personality disorder.* Paper presented at the 10th annual meeting of the Society for the Exploration of Psychotherapy Integration, Buenos Aires, Argentina.

Putnam, F. W. (1989). *Diagnosis and treatment of multiple personality disorder.* New York: Guilford Press.

Rachman, S. (1978). *Fear and courage.* New York: Freeman.

Raw, S. (1993). Does psychotherapy research teach us anything about psychotherapy? *Behavior Therapist, 16*, 75–76.

Raw, S. (in press). A plaintive plea for the deintegration of psychotherapy and psychotherapy outcome research. *Journal of Psychotherapy Integration.*

Reiser, M. (1990). *Memory in mind and brain.* New York: Basic Books.

Renfrey, G., & Spates, C. R. (1994). Eye movement desensitization and reprocessing: A partial dismantling procedure. *Journal of Behavior Therapy and Experimental Psychiatry, 25*, 231–239.

Resick, P. A., Jordan, C. G., Girelli, S. A., Hutter, C. K., & Marhoerfer-Dvorak, S. (1988). A comparative outcome study of behavioral group therapy for sexual assault victims. *Behavior Therapist, 19*, 385–401.

Resick, P. & Schnicke, M. (1992). Cognitive processing therapy for sexual assault victims. *Journal of Consulting and Clinical Psychology, 60*, 748–756.

Richards, D. A., Lovell, K., & Marks, I. M. (1994). Post-traumatic stress disorder: Evaluation of a behavioral treatment program. *Journal of Traumatic Stress*, 7, 669–680.

Ringo, J. L., Sobotka, S., Diltz, M. D., & Bruce, C. M. (1994). Eye movements modulate activity in hippocampal, parahippocampal, and inferotemporal neurons. *Journal of Neurophysiology*, 71, 1–4.

Rogers, C. R. (1951). *Client-centered therapy*. Boston: Houghton Mifflin.

Rosenthal, R. (1976). *Experimenter effects in behavioral research*. New York: Irvington.

Ross, C. (1991). Epidemiology of multiple personality disorder and dissociation. *Psychiatric Clinics of North America*, 14, 503–517.

Ross, R. J., Ball, W. A., Dinges, D. F., Kribbs, N. B., Morrison, A. R., & Silver, S. M. (1990, May). *REM sleep disturbance as the hallmark of PTSD*. Paper presented at the 143rd annual meeting of the American Psychiatric Association, New York.

Ross, R. J., Ball, W. A., Kribbs, N. B., Morrison, A. R., Silver, S. M., & Mulvanye, F. D. (1994). Rapid eye movement sleep disturbance in posttraumatic stress disorder. *Biological Psychiatry*, 35, 195–202.

Ross, R. J., Ball, W. A., Sullivan, K. A., & Caroff, S. N. (1989). Sleep disturbance as the hallmark of posttraumatic stress disorder. *American Journal of Psychiatry*, 146, 697–707.

Rossi, E. L. (1986). *The psychobiology of mind–body healing*. New York: Norton.

Rothbaum, B. O. (1992). How does EMDR work? *Behavior Therapist*, 15, 34.

Rouanzoin, C. (1994, March). *EMDR: Dissociative disorders and MPD*. Paper presented at the 14th annual meeting of the Anxiety Disorders Association of America, Santa Monica, CA.

Russell, M. C. (1992). *Towards a neuropsychological approach to PTSD: An integrative conceptualization of etiology and mechanisms of therapeutic change*. Unpublished doctoral dissertation, Pacific Graduate School of Psychology, Palo Alto, CA.

Rychtarik, R. G., Silverman, W. K., Van Landingham, W. P., & Prue, D. M. (1984). Treatment of an incest victim with implosive therapy: A case study. *Behavior Therapy*, 15, 410–420, 423–425.

Sabourin, M. G., Cutcomb, S. D., Crawford, H., & Pribram, K. (1990, December). EEG correlates of hypnotic susceptibility and hypnotic trance: Spectral analysis and coherence. *International Journal of Psychophysiology*, 10, 125–142.

Salter, A. (1961). *Conditioned reflex therapy*. New York: Capricorn.

Sanderson, A., & Carpenter, R. (1992). Eye movement desensitization versus image confrontation: A single-session crossover study of 58 phobic subjects. *Journal of Behavior Therapy and Experimental Psychiatry*, 23, 269–275.

Sartory, G., Rachman, S., & Grey, S. J. (1982). Return of fear: The role of rehearsal. *Behaviour Research and Therapy*, 20, 123–133.

Scheppele, K. L., & Bart, P. B. (1983). Through women's eyes: Defining danger in the wake of sexual assault. *Journal of Social Issues*, 39, 63–81.

Schindler, F. E. (1980). Treatment by systematic desensitization of a recurring nightmare of a real life trauma. *Journal of Behavior Therapy and Experimental Psychiatry*, 2, 53–54.

Schmitt, R., Capo, T., & Boyd, E. (1986). Cranial electrotherapy stimulation as a treatment for anxiety in chemically dependent persons. *Alcoholism Clinical and Experimental Research, 10*, 158–160.

Scrignar, C. B. (1983). *Stress strategies: The treatment of anxiety disorders.* New York: Karger.

Shapiro, D. A., Startup, M., Bird, D., Harper, H., Reynolds, S., & Suokas, A. (1994). The high-water mark of the drug metaphor: A meta-analytic critique of process-outcome research. In R. L. Russell (Ed.), *Reassessing psychotherapy research.* New York: Guilford Press.

Shapiro, F. (1989a). Efficacy of the eye movement desensitization procedure in the treatment of traumatic memories. *Journal of Traumatic Stress Studies, 2,* 199–223.

Shapiro, F. (1989b). Eye movement desensitization: A new treatment for post-traumatic stress disorder. *Journal of Behavior Therapy and Experimental Psychiatry, 20,* 211–217.

Shapiro, F. (1991a). Eye movement desensitization and reprocessing procedure: From EMD to EMDR: A new treatment model for anxiety and related traumata. *Behavior Therapist, 14,* 133–135.

Shapiro, F. (1991b). Eye movement desensitization and reprocessing: A cautionary note. *Behavior Therapist, 14,* 188.

Shapiro, F. (1992). Stray thoughts: Frozen in childhood/bio-electrical valence. *EMDR Network Newsletter, 2,* 1–2.

Shapiro, F. (1993). Eye movement desensitization and reprocessing (EMDR) in 1992. *Journal of Traumatic Stress, 6,* 417–421.

Shapiro, F. (1994a). Eye movement desensitization and reprocessing: A new treatment for anxiety and related trauma. In L. Hyer (Ed.), *Trauma victim: Theoretical and practical suggestions.* Muncie, IN: Accelerated Development.

Shapiro, F. (1994b). Alternative stimuli in the use of EMD(R). *Journal of Behavior Therapy and Experimental Psychiatry, 25,* 89.

Shapiro, F. (1994c). EMDR: In the eye of a paradigm shift. *Behavior Therapist, 17,* 153–157.

Shapiro, F. (1994d). International update. *EMDR Network Newsletter, 1,* 14–16.

Shapiro, F., & Solomon, R. (in press). Eye movement desensitization and reprocessing: Neurocognitive information processing. In G. Everley & J. Mitchell (Eds.), *Critical incident stress management.* Elliot City, MD: Chevron.

Shapiro, F., Vogelmann-Sine, S., & Sine, L. (1994). Eye movement desensitization and reprocessing: Treating trauma and substance abuse. *Journal of Psychoactive Drugs, 26,* 379–391.

Siegel, B. S. (1989). *Peace, love & healing.* New York: Harper & Row.

Silver, S. M., Brooks, A., & Obenchain, J. (1995). Eye movement desensitization and reprocessing treatment of Vietnam war veterans with PTSD: Comparative effects with biofeedback and relaxation training. *Journal of Traumatic Stress, 8,* 337–342.

Simonton, O. C., & Creighton, J. (1982). *Getting well again.* New York: Bantam.

Solomon, G., & Temoshok, L. (1987). An intensive psychoimmunologic study of long-surviving persons with AIDS. *Annals of the New York Academy of Science, 496,* 647–655.

Solomon, R. M. (1994, June). *Eye movement desensitization and reprocessing and treatment of grief.* Paper presented at 4th International Conference on Grief and Bereavement in Contemporary Society, Stockholm, Sweden.

Solomon, R. M. (1995, February). *Critical incident trauma: Lessons learned at Waco, Texas.* Paper presented at the Law Enforcement Psychology Conference, San Mateo, CA.

Solomon, R. M., & Kaufman, T. (1994, March). *Eye movement desensitization and reprocessing: An effective addition to critical incident treatment protocols.* Paper presented at the 14th annual meeting of the Anxiety Disorders Association of America, Santa Monica, CA.

Solomon, R. M., & Shapiro, F. (in press). Eye movement desensitization and reprocessing: An effective therapeutic tool for trauma and grief. In C. Figley (Ed.), *Death and trauma.* Orlando, FL: G. P. Press.

Solomon, S. D., Gerrity, E. T., & Muff, A. M. (1992). Efficacy of treatments for posttraumatic stress disorder. *Journal of the American Medical Association, 268,* 633–638.

Spates, R. C., & Burnette, M. M. (in press). Eye movement desensitization and reprocessing: Three complex cases. *Journal of Behavior Therapy and Experimental Psychiatry.*

Spector, J., & Huthwaite, M. (1993). Eye-movement desensitisation to overcome post-traumatic stress disorder. *British Journal of Psychiatry, 163,* 106–108.

Spiegel, C., Kraemer, H. C., Bloom, J. R., & Gottheil, E. (1989, October). Effect of psychosocial treatment on survival of patients with metastatic breast cancer. *Lancet,* 888–891.

Spiegel, D. (1984). Multiple personality as a post-traumatic stress disorder. *Psychiatric Clinics of North America, 7,* 101–110.

Spiegel, D. (1993). Multiple posttraumatic personality disorder. In R. P. Kluft & C. G. Fine (Eds.), *Clinical perspectives on multiple personality disorder.* Washington, DC: American Psychiatric Press.

Stampfl, T. G., & Levis, D. J. (1967). Essentials of implosive therapy: A learning-theory-based psychodynamic behavioral therapy. *Journal of Abnormal Psychology, 72,* 496.

Steketee, G., & Foa, E. B. (1987). Rape victims: Post-traumatic stress responses and their treatment: A review of the literature. *Journal of Anxiety Disorders, 1,* 69–86.

Steketee, G., & Goldstein, A. J. (1994). Reflections on Shapiro's reflections: Testing EMDR within a theoretical context. *Behavior Therapist, 17,* 156–157.

Stern, R., & Marks, I. (1973). Brief and prolonged flooding: A comparison in agoraphobic patients. *Archives of General Psychiatry, 28,* 270–276.

Strayer, R., & Ellenhorn, L. (1975). Vietnam veterans: A study exploring adjustment patterns and attitudes. *Journal of Social Issues, 31,* 81–91.

Sutton, J. P., Mamelak, A. N., & Hobson, J. A. (1992). Modeling states of waking and sleeping. *Psychiatric Annals, 22,* 137–143.

Taber, E. (in press). An EMDR case study with a Vietnam combat veteran. *Journal of the Vietnam Veterans Institute.*

Tallis, F., & Smith, E. (1994). Does rapid eye movement desensitization facilitate emotional processing? *Behavioural Research and Therapy, 32,* 459–461.

Teitelbaum, H. A. (1954). Spontaneous rhythmic ocular movements: Their possible relationship to mental activity. *Neurology, 4,* 350–354.

Thomas, R., & Gafner, G. (1993). PTSD in an elderly male: Treatment with eye movement desensitization and reprocessing (EMDR). *Clinical Gerontologist, 14,* 57–59.

Thyer, B. A., Papsdorf, J. D., Davis, R., & Vallecorsa, S. (1984). Autonomic correlates of the subjective anxiety scale. *Journal of Behavior Therapy and Experimental Psychiatry, 15,* 3–7.

Tilly, A. J., & Empson, J. A. (1978). REM sleep and memory consolidation. *Biological Psychology, 6,* 293–300.

Turner, S. M. (1979, December). *Systematic desensitization of fears and anxiety in rape victims.* Paper presented at the 13th annual meeting of the Association for Advancement of Behavior Therapy, San Francisco.

Turner, S. M., & Frank, E. (1981). Behavior therapy in the treatment of rape victims. In L. Michelson, M. Hersen, & S. M. Turner (Eds.), *Future perspectives in behavior therapy.* New York: Plenum.

van der Kolk, B. A. (1987). The drug treatment of post-traumatic stress disorder. *Journal of Affective Disorders, 13,* 203–213.

van der Kolk, B. A. (1994). The body keeps the score: Memory and the evolving psychobiology of posttraumatic stress. *Harvard Review of Psychiatry, 1,* 253–265

van der Kolk, B., Greenberg, M., Boyd, H., & Krystal, J. (1985). Inescapable shock, neurotransmitters, and addiction to trauma: Toward a psychobiology of posttraumatic stress. *Biological Psychiatry, 20,* 314–325.

van der Kolk, B. A., & van der Hart, O. (1991). The intrusive past: The flexibility of memory and the engraving of trauma. *American Imago, 48,* 425–454.

Vaughan, K., Armstrong, M. F., Gold, R., O'Connor, N., Jenneke, W., & Tarrier, N. (1994). A trial of eye movement desensitization compared to image habituation training and applied muscle relaxation in post-traumatic stress disorder. *Journal of Behavior Therapy and Experimental Psychiatry, 25,* 283–291.

Vaughan, K., Wiese, M., Gold, R., & Tarrier, N. (1994). Eye-movement desensitisation: Symptom change in post-traumatic stress disorder. *British Journal of Psychiatry, 164,* 533–541.

Veronen, L. J., & Kilpatrick, D. G. (1980). Self-reported fears of rape victims: A preliminary investigation. *Behavior Modification, 4,* 383–396.

Viola, J., & McCarthy, D. (1994). An eclectic inpatient treatment model for Vietnam and Desert Storm veterans suffering from post-traumatic stress disorder. *Military Medicine, 159,* 217–220.

Watson, J. P., Hoffman, L., & Wilson, G. V. (1988). The neuropsychiatry of post-traumatic stress disorder. *British Journal of Psychiatry, 152,* 164–173.

Watzlawick, P. (1987). If you desire to see, learn how to act. In J. K. Zeig (Ed.), *The evolution of psychotherapy.* New York: Brunner/Mazel.

Wernik, U. (1993). The role of the traumatic component in the etiology of sexual dysfunctions and its treatment with eye movement desensitization procedure. *Journal of Sex Education and Therapy, 19,* 212–222.

Weston, D. (1994, December). *Clinical applications of EMDR in HIV/AIDS care.*

Paper presented at the 6th International Conference on Psychology of Health, Immunity and Disease, Hilton Head Island, SC.

Wilson, D., Covi, W., Foster, S., & Silver, S. M. (1995, May). *Eye movement desensitization and reprocessing and ANS correlates in the treatment of PTSD.* Paper presented at the 148th annual meeting of the American Psychiatric Association, Miami, FL.

Wilson, J. P. (1978). *Identity, ideology, and crises: Part 2. The Vietnam veteran in transition.* Cincinnati, OH: Disabled American Veterans.

Wilson, S. A, Becker, L. A., & Tinker, R. H. (in press). Eye movement desensitization and reprocessing (EMDR) treatment for psychologically traumatized individuals. *Journal of Consulting and Clinical Psychology.*

Winson, J. (1990). The meaning of dreams. *Scientific American, 263,* 86–96.

Winson, J. (1993). The biology and function of rapid eye movement sleep. *Current Opinion in Neurobiology, 3,* 243–247.

Wolfe, B. E. (1994). Adapting psychotherapy outcome research to clinical reality. *Journal of Psychotherapy Integration, 4,* 160–166.

Wolff, R. (1977). Systematic desensitization and negative practice to alter the aftereffects of a rape attempt. *Journal of Behavior Therapy and Experimental Psychiatry, 8,* 423–425.

Wolpe, J. (1958). *Psychotherapy by reciprocal inhibition.* Stanford, CA: Stanford University Press.

Wolpe, J. (1990). *The practice of behavior therapy* (4th ed.). New York: Pergamon Press.

Wolpe, J., & Abrams, J. (1991). Post-traumatic stress disorder overcome by eye movement desensitization: A case report. *Journal of Behavior Therapy and Experimental Psychiatry, 22,* 39–43.

Young, J. E. (1990). *Cognitive therapy for personality disorders: A schema-focused approach.* Sarasota, FL: Professional Resource Exchange.

Young, W. (1992). Observations of using EMDR in patients with a history of sadistic and ritual abuse. *EMDR Network Newsletter, 2,* 10–11.

Young, W. (1994). EMDR treatment of phobic symptoms in multiple personality. *Dissociation, 7,* 129–133.

Young, W. (in press). EMDR: Its use in resolving the trauma caused by the loss of a war buddy. *American Journal of Psychotherapy.*

Zager, E. L., & Black, P. (1985). Neuropeptides in human memory and learning processes. *Neurosurgery, 17,* 355–369.

Zilberg, N., Weiss, D. S., & Horowitz, M. (1982). Impact of event scale: A cross-validation study and some empirical evidence supporting a conceptual model of stress response syndromes. *Journal of Consulting and Clinical Psychology, 50,* 407–414.

Clinical Aids

The following sample checklist format may be helpful to record pertinent data and dates of important communications to the client. Additional spaces or sheets will be necessary for actual use.

EMDR SCREENING AND DATA CHECKLIST

Name: _____ Date: _____

Type and amount of previous counseling: _____

_____

Present medications: _____

☐ Results of objective tests _____

☐ Mental status exam plus dissociative disorder screening

☐ Sufficient rapport (feeling of safety, degree of truth telling)

☐ Ability to use self-control techniques tested positive with

_____

☐ Personal and environmental stability: Factors needing attention are:

_____

☐ Life supports: _____

_____

☐ Physical health (areas of concern include neurological impairment; pregnancy; cardiac, respiratory, and geriatric issues; seizures, and eye problems):_____

_____

☐ Inpatient treatment (medical needs; nature of the traumatic memory; is client a danger to self or others?): _____

_____

☐ Medication needs: _____

_____

☐ Drug or alcohol abuse (supports; program; was briefing given of potential exacerbation?): _____

☐ Legal restraints (processing effects/forensic issues): _____
_____

☐ Systems control: _____

☐ Secondary gains (action planned): _____

☐ Timing considerations: _____

☐ Reporting requirements: _____

☐ Terms in which theory was explained: nervous system, blocked learning, REM, hemispheres, or other? _____

☐ Informed consent: Mention fact that method is new (promising, but no guarantees); that distressing, unresolved memories may surface; that unanticipated reactions may include disturbing emotions or sensations; and that between-session disturbance, such as nightmares or other memories, may occur.

☐ Test eye movement (client's preferences? which movements to avoid? alternative stimuli to be used?): _____

☐ Metaphors (train, tiger, tunnel, other?): _____

☐ Safe place (specify place and word): _____

☐ Stop signal: _____

☐ Other: _____

EMDR TREATMENT PLANNING CHECKLIST

Name: _____ Date: _____

☐ Symptoms: _____

☐ Intrusive images: _____

☐ Negative cognitions: _____

☐ Duration: _____

☐ Initial cause(s): _____

☐ Additional occurrences (or top 10 memories): _____

☐ Additional complaints: _____

☐ Present constraints: _____

☐ Significant people: _____

☐ Desired state: _____

☐ Skills/adjunctive groups needed: _____

s may find it useful to offer clients the following list of sample negative
tive cognitions. Generally, clients can make an appropriate selection,
or use the examples as a starting point to construct choices more suitable to
their particular problem.

LIST OF GENERIC NEGATIVE AND POSITIVE COGNITIONS

Negative cognitions	*Positive cognitions*
I don't deserve love.	I deserve love; I can have love.
I am a bad person.	I am a good (loving) person.
I am terrible.	I am fine as I am.
I am worthless (inadequate).	I am worthy; I am worthwhile.
I am shameful.	I am honorable.
I am not lovable.	I am lovable.
I am not good enough.	I am deserving (fine/okay).
I deserve only bad things.	I deserve good things.
I cannot be trusted.	I can be trusted.
I cannot trust myself.	I can (learn to) trust myself.
I cannot trust my judgment.	I can trust my judgment.
I cannot succeed.	I can succeed.
I am not in control.	I am now in control.
I am powerless (helpless).	I now have choices.
I am weak.	I am strong.
I cannot protect myself.	I can (learn to) take care of myself.
I am stupid (not smart enough).	I am intelligent (able to learn).
I am insignificant (unimportant).	I am significant (important).
I am a disappointment.	I am okay just the way I am.
I deserve to die.	I deserve to live.
I deserve to be miserable.	I deserve to be happy.
I cannot get what I want.	I can get what I want.
I am a failure (will fail).	I can succeed.
I have to be perfect (please everyone).	I can be myself (make mistakes).
I am permanently damaged.	I am (can be) healthy.
I am ugly (my body is hateful).	I am fine (attractive/lovable).
I should have done something.	I did the best I could.
I did something wrong.	I learned (can learn) from it.
I am in danger.	It's over; I am safe now.
I cannot stand it.	I can handle it.
I cannot trust anyone.	I can choose whom to trust.
I cannot let it out.	I can choose to let it out.
I do not deserve . . .	I can have (deserve) . . .
It's not okay to feel (show) my emotions.	I can safely feel (show) my emotions.
I cannot stand up for myself.	I can make my needs known.
I am different (don't belong).	I am okay as I am.
I should have known better.	I do the best I can (I can learn).
I am inadequate.	I am capable.

The following EMDR procedural outline offers reminders and suggested wording that may be helpful for clinicians during initial practice sessions.

EMDR PROCEDURAL OUTLINE

Explanation of EMDR: (Wording of the explanation of the EMDR method depends on age, background, experience, and sophistication of client.)

"When a trauma occurs it seems to get locked in the nervous system with the original picture, sounds, thoughts and feelings. The eye movements we use in EMDR seem to unlock the nervous system and allow the brain to process the experience. That may be what is happening in REM or dream sleep—the eye movements may help to process the unconscious material. It is important to remember that it is your own brain that will be doing the healing and that you are the one in control."

Specific instructions: "What we will be doing often is a simple check on what you are experiencing. I need to know from you exactly what is going on, with feedback that is as clear as possible. Sometimes things will change and sometimes they won't. I'll ask you how you feel from 0 to 10; sometimes it will change and sometimes it won't. I may ask if something else comes up; sometimes it will and sometimes it won't. There are not "supposed to's" in this process. So just give feedback as accurately as you can as to what is happening, without judging whether it should be happening or not. Let whatever happens, happen. We'll do the eye movements for awhile, and then we'll talk about it."

Stop signal: "If at any time you feel you have to stop, raise your hand."
Establishing appropriate distance: "Is this a comfortable distance and speed?"

Presenting issue: "What old memory would you like to work on today?"
Image: "What picture represents the worst part of the incident?"
Negative cognition (NC): "What words best go with the picture and express your belief about yourself now?" (Have client make the statement in the form of an "I" statement in the present tense. This must be a presently held negative self-referencing belief.)
Positive cognition (PC): "When you bring up that picture/incident, what would you like to believe about yourself now?" (This must be a present desired self-referencing belief.)
VOC (for PC only): "When you think of that picture/incident, how true does that [positive cognition] feel to you now on a scale of 1 to 7, where 1 is untrue and 7 is totally true?"
Emotions/feelings: "When you bring up that incident and those words [negaive cognition], what emotion(s) do you feel now?"
SUDs: "On a scale of 0 to 10, where 0 is no disturbance or neutral and 10 is the highest disturbance imaginable, how disturbing does it feel to you now?"
Location of body sensation: "Where do you feel it [the disturbance] in your body?"

Desensitization: "(I'd like you to) bring up that picture, those negative words [repeat the negative cognition], notice where you are feeling it in your body, and follow my fingers."

1. Begin the eye movements slowly. Increase the speed as long as the client can comfortably tolerate the movement.
2. Approximately every 12 movements, or when there is an apparent change, comment to the client, "That's it. Good. That's it."
3. It is helpful to make the following comment to the client (especially if client is abreacting): "That's it. It's old stuff. Just notice it." (Also use the speeding train metaphor.)
4. After a set of eye movements instruct client to "Blank it out" and/or "Let it go and take a deep breath."
5. Ask: "What do you get now?" or "What are you noticing now?"
6. If the client reports movement, say, "Stay with that" (without repeating the client's words). Client should be reporting a 0 or 1 on the SUD scale before doing the installation.

Installation of positive cognition (linking the desired positive cognition with the original memory or image):

1. "Do the words [repeat the positive cognition] still fit, or is there another positive statement you feel would be more suitable?"
2. "Think about the original incident and those words [selected positive cognition]. From 1, completely false, to 7, completely true, how true to they feel?
3. "Hold them together." Lead client in an eye movement set. "On a scale of 1 to 7, how true does that [positive statement] feel to you now when you think of the original incident?"
4. VOC: Measure the VOC after each set. Even if client reports a 6 or 7, do eye movement again to strengthen, and continue until validity no longer strengthens. Go on to the body scan.
5. If client reports a 6 or less, check appropriateness and address blocking belief (if necessary) with additional reprocessing.

Body scan: "Close your eyes; concentrate on the incident and the PC, and mentally scan your body. Tell me where you feel anything." If any sensation is reported, do EM. If a positive/comfortable sensation, do EM to strengthen the positive feeling. If a sensation of discomfort is reported—reprocess until discomfort subsides.

Closure (debriefing the experience): "The processing we have done today may continue after the session. You may or may not notice new insights, thoughts, memories, or dreams. If you do, just notice what you are experiencing. Take a snapshot of it (what you are seeing, feeling, thinking, and the trigger), and keep a log. We can work on this new material next time. If you feel it is necessary, call me."

Client Safety

EMDR was introduced as an experimental procedure during trainings that began in 1990. In order to disseminate this new psychotherapeutic approach responsibly, the training practices and client safety factors were overseen by independent committees of senior, experienced clinicians. Their recommendations form the core of the guidelines provided here, so that readers can review the primary areas of concern regarding client safety.

The first section of this appendix consists of the EMDR Dissociative Disorders Task Force recommended guidelines, which contain a general guide to EMDR's use in the dissociative disorders and a suggested reading list

The second section provides the recommendations of the EMDR Professional Issues Committee (EPIC) that has guided EMDR training policies. A special task force is presently working to establish guidelines for education and competency standards in order to support other organizations and individuals in training EMDR throughout the mental health profession. The goal is to find a way to protect client safety, maintain the integrity of the EMDR methodology, and prevent diluted versions from proliferating in the hands of unlicensed lay practitioners.

Section I

EMDR DISSOCIATIVE DISORDERS TASK FORCE RECOMMENDED GUIDELINES: A GENERAL GUIDE TO EMDR'S USE IN THE DISSOCIATIVE DISORDERS

Purpose: This section of this appendix offers general guidelines in the application of EMDR to the dissociative disorders, with paramount concern for client safety. The intended audience is the *established* clinician who is new to the diagnosis and treatment of dissociative disorders. This guide is not intended to define standards of care or specific training requirements or certification guidelines. Further, it is not intended to supersede expert clinical judgment or training in dissociative disorders or hypnosis.

Assumptions: The following are some assumptions underlying this guide: (1) EMDR treatment of those with a dissociative disorder is best imbedded within a total psychotherapeutic approach and does not stand alone as a treatment; (2)

there is a high prevalence of undiagnosed dissociative disorder in clinical populations; (3) there is a high cost to patient, therapist, and the therapeutic alliance of failing to adequately consider the possibility of dissociative disorders before first using EMDR in a patient's treatment; (4) as our understanding continues to develop, these guidelines may need revision. In the following paragraphs are guidelines for therapists to use in evaluating patients for EMDR and determining whether and at what point EMDR may be safely introduced into a patient's treatment.

Screening: The therapist should screen every patient for the presence of an underlying dissociative disorder regardless of the presenting complaint. Screening approaches include the DES (Bernstein & Putnam, 1986) or the Mental Status Examination for Dissociative Disorders (Loewenstein, 1991). The therapist has not conducted sufficient screening if that screening is limited to in-session monitoring for evidence of "switching." If the index of suspicion for a dissociative disorder is low after screening, the therapist may proceed with the EMDR protocol, including preparatory steps that are appropriate for the presenting problem.

Clarifying the diagnosis: If the index of suspicion for a dissociative disorder is high after screening, the therapist should conduct further diagnostic clarification, using, for example, the Dissociative Disorders Interview Schedule (DDIS; Ross, 1989) or the lengthier Structured Clinical Interview for DSM-IV Dissociative Disorders (SCID-D; Steinberg, 1993) or should obtain appropriate consultation.

When a dissociative disorder is present: If the assessment reveals that a dissociative disorder is present, the decision to proceed with EMDR is best guided by considering both therapist and patient factors, as follows:

1. *Therapist factors:*
   a. It should be determined whether the therapist is sufficiently trained in the dissociative disorders, as evidenced by the therapist's (1) having taken formal courses in the area and (2) having been supervised in the psychotherapy of dissociative patients.
   b. It should be determined whether the therapist is sufficiently skilled in the treatment of dissociative disorders, as evidenced by such abilities as (1) troubleshooting with hostile alters, child alters, and perpetrator alters; (2) anticipating and accommodating transferences; (3) recognizing and working with hypnotic and dissociative phenomena; (4) managing crises; and (5) determining the need for medical and/or inpatient backup.
   c. The therapist should have considerable experience using EMDR on patients without dissociative disorders before attempting it on highly dissociative patients. The therapist needs skill in the "cognitive interweave" interventions and other active interventions described in the EMDR Institute's Level II training.
   d. Unless the aforementioned skills are present, the therapist should either refer the patient or seek additional training in the fields of

dissociative disorders and hypnosis before using EMDR on the dissociative patient (see section on Additional Training).

  e. If the requisite skills and training are present, the therapist may implement EMDR within the context of a thorough treatment plan only if positive patient factors are present (see next section).

2. *Patient factors:* Patient factors are important in planning the treatment of dissociative patients, whether EMDR is used or not. Because of the potential of EMDR for rapid destabilizing, however, patient factors directly affect the risks associated with the procedure.

  a. Assess patient suitability for EMDR treatment by ascertaining if the patient has (1) good affect tolerance; (2) a stable life environment; (3) willingness to undergo temporary discomfort for long-term relief; (4) good ego strength; (5) adequate social support and other resources; (6) history of treatment compliance. The following assessment is a necessary element of the evaluation of any dissociative patient for any treatment. With EMDR, however, the risks associated with failing to adequately assess is more serious because of the power of the procedure.

  b. Determine whether the patient exhibits the following signs, which would tend to argue against the use of EMDR: (1) ongoing self-mutilation; (2) active suicidal or homicidal intent; (3) uncontrolled flashbacks; (4) rapid switching; (5) extreme age or physical frailty; (6) terminal illness; (7) need for concurrent adjustment of medication; (8) ongoing abusive relationships; (9) alter personalities that are strongly opposed to abreaction; (10) extreme character pathology, especially, a severe narcissistic, sociopathic, or borderline disorder; (11) serious dual diagnoses such as schizophrenia or active substance abuse.

  Note: The presence of these signs may not constitute absolute contraindications. However, the risks and complexities that accrue if the therapist proceeds with EMDR in the presence of these signs is considerable. The potential benefits must outweigh these risks, and safety precautions must be in place. Only therapists who are *highly experienced* with managing those complications are prepared to proceed with EMDR for patients evidencing these signs.

Embedding EMDR in the treatment plan: If the aforementioned therapist and patient factors described above are appropriate, EMDR may be one component in a progressive course of treatment. The total treatment plan is best guided by the accumulated knowledge of the field of dissociation and may include hypnosis, EMDR, behavior therapy, cognitive therapy, and other methods.

Preparing for EMDR: The therapist should prepare the patient for EMDR with the intention of minimizing the likelihood and impact of any problems occurring in the middle of EMDR sessions. At the same time, the therapist needs to "expect the unexpected," to use Kluft's phrase. At a minimum, the therapist should carefully explain the procedure with the intent of achieving sufficient informed consent of the entire system, recognizing that this is not a fully attainable goal. To the degree that the system consents, EMDR is likely to proceed smoothly. Suggestions for the entire system to observe, even if parts are reluctant, can prevent surprised alters from aborting the EMDR. The therapist's preparation of the patient for EMDR may be affected by such factors as the following: (1) system complexity; (2) informed consent of the relevant portions of the system; (3) cooperation between parts; (4) permeability of dissociative barriers; and (5) overall system motivation for change. A straight-forward, cooperative, and coconscious system is easier to prepare for EMDR than one that is hostile, complex, and impermeable. Preparation for EMDR may proceed in tandem with other therapeutic activities, including the establishment of rapport and the teaching of affect containment and other skills.

Early treatment phases: Early in the treatment of a dissociative disorder, therapists should refrain from the use of EMDR.

Exceptions may exist under extraordinary circumstances, to be defined in consultation.

Caution: The use of eye movements too early in treatment risks premature penetration of dissociative barriers. This could produce such results as flooding of the system, uncontrolled destabilization, and increased suicidal or homicidal risk. For crisis intervention, the therapist should only attempt eye movements if the risks of failing to intervene are as high without as with the intervention.

Middle treatment phases: Throughout the integration phase of treatment, the therapist may find various uses for EMDR, including, for example, (1) EMDR's prototypic application, the neutralization of trauma through abreaction; (2) facilitation of internal dialogue using Ego State Therapy (Watkins, 1992) during EMDR; (3) restructuring of cognitive distortions used as EMDR targets; (4) building of alternative coping behaviors using EMDR installations; (5) ego strengthening through installations; and (6) fusion.

Final treatment phases: In the postintegration and termination stages of treatment, EMDR may have continued application, including (1) additional coping skills development; (2) generalization into new situations; (3) facilitating the patient in making meaning of life's trauma, pain, and healing; (4) resolving remaining obstacles to the achievement of life goals.

Task force members: The following, in alphabetical order, are the EMDR Dissociative Disorder Task Force members: Catherine Fine, Ph.D., Marilyn Luber, Ph.D., Sandra Paulsen, Ph.D., Gerald Puk, Ph.D., Curt Rouanzoin, Ph.D., and Walter Young, M.D.

Additional Training

Clinicians who seek additional training in the diagnosis and treatment of dissociative disorders should contact the International Society for the Study of

Multiple Personality and Dissociation (ISSMPD), phone (708) 966-4322; and *Dissociation* (5700 Old Orchard Road, 1st Floor, Skokie, IL 60077).

Suggested Reading

The following are a few of the sources available for the study of dissociation:

Bernstein, C., & Putnam, F. (1986). Development, reliability, and validity of a dissociation scale. *Journal of Nervous and Mental Disease, 174*, 727–735.

Braun, B. G. (1988). The BASK model of dissociation. *Dissociation, 1*(1), 4–23.

Braun, B. G. (1986). *Treatment of multiple personality disorder*. Washington, DC: American Psychiatric Press.

Fine, C. G. (1991). Treatment stabilization and crisis prevention: Pacing the therapy of the multiple personality disorder patient. *Psychiatric Clinics of North America, 14*(3), 661–676.

Goodwin, J. (1982). *Sexual abuse: Incest victims and their families*. Boston: Wright/PSG.

Kluft, R. P. (1988). Making the diagnosis of multiple personality disorder. In F. F. Flach (Ed.), *Diagnostics and psychopathology*. New York: Norton.

Kluft, R. P. (1985). *Childhood antecedents of multiple personality disorder*. Washington, DC: American Psychiatric Press.

Kluft, R. P. (1985). The treatment of multiple personality disorder (MPD): Current concepts. In F. F. Flach (Ed.), *Directions in psychiatry*. New York: Hatherleigh.

Kluft, R. P., & Fine, C. G. (1993). *Clinical perspectives on multiple personality disorder*. Washington, DC: American Psychiatric Press.

Loewenstein, R. J. (1991). An office mental status examination for complex chronic dissociative symptoms and multiple personality disorder. *Psychiatric Clinics of North America, 14*(3), 567–604.

Putnam, F. W. (1989). *Diagnosis and treatment of multiple personality disorder*. New York: Guilford.

Ross, C. A., Heber, S., Norton, G. R., Anderson, D., Anderson, G., & Barchet, P. (1989). The Dissociative Disorders Interview Schedule: A structured interview. *Dissociation, 2*(3), 169–189.

Ross, C. A. (1989). *Multiple personality disorder: Diagnosis, clinical features and treatment*. New York: Wiley.

Spiegel, D. (Ed.). (1993). *Dissociative disorders: A clinical review*. Lutherville, MD: Sidran Press.

Steinberg, J. (1993). *Structured clinical interview for DSM-IV dissociative disorders*. Washington, DC: American Psychiatric Press.

Watkins, J. (1992). *Hypnoanalytic techniques*. New York: Irvington.

Section II

EMDR PROFESSIONAL ISSUES COMMITTEE RECOMMENDED GUIDELINES

In 1987 a clinical procedure called Eye Movement Desensitization (EMD) was developed by Francine Shapiro, Ph.D. In her initial study (1989) EMD was used to treat survivors of sexual assault and Vietnam veterans. In 1990 the name was changed to Eye Movement Desensitization and Reprocessing (EMDR) to take into account the cognitive and emotional restructuring aspect of the method. Since it first appeared in the literature, EMDR has undergone a number of modifications, rendering the original articles obsolete.

Over the course of the development of EMDR, a group of clinicians formed a committee whose primary function was to address professional and ethical issues related to the practice of EMDR. This group, called EMDR Professional issues Committee (EPIC), has identified two primary areas of concern—client welfare and training—which are inexorably linked.

Client Welfare

Fundamental to the professional practice of any psychotherapy is the primary concern for client welfare. For psychologists, this concern underlies the American Psychological Association's (APA) Ethical Principles, guidelines to be considered before initiating any type of therapy. (Other professionals who practice psychotherapy have their own, similar codes of conduct.)

The issue of client welfare is pertinent in a variety of ways. For example, prior to beginning treatment clients should be informed about any procedure that is to be used. Of course, this raises the issue of informed consent, which with respect to EMDR includes, among other things, preparing the client for the process itself. This facet of informed consent is particularly important since EMDR has the potential to evoke very powerful emotional reactions from the client. Because of the intensity of emotional arousal, special care should be given to such conditions as cardiac problems, pregnancy, ocular problems, and dissociative disorders. The presence of any one of these conditions requires careful consideration and consultation with appropriate professionals (e.g., physicians, ophthalmologists) before initiating EMDR treatment.

It is important to note that EMDR is not a "quick fix." It should not be applied arbitrarily to all clients. To protect client welfare, a thorough history taking about the presenting problem and a careful screening are both necessary components of EMDR treatment. As clinicians and researchers continue to study and apply EMDR to specific client populations and problems, new protocols are being developed and others refined in order to better address specific issues and client needs.

One of the most important issues that arises with respect to EMDR and client welfare concerns the fact that highly emotional states (abreactions) may occur during the process. Thus, if EMDR is not used appropriately, the client may be retraumatized and may become immobilized in the process (i.e., may experience disturbing affect or physical sensations without any reduction in intensity). Consequently, it is critical that clinicians possess more than sound clinical judgment and an intuitive sense of what to do; they must know how to handle the situation appropriately and effectively under the methodological guidelines set forth in the EMDR trainings.

Training

Therapists, like most professionals, require training, whether it is to acquire new skills or knowledge, enhance existing skills, or brush up on infrequently used techniques. Competence to provide particular services is of such significance that at least two of the APA Ethical Principles have been formulated for psychologists: Principle A (Competence) and Ethical Standard 1.04 (Boundaries of Competence). Similar concerns are expressed in the applicable ethics codes for other practicing psychotherapists. In particular, when new methods such as EMDR are introduced to the mental health community, psychologists must "take reasonable steps to ensure the competence of their work and to protect patients, clients, students, research participants, and others from harm" (APA, 1992, p. 1600). Related to competency is the issue of training in new methods, which is also covered by the aforementioned sections of the Ethical Principles. Thus, there is an ethical mandate for psychologists to first avail themselves of "appropriate study, training, supervision, and/or consultation from persons who are competent in those areas or techniques" (APA, 1992, p. 1600). With respect to the latter, the EMDR Institute has authorized certain individuals to conduct EMDR training. These EMDR-trained clinicians have been using the method for at least two years and have also worked as facilitators who supervise the practicum for trainings led by Dr. Shapiro. Only these individuals are considered to be qualified and competent to teach the EMDR training seminars.

Although EMDR may appear to be deceptively simple to some, its use—not only from an ethical viewpoint but also from the practical perspective of trained and experienced clinicians—demands that training be obtained from EMDR-authorized instructors and training seminars. As stated previously, EMDR has demonstrated that it can elicit very powerful reactions from clients, and it is therefore of utmost importance that clinicians know how to safely and effectively manage these occurrences. It is only through the trainings, which contain close supervision from experienced clinicians, that these and other skills can be adequately taught.

Training is divided into two levels, both of which include a didactic component as well as a supervised practicum that incorporates the utilization skills. In the first level, the fundamental aspects of EMDR regarding trauma applications are covered, as are issues and guidelines concerning client safety. Effective application requires that attention be paid to a variety of areas (affect, images, cognition, physical sensations) in a manner that conveys to the client encouragement, support, and a safe environment. It is also stressed in the first level of training that EMDR is a client-focused approach, which means that the clinician must learn to be nonintrusive. Clinicians are trained to "follow the client's process," and for many this means learning not to intervene in ways that have been derived from traditional models. Without benefit of the Level 1 training, clinicians will lack guidance regarding proper timing and application and may inadvertently get in the client's way (via delayed or too rapid responses, reflecting, interpreting, reframing, etc.), which may adversely affect the client's experience and progress.

The second level of training focuses on the application of more specific EMDR protocols for particular diagnoses and presenting problems. Additionally, a more active version of EMDR is taught, a version that is necessary when working with more highly disturbed clients of any diagnosis. (It should be noted that the second level of training is best utilized after clinicians have had some time to use EMDR with their own clients). Also presented in both levels of training is the most recently derived information needed to provide clients with the opportunity for informed consent. Without participation in the authorized trainings, the clinician cannot be fully informed and experientially guided regarding how to use EMDR, when to use it, with whom to use it, how to identify its potential benefits and risks, and how to address and minimize those risks. If the clinician is not fully informed, then the client cannot be fully informed, thus violating another tenent of the Ethical Principles—Ethical Standard 4.02 (Informed Consent). If the client is not adequately prepared for the experience of EMDR, he may be retraumatized.

In sum, it is the position of EPIC that the safe, effective, and ethical practice of EMDR cannot be achieved unless the clinician has participated in trainings led by authorized instructors. Therapists who have not participated in these trainings are not familiar with, among other things, the experiential utilization of the standard EMDR protocol, the latest treatment implications, research results, most lately revealed contraindications for treatment, and management issues. Current knowledge in these areas contributes to increasing the safety and efficacy of EMDR.

It is EPIC's hope that these guidelines have conveyed the importance of receiving training from authorized EMDR instructors in order to protect the welfare of clients. Given the fact that EMDR is a new and evolving method, it seems prudent and appropriate that clinicians avail themselves of the opportunity to learn from those who are deemed competent to teach (from the EMDR Institute) and to benefit from training and supervision that is appropriate.

EPIC Members: Lois Allen-Byrd, Ph.D., MRI Research Associate; Virginia Lewis, Ph.D., MRI Senior Research Fellow; Marquerite MoCorkle, Ph.D., MRI Senior Research Fellow.

Reference

American Psychological Association. (1992). Ethical Principles of Psychologists and Code of Conduct. *American Psychologist, 47*, 1597–1611.

EMDR Resources

THE INTERNATIONAL EMDR NETWORK

The EMDR Network office is located in Pacific Grove, California, where it was established as a nonprofit mutual benefit corporation. The purpose of the organization is to foster ongoing education, research, and development regarding EMDR, as well as to offer continued professional and educational support of EMDR practitioners.

Members are mental health professionals who have participated in formal training in EMDR and are involved in using it clinically or for research purposes. The organization offers its members opportunities to learn of new applications, concerns, and research, through meetings, articles, audiotapes of EMDR conference presentations, a research data base, and newsletters. The newsletters disseminate clinical results, new protocols, innovations, suggested theories, client cautions, and information on opportunities for international collaboration regarding clinical and research interests.

At this time there are regional coordinators in approximately 25 states and in Europe, Australia, and South America. Regional Network meetings occur three to four times a year and generally include meetings of special interest groups, where interested EMDR clinicians exchange ideas and case material on such topics as anxiety disorders, dissociative disorders, peak performance, personality disorders, psychophysiological disorders, children and adolescents, and substance abuse. The general session consists of a question-and-answer period, research updates, and presentations of the most significant findings of various special interest groups. The reports, of individual and group case findings, are based on a variety of self-report measures, objective assessments, and behavioral measures. The EMDR Network also coordinates study groups, which meet throughout the United States, so that practitioners can exchange case information, request assistance, and discuss recent innovations.

The EMDR Network's Professional Support Committee provides suggested formats for informed consent forms, client education material, and professional presentations. The EMDR Professional Issues Committee (EPIC) addresses ethical and professional issues, responds to complaints in these areas, and recommends policy and training standards to safeguard ethical and professional practices. A special task force is currently evaluating guidelines and proposed standards for adequate independent training/supervision and practice of EMDR throughout the professional community. A Norman Cousins' Research Fund and a Charles and Lena Sumner Scholarship Fund have been established to offer seed money for selected EMDR research projects. A research data base compiles information on completed research and selected studies in progress.

At this time, membership in the EMDR Network is limited to those who have been formally trained by means of an authorized supervised practicum. At a later date, membership status will be extended to students and professionals who are trained according to standards set forth by the EPIC task force. For further information, including new eligibility requirements for membership, contact International EMDR Network, P.O. Box 51038, Pacific Grove, CA 93950.

TRAINING AVAILABILITY

An unfortunate side effect of the widespread media attention surrounding EMDR has been that a number of untrained clinicians and laypersons are using their version of the method with clients. In addition, various workshops in "eye movement therapy" have been springing up all over the country. In all the instances that have been reported, the eye movements are being used without the procedures, protocols, or safeguards that represent EMDR. We feel strongly that clients need to be protected from the potential dangers of the misuse of this therapy. There is a list of all licensed therapists who have been educated in the method which can help clients and professionals make more informed decisions. The EMDR Network acts as a clearinghouse for pertinent information and maintains a directory of all clinicians educated in the EMDR methodology (as described in this volume) by means of recognized training.

An EMDR Network Professional Issues Committee Task Force is currently evaluating standards of recognition for responsible training programs. Training centers that meet these standards would have their graduates eligible for membership in an International EMDR Association. In addition, one of the purposes of writing this textbook was to enable EMDR to be taught in appropriate clinical graduate school programs, and such teaching is already occurring in several of them. To obtain information regarding the professional guidelines, eligibility requirements, and alternative training programs, please contact the EMDR Network.

At present, the EMDR Institute has trained over 10,000 clinicians in the use of EMDR. Affiliated organizations exist throughout the United States, Europe, South America, and Australia. These organizations utilize the presently authorized workshop format under the guidance of instructors and facilitators who have been trained for this educational purpose over the past five years. Trainings entail the presentation of didactic material, the use of treatment tapes, and—most importantly—supervised small-group practice. The use of the logo shown below is restricted to EMDR Institute–authorized trainings and affiliates.

In addition to basic training, the EMDR Institute offers (1) specialty trainings presented by experts who have employed EMDR successfully with a number of diverse clinical populations, (2) all-day supervised practice sessions, (3) case consultants, and (4) an annual conference that includes the latest innovations, clinical applications, and research reports.

For information regarding trainings, equivalency tests, affiliates, consultants, and eligibility requirements, please contact EMDR Institute, P.O. Box 51010, Pacific Grove, CA 93950.

EMDR Clinician Survey

This appendix includes the unpublished results of a survey conducted on the work of the first 1,200 clinicians trained in EMDR with over 10,000 clients. This extensive report was instrumental in the decision to continue the training programs while awaiting the publication of more rigorous controlled studies.

Preliminary results of the survey were presented at the 1992 annual conference of the International Society for Traumatic Stress Studies and the final results were reported in a paper presented at the 1994 annual conference of the American Psychological Association. The survey results are included in this text in order to expedite its availability because it has been extensively referenced at a variety of professional presentations, in a number of published articles, and throughout this text.

Please note that not all of the clinicians surveyed had completed the two-part course, and specific protocols for a number of target populations had not yet been incorporated into the EMDR methodology at the time of the study.

Eye Movement Desensitization and Reprocessing (EMDR): A Quantitative Study of Clinician Impressions of Effects and Training Requirements

Howard Lipke, Ph.D.
DVA Medical Center, North Chicago
Finch University of Health Sciences/Chicago Medical School

While controlled studies are absolutely essential to examine the effectiveness of EMDR, or any other method of psychotherapy, another kind of research— extensive clinical reporting—may also be of vital importance. Controlled treatment outcome studies have practical drawbacks in that the number and type of cases examined must be limited and the use of the treatment must be carefully prescribed. This means that much could be missed about the effects of a therapeutic method in true clinical situations, about the breadth of its applicability, and, of preeminent importance, about the dangers or limitations to its use. Putnam and Loewenstein (1994) made similar points in describing their survey of treatment for multiple personality disorder (MPD).

This study of EMDR, based on methodology used by Shipley and Boudewyns (1980) to examine whether flooding and implosion procedures were as dangerous (i.e., as likely to promote decompensation) as many clinicians feared, looked for danger in general but also asked subjects to comment on a wide variety of possible problems during therapy and attempted to ascertain the types of cases in which there were beneficial results. Structured questions were used to enhance objectivity in interpretation and were supplemented by unstructured questions to allow for maximum expression. Because EMDR training policies have been a center of controversy recently, a specific question on the need for training was also included.

METHOD

Subjects and Procedure

At the time this study was initiated, over 1,500 clinicians had been trained in EMDR by Francine Shapiro. Identifying information was available for all but approximately 25 of these trainees, who participated in small training meetings for researchers at two sites. Between August 15 and September 1, 1992, an extensive survey on EMDR was sent to all 1,295 trainees for whom there was a record of training before February 1, 1992; this date was chosen so that all subjects included in this study would have had at least 6 months to gain experience with EMDR. For trainees at each of the two sites where identification information was not obtained, a representative was asked to distribute surveys to clinicians who took the training.

Because a number of the therapists to whom surveys were sent failed to respond (a typical problem with any survey), it is legitimate to question the representativeness of the sample obtained. Thus, it could be claimed with some justification that people who did not respond are different in some significant way from those who did, rendering the sample nonrepresentative of the population as a whole. Nonresponders might, for example, tend to have an extreme attitude (negative or positive) about EMDR, but for whatever reasons do not wish to make such feelings public. In order to determine if any differences exist between responders and nonresponders, a random sample from this group was mailed a second request.

Therefore, in November 1992, 89 surveys were sent a second time to a randomly chosen 10% of the clinicians who had not responded to the initial mailing. Subjects who did not respond were telephoned at least once (and if not reached, a message was left) to encourage them to participate, if possible, in the study.

To sum up, of the original population of 1,295 EMDR therapists to whom surveys were sent, 408 (31%) responded and, of the random sample of 89 out of 887 initial nonresponders who were mailed a second request, 35 (39% of the sample) responded. Because there were no obvious differences in survey results between the initial responders and second-mailing responders (see Tables 1, 8, 11, 12, below), it is reasonable to combine the results of the two mailings and to conclude that, by means of both direct and random sampling, 58% of the original population is represented by the current sample of 443 individuals. In addition, the similarity between the responses of the two groups also supports the reliability of the present survey instrument. On key questions the two samples are analyzed separately.

Tables 1, 2, 3, and 4 summarize the professional background of the subjects. Table 1 lists all of the subjects once. Tables 2, 3, and 4 include subjects in more than one catagory.

Licensed doctoral level psychologists (LP) subjects are the most highly represented group. The subsample of LP subjects is heavily weighted toward therapists in private practice. The amount of experience, as well as theoretical orientation reported, suggests that subjects had wide-ranging clinical backgrounds. It is interesting to speculate that there is some relationship between work in the private sector and a clinician's awareness of or willingness to investigate innovative treatment.

Materials

The survey contained 26 items, some of which called for multiple responses. Subjects were asked to identify their profession, level of professional training, membership in professional organizations, level of EMDR training, theoretical orientation, type of employment, overall frequency of EMDR use, comfort with the procedure, reasons for lack of use, and recent changes in frequency of use. Item 13 asked subjects to rate EMDR on 13 dimensions and to compare it to other treatment procedures they had used. After responding to this item, subjects were asked to give the specifics of any serious side effects. Item 13 was phrased so that

TABLE 1. Profession of Subjects

	First mailing		Second mailing	
	N	%	*N*	%
Licensed doctoral psychologists	198	49	10	29
Licensed marriage family child counselors	64	16	10	29
Licensed social workers	53	13	6	17
Nonlicensed psychologists	46	11	4	11
Students	14	3	3	9
Psychiatrists	13	3	1	3
Registered nurses	11	3	0	0
Others	8	2	1	3
Total	407	100	35	100

TABLE 2. Subjects' Organizational Membership

Professional organization	N
American Psychological Association	205
Association for Advancement of Behavior Therapy	68
National Association of Social Workers	42
International Society for Traumatic Stress Studies	31
American Society of Clinical Hypnosis	30
American Association of Marriage and Family Therapists	18
American Psychiatric Association	9
American Nursing Association	6

TABLE 3. Number of Years in Practice

Years	N
0–10	136
11+	246

TABLE 4. Subjects' Employment

Type of practice	N
Private practice	296
Veterans Administration	59
State or mental health agency	46
University affiliate	28
Other	25

clinicians would use their non-EMDR practice as an informal control group, thus allowing their responses to be interpreted in a meaningful context.

Items 14 to 16 asked subjects to list populations for which EMDR had been generally harmful, generally ineffective, and generally beneficial. Subjects were allowed unstructured response space to convey their impressions. In Item 17 subjects were asked to report on their results with obsessive–compulsive disorder, seizure disorders, multiple personality disorder, and posttraumatic stress disorder.

On Item 18 subjects were asked to rate their personal experience in the client role in EMDR training (it is been clear that practice sessions in these workshops have a powerful impact on some trainees). On Item 19 subjects were asked to rate the importance of supervised practice in EMDR training, an item developed in response to therapists who have questioned the necessity for practicum training in EMDR (Baer et al., 1992).

Item 20 asked clients to describe the effects of medication or illicit drugs on EMDR results, Item 21 asked about the frequency of use and effectiveness of self-generated eye movements by therapists and clients, and Item 22 asked for comments on any other matter related to EMDR. Items 23 to 26 asked subjects how frequently they use exposure therapy and had them compare exposure with EMDR on effectiveness, client distress, and therapist distress in administration of the procedure.

RESULTS

Extent of Use

Tables 5, 6, and 7 summarize the extent to which subjects have used EMDR.

The strength of an extensive survey of clinicians is that information is made available about a greater number of clients (in this case, over 10,000)—who represent a greater variety of problems and who are treated in a more naturalistic manner—than is possible with controlled studies.

A sufficient number of clients are reported on here to warrant the belief that the conclusions reached by this survey on the possible negative effects of EMDR on target populations are valid.

TABLE 5. Approximate Number of Clients Treated with EMDR

	First mailing	Second mailing
Total	10,756	633
Licensed doctoral psychologists	4,683	

TABLE 6. Number of EMDR Clients Treated per Therapist

Number of EMDR clients in total client load	*N*
0	27
1–10	144
11–50	167
50+	56

TABLE 7. Comfort Level of Therapists Using EMDR

Description of comfort level	*N*
As comfortable as with any procedure	239
Somewhat uncomfortable	86
Very uncomfortable	17
Total	342

Effectiveness

Tables 8, 9, 10, and 11 summarize subject evaluation of the effects of EMDR from various perspectives.

Although the items listed in Table 8 are possible negative effects of EMDR, some of these are temporarily uncomfortable experiences that are part of many successful psychotherapies. The rarity of many of these responses with EDMR is suggested by the fact that so many subjects invented the "not applicable" category for many of the items.

Activity not uncommon to fragile psychotherapy clients—such as suicidal ideation (with and without activity), violence, postsession dissociation, physical illness, cancellation of the next session, and premature termination of treatment—are reported considerably less often with EMDR than with other treatments. The reports of eye damage were difficult to interpret (see problems below). For two items—extreme agitation or panic and in-session dissociation—EMDR was somewhat more likely to be associated with these responses than were other treatments, and EMDR was so overwhelmingly more often associated with emergence of repressed material that this effect could be considered a cardinal feature of the method. Perhaps the most parsimonious reading of the overall pattern of findings is that during EMDR sessions repressed material surfaces and is often accompanied by strong negative affect and/or dissociation. However, these negative effects are limited to the session itself (perhaps because the material is successfully integrated), and therefore there is less suicidal ideation and activity, physical illness, and violence associated with EMDR than with other procedures.

TABLE 8. Subjects' Comparison of EMDR to Other Procedures (in %)

"Compared to other treatment procedures you have used, how often have EMDR sessions led to . . . "	N	More often	As often	Less often	NA
Suicidal ideation	363	6	36	39	20
Suicidal ideation and activity	324	2	38	49	12
Extreme agitation or panic	341	31	31	34	4
Emergence of repressed material	357	86	10	3	2
In-session dissociation	353	29	41	20	10
Postsession dissociation	330	14	46	32	9
Eye damage	329	4	42	23	31
Physical illness	330	8	41	31	21
Violence	322	1	42	36	21
Cancellation of next appointment	326	12	43	33	12
Premature termination of treatment	326	10	49	33	8
General negative side effects					
First mailing	326	8	39	46	7
Licensed psychologists	169	11	43	39	8
Second mailing	23	4	48	30	17
General beneficial therapeutic effects					
First mailing	354	76	20	4	1
Liscensed psychologists	178	76	21	3	1
Second mailing	23	70	26	4	

Note. In percent of subjects selecting degree of frequency. NA = not applicable.

Problems. Based on reports concerning eye damage from an unstructured inquiry it appears that all but two positive incidents of eye damage referred to transitory discomfort. There were approximately 70 other notable (it is a matter of judgment whether an incident is considered notable) negative incidents reported by subjects during the unstructured inquiry. These included three cases of emergence of alter personalities in clients not previously diagnosed with MPD, out-of-session dissociative episodes, violence (a rock thrown at an abuser's car), increased auditory hallucinations in a previously diagnosed psychotic depression, serious suicide gestures, and severe headaches. Some of these responses resulted in hospitalization. In the case of some clients, such incidents were seen as precursors to therapeutic breakthroughs; for others, the course of treatment appeared to be negatively affected.

Limits of Effectiveness. To an unstructured question about problems for which EMDR generally had no effect, obsessive–compulsive disorder (OCD) was clearly the most cited. Responses to a later unstructured question on OCD indicated that about half the subjects reported some positive outcomes, with the remainder indicating little success. One subject reported deterioration in a client and the resumption of self-threatening behavior. It was specifically suggested that EMDR was most effective with OCD patients when combined with other behavioral methods. Personality problems were also frequently cited (about 25 times in the LP group) as nonresponsive to EMDR. These nonresponders were generally reported to have problems with avoidance, hostility, and issues of control.

Beneficial Effects. Posttraumatic stress disorder was listed over 120 times by the LP group alone in a response to an unstructured question about problems for which EMDR was generally beneficial. Often, responses were extremely enthusiastic. Phobias, anxiety, panic, depression, and MPD were each listed by 10 to 25 subjects in the LP group as responding positively to EMDR.

Seizure Disorders. Subjects were asked to summarize the effects of EMDR in treating patients with seizure disorders. One subject reported that EMDR may have led to a mild seizure (the client may have been dissociating); another reported EMDR led to a petit mal seizure. No other subject reported any role of EMDR in eliciting seizures, and one subject reported a decrease in frequency and intensity of seizures. Five subjects reported not attempting EMDR in seizure patients because of the clients' fears. Ten subjects reported having done EMDR with at least one diagnosed seizure patient with no seizure induction. No subject reported seizure activity elicited in a client with previously undiagnosed seizure disorder. These findings suggest EMDR is not contraindicated for seizure patients; however, caution should be exercised.

Medication and Drug Use. All subjects were asked, "From your experience, what effects does the use of medication or illicit drugs have on EMDR results?" Subject responses indicated that the interaction between EMDR and medication is complex. In general, antidepressants did not appear to interfere with EMDR effectiveness, and in some cases were seen to enhance effectiveness. Four subjects singled out benzodiazepines as decreasing effectiveness, while one reported that anxiolytics improved effectiveness. Overall, subjects' reports suggest that medication does not rule out the use of EMDR, and that in some cases, perhaps those with severe depression, medication might provide sufficient stabilization to begin EMDR treatment.

Self-Use. In EMDR workshops it is suggested that clients not attempt self-use of EMDR until the end of treatment. The survey did not inquire into the timing of self-use but in a nonstructured item asked subjects about their own self-use and that of their clients. Seventy-five subjects reported using eye movements themselves, and 61 reported at least some self-use by clients. Three subjects reported that these eye movements elicited new memories and problems. We do not know how many of the self-users used eye movements outside workshop guidelines, so it is difficult to interpret what the three bad experiences mean in terms of potential problems, if self-use was indiscriminate. In general, the reports suggest that the effects from self-use are milder than those elicited by standard EMDR treatment. Sixty-five subjects reported results to be at least mildly positive, especially in promoting relaxation.

Comparison to Exposure Treatments. As Keane (1992) has pointed out, there has been a paucity of controlled research on treatment of posttraumatic stress disorder (PTSD). Most of the treatment studies that have been published are on the use of exposure. In addition, in discussing EMDR, researchers often point to the exposure aspect of the method. For these reasons—and because the design of this study was chiefly influenced by a study on the exposure procedures of flooding and implosion (Shipley & Boudewyns, 1980)—it was decided to include questions directly comparing EMDR with flooding and implosion procedures. It should be noted that there are significant differences between the exposure aspects of EMDR and flooding and implosion procedures. Most salient are the far shorter exposure periods during most EMDR sessions and the use of cognitive restructuring interventions in EMDR, rather than increased exposure to the target scene, in the face of client failure to progress.

The items on flooding and implosion allowed for a comparison of treatment approaches by clinicians experienced in both methods.

TABLE 9. Comparison between EMDR and Exposure (in %)

	N	EMDR more	Equal effects	EMDR less	Variable effects
Effectiveness	91	57	19	19	5
Stress to client	90	11	24	59	6
Stress to therapist	86	21	24	47	8

Note. In percent of subjects selecting each response.

These results reflect an advantage for EMDR in terms of treatment effectiveness and extent of stress for clients (and, to a lesser extent, extent of stress for the therapist). This finding is notable in light of the fact that the subjects are likely to have had more experience with exposure procedures than with EMDR. The experience of subjects who did not often use EMDR and who did not find it generally more effective and less distressing than flooding and implosion may have been due to one or more of the following factors: therapist discomfort with a new procedure, the likelihood of repressed material emerging in EMDR sessions, muscle fatigue from the arm movements, and the lack of relative advantage of EMDR over flooding and implosion in the treatment of severe OCD. Another hypothesis that must also be considered is that flooding and implosion may in fact be more effective than EMDR, or equally effective, but that the subjects in this survey who found EMDR more effective were those who had not been able to effectively implement the exposure procedures.

Subject reports on changes in their use of EMDR are shown in Table 10, where subject use of EMDR appeared to be fairly stable in that a majority of the subjects had not changed use in the past 3 months. Responses to the open-ended part of this item suggest that the most common reason for decreasing the use of EMDR was a change in client load or work situation. Other reasons, in approximate descending order of frequency, were therapist preference of other procedures owing to their success or EMDR's failure, need for more training to feel comfortable using EMDR, client rejection of the procedure, and lack of supervision.

TABLE 10. Change in Clinical Use of EMDR by Subjects

Use of EMDR over past 3 months	*N*
Increased	95
Decreased	77
Stayed the same	207

Therapists' Personal Experiences. During the practicum portion of EMDR workshops trainees participate in both the therapist and client position. This activity is not role-played: Target events are those that trainees find uncomfortable (and sometimes traumatic). The final measure in this study of EMDR's effectiveness was subjects' report of the therapeutic benefit they themselves received in the client role in the workshops.

The results in Table 11 strongly suggest positive effects of EMDR reported by the clients themselves. The fact that the pool of subjects corresponding to this item consists of psychotherapists limits any generalization from this population to a clinical population. On the other hand, the fact that psychotherapists, who presumably have had the opportunity to resolve difficulties from their past, could benefit so much from the EMDR practicum suggests substantial effectiveness for the method.

TABLE 11. Subjects' Ratings of Personal Experience in the Client Role in Practice Sessions of the EMDR Workshop (in %)

		Very harmful						Very helpful
	N	-3	-2	-1	0	1	2	3
First mailing	365	1	2	4	7	28	26	32
Second mailing	30	0	0	0	7	30	27	37

Note. In percent of subjects selecting each position along harmful–helpful continuum.

Need for Training

Some of the controversy surrounding EMDR has related to training criteria. Several clinicians (Baer et al., 1992) have criticized the insistence that training could not be completed in a 3-hour workshop, as well as the implication that it is inappropriate to practice EMDR without extensive training. A question was included in the survey to obtain the opinions of EMDR-trained clinicians on the need for extensive training (i.e., training that includes supervised practice) in order to use this method with clients (see Table 12).

These results overwhelmingly indicate that clinicians who have had Shapiro's EMDR training believe that supervised practice with the method is of significant value, a finding that disputes the Baer et al. (1992) criticism concerning the viability of 3-hour training.

TABLE 12. Importance of Supervised Practice (in %)

"How important is it for EMDR training to include supervised practice?"	N	Extremely important	Somewhat important	Not important
First mailing	377	77	20	3
Second mailing	32	78	22	

Note. In percent of subjects selecting each response.

GENERAL DISCUSSION

At the time Shipley and Boudewyns collected their data, flooding and implosion were being taught at a number of sites, thus making it extremely difficult to take a representative sample of clinician-subjects. They sent 132 surveys and received responses from 70 subjects, who reported using flooding and implosion on 3,493 cases (with a range of 1 to 500). The present study took advantage of the fact that EMDR was initially developed by one person, Shapiro, who had at the time of this survey overseen all training in EMDR. Sampling was not necessary inasmuch as almost the whole population of trained clinicians could be surveyed. An advantage in interpreting this research is that the training for EMDR, unlike the training for flooding and implosion, is standardized. The homogeneity of trainings, however, does have a disadvantage in that these results can only be generalized to similarly trained clinicians; similar results may not be obtained by clinicians who learn EMDR by other means.

Shipley and Boudewyns (1980) used slightly different phrasing when they asked subjects about negative side effects of treatment. Since they were chiefly concerned with exploring the dangers of imaginal exposure, they asked subjects to compare this procedure to others in current use. The present study asked subjects to compare EMDR to procedures subjects had used. This phrasing allowed for the possibility that EMDR treatment had supplanted other forms of therapy for similar problems in a clinician's practice.

To briefly summarize, the data in the present study indicate that a majority of clinicians trained in EMDR consider the procedure to be of considerable value for clients with PTSD and other psychological problems. Subjects reported that negative effects were no more common with EMDR than with other procedures. However, given the reported tendency for emergence of repressed material and subjects' endorsement of the need for practicum training, it may be inferred that there is potential for countertherapeutic results if caution is not displayed. Both the number of respondents to the first round of surveys and the consistency between overall ratings by first round responders and nonresponders who responded to the second mailing suggest that these results are reasonably representative of the whole population.

This study's findings are consistent with the call for continued aggressive research into EMDR. In addition, they are seen as supportive of continued clinical use and training in this method of psychotherapy.

ACKNOWLEDGMENT

This study was approved by Medical Research Service, DVA Medical Center, North Chicago, and partially funded by that medical center. However, this report should not be taken as a reflection of the policy of that medical center or the Department of Veterans Affairs. The author wishes to thank James Alexander, Lynn Lipke, Robbie Dunton, A. J. Popky, William Zangwill, and Francine Shapiro for their assistance.

REFERENCES

Baer, L., Hurley, J. D., Minichiello, W. E., Ott, B. D., Penzel, F., & Ricciardi, J. (1992). EMDR workshop: Disturbing issues? *Behavior Therapist, 15*(5), 110–111.

Keane, T. (1992, October). Keynote address for the Annual Convention of the International Society for Traumatic Stress Studies, Los Angeles.

Putnam, F. W., & Loewenstein, R. J. (1994). Treatment of multiple personality disorder: A survey of current practices. *American Journal of Psychiatry, 150*(7), 1048–1052.

Shipley, R. H., & Boudewyns, P. A. (1980). Flooding and implosive therapy: Are they harmful? *Behavior Therapy, 11*, 503–508.

Index